W9-AUY-164

THE SEVENTY GREAT JOURNEYS IN HISTORY

E R

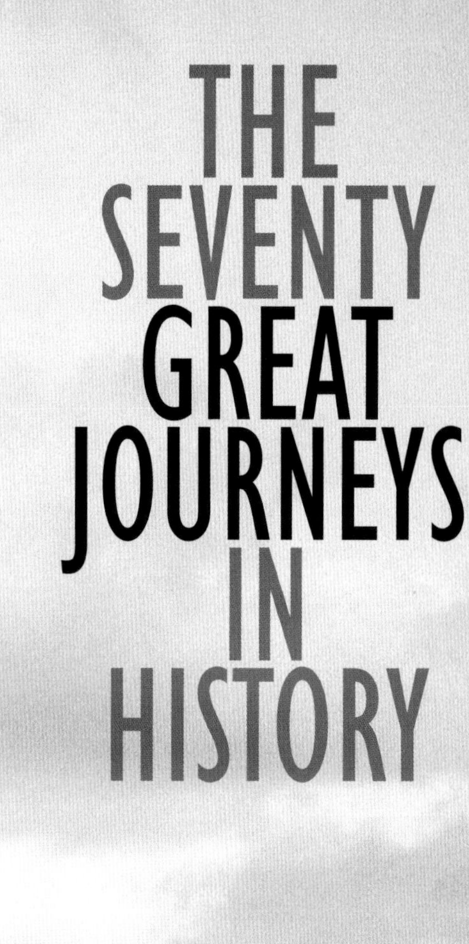

THE SEVENTY GREAT JOURNEYS IN HISTORY

Edited by Robin Hanbury-Tenison

with 420 illustrations, 331 in color

Thames & Hudson

Contents

The Maya pyramid-temple at Tulum, Mexico, by F. Catherwood

Thames & Hudson would like to dedicate this book to the memory of Wendy Gay, to whose picture research it owes so much.

First published in 2006 in hardcover in the United States of America by Thames & Hudson Inc., 500 Fifth Avenue, New York, New York 10110

thamesandhudsonusa.com

Library of Congress Catalog Card Number 2005911291

ISBN-13: 978-0-500-25129-4
ISBN-10: 0-500-25129-0

Printed and bound in China by Toppan Printing

Half-title *A 15th-century astrolabe used in navigation.*

Title page *Working replica of Francis Drake's ship the* Golden Hind *at sea.*

Ancient World

A group of Muslim pilgrims sets off on the Hajj, from The Maqamat

Medieval World

Relief showing a Phoencian trading ship, 2nd century BC

The Renaissance

Painting of insects and banana plant by Maria Sibylla Merian

Cortés greeted by Motecuzoma's emissaries, by Diego Durán

17th & 18th Centuries

19th Century

Frontispiece of a contemporary biography of David Livingstone

Edwin 'Buzz' Aldrin on the Moon, Apollo 11 *mission*

Modern Times

Contributors

ROBIN HANBURY-TENISON is a well-known explorer, author, conservationist and campaigner. He made the first land crossing of South America at its widest point, and the first river crossing of South America from north to south from the Orinoco to Buenos Aires. A regular contributor to newspapers and magazines, he has made several films of his expeditions for television, and broadcasts regularly on radio and TV. His many books include *A Ride along the Great Wall* (1987), *Fragile Eden* (1989), *Spanish Pilgrimage* (1990); he is also the editor of *The Oxford Book of Exploration* (1993). **32**

CHARLES ALLEN was born in India in the last years of the British Raj, and has travelled extensively throughout South and Southeast Asia. An authority on British Indian and South Asian history, his first book on the subject was *Plain Tales from the Raj* (1975) and his most recent *God's Terrorists: The Wahhabi Cult and the Roots of Modern Jihad* (2006). Other books, including *The Search for Shangri-La* (1999), are based on his travels in the Himalaya and Tibet. In 2004 he was awarded the Sykes Gold Medal by the Royal Society for Asian Affairs for his contribution to the understanding of Asian affairs. **33**

SARAH ANDERSON founded the Travel Bookshop in Notting Hill in 1979. She was educated at the London University Colleges of SOAS and Heythrop and now teaches travel writing at City University, writes regularly about her travels for timesonline and gives talks worldwide. Her books include *Anderson's Travel Companion* (1995), *The Virago Book of Spirituality* (1996) and *Inside Notting Hill* (with Miranda Davies, 2001). **64**

ROBERT D. BALLARD is a professor of Oceanography at the University of Rhode Island's Graduate School of Oceanography. For 30 years he was at the Woods Hole Oceanographic Institution, where he pioneered the development of manned submersibles and remotely operated vehicle systems. He participated in the first manned exploration of the Mid-Ocean Ridge in 1973/4, was co-chief scientist of the 1977 expedition that discovered the first active hydrothermal vents and used *Angus* in 1979 to discover the first high-temperature 'Black Smokers'. **68**

WILLIAM BARR is a Professor Emeritus, University of Saskatchewan, where he taught for 31 years in the Department of Geography, and a Senior Research Associate, Arctic Institute of North America, University of Calgary. His recent books include: *Red Serge and Polar Bear Pants. The Biography of Harry Stallworthy R.C.M.P.* (2004), *From Barrow to Boothia. The Arctic Journal of Chief Factor Peter Warren Dease, 1836–1839* (2002) and *Searching for Franklin, the Land Arctic Searching Expedition, 1855* (1999). **34, 53**

PETER BELLWOOD is Professor of Archaeology at the Australian National University in Canberra. He has carried out field research in many parts of Southeast Asia and the Polynesian islands. His publications include *Man's Conquest of the Pacific* (1978), *The Polynesians* (2nd ed., 1987), *Prehistory of the Indo-Malaysian Archipelago* (2nd ed., 1997) and *First Farmers* (2005). **3**

JAMIE BRUCE LOCKHART, a former diplomat, has published three volumes of diaries of travels in Africa by the Scottish explorer Hugh Clapperton (1788–1827) – the latest being *Hugh Clapperton into the Interior of Africa, the Records of the Second Expedition, 1825–1827*, co-edited with Paul Lovejoy (2005) – and articles on other journeys of discovery by Europeans in the central Sahara and Sudan in the 19th century. **47**

PAUL CARTLEDGE is Professor of Greek History, University of Cambridge, and a Professorial Fellow of Clare College. Among his many books are *Alexander the Great. The Hunt for a New Past* (2nd ed., 2005) and *Xenophon. Hiero the Tyrant and Other Treatises* (with Robin Waterfield; new ed., 2006). He is an honorary citizen of Sparta and holder of the Gold Cross of the Order of Honour, awarded by the President of Greece. **6, 7**

JOHN CHRISTOPHER is a professional balloon pilot and author. A former editor of the *Aerostat* and *Airship* journals, he has written four books on lighter-than-air flight, including *Riding the Jetsream* (2001) on the round-the-world ballooning challenge. His latest book, *Brunel's Kingdom* (2006), celebrates the work of Britain's greatest engineer, Isambard Kingdom Brunel. **69**

MICHAEL D. COE is Professor Emeritus of Anthropology at Yale University. His interests include ancient Mesoamerica and the Khmer civilization of Southeast Asia, the historical archaeology of New England and the history of chocolate. Among his many publications are *The Maya* (7th ed., 2005), *Mexico* (5th ed., with Rex Koontz, 2002), *Breaking the Maya Code* (1992), *The True History of Chocolate* (with Sophie D. Coe, 1996), *Angkor and the Khmer Civilization* (2003) and *Final Report: An Archaeologist Excavates His Past* (2006). **45**

VANESSA COLLINGRIDGE read Geography at Oxford before becoming a writer and broadcaster. Her books include *Captain Cook* (2002) and *Boudica* (2005). She specializes in the history of exploration and is currently working on the history of the Antarctic in maps and literature. **36, 37**

BARRY CUNLIFFE is Professor of European Archaeology at the University of Oxford. He is particularly interested in ancient trade and exchange, and has excavated widely in Britain, Brittany and Spain. His many books include *Iron Age Communities in Britain* (4th ed., 2005), *Facing the Ocean* (2001) and *The Extraordinary Journey of Pytheas the Greek* (2001). **8**

CAROLLE DOYLE is a freelance journalist and private pilot who specializes in travel and light-aviation writing in national newspapers and magazines. In 2001 she travelled around the world reporting on the flight of her friend, Polly Vacher, who became the first woman to fly solo round the world via the Pacific in a Piper Cherokee Dakota single-engine aircraft. **62**

FREDERICK ENGLE is an environmental policy consultant in Washington, DC. He is a Fellow of the Royal Geographical Society and was previously the geographer at the National Air and Space Museum, Washington, DC. His publications include *Looking at Earth* (with P. Strain, 1992) and articles on environmental monitoring from aircraft and satellites. He is currently researching the role of remote sensing in shaping environmental policy. **61**

RICHARD EVANS lived in China as a diplomatic language student from 1955 to 1957. He was the British Ambassador to China from 1984 to 1988. He is an Emeritus Fellow of Wolfson College, Oxford and is the author of *Deng Xiaoping and the Making of Modern China* (1993). **63**

BRIAN M. FAGAN is Emeritus Professor of Anthropology at the University of California,

Santa Barbara. An authority on world prehistory, he is the author of many general books on archaeology, including *The Great Journey* (new ed., 2004), *The Little Ice Age* (2002), *The Long Summer* (2004) and *Fish on Friday* (2006). He also edited The *Seventy Great Mysteries of the Ancient World* (2001) and The *Seventy Great Inventions of the Ancient World* (2004). **1, 2, 13, 24, 27**

RANULPH FIENNES was described by the *Guinness Book of Records* in 1984 as 'the world's greatest living explorer'. Among the 32 expeditions he has led are 'first to both Poles, first to cross Antarctica and the Arctic and the Northwest Passage'. In 1979–82 he led the first polar circumnavigation of Earth and in 1993 he and Mike Stroud became the first to cross the Antarctic continent with no outside support by manhauling sledges from the Atlantic to the Pacific coast via the South Pole. He has written 16 books, including the biography *Captain Scott* (2003). **58**

TOM FREMANTLE is a writer and adventurer. His books include *Johnny Ginger's Last Ride* (2000), *The Moonshine Mule* (2003) and *The Road to Timbuktu* (2005), the last focusing on his journey through West Africa on the trail of the explorer Mungo Park. **39**

JASON GOODWIN was joint winner of the *Spectator/Sunday Telegraph* Young Writer of the Year Award in 1987, and has travelled extensively in the Far East and India. His first book, *The Gunpowder Gardens: Travel through India and China in Search of Tea* (1990) was shortlisted for the Thomas Cook Travel Book Awards, and his second, *On Foot to the Golden Horn: A Walk to Istanbul* (1993), won the *Mail on Sunday*/John Llewellyn Rhys Prize. He is also the author of *Lords of the Horizon: A History of the Ottoman Empire* (1998). **17**

PEN HADOW is a Fellow of the Royal Geographical Society, founder of a commercial Arctic Ocean guide service, one of the world's most experienced sea ice guides, and the only person to have trekked successfully solo and without resupply from Canada to the North Geographic Pole (2003). He is the author of *Solo – The North Pole: Alone and Unsupported* (2004). **57**

CONRAD E. HEIDENREICH is Professor Emeritus of Geography at York University, Toronto. His numerous books and articles on exploration, mapping, Natives and European/Native relations of early Canada include *Huronia: A History and Geography of the Huron Indians* (1973); he was also co-editor and contributor to the *Historical Atlas of Canada, Vol. 1* (1987). He is currently working on a new bilingual edition of Champlain's writings to be published by the Champlain Society. **29**

JOHN HEMMING has made numerous expeditions in Peru and among the indigenous peoples and forests of Amazonia. Among his many publications are *The Conquest of the Incas* (revised 1995) and *The Search for El Dorado* (republished 2001). He was director of the Royal Geographical Society for 21 years. **25, 26**

PETER HOPKIRK has travelled widely over many years in Great Game country while researching and writing his six books. He was an ITN reporter and newscaster, a Fleet Street foreign correspondent, then worked for 20 years on *The Times*, five as its chief reporter and latterly as a Middle and Far East specialist. His *Trespassers on the Roof of the World* (1982) deals with the activities of the Pundits. His works have been translated into 14 languages. **54**

LANDON JONES is the author of *William Clark and the Shaping of the West* (2004) and *The Essential Lewis and Clark* (2000). During his publishing career at Time Inc. in New York City, he served as the head editor of both *People* and *Money* magazines and launched several new titles, including *In Style*, *People en Espanol*, *Teen People* and *Who Weekly*. His 1980 book, *Great Expectations: America and the Baby Boom Generation*, coined the phrase 'baby boomer'. **41**

JOHN KEAY is the author of many works on Asian history, including *The Honourable Company* (1991), *Last Post: The End of Empire in the Far East* (1997), *Sowing the Wind: The Mismanagement of the Middle East* (2003), *India: A History* (2000) and *The Spice Route* (2005). He also writes on Scotland and on the history of exploration, editing *The Royal Geographical Society History of World Exploration* (1991) and authoring the two-volume *Explorers of the Western Himalayas* (1975, 1979), *The Great Arc* (2001) and *Mad About the Mekong; Exploration and Empire in South East Asia* (2005). **51**

DUANE KING is Executive Director of the Southwest Museum of the Autry National Center in Los Angeles and was previously Assistant Director of the Smithsonian Institution's National Museum of the American Indian. He was the founding editor of the *Journal of Cherokee Studies* and edited *The Cherokee Indian Nation: A Troubled History* (1979). Among his many publications is *Cherokee in the West* for the Smithsonian Institution's Handbook of North American Indians. **44**

ROBIN KNOX-JOHNSTON, currently Chairman of Clipper Ventures plc, is a Master Mariner and the first person to sail solo non-stop around the world. Of his 14 books *A World of My Own* (1969) remains in print in 11 countries. **66**

DAVID LOADES is Professor Emeritus of the University of Wales, and Honorary Research Professor of the University of Sheffield. He is the author of *The Tudor Navy* (1992), *England's Maritime Empire, 1450–1690* (2000) and numerous other books on Tudor history. He is also the co-editor (with C. S. Knighton) of *The Anthony Roll of Henry VIII* (2000) and *Letters from the Mary Rose* (2002). **28**

JOSÉ-JUAN LOPEZ-PORTILLO studied ancient and modern history at Oxford and is currently researching for his PhD in 16th-century Spanish colonial history under the supervision of Professor Felipe Fernández-Armesto. **20**

DAVID McLEAN has travelled all his life, but his first love has always been South Georgia, Elephant Island and the Antarctic Peninsula. He has focused on Shackleton and his inspiring leadership of men in the *Endurance* expedition. Now a committee member of the James Caird Society, he designed and produced the exhibition 'Shackleton: The Antarctic and Endurance' (2000). **59**

JUSTIN MAROZZI is a travel writer and historian. A Fellow of the Royal Geographical Society, he is the author of *South from Barbary: Along the Slave Routes of the Libyan Sahara* (2001) and *Tamerlane: Sword of Islam, Conqueror of the World* (2004). He is currently researching a history of Herodotus. **5**

PHILIP MATYSZAK studied ancient history at Oxford University where he received his doctorate on the Senate in the late Roman Republic. His publications include *Chronicle of the Roman Republic* (2003), *The Enemies of Rome* (2004) and *The Sons of Caesar* (2006). **9, 10, 11**

ALEXANDER MONRO studied at Durham and Cambridge universities. He has followed the path of Genghis Khan overland from Mongolia to Afghanistan and now lives in Shanghai, where he works as a journalist. He has written articles on the UK and China for the *New Statesman*, Reuters, AFP, *The Times* and *The Sunday Telegraph*. **16**

MALYN NEWITT was Charles Boxer Professor of History at King's College London. He has organized academic conferences in Russia, Uzbekistan and the Cape Verde Islands, as well as in London, where his focus has been on Portuguese colonial history. He is author of *São Tomé and Príncipe* (with Tony Hodges, 1988), *A History of Mozambique* (1995) and *A History of Portuguese Overseas Expansion 1400–1668* (2004). **21**

CHRISTOPHER ONDAATJE founded Pagurian Press in 1967, later the Pagurian Corporation. In 1988 he sold all his business interests and returned to the literary world. He is the author of eight books, including the bestselling Burton biographies *Sindh Revisited* (1996) and *Journey to the Source of the Nile* (1998) as well as *Hemingway in Africa* (2004) and *Woolf in Ceylon* (2005). He was a member of Canada's 1964 bobsled team, is a Fellow of the Royal Geographical Society and a Trustee of the National Portrait Gallery. He lives in London and was knighted by the Queen in 2003. **48**

GHILLEAN PRANCE is Scientific Director of the Eden Project, a visiting professor at the University of Reading and former Director of the Royal Botanic Gardens, Kew. He has conducted many botanical expeditions to Amazonia and is author of 19 books and over 500 scientific and general articles on plant taxonomy, ecology, ethnobotany and conservation. **40, 43**

JANE ROBINSON is an author and lecturer specializing in women's history and biography. Her numerous books include *Wayward Women: A Guide to Women Travellers* (2001), *Unsuitable for Ladies: An Anthology of Women Travellers* (2001) and a biography of Mary Seacole (2005). **60**

JOHN ROSS is a Melbourne-based journalist and publisher. He was Editor-in-Chief of *Chronicle of the 20th Century* (Australian edition, 1999) and *Chronicle of Australia* (2000), and co-author of *200 Seasons of Australian Cricket* (1997). He is author of some 20 books, including *Country Towns* (1975), *One People, One Destiny: The Story of Federation* (2001) and *Voices of the Bush* (2001). **31, 49**

ANTHONY SATTIN is an author, critic and broadcaster whose books include *The Pharaoh's Shadow: Travels in Ancient and Modern Egypt* (2000) and *The Gates of Africa: Death, Discovery and the Search for Timbuktu* (2003). He is a regular contributor to *The Sunday Times* and writes for newspapers and magazines around the world. His 1987 book *Lifting the Veil*, which described the arrival of Europeans in Egypt at the beginning of the 19th century, bred a passion for Burckhardt that has led him to live and travel extensively in North Africa and the Middle East. **42**

ANN SAVOURS (Dr Shirley) writes on the history of polar exploration, including *The Search for the North West Passage* (1999) and *The Voyages of the 'Discovery'* (1992). She is Vice-President of the Hakluyt Society and in 2001 received the Murchison Award from the Royal Geographical Society. She was formerly Assistant Librarian and Curator at the Scott Polar Research Institute, Cambridge, and then Assistant Keeper at the National Maritime Museum, Greenwich. She is currently editing the fourth volume of *The South Polar Times*. **46**

ROBIN SCAGELL is a writer and broadcaster on astronomy. During the lunar landings he photographed the Moon from a French observatory for the University of Manchester, and after a brief spell as a telescope maker he became a journalist, editing partwork magazines on subjects such as photography, history for children, contemporary accounts of the Second World War and space exploration. He now runs a picture library of astronomical images. **67, 70**

TAHIR SHAH is the author of more than a dozen books on cultural and intercultural studies, including *The Middle East Bedside Book* (ed., 1992), *In Search of King Solomon's Mines* (2003) and *The Caliph's House* (2006). He has also published numerous articles and academic monographs in leading journals, and has presented a number of highly acclaimed television documentaries. **15, 18**

STANLEY STEWART is an author whose travel books include *Old Serpent Nile* (1991), *Frontiers of Heaven* (1995) – an account of his own journey through China and across the Karakorams to the sub-continent along much the same route as Fa Xian and Xuan Zang – and *In the Empire of Genghis Khan* (2000). The last two won the Thomas Cook Travel Book of the Year Award. **12, 19**

ROBERT TWIGGER has been described as a 'nineteenth century adventurer trapped in the body of a twenty-first century writer'. He was the first person since 1793 to retrace Mackenzie's exact route, as recounted in his book *Voyageur. Across the Rocky Mountains in a Birchbark Canoe* (2006). Currently he is searching for a new species of beetle in the Brazilian jungle. **38**

JOHN URE is a former British Ambassador to countries as diverse as Cuba, Brazil and Sweden. He has written a dozen biographies, travel and historical books, many of which have been translated into different languages; his latest book is *Pilgrimage: The Great Adventure of the Middle Ages* (2006). He writes regular travel articles for the *Daily* and *Sunday Telegraph*, and book reviews for the *Times Literary Supplement*. **14, 35, 52, 55, 56**

STEPHEN VENABLES was the first Briton to climb Everest without supplementary oxygen, completing a new route up the East Face, one of many first ascents he has made in the Himalaya and other mountain ranges. He has written eight books about his travels, worked on several television documentaries and appeared in the IMAX film *Shackleton's Antarctic Adventure* (2001). He is President of the Alpine Club. **65**

BRUCE WANNELL, linguist and traveller, has lived in many parts of the world covered by the travels of Ludovico di Varthema. **22**

PETER WHYBROW is director of the Semel Institute for Neuroscience and Human Behavior and the Judson Braun Distinguished Professor of Psychiatry and Biobehavioral Sciences at UCLA. In his latest book, *American Mania: When More Is Not Enough* (2005), he discusses at length the temperament of the migrant and its consequences. 'The Migrant Mind' in **1**

TOBY WILKINSON has a doctorate in Egyptology from the University of Cambridge where he is a Fellow of Clare College. He lectures widely on ancient Egypt and has extensive experience of the archaeological sites in the Nile Valley and Egyptian deserts. His books include *Genesis of the Pharaohs* (2003) and *The Thames & Hudson Dictionary of Ancient Egypt* (2005). **4**

GLYN WILLIAMS is Emeritus Professor of History at Queen Mary, University of London. He is the author of a dozen books on exploration and travel, the most recent of which are *The Prize of all the Oceans: The Triumph and Tragedy of Anson's Voyage Round the World* (1999) and *Voyages of Delusion: The Search for the Northwest Passage in the Age of Reason* (2002). **30**

SIMON WILSON STEPHENS worked as a guide in Uganda for four years before retracing Stanley's Trans-Africa Expedition in 2003, cycling and kayaking solo through East Africa. He now lectures and owns and runs Milestones, a specialist travel marketing company, promoting tourism and exploration in Africa. **50**

SIMON WINCHESTER, a former foreign correspondent for the *Guardian*, now writes books on modern history from his homes in New York and western Massachusetts. His most recent work is *A Crack in the Edge of the World: America and the Great California Earthquake of 1906* (2005). **23**

Introduction

Solvitur ambulando: *It is solved by walking.*
St Augustine

Observation is the key to understanding. Throughout history, people have travelled in order to see and make sense of their surroundings. Whether they were the first early humans setting out from their familiar habitats or later men and women making pioneering journeys, whether their travels were military, economic or religious in nature, all were driven by an insatiable curiosity to observe and chart the unknown world.

The journeys that are described here span the whole range of possible reasons for travel, from migration to mysticism, from curiosity to conquest. Each merits inclusion because they succeeded, to a greater or lesser extent, in their objectives. Many, if not most, were recorded at the time by the travellers themselves, some are known to us from the writings of contemporary or subsequent historians, others from the archaeological traces which remain, from great temples and palaces to potsherds and bones.

Recounting the stories of the greatest journeys ever made thus leads us to ask: what is it that drives people to explore? What is it that motivates mankind to set out into the unknown? And what did those who survived their adventures and returned home safely – though tragically not all did – ultimately achieve?

There is an unashamed emphasis on exploration here. My definition of exploration has always been that it changes the world. And so the choice of 'great' journeys in this book includes those which had a significant effect on our view of the planet. Nothing can surpass the thrill of stepping where no human foot has trod before and, from the days of our earliest ancestors to the moment when man first set foot on the Moon, this is certainly one of the motives that has driven us to explore. The same enthusiasm today infuses our reach out into space. And yet, those first migrants in the earliest eras of our existence had populated almost all the habitable regions of earth long, long before historical times. Therefore, almost all the great journeys actually took place through lands already settled by our relations and, as a result, few of the pioneers whose stories are told in this book were really the first.

Epic journeys

So what constitutes a 'Great Journey'? The spread of human adventure since earliest times is far too wide to be accommodated by a single definition, but we have attempted to follow certain criteria in our choices. There has to be an epic quality

Christopher Columbus in a portrait of 1525: his journey to the Americas literally reshaped the contemporary view of the world.

Military reasons lay behind some great journeys: Genghis Khan led his armies immense distances in his seemingly unstoppable conquests across Asia. This detail from a 13th-century manuscript shows him fighting a battle in a mountain pass.

about each journey. Some were group enterprises involving armies, whole peoples, fleets or expeditions. Others were outstanding solo efforts. As far as possible, we have tried to identify the moving spirit behind each enterprise, the leader, because great journeys usually are driven by one person. And as Peter Whybrow tells us in his box on the Migrant Mind, there seems to be something in the genes of certain people which urges them to explore and seek out new lands. Whatever the motive, our world would not be the same had it not been for these outstanding characters.

Constraints of space mean, of course, that many great journeys that could have been included have had to be left out. Instead, we have tried to illustrate the questing nature of the human spirit by including a broad mix of individual journeys along with great migrations, military campaigns and geographical investigations.

The contributors, too, represent a wide and eclectic range of talent, experience and expertise, from distinguished historians and writers to travellers and explorers, including those with first-hand acquaintance of the journeys and places they describe. Their intimate knowledge and enthusiasm for their subjects brings these legendary journeys alive in a way that has not been attempted before.

Travelling through time

The Great Journeys are divided into six sections representing fairly distinct eras throughout history, in each of which the character of travel was different.

In the Ancient World we see the transition from a completely unknown and largely uninhabited world to one where the mists of time part tantalizingly to allow a glimpse of the earliest journeys of exploration, whose motives are often hard for us to understand today. The urge to move, spurred on by hunger and population pressure, which may have led our earliest ancestors out of Africa, gradually evolves into a more focused curiosity, in which the continuing threads of trade and conquest begin increasingly to take shape.

Medieval travellers take this a stage further, often driven by religion: the Chinese in search of sacred Buddhist texts, the Christians and Muslims seeking salvation. There were successive waves of purely military migration, too, such as the regular explosions of fierce people from out of the East. And there were also the first examples of individual travellers motivated largely by curiosity. Marco Polo and his family were traders, but it is his observation that gives him immortality. Ibn Battuta was perhaps the most compulsive traveller ever. Few, even today, could rival the distances he covered.

When we come to the Renaissance we enter a time when the entire globe is revealed and circumnavigated. Columbus's earth-shattering discovery of the New World triggered a hundred years of obsession with the shape of the planet, motivating explorers to undertake some of the most enlightening journeys of all time. The fact that the world had been proved to be round made people seek desperately for ways to exploit this revelation commercially. New routes to the East, through and across the Americas, became vital ingredients in the power struggles of that age. Journeys were usually official government missions designed to stake a claim to new lands, regardless of the diverse peoples already occupying them.

In the 17th and 18th centuries most of the remaining gaps in the global maps are filled.

Above *Thomas Baines painted this view of rapids on the Zambezi River in 1859 on an expedition with David Livingstone. Baines has depicted himself with his sketchbook, but around this time photography was increasingly being used to record journeys and a photographer can be seen, hunched over his tripod, on a rock in the river (right).*

Left *A Calumet pipe, late 1700s to mid-1800s, Missouri River, possibly presented to Lewis and Clark on their expedition across North America.*

Gertrude Bell, photographed in front of her tent in Babylon, 1909. Bell travelled alone into the tribal heartland of Arabia, a significant achievement for a woman at that time and a feat that probably could not be repeated today.

Some of the harsher environments are also tackled. Lands far to the south and in the frozen north are reached, while discoveries of new island peoples leading apparently idyllic lives in places such as Tahiti and Hawai'i add fuel to the fevered search for other such arcadian paradises. Darkest Africa is penetrated for the first time by Europeans, and science, surely the finest reason for travel, becomes the prime motive for a few pioneering spirits.

A dinner held in honour of the birthday of Robert Falcon Scott (at the far end of the table) on board the Terra Nova, *on the ill-fated British Antarctic expedition, 1910–12.*

These investigations explode in the 19th century, when intrepid polymath researchers penetrate pristine regions to apply Linnaean principles of classification to the welter of unknown plants and animals they find. Some also began to recognize and record the experience and wisdom of the people they met. This is the great era of exploration, when most of the remotest, uncharted wilds of Africa, South America and Central Asia are discovered. The search for fame and glory spurs many, while others are driven by religious or patriotic fervour. National pride in simply being the first begins to play a major role, and this is evident wherever flags are proudly

raised, but behind this nearly always lay the global scramble for power and influence.

Finally, in Modern Times, the last and most hostile regions on and above the earth are tackled. Both Poles are reached at last, the highest mountains climbed, the deepest ocean trenches plumbed. Technological developments – whether the sophisticated machinery designed for sea and air, or the new personal equipment and clothing that permit ever greater feats of endurance and bravery – allow new frontiers to be vanquished. Pioneer aviators and sailors demonstrate the extremes to which the human spirit can aspire in overcoming every natural obstacle. And now we are setting out on the last epic journey – into space. At the same time, we begin to suspect that what really matters is not so much the physical achievement of the great journey as the conclusions drawn and the greater understanding of life which it discloses.

Perhaps, in the end, the most important criterion for inclusion in this book is that the journey has had an impact that resonates through the ages. Whether it has opened our eyes to an aspect of the world that was previously unknown, or inspired us by the fortitude of its participants, it will be remembered as having been a journey which made a difference.

Thor Heyerdahl in his reed boat Ra II *battling against the waves. He set out to show that the Egyptians could have reached the Americas by sailing across the Atlantic using the same technology.*

Ancient World

Humankind's early migrations were travels greater than all later journeys put together. During vast unrecorded stretches of time, virtually every corner of the habitable world was discovered and settled. Subsequent journeys followed in the footsteps of these first brave pioneers, who could have had no idea where they were going because no one had ever been there before. Their driving force was perhaps as much a need to find food as curiosity. As our species became more successful, populations grew and required more space for hunting game and, later, to plant crops. The earliest indications – flint arrowheads, traces of fire or paint – tell us that our ancestors were there, and we are now able to date their presence with increasing accuracy.

However, as the box on The Migrant Mind (p. 21) points out, there must have been more to these migrations than simply hunger. There seems to be something in the human spirit that drives certain individuals to seek further. Whether it is indeed genetic, it is this instinct to explore that has brought about the greatest journeys, and we will see it manifest again and again as we follow the travels and travails of those whose journeys we retrace here.

Once those first émigrés from Africa had penetrated the whole of Asia and Europe, and even island-hopped far to the south to reach Australia and Tasmania, they seemed to have found the whole habitable world. Then, some 18,000 years ago, towards the end of the last Ice Age, a land bridge formed between Siberia and Alaska. Within a relatively short time, a few intrepid hunters who made their way across had become

Persepolis, ancient capital of the Persian empire: Herodotus wrote a history of the Greek wars against the Persians, while Xenophon was a Greek who fought for them; Alexander the Great defeated them and set Persepolis on fire.

large groups of diverse peoples, who rapidly colonized the whole of a New World. A world that was to remain isolated from the Old World for thousands of years once sea levels rose again as the ice melted and the land bridge vanished.

The Polynesians, using outrigger and double canoes, made some of the greatest sea journeys of all time, spread over a period of more than 4,000 years. Setting off into a huge, featureless ocean, they sought to strike any one of its numerous tiny scattered islands. If they did, they stayed and founded new societies. By about AD 1200, when they reached New Zealand, they had discovered or colonized all the habitable islands in the Pacific.

Our first tantalizing glimpses of actual records of some of these journeys come with the Egyptians, Phoenicians, Greeks and Romans. Surviving as reliefs carved in stone or wall paintings in tombs, and in texts if we are fortunate, a contemporary history of travel is documented. More often, however, the stories filter down to us through later mentions, swathed in myth and legend, second- and third-hand versions of long-lost originals. Now the motive is usually conquest, sometimes trade.

The Egyptians penetrate Africa and, through the eyes of Harkhuf, we gain a sense of the excitement provoked by his exotic trophies of ivory, ebony and a dancing pygmy. A thousand years later the Egyptians were sending out fleets to explore the African coastline, while those great seafarers, the Phoenicians, were going even farther afield. While empires come and go, the earliest individual travellers start the great tradition of journeying, observing and recording.

Herodotus, the world's first historian and also its first travel writer, brings us the Greeks' celebrated campaigns against the Persians, and much more. And the mercenary Xenophon recounts first-hand his journey from Persia home to Greece. Alexander the Great seems unstoppable, as he overwhelms almost the whole known world, culminating in his epic invasion of the east, on which he finally crosses the Indus, only to die on the return journey. In another military venture, Hannibal takes on the Roman Empire, crossing the Alps with his elephants after a huge campaign through Spain and southern Gaul. Rome's ultimate frontiers were finally to be defined by the emperor Hadrian, who spent most of his rule travelling between the extremes of Egypt and northern Britain, where he built his famous wall.

Meanwhile, Pytheas of Marseille reveals the first glimmerings of an ocean beyond the Mediterranean world, and a mysterious north where the sea 'congeals' and the sun barely sets. St Paul's tempestuous journey from Jerusalem to Rome was chronicled by St Luke. As a result, it had great significance for the development of early Christianity, as well as being one of the best-recorded sea voyages in antiquity.

The fleeing Persian emperor Darius III looks back at the victorious Alexander at the Battle of Issus, in a mosaic from the House of the Faun, Pompeii. Alexander set out to defeat the Persian empire, but did not stop there: he and his army covered over 32,000 km (20,000 miles), reaching as far as Central Asia and India.

BRIAN M. FAGAN

Out of Africa

1

100,000–50,000 years ago

And Adam called his wife's name Eve; because she was the mother of all living people.
GENESIS, III:20

We are *Homo sapiens*, the wise people. We design and make tools, communicate through articulate speech, think logically and plan ahead. These unique abilities enabled us to colonize the world in the first and most ambitious of all human journeys, after 100,000 years ago.

Mitochondrial DNA, inherited through the female line, traces our ancestry back to a primordial African population, whose genes are in every living human being. *Homo sapiens* evolved south of the Sahara Desert some 200,000 years ago; thanks to the discovery of fossils at Omo Kibish and Herto in Ethiopia, we know that the biological developments that led to the appearance of ourselves had already taken place by around 150,000 years ago.

Reconstructed skull from Omo Kibish (Omo I), Ethiopia, which provided evidence of the early development of Homo sapiens.

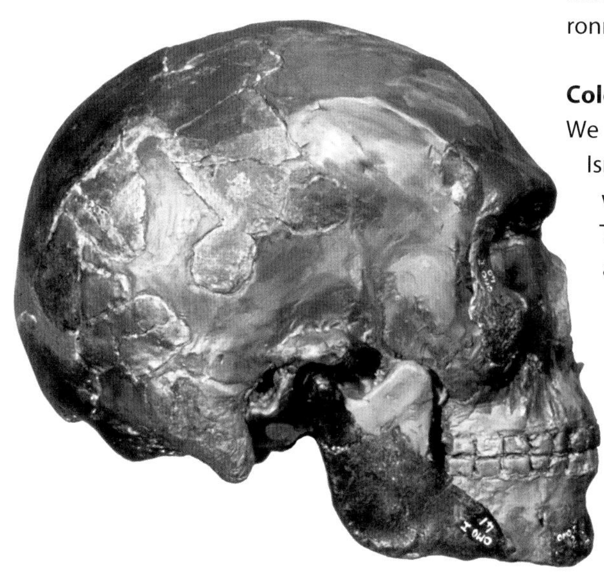

Humanity's first journey

At first, modern humans flourished only in tropical Africa, south of the Sahara Desert. Modern humanity's journey began when small groups of hunter-gatherers hunted and foraged their way across the Sahara into the Nile Valley and then Southwest Asia as early as 100,000 years ago.

Theirs was not a deliberate journey of exploration. A few hundred people, probably no more, lived in small, highly mobile bands, adapted to an existence in open country where food was widely dispersed across the landscape. Every band was in a state of perpetual flux. Sons diverged from fathers; daughters found partners outside the group; people quarrelled and moved away; and everyone covered enormous distances every year. These earliest migrations were part of the fundamental dynamics of hunter-gatherer existence. During the late Ice Age, these dynamics, and the superior adaptability of modern humans, took *Homo sapiens* into almost every natural environment imaginable.

Colonizing Southwest Asia

We know from excavations at Qafzeh Cave in Israel that our ancestors were living in southwestern Asia by at least 90,000 years ago. There they existed in limited numbers alongside a small population of archaic Neanderthals for about 45 millennia. The two populations may have had sporadic contact, but, in the end, the Neanderthals became extinct in the region, probably by about 45,000 years ago. This long period of co-existence saw dramatic changes in human toolkits, and, apparently, a sharp jump in human cognitive abilities.

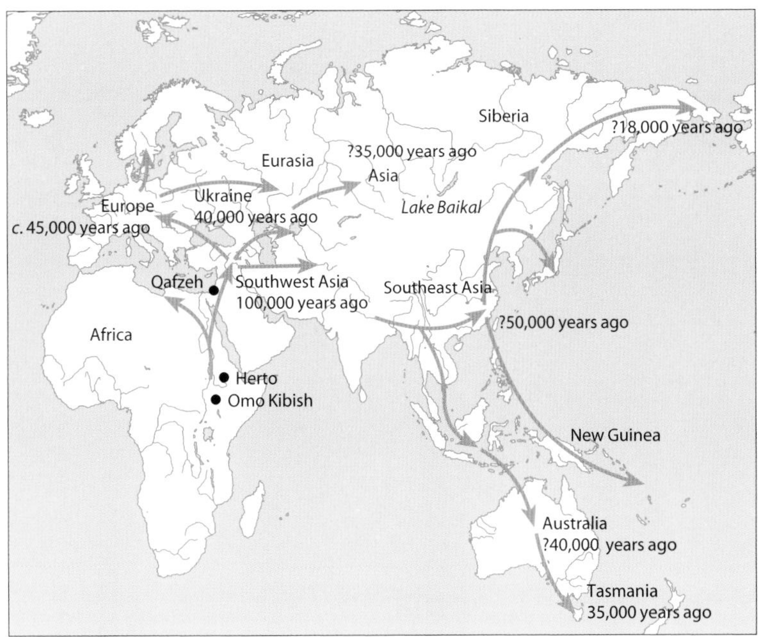

Map showing the the spread of Homo sapiens *in Europe, Asia and Australasia, with dates and major archaeological sites mentioned in the text.*

By 50,000 years ago, modern people living in southwestern Asia had developed more efficient hunting weapons and tool technology. Together with other innovations this may have resulted from much greater cognitive fluidity, allowing people to make connections between environmental, technical and social intelligence. And, in turn, these associations led to much more sophisticated social relations and to the development of visual symbolism, such as the late Ice Age cave art of central and western Europe – some dating to 30,000 years ago. *Homo sapiens* now had a competitive advantage over more archaic people, and modern humans spread rapidly across the Old World after 50,000 years ago.

Asia and Australia

Fifty thousand years ago, the world was a very different place from today. Huge ice sheets covered Scandinavia, the Alps and much of present-day Canada. Vast areas of Eurasia consisted of treeless tundra with nine-month winters. Sea levels were as much as 91 m (300 ft) below modern levels, creating vast continental shelves that joined Siberia to Alaska, and extended far offshore from the coast of Southeast Asia.

We do not know when *Homo sapiens* moved from the Near East into South Asia, but modern people were living in Indian river valleys and on what are now the offshore islands of Southeast Asia by about 50,000 years ago. Around that date, they made the crossing over open water, probably on rafts or in simple dugout canoes, to reach what is now New Guinea and Australia. By 35,000 years ago, Stone Age wallaby hunters were flourishing in the cold climate of Tasmania in the extreme south.

Other *Homo sapiens* groups had long settled in temperate eastern Asia, perhaps moving north from warmer regions in the south as early as

Nunamira Cave (formerly called Bluff Rock Shelter), Tasmania, was visited by ancient wallaby hunters after 35,000 years ago, during the late Ice Age.

35,000 years ago. We know almost nothing of these people, who were probably among the very remote ancestors of the first Americans (p. 23).

A masterpiece of Cro-Magnon bone sculpture: a European bison licks its flank.

Europe and Eurasia

Small *Homo sapiens* groups crossed into Europe from southwestern Asia by about 45,000 years ago. Ten thousand years later, they had settled alongside indigenous Neanderthal bands in the west, the latter becoming extinct around 30,000 years ago. The newcomers adapted brilliantly to the late Ice Age climate of central and western

THE MIGRANT MIND

PETER WHYBROW

I am become a name; for always roaming with a hungry heart.
ALFRED, LORD TENNYSON, *ULYSSES*, 1842

What fuels the migrant mind? What feeds the hungry heart? For a kinship band to walk from Ethiopia to the tip of South America, albeit over many generations, requires greater motivation than a nomadic search for the next meal of mammoth meat or the perfect fruit tree. It suggests daring, curiosity and a love of novelty in the group's leadership that is reflective of those pioneering souls who have undertaken the great journeys throughout history.

Today, neuroscience teaches us that it is the messengers of the brain's dopamine reward system that fuel such novelty seeking. The uncommon drive of the migrant explorer lies at one extreme of the genetically programmed spectrum of behaviour that we call temperament. It is temperament – a pattern of emotional style emerging in childhood – that first shapes whether we are bold or shy, risk tolerant or averse, an adventurer or a homebody.

Variations in temperament are determined by subtle differences, called alleles, in the genes that build the superhighways and receptor systems of dopamine reward. Those individuals of risk-taking temperament have been found to carry a dopamine receptor gene variant, the D4-7 allele that is distinct from that distributed in the general population (D4-4 allele).

Recent research suggests that the distribution pattern of the D4-7 allele among world populations is similar to that of the ancient migratory paths of our species. Based on estimations of the distance travelled by each migrant sub-group from knowledge of the probable origin of their native language, a coherent pattern emerges where those peoples who have stayed close to their ancestral homeland in North Africa and Asia Minor have a high percentage of the common D4-4 allele. In contrast, those peoples whose ancestors crossed the landbridge of the Bering Strait and moved down into the southern hemisphere of the Americas carry a *preponderance* of the exploratory and novelty seeking D4-7 allele.

Chauvet Cave in southeastern France is a Sistine Chapel of Ice Age art, including this frieze of wild horses.

Europe, using elaborate toolkits in stone, bone and antler to make such specialized artifacts as antler harpoons and needles, the latter essential for sewing layered, cold-weather clothing. These Cro-Magnons, compact, round-headed people, developed an elaborate ceremonial life, reflected in cave art and richly decorated antler objects that appear as early as 31,000 years ago.

To the north and east an endless steppe-tundra extended across Eurasia and into northeastern Siberia. Small numbers of modern humans settled in the Ukraine and along the Ural Mountains as early as 40,000 years ago, where they preyed on mammoth and other arctic animals. Extreme cold at the height of the last Ice Age around 20,000 years ago caused these bands to move southward into warmer environments, but settlement across the tundra resumed about 18,000 years ago. By that time, Stone Age hunter-gatherers had settled around Lake Baikal in Siberia, and also in the deserts of Mongolia. A few people had settled north of the Arctic Circle around 27,000 years ago, but they probably later retreated in the face of extreme cold, as did people far to the west. The region east of the frigid Verkoyansk Mountains of northeastern Siberia was not settled by their successors until the climate warmed slightly.

The Ice Age ended after about 18,000 years ago and the world began to warm up. By then, *Homo sapiens* had travelled from their origins in Africa into a much wider world: modern humans had adapted successfully to extreme cold, tropical rainforests and arid landscapes. But the next chapter of this extraordinary journey did not unfold until after the Ice Age, when the first bands of human settlers crossed from Siberia into Alaska and an uninhabited continent – the Americas.

BRIAN M. FAGAN

Into a New World

2

18,000 years ago

Because this could not happen except by the passage of many years and most ancient times, there is not a great argument that the people of these islands and continent are very ancient.

FRAY BARTOLEMÉ DE LAS CASAS, 1542

Eighteen thousand years ago, during the last Ice Age, when so much water was locked up in ice and sea levels were much lower than today, northeast Siberia and Alaska were part of a single landmass known to geologists as Beringia. The low-lying plain that joined the two continents was bitterly cold and devoid of much vegetation, until global warming brought scrub and stunted willows to the land-bridge. Despite prolonged controversy, most experts believe that this inhospitable plain was the route that brought the first human settlers to the Americas.

These ancient Siberians were arctic hunter-gatherers, who covered enormous areas in pursuit of game and plant foods. There was never a single, momentous journey that led to the settlement of the Americas. Instead, there were hundreds of journeys, irregular movements by nomadic hunting bands that took them back and

A glacial landscape in Alaska, part of the mosaic of arctic terrain traversed by the first humans to cross Beringia into North America.

forth, until, generations later, some bands lived full-time along the coasts and in the interior of Alaska – the first Americans.

No one knows exactly when the first settlers ventured on to the landbridge. Some archaeologists believe it was before 25,000 years ago, before the last cold spell of the late Ice Age. But most experts think first settlement came immediately after the Ice Age, as early as 16,000 years ago, when global warming brought more favourable conditions to the far north.

Ice-free corridors and coastal settlement

The earliest known traces of human occupation in Alaska come from the Tanana River, near the modern city of Fairbanks, dating to about 11,700 BC, but people may well have settled in the interior as early as 14,000 BC, perhaps even earlier. That their ultimate ancestry lies in northeast Asia seems a certainty, confirmed by both genetics and linguistic research.

At the time of first settlement, Alaska was ice-free, but surrounded to the east and south by the massive ice sheets that mantled most of modern-day Canada. The vast glaciers, one centered on eastern Canada, the other on the Rocky Mountains, blocked any access to the south. But, by 11,500 BC, some bands passed south of the ice sheets.

How did they move south? Was it through an ice-free corridor between retreating ice sheets? Or did they travel over the continental shelf, following the ice-free southeast Alaskan coast? Unfortunately, any human traces would now lie below modern sea level, but many experts believe that people from the north skirted the ice sheets, then moved inland south when they could; here, their occupation is well documented by 12,000 BC.

The first settlers

Only a handful of archaeological sites, most of them little more than scatters of stone artifacts, document human occupation in the Americas before 11,500 BC. The earliest well-investigated human occupation comes from a hunting camp at Monte Verde, far to the south in Chile, occupied as early as 12,500 BC. There are claims of settlement in Virginia dating to about 14,000 BC, but few experts accept this date. The scarcity of sites is not surprising, for the first settlers moved constantly and used a lightweight, portable toolkit, leaving little behind them.

Everything points to rapid colonization, spearheaded by small numbers of hunter-gatherers, some of whom had settled as far south as the Strait of Magellan by 10,000 BC. The best known of the earliest 'Paleo-Indian' cultures is that of the Clovis people, whose distinctive projectile points are found from Nova Scotia to Texas, and California to Florida. The Label 'Clovis' means little, because by 11,000 BC, there were hunter-gatherers living in every kind of environment imaginable – coastal desert, tropical rainforest and open grassland.

The first settlement of the Americas is one of history's most mysterious journeys. All we know is that Stone Age Siberians migrated east across Beringia into Alaska, and then south as the climate warmed rapidly after the Ice Age. Once south of the retreating ice sheets, they spread rapidly through an uninhabited continent and adapted brilliantly to its environmental diversity.

Right
Meadowcroft Rockshelter, Pennsylvania, one of the sites in North America where human occupation may be documented before 11,500 BC.

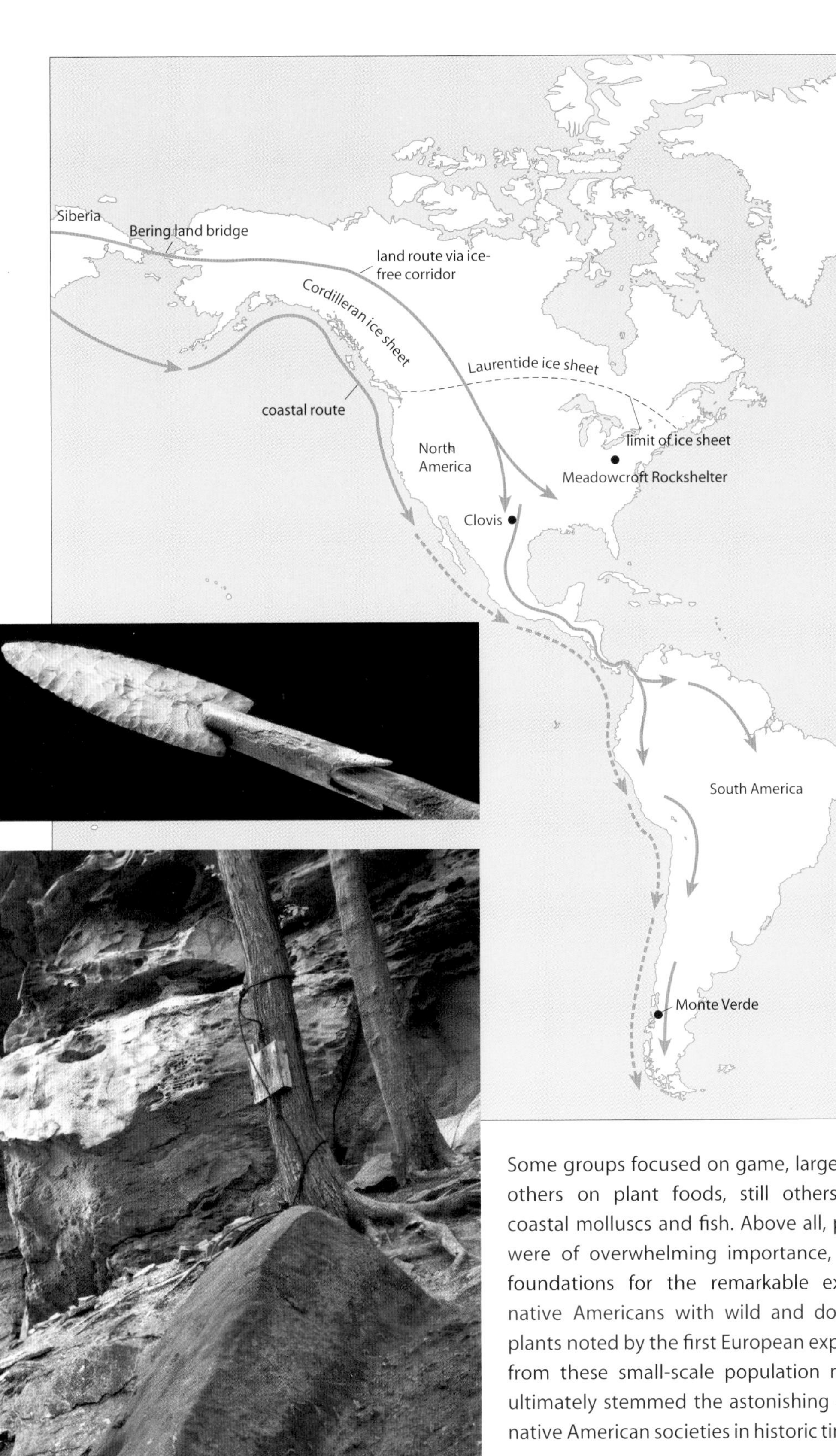

Possible routes used by the first human migrants into the Americas. It is thought that they may either have travelled through an ice-free corridor between ice-sheets, or skirted around the coast.

Some groups focused on game, large and small, others on plant foods, still others exploited coastal molluscs and fish. Above all, plant foods were of overwhelming importance, laying the foundations for the remarkable expertise of native Americans with wild and domesticated plants noted by the first European explorers. And from these small-scale population movements ultimately stemmed the astonishing diversity of native American societies in historic times.

Above centre
A modern reconstruction of a Clovis point, showing the stone projectile head mounted in a short foreshaft, which in turn fits on the spear shaft. When the spear hit its quarry, the head and foreshaft would break off and separate from the main shaft, inflicting a more serious wound.

PETER BELLWOOD

Early Pacific Voyagers

3000 BC – AD 1200

If we are desirous of tracing the races of all these islanders back to any continent, or its neighbourhood, we must cast an eye on a map of the South Sea, where we find it bounded to the East by America, to the West by Asia, by the Indian Isles on its North side, and by New Holland to the South.

GEORGE REINHOLD FORSTER, 1778

George Reinhold Forster was one of the earliest Europeans to ponder the origins of the Pacific islanders, based on their physical appearances and widely shared vocabularies, after his journey across the Pacific with Captain James Cook (p. 143). Forster observed correctly that the Pacific Islands (specifically Polynesia and Micronesia) were settled not from the Americas, Australia or New Guinea, but from Asia and its offshore islands, particularly the Philippines.

Today, scientific research has not only confirmed Forster's insight but has also revealed that the settling of the Pacific was a huge saga of movement, spread over millennia and involving thousands of individual voyages. The Pacific is the largest ocean in the world, its archipelagos stretching for over 20,000 km (12,400 miles) from the Philippines via Polynesia to South America. Although hunters and gatherers crossed short sea passages to settle Australia and New Guinea at least 45,000 years ago, they never reached the open seas beyond the Solomon Islands.

Austronesian-speakers

It was only after 2000 BC that the main, canoe-borne colonization of the Pacific was undertaken by ancestral Austronesian-speaking populations. The Austronesian language family today has almost 400 million speakers and was the most widespread language family in the pre-Columbian world. Carried initially by migrating populations into the vastnesses of Island Southeast Asia and Oceania, it eventually reached New Zealand, via central Polynesia, by AD 1200. This

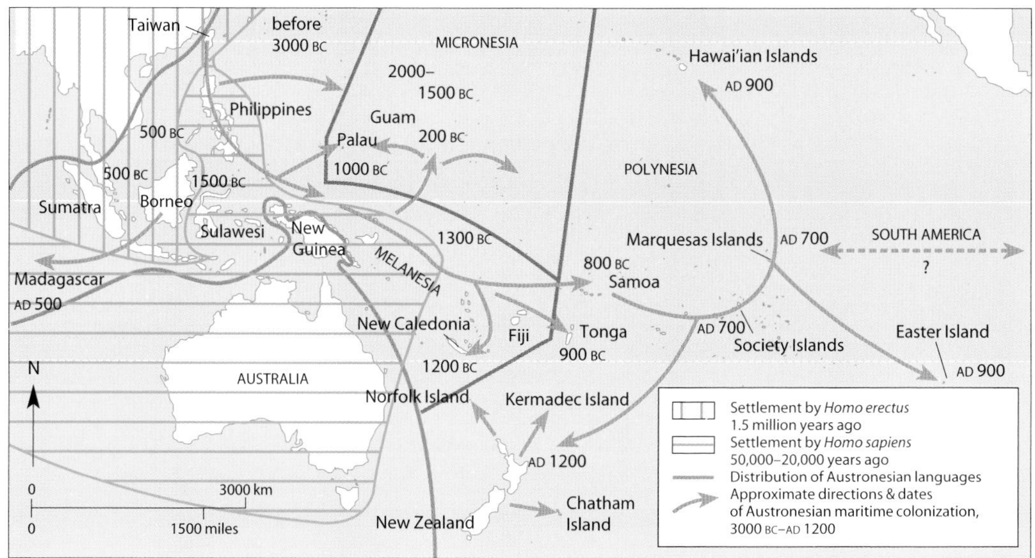

The sequential pattern of human settlement of the Pacific region.

A Bajau stilt village built above an offshore lagoon, Laluin Island, near Halmahera in eastern Indonesia. Remains of stilt villages have been found dating to about 5000 BC in Neolithic China and to 1400 BC in Melanesia (Lapita Culture).

was the greatest 'folk migration' in human history, albeit with myriad smaller movements within the greater migrational trends.

A migration on this scale, stretching over such vast distances of space and time and involving hundreds of generations of pioneers related by language and culture, is impossible to summarize in a few words – the map presents the essential framework as it is understood today.

Linguistic and archaeological records indicate that the roots of Austronesian population expansion lay among cereal (rice and millet) farmers in southern coastal China and Taiwan at about 3000 BC. Their migration involved two apparent major bursts of activity, according to both radiocarbon dates and linguistic reconstructions. The first stage, dating between 2000 and 1000 BC, took settlers across about 8,000 km (almost 5,000 miles) from southern Taiwan and the Philippines, through Indonesia and around New Guinea, to reach Tonga and Samoa in western Polynesia (in around 900 BC and 800 BC respectively).

As far as the Solomon Islands, the new populations were migrating into lands already occupied by humans for many millennia. In the previously unsettled Oceanic islands beyond the Solomons the arrival of humans is marked by the arrival, between 1400 and 800 BC, of Neolithic populations – users of decorated Lapita pottery as far east as Samoa, but without pottery beyond. These people had systems of food production based on tubers (e.g., yam, taro) and tree products (e.g., breadfruit, banana, coconut) and three domestic animals – the pig, dog and chicken.

A standstill followed, lasting about 1500 years. Then, voyaging began again between AD 700 and 1200 when settlers sailed beyond Samoa to all habitable islands in Polynesia, including many that were never permanently settled (such as Norfolk, Pitcairn, Henderson). Austronesians also moved in the opposite direction – westwards – to Madagascar (AD 500).

By AD 1200, when tropical Polynesians reached the temperate shores of New Zealand with its large populations of prodigious flightless birds (*moa*), the migrations were virtually over. Others

Top-knotted stone statues on an ahu *platform at Anakena, Easter Island. These were carved by* c. *AD 1500 by some of the remotest descendants of the Austronesian diaspora across the Pacific.*

A single-outrigger sailing canoe in the Caroline Islands of Micronesia, painted in the 19th century.

had reached Easter Island by about AD 900, eventually to carve the colossal statues in mysterious isolation. Some probably reached South America, to return with the sweet potato and additional stone-carving skills. By this time, Austronesians had spread more than half way around the world.

How and why?

How was it done? According to linguistic reconstructions and ethnographic records, early Austronesian canoes had matting sails and stabilizing outriggers, and were constructed with side planks lashed edge-to-edge through perforated lugs on to a dugout keel, the whole structure lashed in turn against inserted ribs. It is likely that these lashing techniques, using *sennit* (coconut fibre), as described by Forster for large double canoes in Tahiti in 1774, allowed pioneers to voyage over Pacific swells, upon which hull flexibility would have offered key advantages.

The origins of these Neolithic carpentry skills (including dowels, mortises and tenons) and the necessary polished stone adzes and chisels can be traced back into lower Yangtze China, where canoe parts and paddles have been found dating from 6000 BC. The lashing technology was related to that used in the funerary boat of the 4th Dynasty Egyptian pharaoh Khufu, buried beside his pyramid at Giza in the mid-3rd millennium BC. This is not to imply direct diffusion, rather a widespread body of shared human knowledge that must go back in origin far into the coastal and riverine realms of the Old World Neolithic.

Just why so many people undertook so many voyages over so many millennia is an issue that will entertain anthropologists for many generations. The venture was made possible by the acquisition of carpentry and boatbuilding skills, and transportable systems of food production (hunters and gatherers would not have subsisted for long on many of the smaller islands of Oceania). The movements were too rapid to be the result of population growth alone, but naive bird faunas on uninhabited islands, encouraging weather patterns (including periods of frequent El Niño induced westerly winds) and simple human ambition to found new lines of descendants in fresh lands, all doubtless contributed.

Perhaps the first really *long*-distance Pacific voyage on record occurred about 1500 BC, from the Philippines to the Mariana Islands, across 2,000 km (1,240 miles) of open sea. After this, the human settlement of the open Pacific was on course for success.

TOBY WILKINSON

Egyptian Explorers

4

2250, 1460, 600 BC

The majesty of Merenra, my lord, sent me together with my father ... to Yam, to open the way to that country. I did it in seven months; I brought from it all kinds of beautiful and rare gifts, and was praised for it very greatly.

HARKHUF, *c.* 2250 BC

Ancient Egypt is sometimes characterized as an isolationist and introspective civilization, secure within its natural borders, confident of its own superiority and suspicious of foreign countries and their inhabitants. Certainly, the ancient Egyptians counted themselves blessed by a fertile and bountiful environment which they contrasted with the harsher, less familiar lands surrounding them. State ideology emphasized this difference to the point of xenophobia. Yet, behind the official rhetoric, the Egyptians were always open to influences from outside the Nile Valley; they were welcoming to visitors and migrants from neighbouring lands (as long as the newcomers adopted Egyptian culture); and they were, if not curious about the outside world, then certainly eager to exploit its economic potential for the greater glory and prosperity of Egypt.

The journeys of Harkhuf

The oldest account of foreign travel to survive from ancient Egypt, and one of the most important, dates from the 6th Dynasty (*c.* 2325–*c.* 2175 BC), towards the end of the Pyramid Age. On the façade of his rock-cut tomb in the hills overlooking the Nile at Aswan, a man called Harkhuf had an autobiographical text inscribed. This was not unusual: all Egyptians of status wished to perpetuate their good name by having their achievements immortalized in stone. However, in Harkhuf's case, he genuinely had something to boast about: the successful accomplishment of not one, but four separate expeditions to the distant land of Yam. These epic journeys place Harkhuf among the most adventurous of ancient explorers.

It was in his father's company that Harkhuf undertook his first expedition, carried out on the orders of the king, Merenra. The purpose of such a

Relief of Harkhuf, from the façade of his tomb at Qubbet el-Hawa, 23rd century BC.

PHOENICIAN VOYAGERS

With an economy dependent on maritime trade, the Phoenicians were the greatest explorers of the ancient Mediterranean world. From the 15th century BC until their final eclipse in the 4th century BC, Phoenician traders undertook commercial voyages throughout the Mediterranean. Departing from cities such as Byblos, Sidon and Tyre in their Lebanese coastal heartland, the Phoenicians traded far and wide, as attested by archaeological evidence. They established permanent trading settlements on many of the main Mediterranean islands, including Cyprus, Crete, Sicily, Sardinia, Malta and Ibiza; commercial activities in north Africa centred on the city of Carthage, a Phoenician foundation on the Bay of Tunis. In search of precious metals and metal-bearing ores, Phoenician merchants settled the Andalusian coast of Spain and even ventured beyond the Strait of Gibraltar, founding the city of Cadiz and a number of colonies along Morocco's Atlantic coast as far south as Mogador, an island in the Bay of Essaouira.

Impressive as these voyages were for the time, literary accounts suggest that the Phoenicians and their descendants may have ventured even further afield. Ancient authors record Phoenician voyages to Madeira and the Canary Islands, while an unverified discovery of Phoenician coins in the Azores may suggest more far-flung Atlantic exploration. An early medieval manuscript records a voyage in the second half of the 5th century BC by a Carthaginian navigator named Hanno along the coast of west Africa, although the extent of his travels remains disputed. Other ancient historical accounts mention Phoenician sailors travelling to the fabled land of Ophir, probably to be located in east Africa or southern Arabia; while a Carthaginian called Himlico reportedly sailed as far as northern Brittany or perhaps even the south coast of England in search of tin, although there is no archaeological proof of Carthaginian trade with northern Europe.

Relief of a Phoenician sea-going ship with two banks of oars, from the palace of the Assyrian king Sennacherib at Nineveh (modern Iraq), c. 700 BC.

journey would have been to secure trade routes and bring back fine objects for the royal treasury. The destination, Yam, lay in present-day Sudan, along the Upper Nile. To reach Yam required a journey of 900 km (560 miles) from Harkhuf's home town of Abu (modern Elephantine), which was itself 700 km (430 miles) south of the ancient Egyptian capital Memphis. Whether Harkhuf left from the court, or from his own town, is not known; but he proudly relates how he accomplished the journey there and back in just seven months, bringing home a collection of exotic goods for the king.

So successful was this mission that Harkhuf was sent to Yam once more, this time as expedition leader in his own right. He left from Elephantine and returned via a series of small territories in Lower Nubia (the northern Sudanese Nile Valley). He took the opportunity to explore these foreign lands, and returned to Egypt after eight months away. Modern Egyptologists and historians have cause to thank Harkhuf for his curiosity, since his recorded observations during this and his next journey represent our best source for the political development of Nubia at this early period.

Harkhuf's third journey to Yam followed a different route, leaving the Nile Valley further north, in the district of This (modern Girga), and taking the 'oasis road'. This route is still used by camel-trains today, and is called in Arabic the Darb el-Arba'in, 'the road of forty (days)'. It led via the Kharga Oasis through the eastern Sahara to the Darfur region of Sudan, although Harkhuf must have left it at some point, turning eastwards back towards the river. Once he had arrived in Yam, Harkhuf discovered that the ruler, with whom he evidently wished to discuss trade matters, had left to wage a military campaign against the Tjemeh (the inhabitants of southeastern Libya). Undeterred, Harkhuf followed him to Tjemeh-land, successfully concluded his negotiations, and returned to Egypt with a caravan of 300 donkeys, laden with rare products including incense, ebony, precious oil, panther-skins and elephants' tusks. However, the journey home was not straightforward: travelling as before through

Statue of the boy-king Neferkara Pepi II seated on his mother's lap, 23rd century BC. *It was early in this pharaoh's reign that Harkhuf undertook his final voyage to Yam, returning with a pygmy, to the delight of the king.*

Lower Nubia, Harkhuf had to negotiate safe passage from the local ruler. Only the presence of an armed escort provided by the ruler of Yam gave Harkhuf the upper hand. Relieved, he made his way north to the royal residence at Memphis, and was welcomed home by a convoy of ships laden with food and drink.

Harkhuf's fourth and final journey to Yam took place early in the reign of Merenra's successor, the boy king Neferkara Pepi II. For Harkhuf, the proudest moment of this voyage was receiving a letter from the king. In it, Neferkara excitedly urged Harkhuf to ensure the safe delivery of the most exotic of all trophies from Yam: a dancing pygmy. Never before had such a prize been brought from the Upper Nile, and the boy king showed his eagerness, writing to Harkhuf 'Come north to the residence at once! Hurry and bring with you this pygmy … to delight the heart of King Neferkara.'

Egypt and Africa: the first circumnavigation?

In their quest for exotic products, the ancient Egyptians launched regular expeditions down the Red Sea coast to the land of Punt, on the borders of eastern Sudan and Ethiopia. The most famous instance was led by the treasurer Nehsi during the reign of the female king Hatshepsut (*c.* 1473–*c.* 1458 BC), and recorded in detail on the walls of her mortuary temple at Deir el-Bahri near

Map showing the route taken by Harkhuf on his third journey to Yam, and the possible location of Punt (inset), the destination of an expedition sent by Hatshepsut in the 15th century BC.

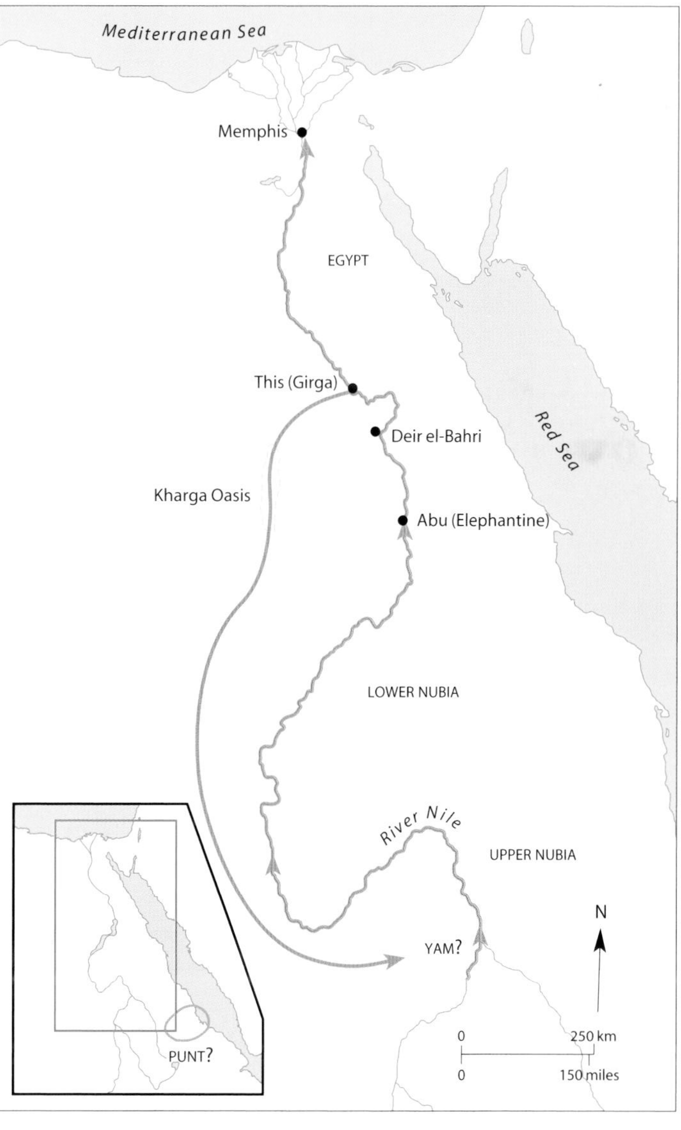

Right *Painted wooden model of a boat, with the crew tending the sail, from Meir, Middle Egypt, c. 1900* BC.

Below *A village of stilt-houses in the land of Punt, depicted in a relief from the temple of Hatshepsut at Deir el-Bahri, 15th century* BC.

Luxor. Such expeditions required a degree of maritime skill, but pale into insignificance beside the sea voyage reputed to have been undertaken in the 26th Dynasty, on the orders of the Egyptian king Necho II (610–595 BC).

According to the Greek historian Herodotus (p. 33), Necho sent a fleet of Phoenician sailors on a circumnavigation of Africa, via the Red Sea and the Indian Ocean, returning via the Strait of Gibraltar. The expedition kept itself supplied by landing periodically, sowing and harvesting crops; the whole journey lasted nearly three years. Tempting as it may be to take this story at face value, there are compelling cultural and literary arguments against it actually having happened. What the story does illustrate, however, is the renowned seafaring prowess of the Phoenicians (see box, p. 30), a skill recognized by their contemporaries throughout the eastern Mediterranean.

JUSTIN MAROZZI

Herodotus

5

c. 450 BC

Herodotus of Halicarnassus here displays his inquiry, so that human achievements may not become forgotten in time, and great and marvellous deeds – some displayed by Greeks, some by barbarians – may not be without their glory; and especially to show why the two peoples fought each other.

HERODOTUS, 5TH CENTURY BC

Thus begins the world's first history book, an epic of storytelling which remains in print almost 2,500 years after its first appearance. It was written by Herodotus, a man of genius and an extraordinary traveller whose life remains fascinatingly obscure. That he came from the ancient city of Halicarnassus, the modern Turkish port of Bodrum, we know only from these opening lines.

Herodotus was born sometime around 484 BC and witnessed at first hand the golden age of Greece, a highpoint of civilization reached after the Persian Wars ended in 479 BC. Among his contemporaries he numbered some of the greatest minds the Greeks ever produced, from Pericles and Protagoras to Socrates, Sophocles and Thucydides. By the time of Herodotus' death in about 425 BC, Plato was just a toddler.

Around 457 BC Herodotus was sent into exile, apparently for conspiring against the tyrant of Halicarnassus, Lygdamis. He probably spent a number of years on the Greek island of Samos before returning to Halicarnassus to help oust Lygdamis from power. After that momentous effort, he seems to have taken to the roads and seas again, making ground-breaking journeys through much of Asia Minor, Babylon, Egypt, Libya, Lebanon, Palestine and Greece, venturing as far north as the Black Sea.

It is thought that he was one of the first settlers to found the Greek colony of Thurii in southern Italy in about 443 BC. Here, he devoted the remainder of his days to writing the *Histories*, a one-volume literary revolution.

Herodotus was the Father of History, the only epithet by which he is popularly known (Plutarch uncharitably dubbed him the 'Father of Lies'). But he was much more than that. He was also the world's first travel writer, a pioneering geographer of distinction, an anthropologist and an explorer, a dramatist and a journalist with an eye for fabulous material to inform and amuse, to horrify and entertain. And as if that was not enough, he was also the writer of the world's first prose epic.

The *Histories*

The *Histories* is his masterpiece, a chronological history of the Greek wars against the Persians – from the invasions of Cyrus in the middle of the 6th century BC through the stories of Cambyses and Darius to the depredations of Xerxes in the early 5th century BC – written with a novelist's, rather than a historian's, flair for narrative suspense and pace.

This is no conventional narrative. The *Histories* is replete with illicit eroticism, sex, love, violence, crime, strange customs of foreign peoples, imagined scenes in royal bedrooms, flashbacks, dream sequences, political musings, philosophical debate, encounters with oracles, geographical speculation, natural history, short stories and Greek myths. It is enthralling reading.

Roman copy of a 4th-century BC Greek bust of Herodotus: although his writings contain a vast amount of detail about the places he visited, surprisingly little is known for certain about the man himself.

Below *Herodotus' distinction as an historian has understandably eclipsed his achievements in the field of exploration. His pioneering travels charted the limits of much of the known world.*

Below right *Scythian warriors depicted on an electrum vessel from a burial mound at Kul Oba, Crimea, 4th century* BC. *Herodotus, though he did not admire them as a people, appreciated Scythian martial prowess. 'No one who invades their country can escape destruction', he wrote.*

Like any tabloid editor who knows instinctively that sex sells, Herodotus understands his audience's desire for titillation. Sex figures prominently in the *Histories*. He describes how every Babylonian woman is forced to sit outside the temple of Aphrodite until a man throws a coin into her lap for the right to have sex with her. Only after that is she set free. 'Tall, handsome women soon manage to get home again,' Herodotus remarks, enjoying himself, 'but the ugly ones stay a long time … as much as three or four years.'

Egypt and beyond

We may not be able to say with precision exactly where Herodotus travelled, just when he was writing from first-hand experience and when he was relying on second-hand accounts. We can surmise that he explored Turkey's Aegean coast, her great cities of Ephesus, Miletus, Priene, Pergamum, Sardis and Smyrna, and in the Black Sea he reached as far as Olbia. We know he sailed among the Greek islands and spent a great deal of time in Samos and Athens. He visited modern Lebanon and Iraq, including the cities of Tyre and Babylon, and probably travelled through Libya, ending his days in southern Italy.

In Egypt, home to the mother of all civilizations, Herodotus found his greatest passion. Here he made his most remarkable journey, sailing

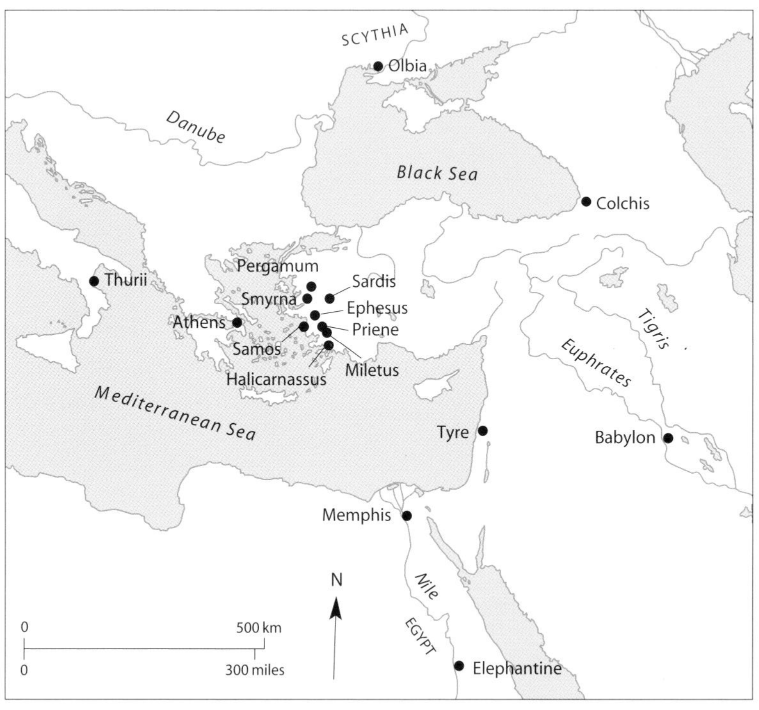

Left *Elephantine was the furthest point south reached by Herodotus in Egypt. His account of Egypt was an important source of information for centuries.*

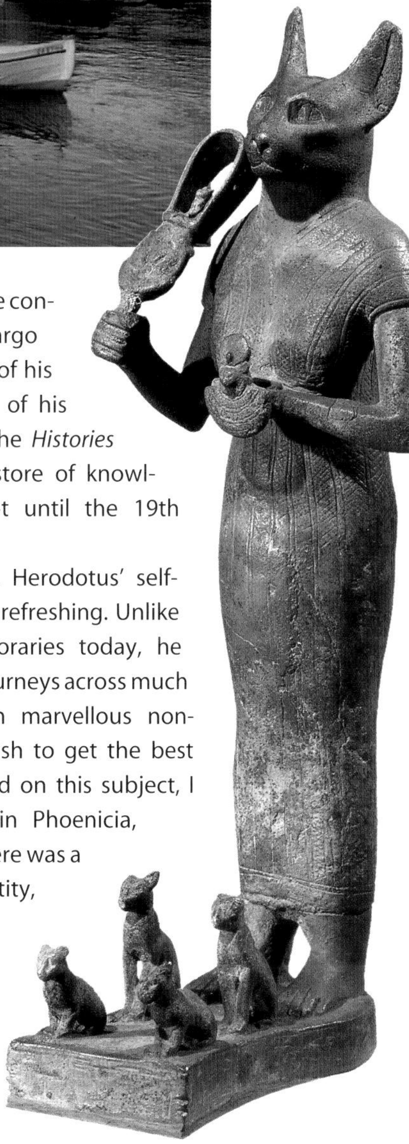

Below *Egyptian bronze figurine of the goddess Bastet, Ptolemaic period. Herodotus described the festival of Bastet in his* Histories.

slowly up the Nile as far south as Elephantine at the first cataract, constantly mesmerized by the great river's mysterious ebb and flow and its seasonal flooding. He writes with commendable accuracy about soundings a day's sail off the mouth of the Nile ('You will get eleven fathoms, muddy bottom, which shows how far out the silt from the river extends'), developing from this observation a theory that the entire Nile Valley was once an arm of the Red Sea. Egypt was therefore a giant alluvial deposit, 'the gift of the Nile'. No mean deduction two millennia before the birth of geology.

Overcome by the antiquity of the place – 'more monuments which beggar description are to be found there than anywhere else in the world' – he recorded almost reverently the local customs, architectural details, diet, farming practices, burial and sacrificial rituals, mummification techniques and instances of necrophilia, anything and everything which contributed to a powerfully realized portrait of Egypt and her people. One moment he recounts how the Egyptian plover removes leeches from the crocodile's mouth, the next he describes the unique construction of the Nile's cargo boats. Such was the depth of his researches and the extent of his travels that Book Two of the *Histories* represented the greatest store of knowledge about ancient Egypt until the 19th century.

For the modern reader, Herodotus' self-effacing modesty is hugely refreshing. Unlike so many of his contemporaries today, he downplays extraordinary journeys across much of the known world with marvellous nonchalance. 'To satisfy my wish to get the best information I possibly could on this subject, I made a voyage to Tyre in Phoenicia, because I had heard that there was a temple there, of great sanctity, dedicated to Heracles,' he writes, as though this were the easiest, most natural jaunt in the world. And he leaves it at that. What a traveller!

PAUL CARTLEDGE

6

Xenophon

401–400 BC

At once Xenophon proceeded to pour a libation himself and ordered that a cup be filled for the young men and that prayers be offered to the gods who had revealed the dream and the ford, so that they might accomplish other blessings too.

XENOPHON, *c.* 428–354 BC

The *Anabasis* or 'Journey upcountry' by Xenophon is a work on which many schoolchildren starting ancient Greek used to cut their teeth. Xenophon, an Athenian former pupil of Socrates and conservative political exile, signed up as an ordinary mercenary in the service of a Persian pretender, along with a large band of other Greek mercenaries in 401 BC. Their journey up country took them to a decisive engagement in southern Mesopotamia. But Xenophon's memoir described also their *Katabasis* – the return march to the Black Sea completed by rather fewer mercenaries in 400 BC. By that time Xenophon had risen to become the band's overall commander. He then recounted too a *Parabasis*, their journey westwards along the southern shore of that sea to Byzantium and beyond.

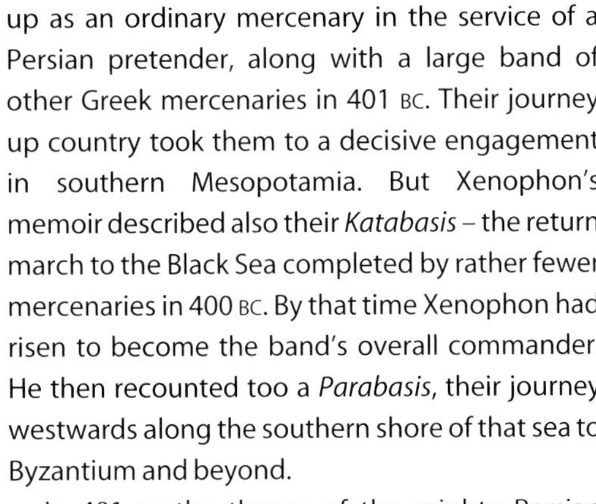

The Cilician Gates, a key pass in the Taurus Mountains. Both Xenophon and Alexander passed through.

In 401 BC the throne of the mighty Persian empire, stretching from the Aegean to the Hindu Kush Mountains and from the Syr-Darya River to the Nile, was contested. Great King Artaxerxes II was faced with a pretender, his younger full brother Cyrus, aged just 21 or 22. Cyrus had had dealings with Greeks, and more specifically had aided the Spartans, in the closing phase of the great Atheno-Peloponnesian War (431–404 BC). In 401 BC, with the connivance of Sparta, he recruited the largest band of Greek mercenaries yet known, some 13,000 strong. Their long march began in spring at Sardis, the capital of the Persians' westernmost Asian satrapy (administrative province) of Lydia.

The turning point

In September 401 BC at Cunaxa, not far from Babylon, the decisive battle took place. The Greek mercenaries by all accounts fought well, but the death of Cyrus robbed their participation of its point and themselves of a paymaster and protector. In the immediate aftermath, moreover, they

were outwitted by Tissaphernes, longtime satrap of Sardis. Most of the mercenaries' leaders fell into a trap and were murdered. The temporarily rudderless survivors nevertheless soldiered on, braving Tissaphernes' best efforts to destroy or at least obstruct them.

Setting out on their long march home, the Greeks passed by the 'Median Wall', following the Tigris upstream in a roughly northerly direction. That would bring them, eventually, to the southeast corner of the Black Sea (Pontos Euxeinos, the 'hospitable sea', as it was euphemistically called in Greek). They journeyed first through Opis (roughly on the site of Baghdad), then over the confluences with the Lesser Zab (omitted by Xenophon) and with the Greater Zab to what the Greeks called Larisa (Nimrud) and Mespila (Assyrian Nineveh). They were now entering the territory of the Cardouchian people living to the south of Lake Van in eastern Armenia. Rather than follow the Tigris all the way to its source, they branched off in a northerly direction following one of its tributaries towards modern Bitlis and Mouch. They were entering upland country, above 1,000 m (3,280 ft), and by now winter (401/400) was setting in.

Xenophon's graphic description of the snow- and ice-bound passage through the territory of the Chalybians contains many memorable passages: 'From there they marched through deep snow over a plain in three stages, a distance of thirteen parasangs. The third stage proved hard. The north wind blew directly in their faces, blasting everything and freezing the men. One of the seers then told them to make animal sacrifice to the wind' – a course of action the pious

One of a pair of massive gold armlets with lion-griffin terminals from the Oxus Treasure (in the British Museum). Xenophon notes that armlets were among the items considered as gifts of honour at the Persian court.

Detail of the 'Nereid Monument', the funerary monument of a local dynast, from Xanthos in Lycia, southwest Turkey. At right is a city under siege; at left, Greek heavy-armed infantrymen mercenaries are distinguishable by their characteristic two-handled shield and crested helmets.

The famous shout 'The Sea! The Sea!' was raised by mercenaries among the 10,000 on viewing the southeastern corner of the Black Sea not far from Trapezous (modern Trabzon). This view well captures the rough and undulating terrain the mercenaries had to contend with on their approach.

Map illustrating the route taken by the 10,000 through much of the western half of the Persian empire, from Sardis in Lydia to southern Mesopotamia and back via Kurdistan to the Bosporus.

Xenophon (see epigraph) regularly approved. By then, with military losses and casualties due to the winter and the terrain, the original 13,000 or so had been reduced to much nearer the canonical 10,000 (a convenient round number). But by early summer 400 relief was literally in sight: in May directly above modern Boztepe the advance guard of a now very straggly column descried 'The sea! The sea!' ('Thalatta! Thalatta!'). The Black Sea, that is, and in the territory of the Colchians at the furthermost point from the sea's gateways to the Aegean. The Katabasis had ended, the Parabasis begun.

Greek civilization regained

In June-July 400 BC they reached the Greek city of Trapezous (Trebizond, Trabzon). Ahead lay two more Greek foundations, Cerasus and Cotyora, which abutted the territory of the Mossynoeci, a non-Greek people considered by Xenophon the most removed of all from a civilized condition since they weren't even eaters of bread. It was at Cotyora that Xenophon proposed transforming the 10,000 from a virtual Greek polis (city) on the march into a fixed coastal settlement, somewhere between there and the next Greek city, Sinope (Sinop). The proposal received a dusty reception: by then the great majority had 'home' fixed firmly in their sights. Moreover, they were now at last in a position to travel as Greeks normally did in coastal situations, by sea rather than by land, from one navigable harbour to the next.

Thus were they transported from Cotyora via Sinope to Heraclea and thence to the Port of Calpe at the southwest end of the Black Sea. Another, relatively undemanding, traverse across dry land took them to Chrysopolis, on the Asiatic side of the Bosporus opposite Byzantium, where a Spartan governor ruled. He apparently saw them as a liability and threatened enslavement, but Xenophon as their leader won time and resources by taking large numbers to fight on behalf of a non-Greek Thracian ruler to north and west of the Propontis (Sea of Marmara) during the winter of 400/399 BC. Sparta then, abruptly reversing its foreign policy, decided to liberate the Anatolian Greek cities from Persia. So in 399, led still by Xenophon, the remnant of the 10,000 were recruited into a Spartan expeditionary force as 'Cyrus's men'. Xenophon himself survived to a ripe old age, well into the 350s, and wrote many other extant works of a didactic nature apart from the *Anabasis*.

PAUL CARTLEDGE

Alexander the Great

7

334–323 BC

For my part I can say one thing without fear of contradiction, and that is that he would not have stopped conquering even if he had added Europe to Asia and the Britannic Islands to Europe. On the contrary, he would have continued to seek beyond them for unknown lands, as it was ever his nature, if he had no rival, to strive to better the best.

ARRIAN, 2ND CENTURY AD

Alexander was one of the world's best ever horsemen and world-beating conquerors. He learned to ride young, and regularly thereafter commanded, fought, hunted and journeyed on horseback. He famously 'whispered' the great Thessalian stallion Bucephalas from whom he was virtually inseparable both in war and in peace for some 20 years. But he also walked at times, sharing the regular lot of his many thousands of men and their female camp followers when necessity called. They covered altogether over 32,000 km (20,000 miles), from their starting point in mainland Greece in the mid-330s BC, marching huge distances across Anatolia, Persia, the Near East, Egypt, to Afghanistan and into Central Asia and India, and finally back to Babylon in Mesopotamia, where Alexander died in June 323. He was almost literally unstoppable, as his best surviving historian Arrian well noted.

Alexander's was, both in distance covered and in achievements, one of the greatest journeys on human record. It began by ship, in spring 334. Alexander, who now commanded the expedition against Persia launched two years earlier by his father Philip II of Macedon, made a point of being the first to set foot on Asian soil, on the southern shore of the Hellespont (Dardanelles). A detour to what was considered to be Homer's Troy enabled the new Achilles and his Patroclus (Hephaestion) to pay their respects to their heroic Greek forebears' alleged tombs. In May Alexander won the Battle of the River Granicus in the Troad, the first of his three set-piece victories over the forces of Great King Darius III and his satraps (viceroys). Disbanding most of his allied fleet, from May to August Alexander campaigned by land in western Asia Minor.

Bronze equestrian statue of the 1st century BC, depicting Alexander wearing a royal diadem astride Bucephalas and striking at an opponent with his (lost) spear. Thought to be a copy of an original by Alexander's court sculptor, Lysippus of Sicyon, it was found at Herculaneum, in Italy, in 1751.

Bas relief from a temple at Luxor, Egypt. Alexander is depicted on the right in his role as de facto *Pharaoh, and so himself an object of divine worship, paying homage to the native Egyptian god Min.*

In spring 333 he was active in the satrapy of Great Phrygia in central Anatolia, most memorably making short work of the Gordian knot. Summer of that year found him at Ancyra (Ankara), whence he proceeded south, through the Cilician Gates, to Tarsus and Soli. His second major pitched battle was fought in November, at Issus in Cilicia, on the banks of the Payas River, not far from modern Iskanderun (the name derives from Alexander). This opened the way to the Levant. From January to July/August 332, Alexander was tied down by the siege of Phoenician Tyre, then a fortified offshore island. Following the easier siege of Gaza, Alexander could contemplate entering Egypt, which fell into his lap, and early in 331 as Pharaoh, he founded a new, eponymous capital at Alexandria before embarking on a dangerous 500-km (310-mile) detour to consult the oracle of Ammon (Amun) at the Siwah Oasis in the western desert.

The Battle of Gaugamela

In the spring of 331 BC Alexander returned from Memphis in Egypt to Tyre, then crossed the upper Euphrates in high summer at Thapsacus, before advancing further east across the Tigris to meet and decisively defeat Darius at Gaugamela, not far from Nineveh, on or about 1 October. During the remainder of 331 Alexander progressed through Babylonia (southern Mesopotamia) via Babylon and the territory of Sittacene to Iran. First he made sure of the old Persian administrative capital of Susa; then over the winter he marched on to the old Persian ceremonial capital and royal burial-ground of Persepolis. A spring campaign in 330 was conducted in the interior of Iran, followed by a return to Persepolis, and the controversial burning of its ancient palace complex. Alexander departed thence for Media (northern Iran) via the original Persian capital of Pasargadae and by June had reached Rhagae (site of modern Tehran).

In July he advanced into Hyrcania, at the southern shore of the Caspian Sea, and in August proceeded on to Areia, in the northwest of what is today Afghanistan, founding Alexandria of the Areians (modern Herat). Alexander then turned south towards Drangiana and Seistan. Defying the winter, he proceeded into Arachosia, where he founded another Alexandria (now Kandahar) on the site of an older Persian fortress. Thence on through Paropamisadae to the foot of the Hindu Kush, founding in winter 330/329 Alexandria-ad Caucasum (north of Kabul, near Begram and Charikar).

Into India

In spring 329 the formidable Hindu Kush range was crossed, and Drapsaca (Kunduz) and Bactra (Balkh) in Bactria (northeast Afghanistan) reached. Crossing the Oxus River, Alexander advanced to Maracanda (Samarkand), summer capital of Sogdiana (in modern Uzbekistan), to the River Jaxartes (Syr-Darya). Foundation of Alexandria Eschate (Khodjend) put down a permanent marker of the extreme northeastern limit of his great journey.

Persepolis, in modern Fars in the deep south of Iran, was the chief ceremonial capital of the Persian empire. Built first under Darius I (520–486 BC) and enlarged by several royal successors, it was set on fire by Alexander. In the foreground is the Palace of Darius, in the background is the Apadana or ceremonial audience-hall.

Right *Alexander's conquest of what is today Afghanistan produced a fusion of Greek and oriental artistic styles and some sort of religious syncretism, as at Hadda, where a small-scale Greek Hercules was depicted (left) in the company of the Buddha.*

The winter of 329/328 was spent at Bactra, and in late summer 328 Alexander returned to Maracanda. Winter quarters for 328/327 were established at Nautaca, followed by the capture in spring 327 of the Sogdian Rock (Baisun-Tau?) and the Rock of Chorienes (Koh-i-Nor). To seal his control of the region, Alexander married Roxane, daughter of the local Sogdian warlord. In late spring he departed at last from Bactria, recrossed the Hindu Kush to Alexandria-ad-Caucasum, and then embarked on yet another adventure – the invasion of 'India' (Punjab), which had long ceased to be part of the old Persian empire.

Winter quarters for 327/326 were established in Assacene (Swat and Buner), before the capture of Massaga and the mighty Rock of Aornos (Pir-Sar) and advance to the no less mighty Indus

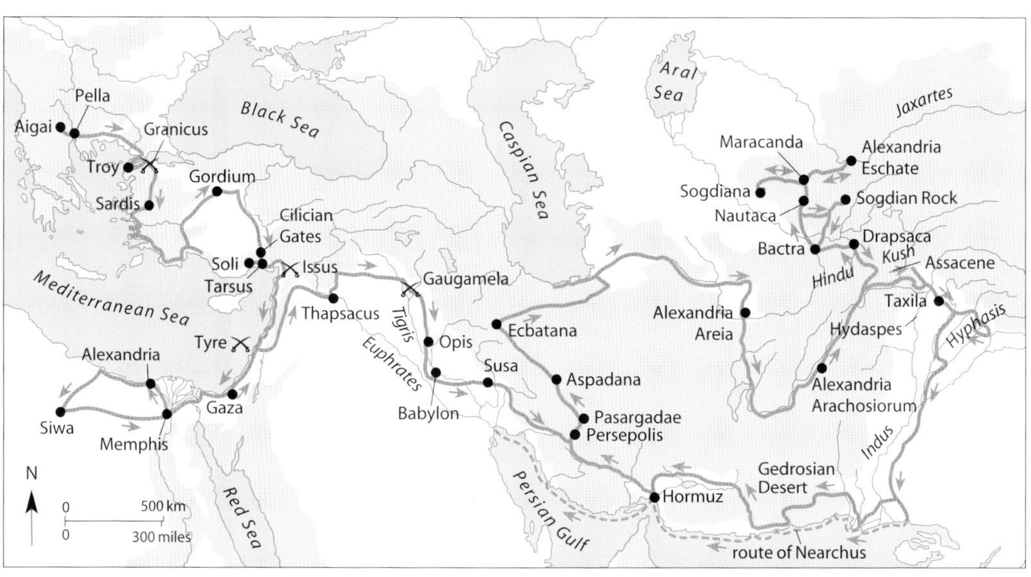

Alexander and his forces marched more than 32,000 km (20,000 miles) in all, from European Greece to the northwest of the Indian subcontinent and back ultimately to Mesopotamia.

River. Progressing unopposed through the local kingdom whose capital was Taxila, Alexander in May encountered fierce resistance from Porus (the rajah of the Pauravas) at the Battle of the River Hydaspes (Jhelum). Defeating and taming Porus, Alexander advanced in late June across the Acesines (Chenab) and Hydraotes (Ravi) rivers to the Hyphasis (Beas) River. Here, though, his footsore, homesick and monsoon-drenched troops finally mutinied.

Alexander complained mightily that he had 'defeated Persians, Medes, Bactrians, Sacae [and any number of other oriental peoples], passed over the Caucasus, crossed the rivers Oxus, Tanais, even Indus, Hydaspes, Acesines and Hydraotes' and would have crossed the Hyphasis too, but for his men's recalcitrance.They forced Alexander to return west to the Hydaspes, where fleets were prepared. In November these were ready to begin the journey to the mouth of the Indus.

The final years

Many adventures remained, however. In 325 Alexander was near-fatally wounded as he sought to reduce the Malli tribe centred on modern Multan. But in July Pattala (Hyderabad?) was reached, and in August he divided his forces. The cashiered troops were sent back by the easier inland route to Iran via Seistan and Carmania, and a fleet under Nearchus was despatched along the Indian Ocean and Persian Gulf. He himself set off in September, still with many thousands of troops and their companions, through the waterless Gedrosian Desert (the Makran). The anticipated rendezvous with the fleet failed to materialize, however, and many soldiers, animals and camp-followers perished, paradoxically from both lack of drinking water and drowning in flash floods. By mid-December 325 Nearchus reached Harmozeia (Hormuz), and late that month he and Alexander were reunited in Carmania (perhaps at Gulashird, site of another Alexandria).

Early in 324 Nearchus left Hormuz, and sailed on to the Persian Gulf. In January, or thereabouts, Alexander reached Pasargadae in southern Iran, and in March Alexander and Nearchus were once more reunited at Susa. Still restless, in June Alexander faced, and faced down, a second mutiny, at Opis on the Tigris (roughly Baghdad). The following winter, 324/323, was spent campaigning brutally against Cossaean nomads south of Ecbatana (Hamadan).

Early in 323 Alexander returned to Babylon, and set in motion preparations for his next major campaign, against the Arabians. But early in June he died, probably of a malarial fever. On its way back to his Macedonian homeland for burial, Alexander's body was taken instead to Alexandria, the city he founded in Egypt. The never-ending journey ended, perforce.

Opposite right
A number of these huge gold medallions, worth 10 drachmas or more, were found in the Oxus Treasure (see p. 37). They were struck in or soon after 326 BC to commemorate the remarkable victory of Alexander (on horseback) over the Rajah Porus (depicted on his war elephant) at the Battle of the River Hydaspes.

Mosaic from the House of Dionysus, Pella, Macedonia, which originally adorned a luxurious Hellenistic-period mansion at the Macedonian capital. It may depict Craterus (right) supporting a heroic Alexander (left) in a lion-hunt in a game park in Syria.

BARRY CUNLIFFE

Pytheas the Greek

320 BC

It would appear that Pytheas the Massaliot was in fact present in these regions [the north]. He says among the observations recorded by him in On the Ocean: *The barbarians pointed out to us on several occasions the place where the sun lies down. For it happens around these places, that the night is extremely short … so that after setting … the sun straightaway rises again.*

GEMINOS, *c.* AD 50?

Around 320 BC Pytheas of Massalia (Marseilles) returned home after an epic journey that had taken him into the Atlantic, around Britain and possibly even to Arctic waters beyond. On his return he recorded his experiences in a book entitled *On the Ocean* – a work which became widely known among contemporary Mediterranean scholars, such as the historian Timaeus and the geographer and astronomer Dicaearchus, and later was referred to by the polymath Eratosthenes, chief librarian of the Great Library of Alexandria. All three quoted extensively from Pytheas and through this network reports of the marvels of the Atlantic fringes – of its fierce seas and great tides and of the curious people who inhabited these regions – entered the Mediterranean consciousness.

Not all believed the stories Pytheas had to tell. Polybius and Strabo were scathing critics, largely because Pytheas' observations did not match their own preconceptions, but nonetheless they quoted him, if only to poke fun. Of the fate of the original book we know nothing. Like so many of the great texts of the Classical world all we have are the fragments that come down to us in the surviving works of his admirers and detractors.

What manner of man was Pytheas? There is surprisingly little that can be said. Above all he was an explorer whose curiosity was sparked by stories of rich sources of tin from the Atlantic shores and amber from the far north, commodities brought to Massalia by traders. But he was more than just an entrepreneur. His observation of people and of natural phenomena showed a keen scientific mind. Particularly telling is his scheme for estimating the distances he travelled. By taking measurements of the length of the shadow cast by the sun at midday on the summer solstice at various points along his journey and comparing them to similar measurements taken at Massalia he was able to calculate the distances he had travelled northwards. These measurements were later used by Hipparchus to calculate latitudes and show that the measurements taken correspond to the latitude of the north coast of Brittany, the Isle of Man, the Isle of Lewis and the north of Shetland. There was no equivalent way of measuring longitude, but his sense of how far west he had gone was assessed by calculating the distance from travelling time by sea. Thus he was aware of Brittany as a great westerly projecting peninsula and he was able to give a remarkably accurate estimate of the shape and size of Britain.

The surviving texts are sufficient to reconstruct his epic journey in broad outline. He probably travelled overland from Massalia via the Aude valley to the Garonne and downriver to the Gironde estuary where he saw the Atlantic Ocean for the first time. From here he sailed, using local vessels, north to Brittany and across to Cornwall, where he observed the marketing of locally produced tin.

For this leg of the journey he would simply have been following backwards the long-established tin route which supplied

Centre *Necklace of amber and glass beads from a grave at Saint-Sulpice, France, second half of 5th century* BC. *Amber from the coast of Jutland and the Baltic was an important item of trade in the 1st millennium* BC *and little was known of its origins until Pytheas published his book.*

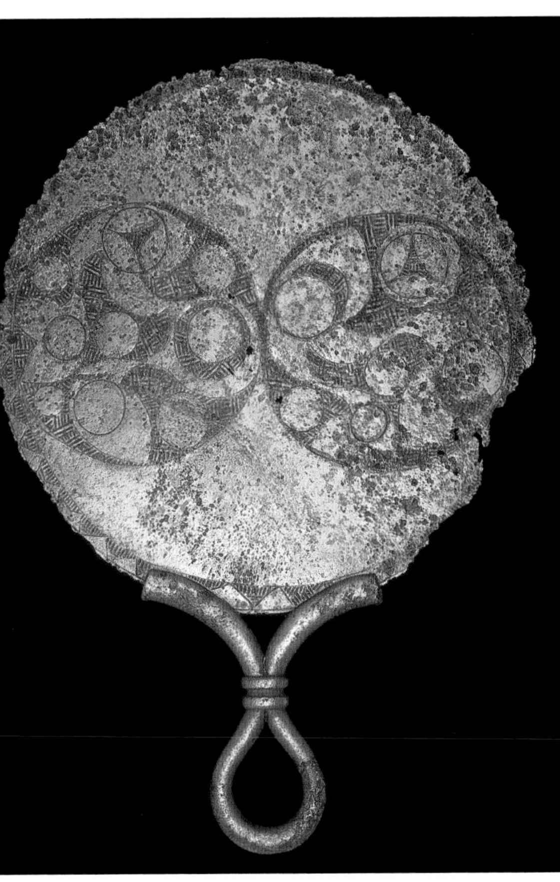

Decorated bronze mirror, 1st century BC, from Trelan Bahow, St Keverne, Cornwall. It was found in a grave with brooches, glass beads and bracelets, suggesting that it might have been the burial of a local wealthy lady – perhaps one of the descendants of the local tin workers whom Pytheas met.

Massalia. Having got thus far he set about exploring Britain by land and by sea. His journey seems to have taken him up the west coast, via the isles of Man and Lewis, and on to Shetland. What happened then is less clear. He mentions the island of Thule, which could be reached by six days' sailing. Here, he says, the sea is 'congealed' and the nights are very short, two to three hours at the most. From all the fragments of evidence available to us a circumstantial case could be made that he is describing Iceland. This need not mean that he actually visited Iceland, but at the very least he seems to have talked to people who had.

From the far north he travelled down the east coast of Britain, possibly making a detour across the North Sea to the amber-producing region of Jutland. He writes extensively of amber but it is possible he picked up the information from Britons who had made the crossing. The final leg of the journey, westwards across the Channel, would have allowed him to estimate the length of the southern face of Britain before returning via Brittany to Massalia. Pytheas' journey to the Atlantic was of epic proportions. He may not have been alone in exploring the Ocean and its far-flung islands, but he was the first to return safely home and to write a book on his adventures.

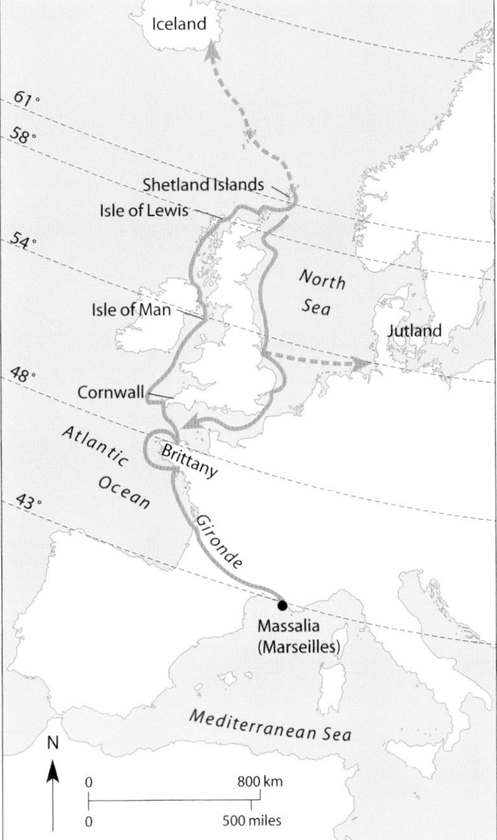

Map to show the possible route taken by Pytheas. The latitudes marked are those which Pytheas measured taking sun heights. It is an open question whether he visited Iceland and the amber-producing coasts of Jutland, or gained his information from those who had.

PHILIP MATYSZAK

Hannibal

220–203 BC

Scipio had never thought that Hannibal would attempt to cross the Alps, but if he had, he would have assumed that the expedition was doomed to failure. Because of these opinions, when he discovered that Hannibal was safe and already besieging cities in Italy, he was amazed at his opponent's daring and audacity.

POLYBIUS, 2ND CENTURY BC

Marble bust, thought to be of Hannibal: so hated was Hannibal's memory by the Romans that few depictions of this great tactician have survived.

Hannibal Barca was born in Carthage (a city near modern Tunis), which had been engaged in a bitter struggle with Rome for mastery of the western Mediterranean. A war lasting from 264 to 241 BC had exhausted both cities, though Rome finally struck the winning blow. Hannibal's father, Hamilcar, had been a leading general in that war, and legend says that he made his son swear never to be friends with the Romans.

Hannibal grew up in Spain, where the Carthaginians were building a new empire, replenishing their depleted reserves with Spanish silver and manpower. Hannibal became a favourite of the troops, who admired his daring, and after Hamilcar's death leadership of the Carthaginians in Spain eventually fell to him.

In 220 BC Hannibal took his army beyond the River Tagus, beginning an odyssey that was to last 17 years. As he advanced, the city of Saguntum started a war with his allies. Hannibal was faced with the decision whether to get involved. It was no easy matter – Saguntum was a Roman ally. Hannibal, however, attacked the city, knowing that this act meant war with Rome. When Saguntum fell in 218 BC, Hannibal marched on Italy even before war was formally declared.

The army on the move

This was a daring manoeuvre, involving a 2,415-km (1,500-mile) march through mountains with treacherous passes and inhabited by equally treacherous tribes. And even before the formidable barrier of the Alps, the wilderness of northern Spain and the rivers of southern France had to be crossed. To compound his difficulties, Hannibal took his elephants with him, deciding that their effect on inexperienced Roman cavalry was worth the effort of getting them over the moun-

tains. However, it was impossible to take a siege train, which meant that desertions and betrayal would be needed to capture any major city in Italy. Hannibal was taking not just a military gamble that he could get his army to Italy, but also a political gamble that the peoples of Italy, many of whom had only come under the control of Rome in the recent past, would see Hannibal as a liberator and join his cause.

Hannibal left Spain in the care of a younger brother, Hasdrubal, while another brother, Mago, accompanied him. His army consisted of about 90,000 men, including 12,000 cavalry, as well as three dozen elephants. In the next few months, they marched from the Ebro to the Pyrenees and then to the south of France, the army moving about 16 km (10 miles) a day – almost every step of which was opposed by local tribesmen.

The Carthaginians anticipated even stiffer opposition from the Romans, but Scipio, the Roman commander, had been delayed by a Gallic uprising in northern Italy. Hannibal crossed the Rhône, though the elephants fell off their rafts into the river and finally swam across using their trunks as snorkels.

The Allobroges, the local Gallic tribe, harried the Carthaginian approach to the Alps. But Hannibal intervened in a local civil war in a tribe living on the Durance (a tributary of the Rhône), and the grateful victor allowed Hannibal to rest and re-equip his army for the Alpine crossing.

Crossing the Alps

Hannibal's route through the Alps is controversial. Strabo, the ancient geographer, refers to 'the pass to the Taurini, which Hannibal went through'. (In fact Hannibal fought a brief campaign there and sacked the tribe's principal town.) The obvious pass for Hannibal to have used is the Col de Larche, but this relatively easy passage cannot be the high and difficult pass which the historians describe. Hannibal's route may have changed either through the treachery of his guides or the ferocity of mountain tribesmen. Not only did the Allobroges launch a valedictory attack (probably along the gorges of the Drac), but in the middle stages of the march,

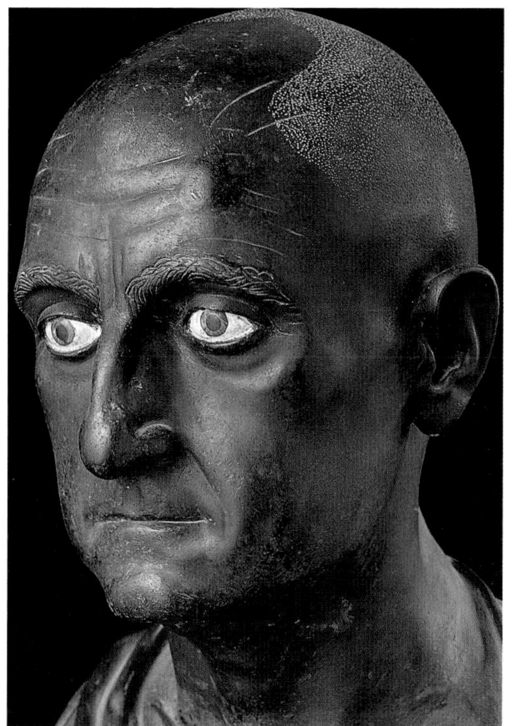

The Roman commander who had to face the threat from Hannibal was P. Cornelius Scipio Africanus, seen here in a contemporary sculpture showing him in later life, now in the Archaeological Museum, Naples.

such as at modern Argentière la Bessée, hostile tribesmen rolled boulders down on Hannibal's men or charged the pack animals on narrow paths, causing many to fall to their deaths.

Hannibal fought back with tenacity and skill, and the casualties on both sides were heavy. Three days into his march, Hannibal captured another Gallic town, and was able to garner a few days' more supplies for his men, as well as a welcome respite. He also recaptured some of his own pack animals which the tribesmen had seized in raids on his column.

The tribesman professed to have learned their lesson from the capture of their town, and they offered Hannibal unmolested passage thenceforth. Hannibal was deeply suspicious, and rightly so, as it turned out that the tribesmen merely wanted to gather themselves unmolested into the best place for a treacherous ambush. Hannibal's precautions, and his use of elephants as shock troops, took the Carthaginians through the danger, but losses were again heavy.

The Gallic pressure was unrelenting and a few days later Hannibal was forced to camp his army on an expanse of windswept bare rock to cover

Opposite right *A war elephant depicted on a silver coin from Carthage. Despite the difficulties involved, Hannibal decided to take his elephants with him on his march into Italy because of the effect they would have on the Roman cavalry.*

The Great St Bernard Pass is one of several routes which Hannibal might have taken through the Alps, but his exact route is still debated among historians.

the passage of his pack animals in the defile below. As the army struggled to the summit of the pass, snow falling on older, hard-packed snow made the going slippery – often lethally so. Hardly had the descent begun when a landslide obstructed their march. One large rock which blocked the narrow track was heated by fires at its base, and doused with vinegar to crack it to pieces. But now the Po valley was in sight, and Hannibal was able to raise his men's morale by pointing to the lush plains of Lombardy, and describing the rich pickings waiting below.

Finally, after 15 days, Hannibal's army staggered into Italy. In their five-month journey, over half his men had perished or deserted. Less than 36,000 Carthaginians remained to face the Romans. At the River Trebbia near Pavia, Hannibal displayed his tactical genius, defeating the Romans and pushing south. He was stopped at the Apennines by the terrain and winter storms, which killed all but one of the elephants he had painstakingly brought over the Alps.

The march through Italy

In the spring of 217 BC, the Romans marched against him once more, but Hannibal ambushed their army near Lake Trasimene, killing the Roman consul and 12,000 legionaries.

For the next year Hannibal moved southward, and pillaged Campania. Then, in 216 BC, the Romans sent a massive army to destroy him near the town of Cannae. Hannibal's response was an envelopment manoeuvre which has become a classic of battle tactics, killing 45,000 Romans and effectively destroying their army.

This was the climax of Hannibal's campaign. Militarily, the march had been huge success. Politically, however, it was a complete failure. Rome's allies did not rebel, and without them Hannibal could not overcome Rome's superior resources and manpower.

In 203 BC the Romans struck back, bypassing Hannibal in Italy, and invading Africa, forcing the Carthaginians to recall their army. Hannibal left Italy, this time by sea, sailing from the

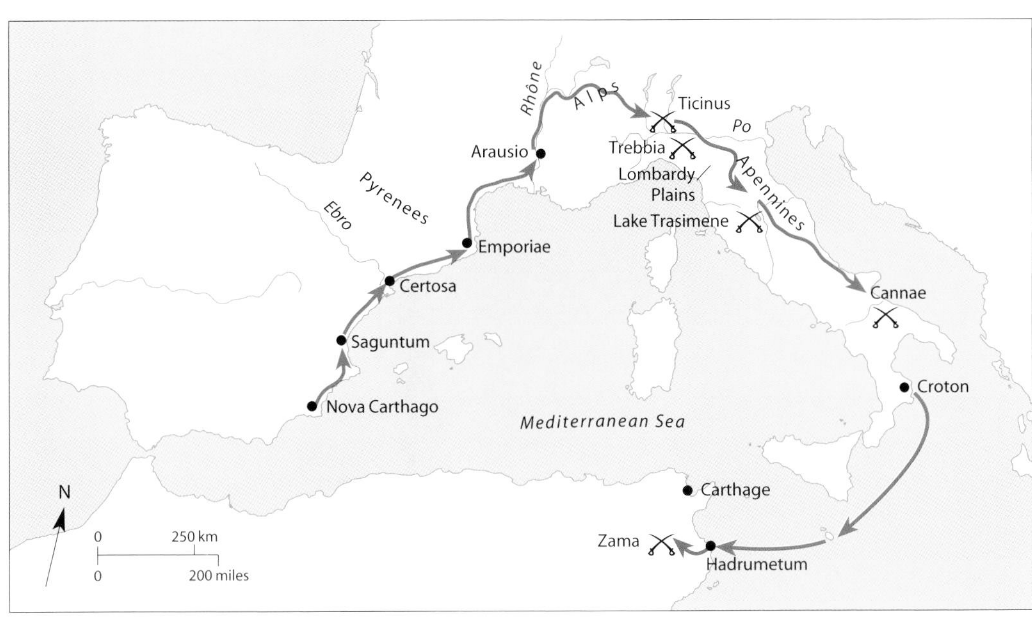

Map showing the route of Hannibal and his army from Nova Carthago, through Spain and France and across the Alps into Italy. After various battles he took ship from the toe of Italy back to North Africa, where he was finally defeated by the Romans at Zama.

south coast. The man who had been 29 when he set out on his epic journey returned at the age of 45.

His homecoming was not happy. Rome defeated him at Zama in 202, forcing him to make peace. Exiled by political foes, Hannibal was hounded across the Mediterranean. The Romans cornered him in Bithynia in 183 BC, 20 years later, where Hannibal defiantly committed suicide. But still, centuries later, mothers quietened restless children by whispering *Hannibal ad portas!* ('Hannibal is at the gates').

Below *A view of Carthage, with remains of the ancient city. Though Hannibal spent most of his life fighting for Carthage he left the city as a boy and returned briefly over two decades later.*

PHILIP MATYSZAK

St Paul

AD 60

Fear not, for none shall be lost but this ship itself, for this night an angel appeared to me … saying 'be brave Paul, you must appear before Caesar and God has given you all who sail with you, so now, be of good cheer'.

ACTS 27:21–22

When Porcius Festus took office as governor of the Roman province of Judaea in AD 60, among the unfinished business left by his predecessor was the matter of Paul of Tarsus, an itinerant preacher accused by Annias, High Priest in Jerusalem, of bringing Gentiles (non-Jews) into the Temple. As a Roman citizen, Paul had exercised his right to be tried before the emperor in Rome – thus avoiding the kangaroo court which his opponents had prepared for him in Jerusalem.

Paul had already languished in jail for two years, but now, after a brief hearing, he was dispatched to Caesarea, there to take ship to Rome. Paul was a person of some standing, being both the principal spokesman for the fast-expanding religion of Christianity, and a member of a prominent and well-respected family. Consequently, he was allowed to take at least one friend with him in the guise of a personal servant. This was St Luke, whose account in the Gospels makes Paul's journey to Rome one of the best-recorded sea voyages in antiquity. It helps that Luke was no sailor, and so he explains much that a hardened sea-salt would take for granted. Also on the voyage was a centurion called Julius, whose task was to escort Paul and other prisoners to Rome.

By now August was more than half gone, and it was late in the sailing season. Consequently, Julius was unable to find a ship sailing directly to Rome and had to settle instead for a merchant ship going to Myra in Asia Minor. Myra was a major port, from where it would be relatively easy to seek passage onward. Thus Paul and his fellow detainees started their voyage on a small coaster, probably about 21 m (70 ft) in length, with a crew of about half a dozen sailors who steered their craft with an oar thrust over the ship's high stern. The prisoners, and possibly the centurion, would have slept on the open deck – unless the centurion used his rank to usurp the captain's cabin.

At Myra, the group transferred to an Alexandrian vessel. This was probably a much larger ship involved in the massive annual trade in corn from Egypt which supplied the bread for Rome's plebeians. Paul's ship battled adverse weather to find haven at Lasea in Crete, probably arriving in mid-September.

There the party remained, waiting for the weather to improve. The delay took the voyagers right to the very end of the safe sailing period, for the Mediterranean in winter is infamous for sudden violent storms and squalls. Under the circumstances, Julius decided to call a *concilium* to decide what to do next. As a wide-ranging traveller, Paul's opinion would have been sought, even if his social position in the little group had not demanded that he be present anyway.

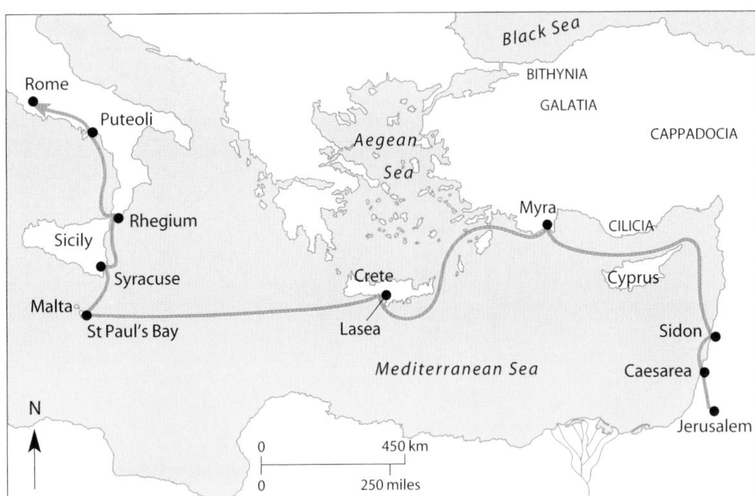

St Paul's epic voyage from Caesarea to Rome is one of the best-recorded sea voyages in antiquity.

Storms at sea

After the council, Paul told Luke his forebodings that 'they had made a mistake in not taking the prudent course' by waiting out the winter in their safe haven. That the final decision had been made by the centurion strengthens the suspicion that the vessel in which Paul travelled was a grain ship in imperial service.

Taking advantage of a fair southerly wind, the party set sail. But before they had even left Crete behind, a sudden squall had them scudding for calmer waters in the lee of the island of Cauda. The wind now set in from the northeast, driving the ship towards Africa in a ferocious gale that continued for days. The sailors tried to strengthen their vessel by passing cables under the hull and looping them around the ship, but the timbers were under massive strain, and the ship started to take on water alarmingly. First the cargo was jettisoned, then the personal effects of the passengers, then the very fittings of the ship itself.

Paul calmly told passengers and crew that no one was in danger. It may have reassured the others that Paul had been shipwrecked before, and survived. This time, after the ship had withstood almost two miserable weeks of rough weather, the mariners heard the sound of waves breaking, and knew that land was near. This was the island of Malta, probably the point of Koura which guards what is today called St Paul's Bay.

The sailors ran their floundering ship ashore, and everyone disembarked in safety, even as the waves smashed the ship to pieces behind them. The natives of the island generously helped the castaways, and thanks to Paul's prudent advice, supplies had been evacuated from the ship along with the passengers. Paul was bitten by a snake

Opposite *Aerial view of Caesarea, the port from which St Paul set out on his sea voyage to Rome. Parts of the ancient harbour are still visible beneath the water.*

Left *Mosaic of St Paul from the Arrian baptistry in Ravenna. During his mission to spread the gospel, St Paul suffered hardship and physical danger, including arrest and two shipwrecks.*

Wall-painting of a busy harbour, perhaps Puteoli in Italy, the end of St Paul's sea journey. He continued on to Rome by land.

while throwing wood on the cooking fire, and deeply impressed the natives by not suffering from the snake's venom (not all snakes invariably inject venom when they bite, and since there are no snakes on Malta today we do not know what species bit St Paul).

Another Alexandrian grain ship, the *Discouri*, had been wintering at Malta, and the centurion was able to put his charges on this ship when it sailed three months later. Perhaps a combination of good weather and favourable winds enabled the party to reach Puteoli (modern Pozzuoli) a few days later. The ship and its cargo probably sailed on to Ostia, the port at the mouth of the Tiber that served Rome, but Puteoli was the passenger port of choice for Rome. It had an established Christian community, so Paul spent some time here before the short journey up the Appian Way to Rome.

At this point our information about Paul becomes scanty. It appears that the emperor Nero was in no hurry to hear his case, and that Paul had a certain degree of liberty. 'He remained two whole years in his own hired lodging ... preaching the kingdom of God and teaching the things which concern the Lord Jesus Christ, with all confidence, without prohibition' (Acts, 28:30–31). The Acts of the Apostles concludes at this point, and while some think he was executed, it seems probable that Paul was acquitted of the charges against him and returned to his travels, perhaps, as he intended, to Spain.

A view of the Appian Way, which St Paul followed to Rome. This most famous of Roman roads remains in good repair for much of its length, and is still walked by many travellers today.

PHILIP MATYSZAK

The Emperor Hadrian

11

AD 121–134

I wouldn't want to be Caesar, to roam among the Britons and endure the frosts of Scythia.
(The poet Florus to Hadrian)
And I wouldn't want to be Florus, meandering in the taverns and lurking in cheap eateries.
(Hadrian to Florus)
LIVES OF THE LATER CAESARS, 4TH CENTURY AD(?)

Almost every Roman emperor spent a part of his career outside Rome, whether touring the provinces or on campaign. But no emperor travelled as did Hadrian – his restless spirit took him from Rome to Britain to Egypt in a journey which, with a three-year interruption in Rome, lasted from AD 121 until 132.

Trajan, Hadrian's immediate predecessor (and his father's cousin), was an outstanding administrator and soldier who enlarged Rome's empire to its greatest extent, with conquests in Babylonia and Dacia. Hadrian served in Dacia with Trajan and later governed Lower Pannonia (an area including parts of modern Hungary and the Balkans). In AD 108, after becoming consul, the pinnacle of a senatorial career, Hadrian withdrew to Athens. Here he indulged his Philhellenism – a love of Greek life and culture – a taste which he shared with many elite Romans.

Adopted by Trajan, Hadrian became the emperor's heir and succeeded him in AD 117. Rome's new master was sophisticated, highly intelligent, and possessed an inquiring mind. His vision of the empire was markedly different from his predecessor's. Some of Trajan's conquests were immediately abandoned, as Hadrian put the empire on the defensive footing it retained more or less continuously thereafter. Within the empire, Hadrian aimed at making its numerous peoples more like citizens and less like subjects. This inclusionist policy, combined with his instinct to take personal charge of everything, was partly the motive for Hadrian's travels. Another powerful motivation was that he was highly unpopular with the senatorial class in Rome; many had opposed his accession, and four senior senators were executed for plotting treason.

Setting out

In AD 121, after less than three years in Rome, Hadrian departed, probably with considerable relief. After first inspecting the legions of the Rhineland, he crossed to Britain. Until this point his entourage had included the biographer Suetonius, who was now dismissed for reasons which remain obscure. In both Britain and Germany, Hadrian established a system of fixed frontier defences. This had never been done before, since

A restless spirit, Hadrian spent most of his years as emperor travelling around the Roman empire. This marble bust was found in his villa at Tivoli.

it had been assumed that the frontiers would keep expanding. But Hadrian believed the empire had reached its natural limits. In Germany he set up a series of palisades along the *limes* (frontiers), and in Britain he ordered a massive wall, which stretches for 114 km (71 miles) from Wallsend-on-Tyne to Bowness-on-Salway in northern England. A bridge at one end bears the emperor's name, perhaps because he designed it personally – Hadrian was also an amateur architect.

From Britain Hadrian proceeded through southern Gaul, always paying particular attention to the training and tactics of the local troops. Arriving in Spain, Hadrian surprised many by not calling at Italica, the home town of Trajan. Instead he sorted out administrative affairs in the province and left for Africa, where a Moorish uprising had left things unsettled. He was never to return to the western provinces.

To the east

Hadrian travelled on to Asia Minor. En route he stopped to rebuild the town of Odrysai into the city of Hadrianopolis (Adrianople), and settled there a large number of Jews displaced by a recent uprising. The main reason for extending his journey to the east was to confirm peace with Parthia – a constant theme of Hadrian was that the empire should have peace on its borders and harmony within them. After touring Asia Minor, Hadrian returned to Athens. As a boy his fondness for things Greek gained him the nickname of *Graeculus* 'little Greek'. Now Hadrian immersed himself further in that culture by being initiated into the Eleusinian Mystery cult.

Hadrian returned to Rome, but was not able to remain within the confines of the city for long. In AD 128 he was off again, first to North Africa, then to Athens, and onward to Syria and Arabia. Such journeying not only satisfied the imperial wanderlust, but also bound the provinces more tightly to the empire, and made Hadrian seem emperor of all his subjects rather than a ruler in distant Rome. One measure with profound implications for European culture was his attempt while in Judaea to Hellenize the Jews. The measures Hadrian instituted led to a massive uprising, and indirectly to the diaspora of the Jewish people.

On his second visit to Asia Minor, Hadrian met and was smitten by a beautiful 18-year-old youth called Antinoüs, who became his travelling companion until AD 130, when tragedy struck in Egypt.

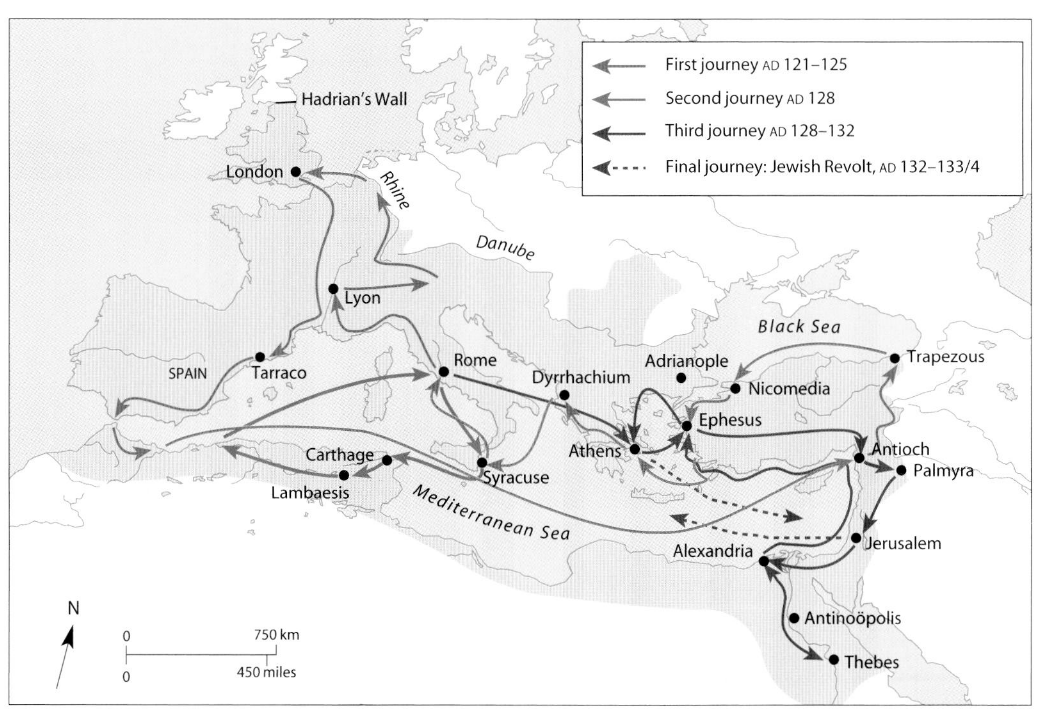

The peregrinations of an emperor: Hadrian's 'hand's on' style of government involved his visiting almost every part of Rome's empire, driven partly by wanderlust and partly by his mutual antipathy with the Roman senate.

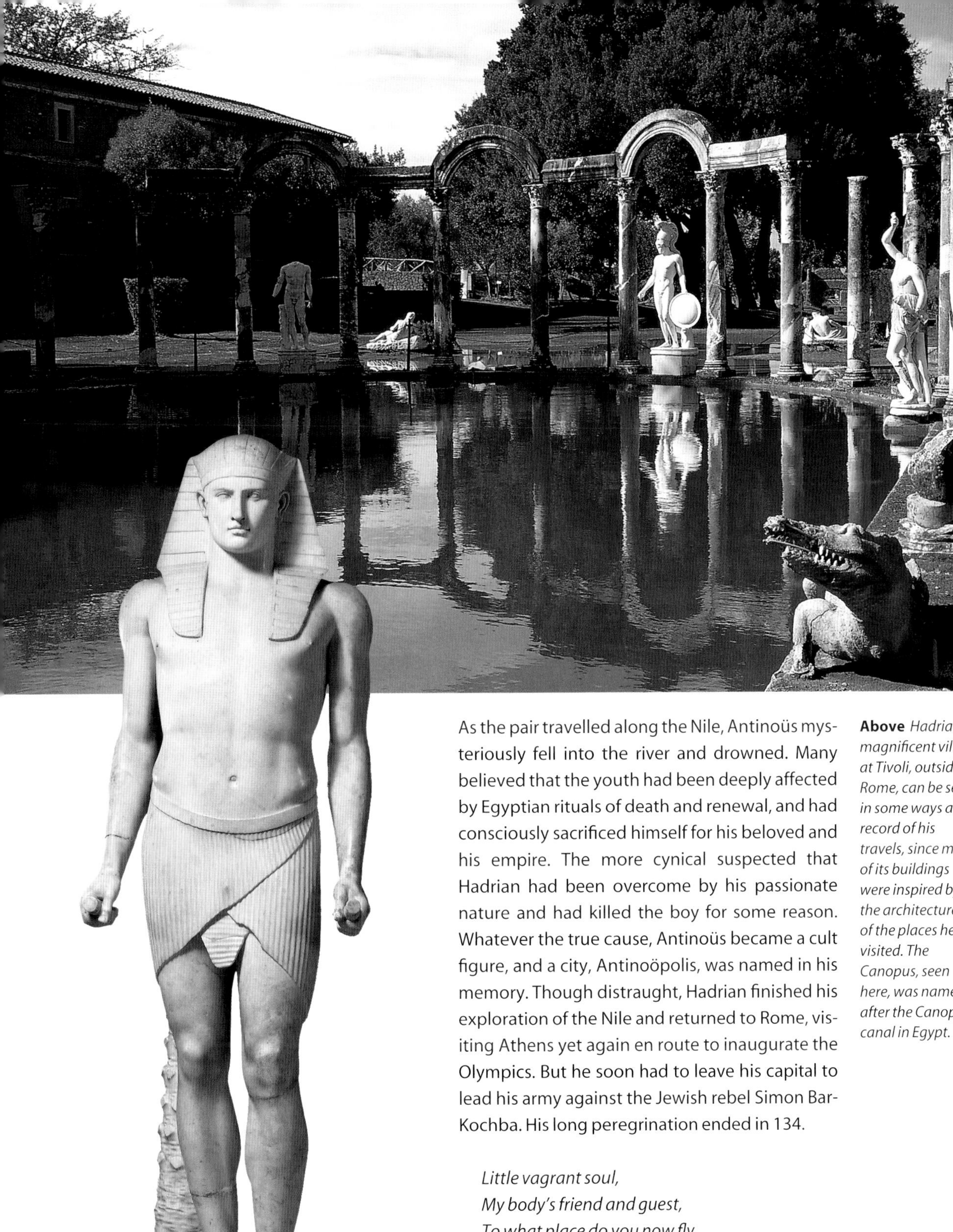

As the pair travelled along the Nile, Antinoüs mysteriously fell into the river and drowned. Many believed that the youth had been deeply affected by Egyptian rituals of death and renewal, and had consciously sacrificed himself for his beloved and his empire. The more cynical suspected that Hadrian had been overcome by his passionate nature and had killed the boy for some reason. Whatever the true cause, Antinoüs became a cult figure, and a city, Antinoöpolis, was named in his memory. Though distraught, Hadrian finished his exploration of the Nile and returned to Rome, visiting Athens yet again en route to inaugurate the Olympics. But he soon had to leave his capital to lead his army against the Jewish rebel Simon Bar-Kochba. His long peregrination ended in 134.

Little vagrant soul,
My body's friend and guest,
To what place do you now fly,
Pale, cold, and naked,
Stripped forever of merriment and joy?

Hadrian wrote these quizzical lines soon before he died in AD 138. Typically, he saw death as his soul embarking on yet another journey.

Above *Hadrian's magnificent villa at Tivoli, outside Rome, can be seen in some ways as a record of his travels, since many of its buildings were inspired by the architecture of the places he visited. The Canopus, seen here, was named after the Canopus canal in Egypt.*

Left *A statue of Antinoüs, Hadrian's young travelling companion, in Egyptian dress.*

Medieval World

During the Middle Ages improved ship-building techniques helped to trigger an explosion in long-distance travel. The Norsemen began to sail westward across the north Atlantic in their solid merchant vessels, using oars and square sails, and their remarkable navigation skills. They settled Iceland and Greenland and then continued to the coast of the New World, which they were almost certainly the first Europeans to visit.

Later, in the 15th century, the Chinese emperor of the time, in a rare expansionist moment, sent a series of vast fleets of huge ships to explore the whole of the Indian Ocean. In 1405 Zheng He, known as the Grand Eunuch, led an expedition of 63 junks out of the Yangtze. They must have been a spectacular sight – some had nine masts and were ten times the tonnage of the ship in which Columbus was later to sail to the Caribbean. The Chinese could have conquered the known world had they chosen to do so, but instead seem to have been interested simply in making friends and allies, before retiring for another 500 years into their traditional Confucian isolation.

Routes on land and by sea could be equally perilous at this time, though the increased availability and efficiency of ships tempted some on to the waves. Chinese Buddhists travelled along the Silk Road to India to visit sacred sites and to search for Buddhist texts and relics. Fa Xian brought back his manuscripts to China by ship, although Xuan Zang went overland, transporting part of his enormous collection back over the Himalaya on an elephant.

Numerous Chinese pilgrims travelled to India in search of Buddhist relics. On this silk scroll from Dunhuang, priests and officials greet Xuan Zang on his return to China, with a procession of horses loaded with boxes of texts.

Marco Polo and his family trekked overland to China, where Marco spent 23 years before returning by sea, escorting a Mongol princess sent to marry a Persian prince. He spent his time observing the customs and practices of a then unknown world, and his stories began to open the eyes of Europeans to the power and mystery of the Orient. Ghengis Khan and his Mongol hordes instead struck terror into European hearts, as they swept across the steppes and penetrated ever closer. The sea played no part in the lives of these consummate horsemen, as they covered immense distances, ruthlessly massacring those who stood in their way

Religious pilgrimages, which were such a feature of the medieval world, also often took to the sea. The Christians sailed from Venice to the Holy Land in galleys, risking piracy and slavery, and some boarded ships in Cornwall for Santiago de Compostela in Spain. Most pilgrims, however, trudged across Europe to Santiago or to Rome, braving the dangers of robbery or imprisonment as they crossed the Alps. For many it was the only long journey they would ever make.

As Islam spread around the world, Muslim pilgrims often had greater and greater distances to travel to reach Mecca on the *Hajj*. From the Far East they came by ship, while those from Africa and Asia joined the huge caravans which gathered the faithful from all corners of the land. For them it is the arrival at Mecca that matters and the journey itself is of little consequence. But it is a journey that every Muslim must try to make once in a lifetime.

Even Ibn Battuta, that most inveterate of overlanders, was shipwrecked on the Malabar coast and lost the treasure he was taking to the Chinese emperor. For almost 30 years he wandered halfway round the world, bringing back a lively description of the whole of Asia. He and Marco Polo began to popularize the idea of travel by writing about the foreign countries they had visited in such a way that others were inspired to follow them and see the wonders for themselves.

The harvesting of pepper in Coilum, India, from a book of travels in the Orient, including those of Marco Polo, by the Boucicaut Master, early 15th century. Travellers such as Ibn Battuta and Marco Polo began writing accounts of their journeys, recording the strange and wonderful sights they had seen.

Early Chinese Travellers on the Silk Road

12

AD 399–414, 629–45

The western routes are bad and dangerous. At times streams of drift sand bar the traveller's way, at other times demons and burning winds. If they are met, no man can escape their fury. Often large caravans are lost and perish utterly.

CHANG YUEH, 7TH CENTURY AD

Buddhism arrived in China with the footsore merchants of the Silk Road. By the 4th century AD it had percolated into every province to become a major religion in a country notoriously averse to foreign influences. Among the earliest Chinese travellers to venture westward into the lands beyond the Great Wall were Buddhist pilgrims eager to visit sacred sites in India, just like generations of European pilgrims to the Holy Land and Muslims to Mecca.

For scholars there was an added impetus for these journeys to India. Buddhist studies in China were handicapped by considerable confusion about texts. As Buddhism had made its way along the Silk Road its meanings and translations had suffered from 'Chinese whispers'. Chinese Buddhist scholars wished to visit India in order to obtain original copies of the scriptures. In the history of journeys, this was a rare impulse. They crossed half of Asia, not for trade or conquest, not for fame or fortune, but for second-hand books.

Pilgrimages began as early as the mid-3rd century AD, but the first substantial record of a Chinese journey to India is that of Fa Xian, who set off from Xian in AD 399. Travelling along the Silk Road, he crossed Lop Nor Desert, one of the Road's great obstacles, where only 'the rotting bones of dead men ... point the way'. In the precipitous gorges of the upper Indus, he found the road cut in the cliff faces so steep 'the eye becomes confused, and ... the foot finds no resting place'.

In India Fa Xian spent six years visiting Buddhist monasteries and the holy sites of the Ganges Valley, as well as collecting holy scriptures. When it was time to turn homeward, he decided to forsake the dangers of the land route for those of the sea. After a stay in Ceylon, already an important Buddhist kingdom, he took passage on trading ships to Java and thence to China. In Nanking, he wrote his memoirs, *A Record of the Buddhist Kingdoms*, among the first travel books. This revealed a wider world to the Chinese and showed the possibilities, and the dangers, of both the overland and the sea route to India.

Map to show the routes taken by Fa Xian and Xuan Zang from China to India. Both set out along the Silk Road, but Fa Xian decided to return by sea.

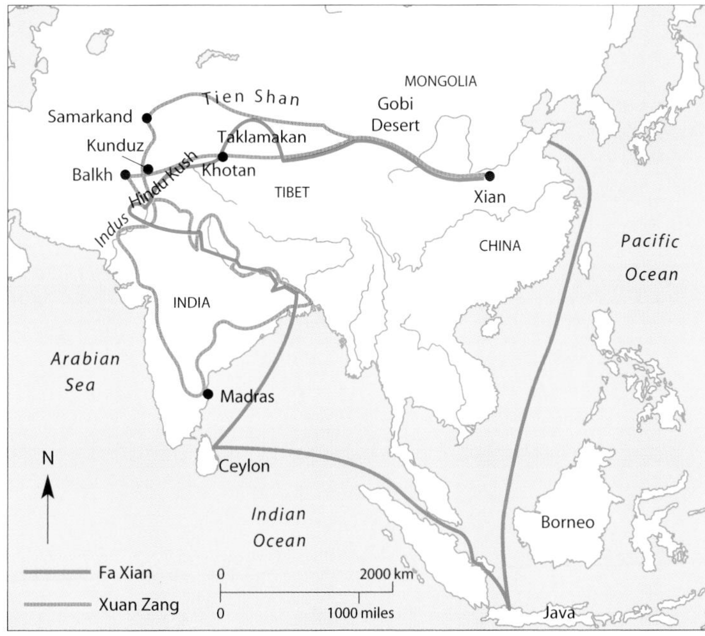

A 10th-century coloured woodcut showing the traveller Xuan Zang carrying scrolls on his back and holding a fly-whisk to drive away evil spirits.

The Master

Two hundred years later another remarkable monk followed in Fa Xian's footsteps, destined to become the most celebrated traveller in the history of Chinese exploration and literature. As with his predecessor, Xuan Zang's epic journey to India was initially a literary quest to acquire the Buddhist scriptures in their original form and thus to correct the many mistakes he rightly assumed had found their way into Chinese translations. But its status was far greater, for Xuan Zang was already a scholar famous throughout China when he set his heart on India. To his many followers, Xuan Zang was known simply as the Master.

Travelling incognito, to avoid an imperial ban on foreign travel, Xuan Zang set off in 629 on a journey that would eventually be subsumed into Chinese literature as myth. In the deserts of Taklamakan, he wrestled with thirst, sandstorms and hallucinations. In eastern Turkestan he dodged assassination attempts and frontier posts. In the Tien Shan mountains, where blizzards howled, he mentions, somewhat casually, that 14 of his caravan perished. In the Hindu Kush he waded through snowdrifts 9 m (30 ft) deep. In Kunduz, in Afghanistan, he became embroiled in a series of court intrigues as a young queen poisoned the king in order to marry his heir, her stepson.

It is little wonder that the travels of Xuan Zang became embellished in a cycle of legends, the most famous of which was Wu Ch'eng-en's 16th-century classic *Monkey* or *Journey to the West*. But archaeological and historical enquiry have proved the accuracy of much of the published record of his travels.

Xuan Zang spent 12 or 13 years in India, travelling the subcontinent, collecting manuscripts and visiting Buddhist sites and monasteries. When he began to plan his homeward journey he was given an elephant by King Harsha, who ruled most of northern India, to help carry his collection of manuscripts and relics – some 657 items packed into 520 cases. When he arrived home in Xian in the spring of 645, he was greeted by vast crowds, with people trampling one another to catch a glimpse of the famous traveller.

Travel and exploration were never the priority in China that they became in Europe. Traditionally China has seen itself as a self-sufficient world, needing little from outside, and historically its contacts with other worlds have been limited. The journeys of Fa Xian and Xuan Zang, remarkable in any age, and from any nation, are a break with that tradition. Not only do they offer a fascinating portrait of Central Asia and India, from a time when few records survive, but they cast light on a rare phenomenon – China looking outward.

Xuan Zang leading an elephant carrying scrolls and relics, depicted in a painting from Cave 103 at Dunhuang.

BRIAN M. FAGAN

Early Voyagers to America

13

6th–10th centuries AD

They went ashore and looked about them. The weather was fine. There was dew on the grass, and the first thing they did was to get some of it on their hands and put it to their lips, and to them it seemed the sweetest thing they had ever tasted.

GRÆNLENDINGA SAGA, 12TH CENTURY

The Western Ocean defined the outer limits of the European world, seemingly limitless, dotted with mysterious islands and holding the lure of paradise. Irish monks in search of paradise and solitude first ventured offshore in skin boats as early as the 6th century AD, when St Brendan of Clonfert is said to have sailed to the Hebrides and to an island far offshore. St Brendan's Isle and a mythical Brendan's Rock remained on British Admiralty charts until the 19th century.

St Brendan's mythic wanderings symbolize the collective sea experience of generations of Irish mariners. St Columba and others made extraordinary voyages, settling in religious communities on the fretted Scottish coast. By 700, a few monks had settled on the remote Faroe Islands. Others sailed to Iceland by 795, where they observed that there was enough light in June 'even to picking the lice out of his shirt'.

Norse settlement of Iceland and Greenland

Norse journeys westward to Iceland and beyond began during the 9th century. The Northmen were consummate sailors and shipwrights, who lived in a mountainous land where most communication was by sea. Their seaworthy warships and merchant vessels developed out of an ancient boatbuilding tradition. The Norse used oars, square sails and an intimate knowledge of their maritime environment to make passages far from land – quick raids across the North Sea and down the English Channel, but also, more often, trading voyages deep into the Baltic Sea and even as far south as the Bay of Biscay. During the 9th century, Norse merchant vessels sailed westward to the Faroes and Iceland.

Replica of a Norse knarr: this type of merchant ship sailed to Iceland, Greenland and beyond.

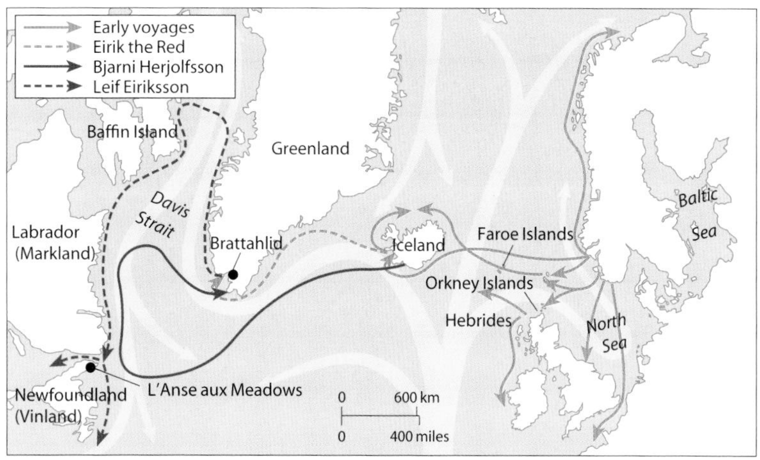

Map showing Norse voyages in the North Atlantic.

A reconstructed house at L'Anse aux Meadows in Newfoundland. The only known Norse settlement in North America, it is perhaps where Leif Eiriksson and his men overwintered.

Norse emigration westward stemmed from many causes, among them population growth, land shortages and endemic warfare. The voyagers took entire households and their animals with them. By 900, some 2,000 people had settled in Iceland, quickly driving out their Irish predecessors. The mariners watched the sky and the winds, the set of the swells and the flight of birds. They relied on crude navigation, using dead reckoning, the stars when they could be seen and, above all, their intimate knowledge of rocks, islands and coastlines, acquired by hard experience. Inevitably, there were feuds and disputes in what was a volatile social environment.

In about 980, the quarrelsome Eirik the Red was exiled for three years. He sailed westward to an unvisited coastline known to exist there, where he found better grazing than at home. He persuaded others to follow him, to establish Norse settlements in what he called Greenland. Soon, the settlers were exploring the rugged coastline to the north, which abounded in fish and sea mammals. They inevitably became aware of snowbound islands across from their new homeland. Archaeological finds in Baffinland in the Canadian Arctic tell us that the Norse traded sporadically with Inuit hunter-gatherers.

Markland and Vinland

In about 985, Bjarni Herjolfsson, blown off course when sailing to Greenland, sighted the forested coast of southern Labrador. He was severely criticized for not landing. In the 990s, Leif Eiriksson, son of Eirik the Red, crossed to the western side of the Davis Strait, then sailed southward along an increasingly forested coast until he was well south of the latitude of southern Greenland. He and his 35 men overwintered at L'Anse-aux-Meadows in northern Newfoundland, surviving an unusually mild winter. They explored the surrounding country, loaded up with timber, and then returned home on the prevailing westerlies.

Leif Eiriksson never returned to the lands he called Markland (Labrador) or to Vinland, an unknown location where the Norse found wild grapes. His brother Thorvald followed in his footsteps, but was killed in a skirmish with local people. More sporadic and unrecorded voyages ensued, many of them in search of timber, but the Norse kept their discoveries to themselves for centuries. They never settled permanently in North America, owing to the hostility of the local people and the harsh climatic conditions.

Norse voyages to Markland ceased by 1350. Nearly a century-and-a-half passed before the Italian John Cabot (Giovanni, or Zuan, Caboto), sailing out of Bristol, landed on Newfoundland and discovered its cod fisheries.

JOHN URE

Christian Pilgrimages

14

4th century AD onwards

There's no discouragement
Shall make him once relent
His first avowed intent
To be a pilgrim.
JOHN BUNYAN, *c.* 1680

The earliest Christians, in contrast to the earliest followers of Muhammad (p. 68), did not immediately think of revisiting the sites and scenes of the life of the founder of their faith. Pilgrimage grew comparatively slowly in the Christian world, and it was not until the 4th century, with the conversion of the Roman emperor Constantine to Christianity and the enthusiastic visits to Palestine by his mother – the Empress Helena – that the practice became established. Thereafter the Holy Land, and the desert retreats of the Early Fathers such as St Jerome, became a focus of travel. A trickle of Western pilgrims attached themselves to merchant caravans or travelled independently through the Byzantine empire and the Levant to Jerusalem. A right of passage came to be assumed.

All that changed in the 11th century with the invasion of Asia Minor by the Seljuk Turks and the capture of Jerusalem. The old tolerance was gone and the West's response was the launching of the First Crusade, ostensibly to keep the pilgrim routes open. With the recapture (albeit short-lived) of Jerusalem by the Crusaders, and the founding of the Orders of the Knights Templar and Knights Hospitaller to protect the overland pilgrim routes to the Holy Land, a new, more combative era of pilgrimage began.

Throughout the heyday of Christian pilgrimage, from the end of the 11th century until the Reformation in the 16th, pilgrims from all over Europe made the journey to the Holy Land both by overland routes and by sea – in the latter case generally from Venice, where a regular service of galleys was set up. The main hazards were Turkish and Moorish pirates, who attacked shipping in the eastern Mediterranean and sold their captives into slavery in the markets of the Orient.

Even after a safe passage to Jaffa, on the Palestinian coast, weeks of frustration at the hands of the local Arab authorities lay ahead of pilgrims

A 13th-century map depicting Jerusalem as the centre of the world. Such theologically based maps were a hindrance rather than a help to explorers.

making their way to Jerusalem, Bethlehem, the Jordan river and other related sites, and many died of disease or exhaustion. To help alleviate this, different European countries set up their own hostelries in Jerusalem to succour and assist their own nationals. Despite all these hardships and difficulties, the Holy Land long remained the ultimate, if most dangerous, pilgrimage.

Rome: the Eternal City

A lesser, but much patronized, Christian pilgrimage was that to Rome, where there were many attractions: this was the scene of the martyrdom of St Peter and possibly of St Paul; it was the seat of the Papacy; it was the repository of an unprecedented collection of relics; and it was – especially for those who combined an element of tourism with their spiritual objectives – one of the cradles of Classical civilization.

But the journey to Rome had its own hazards. Principal among these was the crossing of the Alps, and many pilgrims – including Archbishop Aefsige of Canterbury in AD 959 – froze to death in the Alpine passes. Also, during the periods in the Middle Ages when there was an anti-pope – a rival to the Pope in Rome backed by the Holy Roman Emperor or the King of France – many pilgrims were intercepted and imprisoned. Brother Samson from England was seized by order of Frederick Barbarossa in 1161 and lost all his possessions, being lucky to get away with his life; Peter of Blois was similarly seized by the Emperor's 'executioners'. Others were targets on account of their wealth or status: in the 11th century Archbishop Anselm of Canterbury was arrested by the Duke of Burgundy who was greedily attracted by the 'great weight of gold and silver' Anselm carried with his retinue.

In years when the Pope declared a jubilee year – as in 1300 – and granted exceptional 'indulgences', Rome was particularly inundated with pilgrims. In 1350 the jubilee overlapped with the spread of the Black Death and caused much anxiety as pilgrims were perceived as carriers of the disease. The sheer volume of numbers could also cause disasters, as when in 1450 on the Ponte Molle 200 pilgrims were crushed to death and many others drowned in the Tiber. The sale of

A party of pilgrims arriving at Rome in 1300 for the jubilee; from Giovanni Sercambi, Chronicles, *early 15th century.*

Medieval illumination showing pilgrims on the route to Jerusalem. Not all pilgrims had as tranquil a journey as that illustrated.

Right *Doorway of the cathedral of Santiago de Compostela: the ultimate objective of the pilgrims' long trek across France and Spain.*

indulgences was manipulated to fleece unwary pilgrims: priests used casino-like equipment at St Peter's to rake in the vast quantities of coins donated. The pilgrimage to Rome – like Jerusalem – was not a journey for the faint-hearted.

Santiago de Compostela

The other great medieval pilgrimage in Europe was to Santiago de Compostela, in Spain. Here the attraction was the tomb and shrine of St James the Apostle who, according to legend, had visited Spain in his lifetime and whose body had been miraculously transferred there after his death. To the Spaniards St James had a particular and patriotic appeal as he was believed to have intervened in a number of battles during the Reconquest of the country from the Moors and had been granted the title of 'Matamoros' – the Moor-slayer.

Following the re-establishment of Christianity on the Iberian peninsula, the road to Santiago became popular throughout Europe. In the 12th century the present great basilica was constructed and routes established not only across northern Spain but through France and by sea from England. Chapels and great churches sprang up along these routes to inspire and encourage the pilgrims; and monasteries and abbeys opened their doors to those making the journey on foot or on horseback. In the Pyrenees, Cluniac monks peeled their bells on foggy nights to guide pilgrims to shelter, and wealthy landowners built bridges and repaired paths and roads to help dedicated

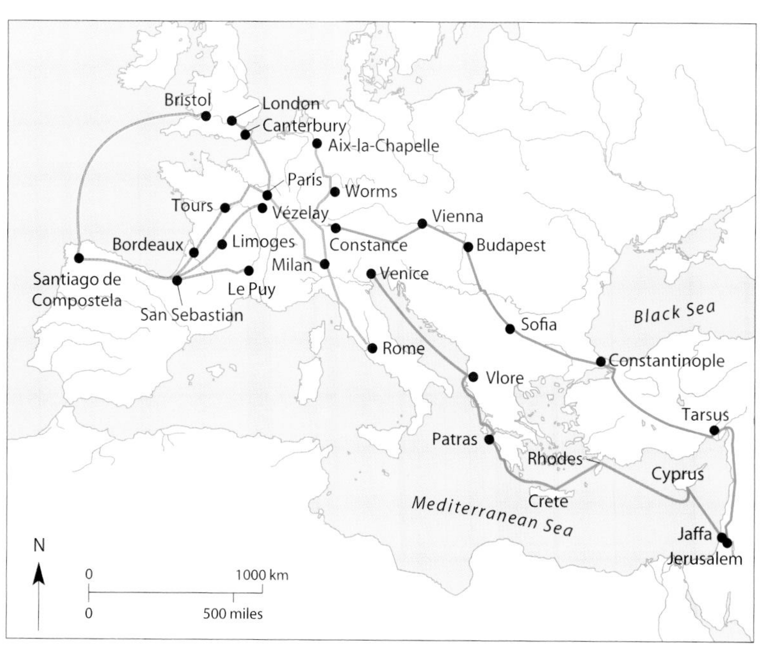

Below *Map showing the main pilgrim routes across Europe to Santiago, Rome and Jerusalem.*

Below right *A 16th-century jet rosary bead from Santiago de Compostela, showing St James the Apostle with his traditional emblem of the scallop (or cockle) shell: pilgrims to his shrine would wear them on their clothes or hats.*

travellers. Immunity from tolls was granted and the archers of Santa Hermandad patrolled and tried to police the roads.

From its inception the Santiago journey attracted many notable pilgrims. St Francis of Assisi went there in 1212; St Bridget of Sweden in 1341; John of Gaunt in 1386, and Sir James Douglas – also in the 14th century – brought the heart of Robert the Bruce there on his way to fight the Moors. For dedicated pilgrims like Margery Kempe of Norfolk in the 15th century, Santiago was a necessary destination.

But despite the celebrity of some of the pilgrims and the measures taken for their assistance, the route to Santiago was not without risks. A proportion of those on the road had been sent as a penance or even as a penalty (which sometimes included travelling in fetters) after a criminal conviction; such 'companions of the road' were often trouble-makers. There were also minstrels, jugglers, beggars and unconvicted criminals on the run, all seeking to live off their more opulent companions. One robber – known as John of London – operated near Estrella in 1318, and a whole gang of English footpads was arrested near Pamplona in 1319. Dishonest inn-keepers not infrequently murdered passing pilgrims in their beds for the sake of their possessions; one French hotelier's woodshed revealed 88 corpses after a nearby monastery became suspicious about the number of pilgrims who were not reaching the next religious house on their route.

All these problems led to others. Because governments found a stream of pilgrims of doubtful provenance a threat to law and order, they began to impose regulations: Philip II of Spain insisted that foreign pilgrims had a licence from their own government or local bishop; Louis XIV of France shipped off unlicensed 'pilgrims' for service in the galleys; English pilgrims were restricted in the amount of money they could take abroad and had to swear not to disclose state secrets about the ports from which they sailed. Despite this, many pilgrims to Santiago not only made the journey but struggled back with notable relics: William the Conqueror had a horse brought from Santiago by one of his knights, and the daughter of Henry I of England even managed to acquire part of St James's mummified hand.

Detail of a stained-glass window in Canterbury Cathedral, with pilgrims travelling to the shrine of St Thomas there, early 13th century. Canterbury was a popular destination for pilgrimages until King Henry VIII discouraged them as part of his religious reforms.

Eventually the great age of pilgrimage came to an end. Henry VIII of England discouraged pilgrimages after his breach with Rome, and Luther declared that 'justification is by faith and not by pilgrimage'. Even the Pope recognized at the Counter-Reformation that preoccupation with relics and indulgences had become obsessive.

Be that as it may, for the five centuries prior to the Reformation, those Europeans who had the opportunity to go on pilgrimage – be it to Jerusalem, Rome or Santiago – had their one chance of travel beyond the confines of their own country, county, estate, diocese or parish, and consequently had the adventure of their lives. Later centuries were to find new destinations – Lourdes or Fatima among others – and to seek healing as well spiritual rejuvenation. But the greatest journeys were undoubtedly those of the medieval epoch, when the quest for absolution from sin in the next world was linked with the quest for adventure in this.

TAHIR SHAH

Muslim Pilgrimages

7th century AD – present

This caravan contained also bustling bazaars and great supplies of luxuries and all kinds of fruit, they used to march during the night and light torches in front of the file of camels and litters, so that you saw the countryside gleaming with light and the darkness turned into day.

IBN BATTUTA, 14TH CENTURY

Five times each day, every practising Muslim in the world turns to face the holy city of Mecca to pledge devotion to God. The prayers form one of the five Pillars of Islam; the others include the profession of faith, the act of charity and abstinence during the month of Ramadan. The fifth Pillar of the Islamic faith is the *Hajj* – the pilgrimage. Once in their lifetime every Muslim, with the means and physical strength, is expected to journey to Mecca and to pray in the birthplace of the religion.

Getting there

In the centuries after the Prophet Muhammad's death in AD 632, Islam spread east and west from Arabia like wildfire, converting vast swathes of the known world. As the religion swept across North Africa, into southern Europe, and through Asia to the Far East, the distances the pilgrims had to travel to Mecca became longer and the journey ever more arduous. Muslim devotees crossed the Sahara in sprawling caravans, ventured over the mountain ranges of Central Asia, and hastened to Mecca by dhow and ship from the Orient; recognized routes set out from Cairo, Baghdad and Damascus, and large caravans formed in these cities before setting off to cross the deserts.

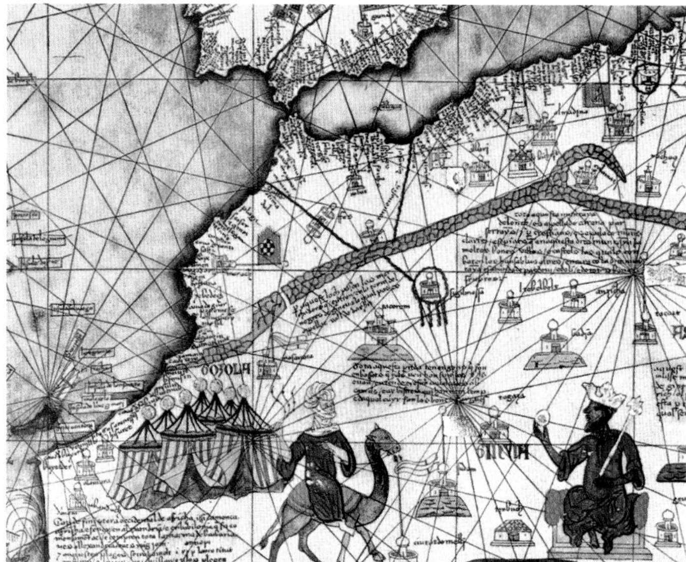

Mansa Musa, ruler of Mali, in a detail from the Catalan Atlas of 1375. His pilgrimage to Mecca comprised an estimated 60,000 people.

For the pilgrims it was a journey fraught with danger – bandits, shipwrecks and illness ensured that many never returned home. The individual tales are almost all lost now, their fragments embedded in the folklore of Arabia and the East. Literate pilgrims have always tended to record their impressions of the ritual and the sacred city alone, and to forget the trials and tribulations of how they got there. For Muslims, nothing is of such little consequence as the physical journey itself. As far as they are concerned, the *Hajj* begins the moment they set foot in Mecca.

Of the few existing tales of travel, the most celebrated is surely the one describing the lavish procession in around 1320 of Mansa Musa, ruler of Mali, from Timbuktu to Mecca. Vast in scope, his caravan, which snaked its way eastward through the Sahara sands, was beyond comparison. Some historians have suggested it comprised as many as 60,000 souls – soldiers and courtiers, ministers, slaves, and the Sultan's senior queen with 500 of her attendants. There were 15,000 camels laden with gold, jewels, perfume and salt. Along the way, the Sultan gave away so much wealth in charity that, when he left Cairo, the gold price was said to plunge. It didn't recover for more than a decade.

The hardships through which pilgrims struggled to reach Mecca in early times contrast with the comparative ease facing most Muslims setting out on the *Hajj* today. Mecca's accessibility now means that every year numbers increase sharply. In 2004 more than two million people travelled to the holy city from all corners of the Earth.

A spiritual journey

The pilgrimage is far more than a simple visit to a sacred place. Rather, it is an opportunity to take part in an ancient ritual, to affirm one's commitment to God, and to be bonded to Muslims of all races in a genuine community. It is almost impossible to overstate the grave significance of taking part. To Muslims, *Hajj* is a time when one shuts out the mundane world and sets out on a spiritual journey, entering into a direct dialogue with God.

The timeless rituals, set out by the Prophet, have not changed in 14 centuries and have been repeated down the ages. Beginning on the seventh day of the last month in the Islamic calendar, pilgrims flock to Mecca, most arriving wearing *Ihram*, the simple two-piece seamless white cotton garb that signifies dedication to God. Before leaving home they have performed a special ablution and will refrain from cutting their hair or fingernails until the pilgrimage has ended.

The rites take in various key locations in and around Mecca, and are centred at a sacred shrine, known as the *Kabah*, in the city's Great Mosque. The *Kabah*, a cubed structure of grey stone and marble, covered in a black cloth called the *Kiswah*, is considered by Muslims to be the most sacred place on earth. Set into the eastern corner is the Black Stone of Mecca, touched and kissed by every pilgrim. Legend has it that it was on this site Abraham built the first House of God.

A sea of humanity

From the moment they arrive at Mecca, the pilgrims are afloat amid a sea of fellow devotees. The sheer mass of humanity, all dressed in white

A human whirlpool forms as the great throng of pilgrims in Mecca circle the Kabah seven times.

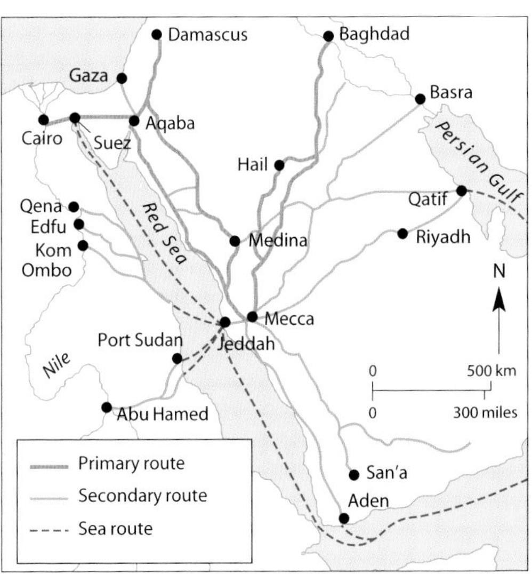

Major pilgrim routes set out from three main assembly points – Baghdad, Damascus and Cairo – for caravans to cross the deserts to Mecca. As Islam spread across the world, some pilgrims had to travel ever greater distances, arriving from North Africa and Asia and the Far East.

cotton, emphasizes the sense of selflessness that is at the core of Islam. The ritual, as performed by Muhammad himself, begins with the *Hajjis* greeting the *Kabah*, and circling it seven times; the first three circuits are made at a jogging pace. The act is near impossible to complete, as the waves of pilgrims form a human whirlpool, centred around the sacred Black Stone.

The devotees pray at several stations of the Great Mosque, drink from the sacred Zam-zam well, fill their water-bottles with its cool waters and prepare themselves for the next stage of their journey. Seven times they walk between the nearby hills of al-Safa and al-Marwa, a distance of a mile and a half, before making their way to Arafat, where the Prophet Muhammad preached his last sermon. The pilgrims are expected to stay at Arafat for a day and a night to contemplate life and to greet the sun rising on a new day.

Given the huge numbers involved, friction might be expected, but, on the *Hajj*, all Muslims are travelling in a tight-knit community, bonded by their belief. There are Africans from oases deep in the Sahara, fair-skinned Berbers from the Moroccan Rif, Chinese Muslims, and others from Malaysia and the Middle East, from Europe and from the mountains of the Hindu Kush.

The pilgrims camp out in a city of white tents, waiting for dawn, spending their time saying prayers and reading the Qur'an. Some stroll around in meditation, others sit alone or in groups, listening to the *Imams*, religious scholars, preaching sermons from where the Prophet gave his last address.

The final stage

From Arafat, the pilgrims hasten towards Mecca, and stop at Muzdalifah to perform a rite laid down in the Qur'an. Evening prayers are given there, and the pilgrims search the ground for 49 pebbles, the size of marbles. They will be used the following day at Mina, the next stage towards Mecca. The pilgrims stay there in yet another tent city for at least three days and nights. Over that time the pebbles gathered at Muzdalifah are thrown with force and meticulous ceremony at three sacred pillars at the Mina site. The act symbolizes the stoning of the Devil.

Mina is also where the Feast of Sacrifice takes place. An animal is slaughtered for every pilgrim at the festival of *Eid*. The scale of the sacrifice is astonishing. With the heat and the sheer quantity of carcasses, only a little of the meat is eaten, and the rest destroyed. Afterwards, the pilgrim may symbolically cut three hairs from his head and remove his cotton garment, before re-entering ordinary life. Each pilgrim returns to a life far away, a different person, cleansed by ritual, by faith and by the journey of a lifetime.

Today the journey to Mecca may be easier – here an Egyptian pilgrim records his journey by air – but the significance of the Hajj to Muslims remains unchanged.

ALEXANDER MONRO

Genghis Khan

16

1206–27

My descendants will be clad in cloth of gold, they will be mounted on superb chargers and they will embrace the most beautiful young women. And they will have forgotten to whom they owe all this.

The Secret History of the Mongols, mid-13th century

In the late 12th century three brothers rode out along the grassy banks of the Tuul, the river that flows into Lake Baikal. After the murder of their father, a minor tribal chieftain, the young men had decided on a diplomatic gamble. They approached the Kerait, a Nestorian Christian tribe, whose chief, To'oril, was an old friend of their late father.

To'oril received them, accepted their prestigious gift of a coat of sable fur and offered to sponsor Temujin, leader of the three brothers. This first diplomatic mission through a land of nomadic tribes with no single ruler would spawn the wildest military torrent in history and a mass migration of nomads out from Central Asia.

Temujin was born and raised in Dadal province in northeast Mongolia. The annals say that at birth he held in his hand a blood clot the size of a knucklebone, auguring greatness. His childhood landscapes were fertile and unspoilt steppe, marked only by hills and rivers and *gers*, the round Mongol tents that still decorate the country to this day.

His first close friend was Jamuqa. As children they swore *anda*, exchanging blood with a handshake and swearing to protect one another as brothers. Having shared leadership as adults and even, the annals suggest, a bed, they parted company suddenly and mysteriously. They next met as enemies – rivals for domination of the steppe. Jamuqa was captured and Temujin offered him freedom. But the offer was declined; Jamuqa died an honourable Mongol death, without the spilling of blood.

Journeys of conquest

The restless Temujin now led his forces through the quiet mountains of the north, the desert of the south and the steppe of central Mongolia, gathering loyal followers and uniting the peoples of an unruly world. In 1206 the tribes pronounced him Genghis (or Chinggis) Khan, 'lord of the oceans', in a country without a sea. Thus Mongolia was born; but Genghis turned his eyes quickly south to China, the nomads' oldest enemy.

When the Mongols crossed the Gobi Desert their army of 110,000 men faced a divided country of 50 million. Riding on stocky horses, whose blood was sometimes their only sustenance, the Mongol soldiers began to pick off the

A later painting of Genghis Khan, showing him as an old man. Portraits of the country's founder still hang in gers *throughout Mongolia's steppe and desert.*

Genghis Khan addressing the people of Bukhara from the steps of the mosque where, like so many Central Asian leaders since, he made religious claims to shore up political support.

cities of northern China. These fell time and again to Genghis's stratagems.

At Wulahai the Mongols offered the city's mayor a deal, say the annals. If he would hand over every cat and bird inside the walls, the invaders would end their siege. The animals were rounded up and handed over to the Mongols, who attached flammable material to their tails and set them alight. Terrified, the cats and birds fled home. In the flames and confusion that ensued, the Mongols stormed in.

Turning west

Following a siege and massacre at Peking, Genghis formed an administration and was content for the moment to turn peaceful despot. To increase trade, he sent envoys to the Khwarazm Shah, Muhammad, whose vast empire spanned northeastern Persia, Afghanistan, Turkmenistan, Uzbekistan, Kazakhstan, Kyrgyzstan and Tajikistan.

The envoys arrived with gifts of gold bars, jade, ivory and white felt for the Shah. He sent them back without a message, so Genghis sent another party. A caravan of 300 camels loaded with beaver and sable fur made the journey to Oytrar in Kazakhstan. The town's mayor had them all murdered. When Genghis sent a further mission to the Shah to demand a trial of the mayor, he received back only the heads of his two messengers. Their hair and beards had been burned off.

In 1219 Genghis declared war, leaving the security of his broad oriental empire for the unknown lands of Islam. His armies travelled 3,200 km (2,000 miles), through deserts and over the snow-heaped passes of the Heavenly Mountains. Picking off the smaller towns of east and central Turkestan, Genghis aimed for Bukhara, one of the stateliest cities in the medieval world. Watered by canals, it was the intellectual and religious hub of the region; Bukhara carpets were sold in the bazaars of Egypt.

Genghis hired a Turkoman guide to lead his troops across the red sands of the Kyzyl Kum Desert. The townsfolk had expected a conventional approach followed by a prolonged siege, as the northern desert was judged impenetrable. Instead, the city was taken in just ten days, as its mullahs encouraged capitulation.

From the steps of the Friday mosque, Genghis informed the locals 'I tell you that I am the

The Kalon complex, Bukhara: the minaret dates to c. 1127 and overlooks a madrasa that functions to this day. Legend has it that Genghis Khan was so impressed by the minaret that he ordered that it should not be destroyed.

scourge of Allah. And if you had not been great sinners, Allah would not have brought my wrath upon your heads.'

In a great sweep, Genghis took the remaining cities of Central Asia and massacred their populations. In both Merv, in modern-day Turkmenistan, and Balkh, in northern Afghanistan, 700,000 were killed. Like Alexander over a thousand years earlier, Genghis all but ignored the Indian subcontinent. Instead, he continued west, killing 1.5 million at Herat, on Afghanistan's Persian frontier, and the same number at Nishapur, in Persia proper. As for the Shah, he died alone on an island in the Caspian Sea, a fugitive in his own kingdom.

The legacy of Genghis Khan

Genghis spent 1222 in the pastures that flank the Hindu Kush mountains. He sent for a Chinese priest called Changchun, a Taoist ascetic who had rejected the Jin emperor's offer to work at the court in Peking. Even in his administration, Genghis chose Chinese methods.

TIMUR

Bust of Timur, modelled from his skull.

In 1336 a baby was born in Kesh, the green city, in present-day Uzbekistan. Where Genghis's name meant 'strength', Timur's means 'iron', and he too was the son of a modest tribal chief. But where Genghis was challenged by rivals, Timur suffered severe arrow wounds in his 20s. Persians dubbed him Timur-i-lang, 'the lame'; known to history as Tamerlane or Tamburlaine.

Timur approached the Mongols for patronage after their 1361 reconquest of Transoxiana, the lands between the rivers Oxus and Jaxartes. In time, his courtship of local populations won him greater popularity than other pretenders to the local throne and he soon controlled the region, building his capital at Samarkand. For the remainder of his life Timur existed in transit, a wanderer who never stayed in one place longer than two years. From Transoxiana he ventured abroad to conquer western China, Afghanistan, Persia, Georgia, Armenia, northern India, Iraq, Syria and Turkey.

Timur governed his empire from the east, from lands where Zoroastrianism had been born and the Buddha had made his crucial pilgrimage. Although Timur's personal religious convictions are disputed, his empire was avowedly Muslim, and its artistic production was in this tradition, even though it built on older foundations of Parthian, Samanid, Chinese, Indian and Gandharan art, influences that had travelled along the Silk Road for centuries.

Islam provided a new unity, religious and artistic, but its doctrinal exclusivity and originality belied the diverse origins of the new artistry. In India, Timur recruited artists and craftsmen. In Herat, Samarkand and Bukhara he patronized miniature-painting, book decoration and poetry. He oversaw the region's largest single building program, the legacy of which stretches from Iran to western China in the mosques, madrasas and mausolea of its many oasis cities. Timur's brilliance as an empire-builder is thus reflected in high Timurid culture, the refined product of a hectic medley of artistic influences.

His influence spread far beyond Transoxiana: a century after his death, one of Timur's descendants set out on a journey south from Samarkand. Stopping in Afghanistan he ruled from Kabul for two decades before leaving for Delhi. His name was Babur and his dynasty the Mughals, whose name is a corruption of 'Mongol'.

So it was that under Timur, who claimed descent from Genghis, the *Pax Mongolica* made the final steps of its journey from wild nomad origins to one of Asia's greatest artistic awakenings.

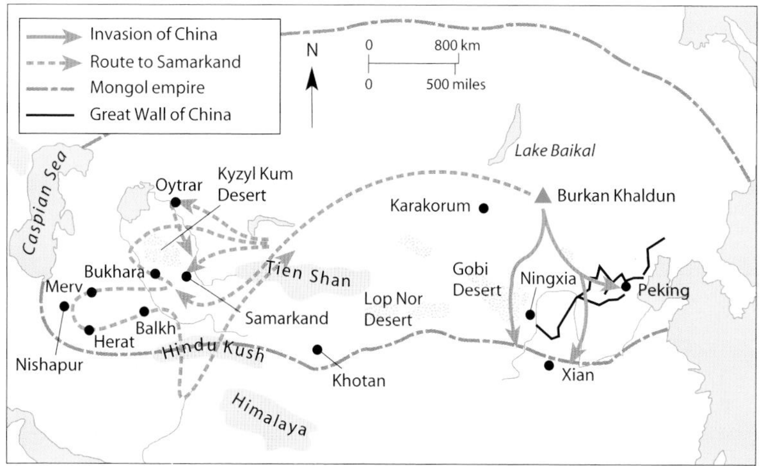

Above *Map showing the route of Genghis Khan on his conquests and the extent of the Mongol empire at his death.*

Below *A Mongol siege, from a manuscript of Rashid ad-din. It is reckoned that the Mongols brought the plague to Europe, because one technique was to catapult plague-ridden animals into the cities they were besieging.*

Here is the paradox of Genghis's imperialism. Born a Mongol nomad, he led a Mongol army over vast distances to victory over northern China, Central Asia and Persia. But beyond ruins and corpses, the Mongol legacy to these areas was negligible. Instead, as Genghis moved from place to place, he acquired the habits, policies and interests of his new-found subjects.

Travelling to the Uighur homeland north of Tibet, he discovered the importance of writing. Genghis employed Uighur scholars to draw up Mongolia's first script, taking the Uighur script as an alphabetical and stylistic guide. The Mongols were soon able to record their own national epic, a building block of Mongolian identity. In China, Genghis's armies discovered the gunpowder, siege engines, catapults and battering rams of Chinese warfare. In time, the Mongols would even move their imperial capital from Karakorum, the 'city of tents' on the steppe, to Peking, the walled metropolis of China's northern emperors. In Transoxiana and Persia, Genghis grew fond of the Shiraz grapes from southern Iran and of the lithe Arab horses, so much faster and finer than the squat steppe breeds he had grown up with. Even the Ilkhanid dynasty that the Mongols founded in Central Asia would be famous not for its horsemanship or terror so much as its artistic genius – a genius displayed in the region's Islamic books and monuments.

Genghis died near Ningxia in northern China. His body was carried back to northeast Mongolia and ended its journey near Burkan Khaldun, the mountain from which he had entreated Tenggeri, the Mongol god of the blue sky, throughout his life. His body was buried in secret among the northern hills of his homeland. According to legend, all who were involved in the funeral, and all who witnessed it, were killed.

In the 12th century one man set out to conquer the earth. But he, his house and his people were changed forever by the places they encountered, while his own influence, like his name, shrank back into obscurity. The world-conqueror and his people had become the subjects of their own quest.

JASON GOODWIN

Marco Polo

17

1271–95

To this day there has been no man, Christian or Pagan, Tartar or Indian, or of any race whatsoever, who has known or explored so many of the various parts of the world and of its great wonders as Master Marco Polo.
Marco Polo, 1298

Genoa, 1298: at the end of a brief war with Venice, a French romance writer called Rustichello is locked up with a Venetian merchant called Marco Polo. Out of this chance encounter comes an extraordinary book, which continues to madden and amaze its readers over seven centuries later. Polo's *Travels*, or 'A Description of the World', is an account of a 23-year sojourn in the Far East.

Marco Polo was born in 1254, and grew up in Venice, the commercial centre of the Mediterranean. The Polos were a merchant family with links to the Crimea, and in 1260 Marco's father and uncle left from there to explore trading possibilities on the Volga. The outbreak of local hostilities saw them stranded in Bukhara for three years. They were rescued by a visiting Mongol ambassador, who took them across Central Asia to Peking (Beijing), from where Kublai, the Great Khan, ruled his new conquests in China.

Kublai Khan questioned his Latin guests about Christianity and Europe, and eventually sent them back under imperial protection with a letter to the Pope, inviting 100 learned men to visit, and asking for oil from the lamp from the Church of the Holy Sepulchre in Jerusalem. Marco was 15 when his father and uncle reappeared in Venice.

Two years later, in 1271, the young Marco accompanied them on their return journey to China. They carried the oil and letters and were accompanied by two friars, who shortly abandoned their mission and went home. It is Marco's acute eyewitness report of his 23 years spent travelling in the Far East that made his *Travels* a literary and historical sensation.

The journey to Cathay

Journeying through Georgia and along the western coast of the Caspian Sea, the Polos reached Hormuz on the Persian Gulf. Regarding the ships as 'wretched affairs ... only stitched together with twine made from the husk of the Indian nut', they abandoned their plan of sailing to Cathay, as China was known in the West, and chose to go overland instead, passing through Herat and Balkh. After an illness which delayed them for a year, they crossed 'the highest place in the world, the Pamirs', before descending to the

In this French 14th-century miniature, from The Travels of Marco Polo, *the two Polo brothers have an audience with the Emperor Baldwin at Constantinople and are blessed by the Patriarch before setting off to sail through the Black Sea.*

Detail from the Catalan Atlas showing European merchants – much like the Polos – travelling along the Silk Road with horses and loaded camels.

Taklamakan Desert. Visiting Yarkand, Khotan, Cherchen and Lop Nor, they pressed on over the terrifying Gobi, spent a year in Suchow (Dunhuang), and finally arrived at the Khan's summer residence in May 1275.

The Polos had already travelled further than any other Westerner before them; but for Marco their three-and-a-half year journey that had taken them 9,000 km (5,600 miles) was just the beginning.

A Mongol passport, such as Marco Polo might have been issued with to enable him to travel through the Mongol empire, though his was said to be of gold; 13th century, Yuan dynasty.

The wonders of the East

The Great Khan, Kublai, was delighted with the young Venetian, for whom China was as strange as it was, perhaps, to the Mongols themselves. Mastering four languages, Marco was brought into Kublai's administration and acted as a special envoy for him in China, Burma and India.

Medieval Europe knew nothing of the civilizations of the east: Polo's *Travels* would open a door into an unimagined world. Ever the dry-eyed commercial realist, he catalogued the customs of the people, their products and their practices, over a huge region that was culturally and materially well in advance of the Mediterranean world. He described the Khan's great hall, sitting 6,000 people to dinner, and an imperial post so well regulated that a

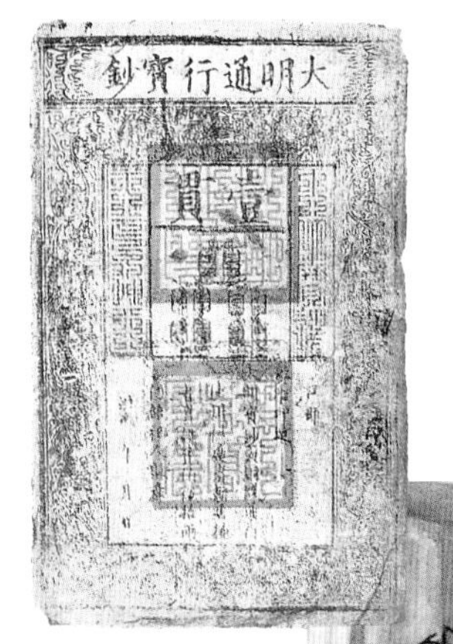

Left *One of the wonders that Marco Polo saw in China and recorded in the account of his travels was paper money: this bank note is from the Khan's first issue of 1260–87.*

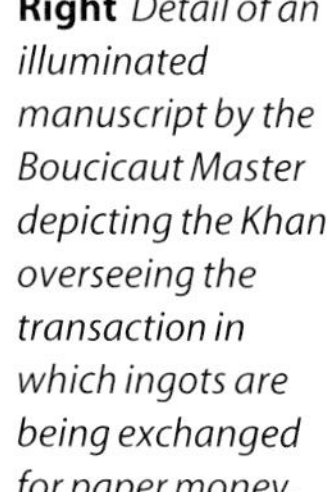

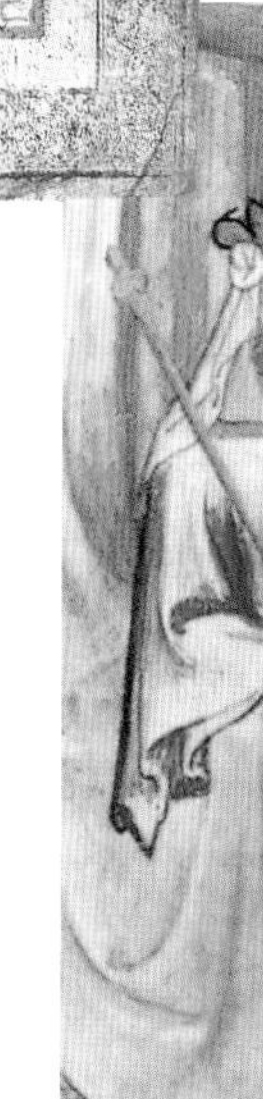

Right *Detail of an illuminated manuscript by the Boucicaut Master depicting the Khan overseeing the transaction in which ingots are being exchanged for paper money.*

courier could travel 185 km (300 miles) in a day, from the Pamirs to the Pacific. The trade between China's great cities, often linked by canal, easily dwarfed that of Venice, and was underpinned by sophisticated credit facilities and the world's first paper money, which astonished Marco Polo. So, too, did many of the products of the country, including coal, a stone that burned, and asbestos, a cloth that wouldn't. Iron was produced on a scale which wasn't to be matched in Europe for another 500 years.

By his own account, Marco was appointed to the Khan's Privy council in 1277, and worked for three years as a tax inspector in Yanzhou on the Grand Canal. But after 17 years, having amassed a fortune, the Polos were anxious to leave while the Khan was still alive and in good health. Reluctantly, the Khan made them part of an imperial escort taking a Mongol princess to marry a Persian prince, and they finally returned to Venice by way of Trebizond (Trapezous) and Constantinople (now Istanbul) in the winter of 1295.

Did Marco Polo go to China?

Widely known to contemporaries as a fabulous compendium of astonishing lies, Marco Polo's account of his travels was written three years later, and became, for its time, a bestseller. Marco was to marry in Venice and died there at the age of 70. To a friar who begged him to confess his lies on his death bed, his retort was: 'I have not told the half of what I saw!'

Was Marco lying? Did he and Rustichello merely spice up rumours picked up in some Central Asian bazaar? We seem to stand, like Polo in the Gobi, on the whispering sands of history, drawn back and forth by suggestive echoes of truth and fiction. What Marco Polo told his audience was true: that to the east there indeed lay a vast and impressive civilization, in many respects way in advance of Europe. Again and again, his details fit with what we know now to be the truth: even his style, such as it is, has more than a whiff of the commercial ledger. Yet some scholars have found cause for doubt. Polo does not mention the Great Wall, tea, foot-binding or the Chinese art of calligraphy. Chinese annals make no mention of him. And there is the troubling presence of Rustichello himself – the writer of romances.

Finally, we are faced with an irony of history. Polo challenged the accepted order of the universe, as it was seen from Christian Europe: he reported, as it were, from a better world – one in which Christ's teachings had never been heard. But his book played a role in extending the influence of Europe, not China, across the globe, when in 1492 Columbus was inspired to seek a western passage to Cathay, carrying with him his own heavily annotated copy. He found instead a world about which Europe knew nothing at all.

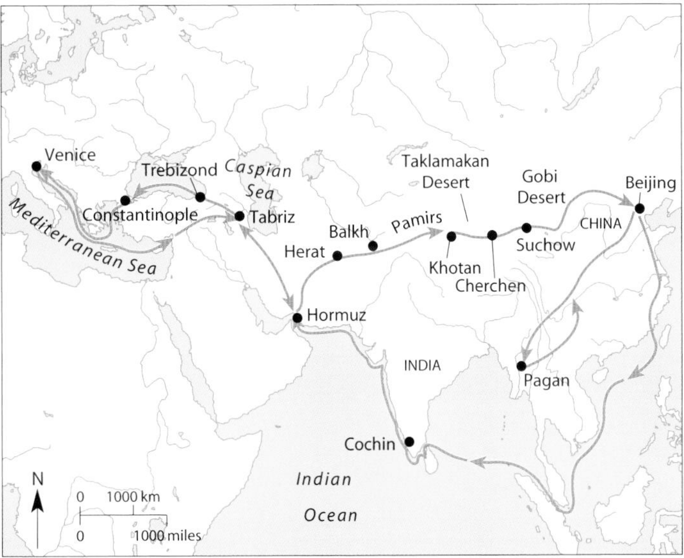

Marco Polo's impressive journey lasted 23 years and covered around 38,625 km (24,000 miles). He set out for China with his father and uncle along the Silk Road, but returned mostly by sea.

Ibn Battuta

1325–54

I braced my resolution to quit all my dear ones, female and male, and forsook my home as birds forsake their nests.
IBN BATTUTA, 14TH CENTURY

On the June morning in 1325 that Ibn Battuta set out for the *Hajj*, the Muslim pilgrimage to Mecca (p. 68), he could not have known that the journey would turn into one of the longest and most remarkable feats of travel of any age. He was just 21 years old when he rode off alone on a donkey from his native city of Tangier, in Morocco's northwest. When returned 24 years later, Muhammad Ibn Battuta strode through the city gates as a wealthy and celebrated adventurer, with a retinue of servants and followers. He had traversed 120,000 km (75,000 miles) of ground, as far apart as al-Andalus in Spain and Malabar, had met more than 40 heads of state, been appointed as an ambassador and a judge, taken several wives, sired children, survived innumerable close encounters and completed the pilgrimage to Mecca many times.

Dyers' vats in the Moroccan city of Fès, a scene that has probably changed little since Ibn Battuta's day. He returned to this city after his long travels and dictated the memoir of his voyages to the scholar Ibn Juzayy.

Setting out on pilgrimage

Ibn Battuta was born in 1304 into a Berber family respected for their scholarship and knowledge of Islamic jurisprudence. After receiving a good education, Battuta decided to embark on the pilgrimage, and to further his studies under various Sufi scholars in the Middle East.

He crossed North Africa, travelling to Tunis and Alexandria, and then on to Cairo, determining that wherever possible, he would never venture down the same road more than once. While en route to Mecca, he travelled to Jerusalem, Aleppo and Damascus (where he witnessed the Black Death), and was received by the Sultan of Egypt, who presented him with gifts and gold. He reached Mecca in October 1326, and was stirred by the astonishing assembly of pilgrims from all over the Islamic world. For Ibn Battuta, the *Hajj* was a catalyst. He had set out like any other as a pilgrim but, having set eyes on the melting pot of peoples at the Holy City, he suddenly comprehended the scope of the known world, and wanted to see it for himself.

An Indian ship depicted in an Arab manuscript of 1238. Such ships sailed with the monsoon winds across the Indian Ocean and down the east coast of Africa following well-established trade routes.

From Mecca he travelled across the Arabian Desert to Baghdad, and on through southern Persia, before returning to Mecca. He then sailed down the East African coast as far as Mombasa in what is now Kenya, before heading north once again, back to the Middle East, and up through Anatolia to the Black Sea. Battuta continued northward to the Crimea and the northern Caucasus before retreating, driven back by the cold. He travelled on to Constantinople, where he had an audience with the Byzantine Emperor Andronicus III, who presented him with a horse, a saddle and a parasol. Leaving the Bosporus behind him, he ventured on to Bukhara, Samarkand, then eastward into Afghanistan and across to India.

Ibn Battuta arrived accompanied now by an entourage of followers, attendants and a harem of wives. He commented later on the strange culture he found, mentioning seeing yogis doing magic tricks, and expressing his shock at witnessing *suttee*, the Hindu practice of a wife climbing atop her husband's burning funeral pyre. Once at Delhi, he made his way to the palace of Sultan

A 13th-century manuscript illumination depicting a camel caravan and a caravanserai – a rest-place for merchants and travellers – in the background.

Muhammad Tughlaq, who bestowed upon him honours and more gifts. The Sultan, who would dote on his guests one minute and slit their throats the next, appointed Ibn Battuta as his *Qadi*, Chief Judge. The Morocccan traveller stayed in Delhi for eight years, until posted to China as the Sultan's ambassador in 1342.

The journey to China was fraught with danger and catastrophe. His entourage was attacked by brigands near Aligarth and Battuta himself was captured and almost executed. There were warring tribesmen to contend with and, then, on the Malabar Coast, Battuta was shipwrecked. He lost his own fortune and all the gifts the mercurial Sultan had sent with him for the Chinese emperor. The adventures continued, through Ceylon and the Maldives, to Bengal, Assam, Sumatra and, eventually, to China itself.

Ibn Battuta was skilled at ingratiating himself to leaders. Most of his journeys were made within the vast new lands of the Islamic world, where his impeccable Muslim credentials could be used to gain entry into any royal court. In an era when few dared to travel for the sake of travel, Ibn Battuta was fêted, lavished with gifts and frequently found himself received as royalty, particularly as he travelled with a large entourage. The success of his travels was partly based on his timing. The cloak of Islam stretched from southern Europe in the west, to China in the east, allowing Ibn Battuta to move with comparative ease in lands off-limits to a Christian.

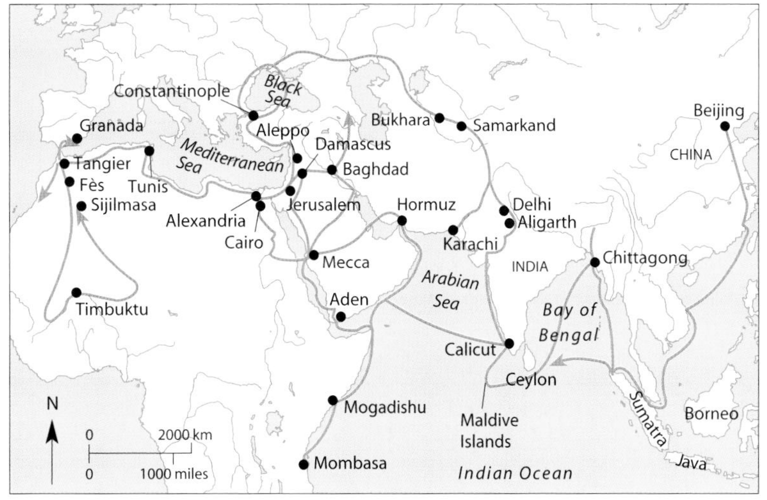

Map indicating Ibn Battuta's epic voyages. Over the course of 29 years he travelled across North Africa, Asia, India and to China and back.

Heading home

The great Arab traveller returned to Morocco in November 1349. The Sultan Abu 'Inan received Battuta at his capital, Fès. After two further journeys – to Andalusia in Islamic Spain, and to the Saharan outpost of Timbuktu – from which he returned in 1354, the Sultan ordered Battuta to write a memoir of his travels. The reminiscences were dictated to the Andalusian scholar Ibn Juzayy, and were presented as a book entitled *Tuhfat al Nuzzarfi Gara'ib al-Amsar wa Aja'ib al-Asfar*, 'Gift to Observers, Dealing with the Curiosities of Cities and the Wonders of Journeys'. More commonly known simply as *Rihla*, 'Travels', it is regarded as one of the most important accounts of life, society and culture from the medieval Islamic world.

Battuta paints a picture of himself as a man of piety, of both virtues and failings, who was willing to eat with beggars and feast with kings. Beyond that, he shows himself to be a man always ready to seize any opportunity to set out on a journey and make the most of circumstance.

Ibn Battuta lived out the last years of his life quietly in Morocco and, when he died in 1377, he was buried in his native city of Tangier.

STANLEY STEWART

Zheng He, the Grand Eunuch

19

1405–33

We have traversed more than one hundred thousand li ... and have beheld in the ocean huge waves like mountains rising sky high, and we have set eyes on barbarian regions far away hidden in a blue transparency of light vapours, while our sails, loftily unfurled like clouds day and night, continued on their course as rapidly as a star, traversing those savage waves as if we were treading a public thoroughfare....

TABLET ERECTED BY ZHENG HE, CHANGLE, FUJIAN, 1432

Eighty years before Columbus set sail across the Atlantic hoping to find a new route to China, a remarkable Chinese admiral embarked on a series of naval expeditions whose scale would have astonished the discoverer of the New World. The seven epic journeys of Zheng He, ranging from Taiwan to Africa, extended Chinese influence in an unprecedented manner at a point when Europeans were still struggling to emerge from the Mediterranean. But for a curious twist of history, China, rather than Europe, might have become the great colonial power.

Born in 1371 in China's Yunnan province, Zheng He was a Chinese Muslim. Entering the service of the Ming court at the age of 10, he was castrated in accordance with imperial protocol. After a time in the household, he joined Zhu Di, the emperor's uncle, in campaigns against the Mongols, where he proved himself a man of considerable valour and leadership.

When Zhu Di usurped the throne in 1402, and declared himself the emperor Yongle, he commissioned Zheng He to mount a series of naval expeditions to 'the Western Oceans'. It was a rare moment in Chinese history, in the early years of the Ming dynasty, when expansionist desire overcame traditional isolationism. Militarily and politically strong, Yongle wanted to assert Chinese suzerainty over the barbarian lands beyond the sea and to secure the kind of overseas luxuries that would enhance his court and his reputation.

Chinese seafaring was already far ahead of that of Europe. The Chinese had invented the compass as early as the 8th century AD, and it was in common use by Chinese navigators by the year 1000, some three centuries before its general use

Zheng He is shown on the right in this woodcut from a 1597 edition of The Western Sea Cruises of Eunuch San Pao *by Lo Mon-teng.*

in Europe. By the 14th century, the Chinese had developed a sophisticated cartographic system based on a rectangular grid which allowed for relatively accurate representation. Marco Polo had noted the superiority of their ships, built with huge central rudders that acted as drop keels, and bulkheads that could seal off leaking sections of the hull, an idea not introduced in Europe for many centuries.

Right *Zheng He's treasure ships would have vastly overshadowed the ships in which Columbus sailed to the Americas around 80 years later, as seen in this diagram comparing their sizes.*

A vast fleet

Zheng He's first expedition left the mouth of the Yangtze in 1405. It was a spectacular sight, consisting of 63 ocean-going junks. The largest, known as *bao chuan*, or treasure ships, had nine masts. Almost 137 m (450 ft) long and 55m (180 ft) wide, they were ten times the tonnage of Columbus's *Santa María*.

This fleet carried up to 28,000 men, including civil and military administrators, scientists, doctors, merchants, accountants and translators, as well as seamen and soldiers. They also carried a vast cargo of porcelain, silk and lacquer ware for trade. Such an armada – not to be surpassed until the First World War – was obviously not just a merchant fleet. Zheng He had been despatched to inform rulers throughout southern Asia that they were vassals of the Chinese emperor. Most of them took the news rather well, as it required only nominal obeisance, though a few recalcitrant princes had to be replaced with more compliant figures.

A Chinese painting showing the port of Quanzhou, the last stop in China before Zheng He set out on his voyages into the wider world.

In a series of seven voyages between 1405 and 1433, Zheng He's fleets travelled through the Indonesian archipelago, along the coasts of Thailand and Malaysia, and across the Indian Ocean to Ceylon and the trading cities of Cochin and Calicut on India's Malabar Coast. In the later voyages they pushed on to the Persian Gulf and the southern shores of Arabia, from where Zheng made a pilgrimage to Mecca, and eventually reached the coasts of East Africa.

Along the way trading stations were established and treasure collected – rhinoceros horn, ivory, tortoiseshell, rare woods, incense, spices, medicines, pearls and precious stones. Envoys accompanied them home with gifts for the Son of Heaven, the most famous of which was a giraffe, sent by the Sultan of Malindi, which was treated as a grand and auspicious omen in the Forbidden City in Beijing.

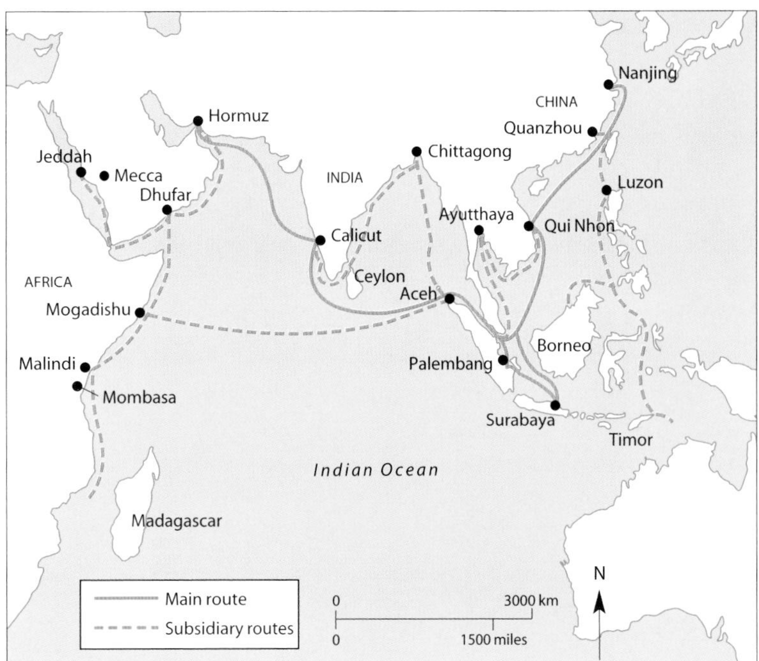

Map showing the main and subsidiary routes taken by Zheng He's fleet.

These Chinese exploratory voyages were in striking contrast to those of later generations of Europeans, for whom such expeditions led inevitably to conquest and empire. The Chinese fleet may have made a show of force, but in seven voyages Zheng He resorted only twice to military action, and once was against a pirate. Primarily diplomatic and commercial missions, their aim was to make friends and allies in the wider world. Compare this to the atrocities committed by the Portuguese along the Indian coasts in the early years of the following century.

In 1433, either at sea or shortly after his return from his last voyage, Zheng He died. His accomplishment was remarkable. He had visited some 35 countries, established a wide diplomatic and trading network and vastly increased Chinese knowledge of the outside world.

The death of the great admiral, known as the Three Jewel Eunuch, coincided with a return to China's more traditional isolationism. Confucian aloofness began again to dominate Chinese policy, which viewed the rest of the world with indifference. Foreign voyages were banned, Zheng He's accounts of his journeys, entitled *The Triumphant Vision of the Boundless Ocean*, were partially destroyed, and his great fleet rotted at its moorings. The brief and spectacular Age of Chinese Exploration had come to an abrupt end.

Zheng He returned to China with a giraffe, a gift for the emperor from the Sultan of Malindi (on the east coast of Africa). The animal was treated as a grand and auspicious omen when presented at court, as depicted in this painting by Shen Du.

The Renaissance

When first Columbus stunned the world by reaching what was to become known as America, and then, just over five years later, Vasco da Gama sailed round Africa to India, everything changed. Suddenly there was no doubt that the world was round. The economic possibilities were soon recognized and the race to dominate the ever-expanding new lands and trade routes was truly on.

The potential riches of the recently encountered New World and the lucrative spice trade with the Far East were the driving forces behind many of the voyages of exploration during the Renaissance. It was not long before the landmasses of both North and South America were crossed and the Pacific Ocean sighted – at a time when central Africa, so close to Europe, was still *terra incognita*. For now, the major powers of the Old World were intent on carving up the newly found territories between them, and the main competitors initially were the Portuguese and the Spanish.

Varthema was perhaps the ultimate adventurer. He claims to have been almost everywhere that anyone had heard of east of Egypt, often disguised as a Muslim so that he was able to visit Mecca and gather information on the Spice Islands. If even half his tall tales were true, he was one of the greatest travellers of the age.

Magellan – Portuguese but sailing for Spain – was instrumental in the first circumnavigation of the globe by discovering the channel in Tierra del Fuego, now named after him, even though he himself did not complete the journey, dying when still only half way round. A few survivors of his crew eventually made it back, but it was a

Vasco da Gama, the first European to sail round Africa to India, is greeted by the ruler of Calicut as he disembarks at this busy Indian port; early 16th-century Flemish tapestry.

Moluccan slave who was actually the first person to go round the world.

Cortés and Pizarro between them subdued the two greatest civilizations of the New World, and they did it with extraordinary ease, through boldness and subterfuge. The greed and cruelty shown by these two conquistadors was to set a trend of savagery which endured for several centuries. From then on the fate of the indigenous inhabitants was sealed. None were able to withstand the superior weaponry of the invaders, nor the diseases which they brought with them.

The geography of the New World was rapidly, and often brutally, revealed. Over a bare 20 years much of the southern part of North America was ravaged by explorers, such as Coronado and de Soto, desperately searching for gold, while the southern continent was crossed by accident. Stranded in rainforests on an expedition to find the fabled El Dorado, 'the gilded man', Orellana was sent with some men to find food for his companions. He built a boat on a river a mere 200 km (125 miles) inland from the Pacific coast, just over the Andes in what is today Ecuador, and set off downstream. He emerged some seven months later at the mouth of the Amazon on the Atlantic.

The English enter the picture with Drake's remarkable circumnavigation of the globe in the *Golden Hind* – the first ship to do so under the command of its captain and only the second ever to complete the journey. Drake's feat meant that England now became a major player in the global game, much to the annoyance of the Spanish.

Equal effort was put into searching for northern routes from the Atlantic to the Pacific. At first it was hoped that the great St Lawrence River was the start of a way through the continent to China. Cartier and Champlain demonstrated that this was not the case by making extensive journeys to the many rivers and lakes of the Canadian interior. At the same time attempts were made to find a sea route further north: the fabled Northwest Passage. Frobisher and Davis were the first in a long line of brave sailors who made arduous and ultimately pointless searches through this most hostile and treacherous region. They were followed by Hudson and Baffin, Foxe and James, all of whom failed to find the elusive channel.

Abraham Ortelius's map New Description of America, or the New World, *from his* Theatris Orbis Terrarum *of 1570, showing the then current state of knowledge of the shape of the recently discovered continent.*

JOSÉ-JUAN LOPEZ-PORTILLO

Christopher Columbus

20

1492–93

Your Highnesses ... thought of sending me, Christopher Columbus, to the regions of India ... and ordered that I should not travel overland to the east, as is customary, but rather by way of the west, whither to this day, as far as we can know for certain, no man has ever gone before.

CHRISTOPHER COLUMBUS, PROLOGUE TO LOG-BOOK, 1492

On 21 April 1493, Columbus rode triumphantly through the streets of Barcelona with his patrons King Ferdinand of Aragon and Queen Isabella of Castile (the 'Catholic Kings' of Spain) at his side. By then, news had spread of his voyage across the 'Ocean Sea', as the Atlantic was known. As the crowds cheered in Barcelona, it was commonly believed that he had achieved his unlikely objective of finding a viable sea route to Asia via the west rather than the east. In doing so, it seemed the Spanish kings had beaten their rival in Portugal to the prize. Soon, however, people began to doubt what exactly Columbus had stumbled upon. And by 1 November 1493, Peter Martyr rightly called those lands a 'new world', the continent we now know as America.

Genesis of the expedition

The desire to find a viable sea route to the fabled wealth and goods of Asia places Columbus within an ancient tradition. In the 15th century this aim was pursued most vigorously by the Portuguese in their attempts at rounding Africa. Although it was sponsored by the kings of Spain, Columbus's expedition should be seen as a product of the Portuguese environment in which he had lived and worked until 1485. But Columbus was convinced that Asia could be reached faster by sailing west rather than east.

The notion that Asia could be reached by sailing west was unusual, but not original. Most

Previous page The Virgin and the Navigators, *by Alejo Fernandez (*c. 1510*). The kneeling figures include Columbus, King Ferdinand (at left), Bishop Fonseca, Vespucci and one of the Pinzón brothers (right). Divine providence was seen as guiding Spain's discoveries.*

Right *Modern reconstructions of the* Niña, Pinta *and* Santa María. *They were small ships (around 18 m/59 ft in length) and cramped, but their lateen rigging made them versatile.*

educated people were aware that the world was spherical, making a western passage possible in principle. Some had even attempted it, such as the Vivaldi brothers in 1291, or the Fleming Ferdinand Van Olmen in 1488 (sponsored by John II, the Portuguese king who rejected Columbus), but had never returned home. The risks of sailing into unknown seas for an indefinite amount of time were enough to deter most men. But Columbus thought he knew what others did not. After much research and consultation with like-minded individuals throughout Europe, he became erroneously convinced that the world was about 20 per cent smaller than was generally believed. He was confident enough to draw up his own map of the world – perhaps the same map he would use on his voyage. All he needed was to persuade a monarch to back him.

Royal patronage was essential to any explorer at that time – lending legitimacy and ensuring that any titles and claims would be protected and upheld. It took Columbus eight years, until 17 April 1492, to be awarded the mandate he so desired with the extravagant titles he requested. He never convinced any committee of experts in Portugal or Spain, however. In the end, his extraordinary perseverance and his charm proved more important: 'If it strikes often enough a drop of water can wear a hole in a stone', he once remarked.

Queen Isabella had been fond of Columbus since their first meeting and she saw that the potential benefits of his scheme could outweigh the risks or costs. Now that Spain had finally captured the Muslim city of Granada (1 January 1492), completing the reconquest of the Iberian peninsula, she ignored the advice of her experts and embraced Columbus's venture, granting this son of a weaver from Genoa in Italy the titles of Admiral of the Ocean Sea, Governor General and Viceroy over any lands he might discover.

The Atlantic crossing

Columbus had acquired extensive knowledge of the wind systems in the Atlantic through his years in Portuguese service. His experience and later investigations led him to believe that a circular wind system operated in the Atlantic. The winds known as 'las brisas' (the northeast trades) were well known and could be relied upon to push his ships west from the latitude of the Spanish Canary isles. The real gamble for Columbus was whether the 'westerlies' known further north in Europe blew from the lands he was hoping to reach back home to known waters.

Notwithstanding any doubts, three caravels, *Niña*, *Pinta* and *Santa María*, with their 90 crewmen set off from Palos on 3 August 1492. After a stop in the Canaries, they sailed into the unknown from the port of La Goletta on 6 September. All they had to steer by was the imprecise nautical technique of 'dead reckoning' through uncharted waters, combined with primitive celestial navigation: Columbus had navigational instruments with him but used them only for show. Remarkably, the expedition's trajectory would be very near to the ideal course followed by the trans-Atlantic galleons of the Spanish empire for centuries to come.

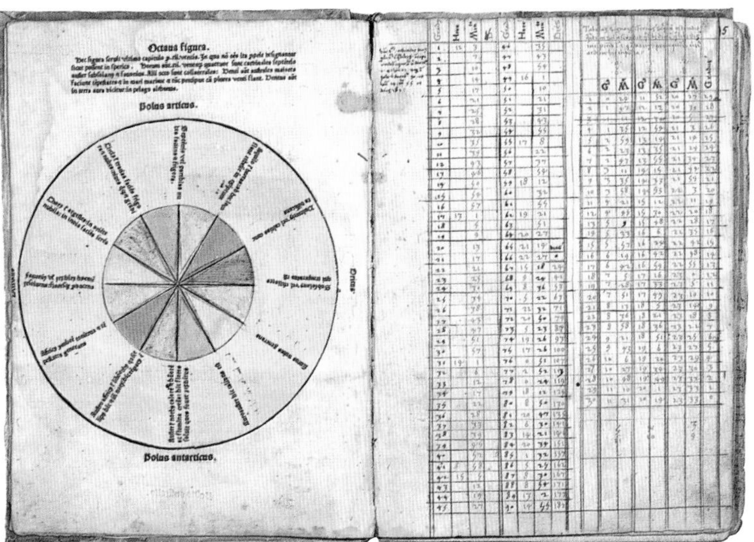

Top *A compass, coloured by Columbus, and a table of winds and hours of light at different latitudes. Columbus had given much thought to his plans for his journey.*

Above *Columbus used navigational equipment – this drawing shows how to use a sextant – along with other tricks, to reassure his nervous crew.*

On 12 October, after perhaps the longest period any European ship had spent out of sight of land, including a time becalmed in the Sargasso Sea, the ships arrived at an unidentified island of the Bahamas. Columbus named the island San Salvador and impetuously claimed it for Spain. Here, the first meeting took place between Europeans and Americans.

Every island the expedition encountered was inhabited by people that Columbus immediately began to call 'Indians', wrongly believing he had arrived at 'the Indies', a name commonly given to Asia. His attitude towards them was ambivalent, presaging the attitudes of the Spanish empire he unwittingly helped to found. On the one hand he had a benevolent, paternalistic affinity for what he saw as the Indian's peaceful and uncorrupted nature; presciently he declared they would make excellent candidates for conversion. On the other hand, their naivety could be used to exploit them. Columbus did not hesitate to abduct 10 of them to take back as guides to navigation in the region and as showpieces for his sponsors in Europe.

For about three months after the initial landfall Columbus continued exploring the islands he encountered in the vain hope of finding evidence of the fabulous empires of Cipangu (Japan),

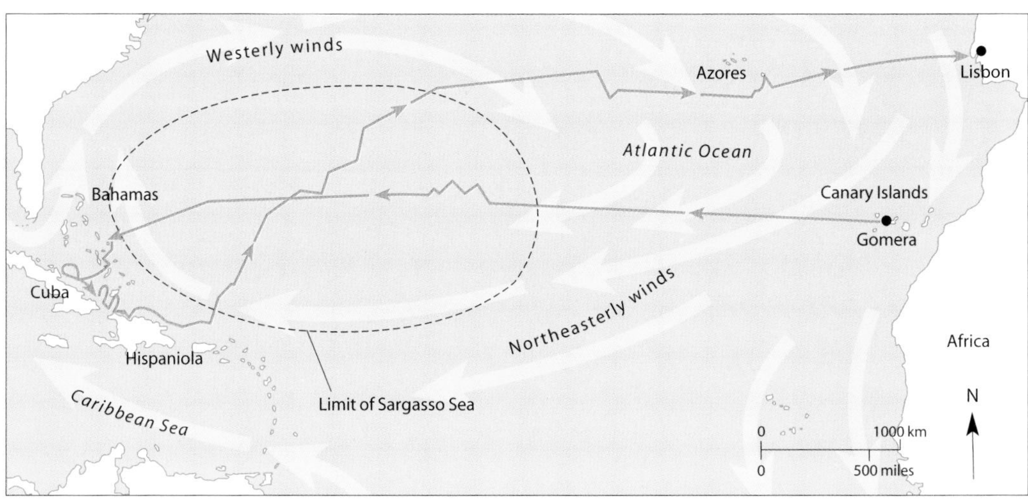

Map showing Columbus' route on his first crossing of the Atlantic. The Atlantic wind system made this the optimal route and it was later followed by the galleons of the Spanish empire.

Cathay (China) or India. But already by 21 November a frustrated Martin Pinzón, captain of the *Pinta*, effectively mutinied and abandoned 'the Admiral' to hunt for gold. Little of value had been found on the islands so far, despite their natural beauty. It was only the discovery of gold on the large and fertile island of La Española ('Hispaniola', now Haiti and the Dominican Republic) that would justify the expedition and elevate the status of Columbus's discoveries to more than just another desolate archipelago in the middle of the Ocean Sea (like the Azores for example).

Columbus made the most of the situation, even turning the disaster of the *Santa María* running aground into an opportunity for establishing the first European colony in America, leaving her 39 crew to trade for gold while he returned to Europe. On the way, Pinzón rejoined the expedition with even more gold and Columbus diplomatically allowed him to do so.

The expedition's big gamble paid off when Columbus headed north from the Caribbean with his two remaining caravels in search of the homeward bound 'westerlies', finding them on 16 January 1493. On 18 February he finally returned to known waters and the Portuguese outposts of the Azores.

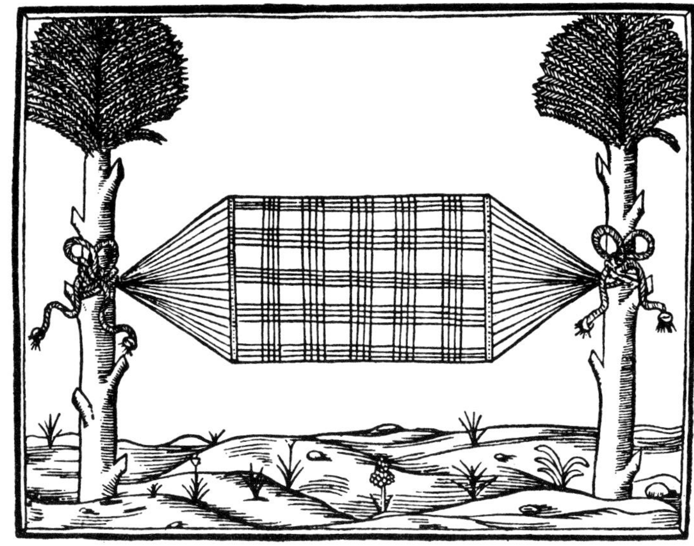

Drawing of a hammock, from Fernández de Oviedo y Valdés' Historia general y natural de las Indias. *Columbus's sailors were the first to see hammocks. The native word was then taken up and survived as hammocks became widely used on ships.*

Aftermath

The excitement aroused in Spain by Columbus's return led to vigorous diplomatic moves by Ferdinand and Isabella, resulting in the Treaty of Tordesillas with Portugal (7 June 1494) that recognized Spain's claim over Columbus's discoveries and any new lands west of an imaginary line '370 leagues west of Cape Verde' (see also p. 98). This claim, above all, laid the foundations of the Spanish empire in America.

Out of pride and for the sake of his titles, Columbus never abandoned the claim that he had found a new route to Asia. This intransigence proved fatal to his reputation and career. Although he made three more voyages to the Americas, he was soon undermined by rivals and found himself alienated from royal patronage. Bitter and incoherent, the discoverer of the 'New World' died in 1506 at the age of 55.

MALYN NEWITT

Vasco da Gama

21

1497–98

A young man in their company ... had come from a distant country, and had already seen big ships like ours. These tokens gladdened our hearts, for it appeared as if we were already approaching our desired destination.

ÁLVARO VELHO, 15TH CENTURY

On 8 July 1497 four ships left Lisbon on a journey that was to change for ever relations between Europe and Asia. The commander was Vasco da Gama, an unknown Portuguese knight of the Order of Santiago. Other ships were captained by da Gama's brother, Paulo, and by Nicolau Coelho, while the fourth vessel was a storeship. Until the accession of João II in 1481, the Portuguese had been preoccupied with the trade in gold and slaves from Africa, but the new king gave Portuguese enterprise a clearer sense of direction, sending ships to map the coasts of Africa and to contact Christian communities in the East.

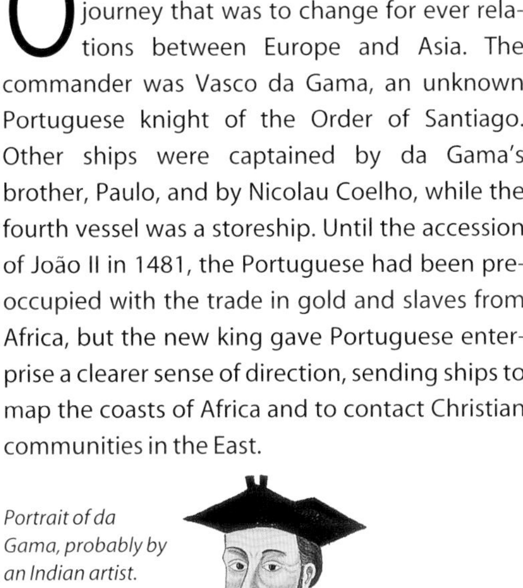

Portrait of da Gama, probably by an Indian artist.

Between 1482 and 1486, two previous expeditions had battled against head winds down the African coast, the second turning back when its commander Diogo Cão died on the coast of

Da Gama's fleet, from the Memoria das Armadas, *1568.*

modern Namibia. A third expedition under Bartolomeu Dias departed in 1487. Dias also struggled south against head winds until forced out to sea by a storm. When he turned back towards the African coast he discovered that the shoreline now ran eastwards. Without knowing it he had rounded the southern cape of Africa and found the sea route to the East. At this point Dias's men demanded to return to Portugal, which was reached again in 1489.

Dias had discovered the westerlies that blew in the southern latitudes and realized that the south Atlantic was dominated by a circulating wind system (as Columbus also discovered in the north Atlantic). A sailing ship wishing to round the southern tip of Africa would first have to make a sweep to the southwest to pick up these winds.

Around Africa

João II never followed up Dias' discovery and it was not till 1497 that the new king, Dom Manuel, reluctantly agreed to another voyage. Short of money, the king did not provide gifts suitable for a diplomatic mission and had to allow the Italian Marchioni bank to provide one of the ships. Da Gama set out with only 150 men, but among them were some of the most experienced pilots of the day, as well as men who could speak Arabic and the African language of the Congo.

The first, familiar, stage of his voyage was to the Canaries and Cape Verde Islands, before setting off into uncharted waters. For the first time, a Portuguese fleet set course southwest into the Atlantic with the intention of picking up the westerlies which had blown Dias round the Cape. After just four months at sea, the ships sighted St Helena bay on the coast of South Africa 'and we saluted the captain-major by firing our bombards, and dressed the ships with flags and standards'. It had taken Dias over a year to reach this same place.

Concerned to keep his ships supplied, da Gama sent his men ashore to meet the local inhabitants. On one occasion they kidnapped a Khoi honey gatherer who was fed at the captain's table, at others the Portuguese and Africans entertained each other with music, but suspicion

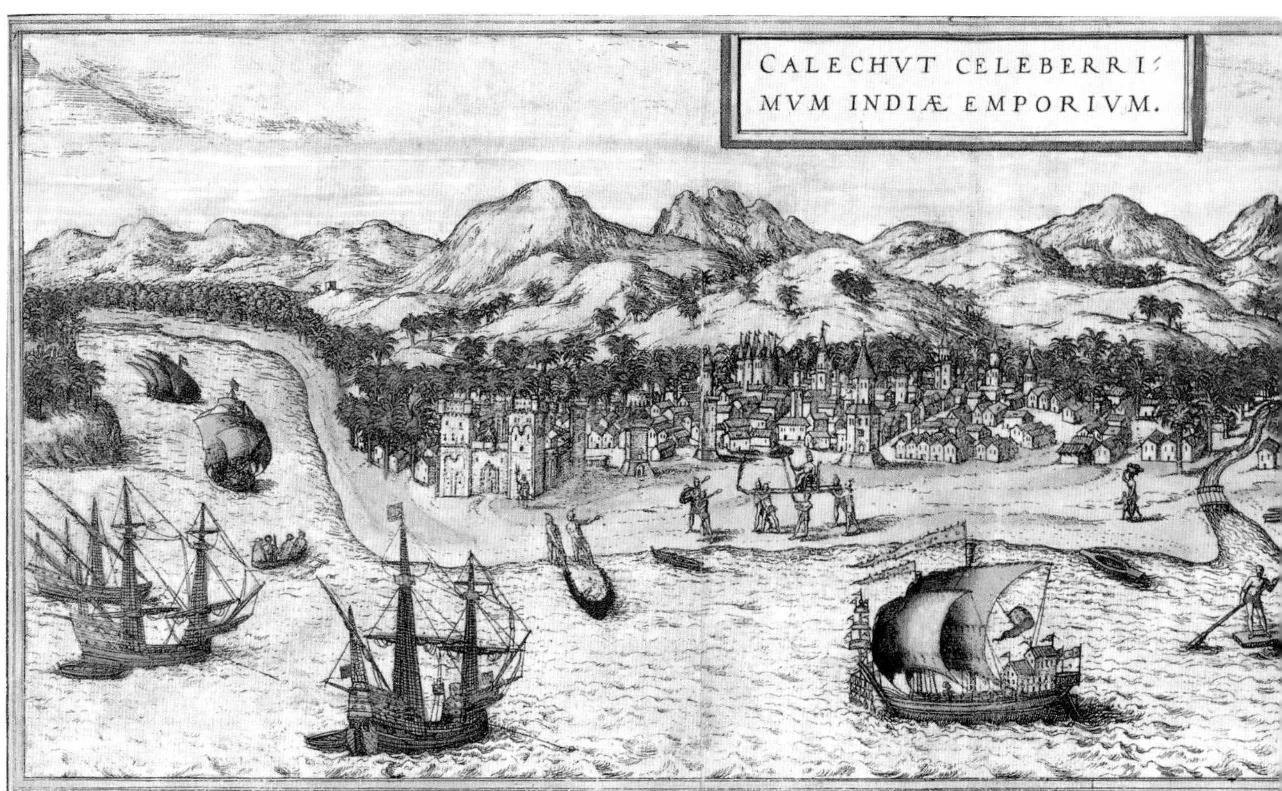

A 16th-century view of Calicut, da Gama's destination on the coast of India and the principal port for the pepper trade; from Georg Braun and Frans Hogenberg's Civitates Orbis Terrarum, *1572.*

eventually erupted into violence, with spears thrown and crossbows fired.

Further along the coast in the bay of São Brás, while the Portuguese amused themselves firing at basking seals, the store ship was broken up. After a month on the coast of South Africa da Gama sailed north, keeping close in shore. At the end of December the three ships passed the land which da Gama named Natal, the Portuguese for Christmas. One ship lost an anchor and sprung its mainmast, but it was shortage of water that forced the fleet to anchor in the estuary of the Inharrime on 11 January 1498. The Portuguese were welcomed by large crowds, mostly of women who wore copper ornaments 'on their legs and arms and twisted in their hair'.

After passing without mishap through the dangerous waters of the Mozambique Channel, da Gama anchored in the northernmost arm of the Zambezi, which he called the River of Good Omens. Here he remained 32 days taking in water, resting his men, who were suffering from scurvy (a potentially fatal disease caused by a deficiency of vitamin C that blighted many voyages until its cause was realized), and careening the ships. Traders wearing silks and Islamic skull caps came to meet them, and for the first time the Portuguese found themselves near to a civilization whose signs they recognized.

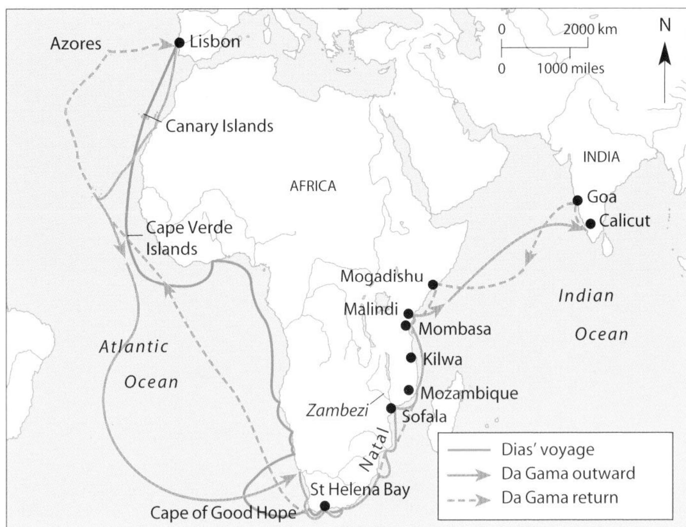

Map to show the routes of Dias and da Gama: Da Gama's outward route shows the knowledge of the wind systems of the South Atlantic that made his voyage possible.

A few days' sail brought the fleet to Mozambique Island, where Coelho's ship ran aground on entering the harbour. Mozambique was a busy port for ships trading from India and da Gama was able to hire pilots and obtain information about Indian Ocean trade. He also quarrelled with the local population, firing his guns at a crowd on the shore and leaving convinced of a Muslim conspiracy to ruin him.

Da Gama's pilots took him safely past Kilwa, where the Portuguese eagerly recorded rumours of a Christian population, and on to Mombasa, where the Portuguese again fell foul of the local population and seized a ship laden with gold and silver. Da Gama's violent actions threatened to ruin the expedition, but they received a friendly reception at Malindi (Melinde), the next city along the coast. Here a fresh pilot was obtained for the passage to India and the Portuguese were fêted with fireworks and music.

The first encounters with India

Blown gently by the seasonal monsoon, the crossing to India was made in 23 days and on 20 May da Gama cast anchor off Calicut, the most important centre of the pepper trade on the Malabar Coast. Here the credulous Portuguese thought they had found the Christians they were seeking and worshipped in a Hindu temple, their suspicions apparently not even aroused by the images 'with teeth protruding an inch from the mouth, and four or five arms'.

Da Gama's diplomatic mission nearly failed when, having boasted of the power and magnificence of his king 'exceeding that of any king of these parts', he presented the Samorin of Calicut with worthless presents including strings of coral and fishermen's hoods. Da Gama's lack of diplomatic skills daily became more dangerous and embarrassing, but eventually he was able to leave Calicut on 29 August, taking with him samples of spices and a great deal of knowledge of the languages and geography of the Indian Ocean.

Da Gama lingered on the Indian coast till October, capturing some ships, taking and torturing hostages and laying down a store of suspicion and hatred for the future. It took three months to return across the Indian Ocean to Africa where one of his remaining ships had to be burnt and abandoned. Da Gama sailed for home on 11 January 1499, rounded the Cape on 20 March and reached the island of Santiago in only 27 days. Here Paulo fell ill and Vasco took him to the Azores where he died. Coelho meanwhile had sailed directly to Lisbon, which he reached in July 1499. In all, 55 men had died on the return voyage.

The significance of the voyage

As a result of da Gama's voyage, the shape of half the world became known and the viability of a sea route between Europe and Asia was convincingly demonstrated – a sea route which was to lead inexorably to European dominance of Asia and to the growth of a global economy. This first European voyage to India by sea around Africa had been made without serious mishap, thanks to the skills of navigators, chart makers and shipwrights acquired over half a century. Da Gama also greatly profited from the knowledge of the Indian Ocean pilots who guided him to his destination.

Da Gama's voyage was an epoch-defining achievement, easy to underestimate because of its successful outcome, but as an heroic figure da Gama was seriously flawed. His violence, suspicion and undiplomatic behaviour meant that Europe's relations with India and Africa got off to the worst possible start.

A Portuguese artist recorded scenes of Indian life, here women wearing colourful saris filling water jars (c. 1540, from the Biblioteca Casanatense, Rome). Da Gama's voyage opened up the sea route to Asia and the Portuguese soon realized the importance of the trade in cloth from Cambay, occupying the northern port of Diu in 1534.

BRUCE WANNELL

Ludovico di Varthema 22

1501–08

When I heard this, I told him I was a Latin and had become a Mameluke in Cairo. On hearing this, he was very happy, and honoured me greatly.
LUDOVICO DI VARTHEMA, 1510

The *Itinerario* of Ludovico di Varthema was a Renaissance bestseller from its publication in Italian in Rome in 1510. Translations into Latin, German and English followed. By 1517, the author was dead and had left no heirs. The new print technology ensured that the account could be massively reproduced to meet the demand for information on the discoveries and conquests of the Portuguese in the Atlantic and Indian oceans.

Varthema referred to himself either as Bolognese or Romano. His family name is unknown in the annals of Bologna, and he may have been Central European and called Ludwig Wertheim, italianized as Varthema. A man of many disguises, he was proud to boast, when relating his exploits, of his duplicity as a spy or a counterfeit dervish, a feigned lunatic and the Mameluke Yunus, lover of the Sultana – among many other things.

However, such boasts ultimately served also to cast doubt on the authenticity of his more sensational claims as a traveller, notably that he was the first European to visit the Spice Islands of the Moluccas. Already in 1563 Garcia de Orta, a Portuguese physician in Goa, wrote that Varthema's travels beyond Calicut and Cochin, dependent on monsoon sailings, would have been impossible in the time available. These doubts were echoed by 19th-century scholars and recent scholarship has confirmed them beyond hope of appeal.

A soldier of fortune

Varthema was one of those European soldiers of fortune who joined the Mameluke troops in Egypt and Syria, converted to Islam and were rewarded with a degree of social advancement seldom possible in feudal Christian Europe. Ludwig (or Ludovico or Yunus) had saleable skills as an artilleryman, and few scruples.

His journey began when he sailed from Venice to Alexandria in Egypt in the autumn of 1501 to join the Mamelukes, dressed as a Muslim. He then went to Damascus, learned some Arabic and was accepted (according to himself) as a Muslim by the local population. His later arrest and imprisonment in Yemen, however, indicates that, as often the case with 'Latin' Mamelukes, he may not have made a completely convincing Muslim.

On 8 April 1504, he joined the 60-strong Mameluke guard on the pilgrim caravan from Damascus to Mecca on the *Hajj* (of which he provides the first extensive European account), then continued to Jeddah and on by sea to Aden in Yemen. He was arrested and taken to the inland capital, Rada', arriving on 9 September 1504 in time to join the campaign to besiege San'a, which

A caravan en route to Mecca, from an engraving in the German edition of Varthema's account of his travels, by Jörg Breu of Augsburg.

A view over San'a, in Yemen, perhaps much as Varthema might have seen it.

Map of Varthema's route as far as Calicut; he returned via Mozambique and around Africa.

fell after six months' siege in early March 1505. Later in the same year Varthema sailed from Aden to Calicut to help resist the Portuguese blockade of the traditional spice and luxury trade from the Indian Ocean to Egypt and Venice – leading to the eventual economic collapse of both these powers, hence their co-operation in confronting this new threat. His vaunted stop-over in Hormuz and Persia is unfortunately vague and contradictory – and chronologically impossible.

Varthema defected to the Portuguese at Cananor on the Malabar Coast on 5 December 1505, bringing urgent news of impending naval attack by the ships of the Samudri Raja of Calicut and his Muslim allies. After joining naval and land battles in the Portuguese war against Muslim traders, Varthema was rewarded with the lucrative post of trade overseer in Cochin and Cananor. There he observed local life and gathered information about places further afield, questioning local traders who went to the Spice Islands.

After the Battle of Ponani, Varthema was knighted on 4 December 1507 by the viceroy Almeida, just before sailing with Tristan da Cunha. Stopping in Mozambique in January, they reached Lisbon in June 1508, where Varthema was debriefed by the Portuguese King Dom Manuel and had his knighthood confirmed.

Varthema the travel writer

Apostasy from Christianity carried heavy penalties in Europe, hence the smoke-screen of vagueness and distortion that covers the bare bones of Varthema's account – but these very distortions gave rise to a marvellous picaresque romance. For the early part of his seven-year trip (the total length of his travels, as he states in his dedicatory letter of 1511 to Vittoria Colonna, recipient also of Michelangelo's sonnets), Varthema's narrative is peppered with phrases in bazaar Arabic, and for his Indian years with colloquial Malayalam. He knew no Persian, in spite of inventing the figure of Hajji O'Nur, the Persian merchant, as his companion in the east.

Varthema remains almost unrivalled among those who wrote about their travels at this period. Soldier and bombardier, brave and adventurous, curious and observant of social realities, he was keenly questioned by educated audiences in Lisbon, Venice and Rome, eager to correct the classical authorities on geography and update their political and commercial information. But, as is the case with many lionized authors, especially in the tradition of the unlearned 'everyman' travel writer, 'world travellers always tell tall tales'.

Ferdinand Magellan

1519–92

The Captain-General wept for joy. He then named the headland Cape Desire, for we had been desiring it for a long time ... we then debouched from that strait, engulfing ourselves in the Pacific sea.

ANTONIO PIGAFETTA, 28 NOVEMBER 1520, ON REACHING THE PACIFIC

Like so much else that is concerned with the 16th-century exploration of the world, the story of Ferdinand Magellan has a great deal to do with nutmegs and cloves and other familiar but still exotic spices, and much also to do with a declaration of a long-dead Pope. And in common also with many other expeditions, it is a story complicated beyond reason and one in which many of the facts have become hopelessly blurred by legend – not the least of them being the widely accepted notion that Magellan was the first man to circumnavigate the world.

Actually, he did not circumnavigate the world at all; the otherwise little-known Sebastian d'El-cano, a member of Magellan's expedition, was the first man to achieve this in one go – and that because his master had been left behind, killed on an island in the Philippines only halfway to his goal.

This melancholy fact, however, does not diminish Ferdinand Magellan's achievement. He – Portuguese, but sailing for the Spaniards as an act of considered defiance after a row – created and organized the flotilla of five tiny vessels – the *Victoria*, the *Trinidad*, the *San Antonio*, the *Concepción* and the *Santiago* – and led them out of the mouth of the Guadalquivir River in September 1519 to forge a route into an unknown of staggering dimension and danger. Just one of his five ships returned, and only 18 of his 237 men: today, his achievement is regarded as one of the greatest feats of courage and navigational genius in all

Below left *A self-taught master of Portuguese carracks and caravels, Fernao de Magalhaes (Magellan), here in a 16th-century portrait by an unknown artist, sailed under the sponsorship of Spain.*

Below right *Magellan's ship,* Victoria, *90 tons, bought in Cadiz for little more than £250.*

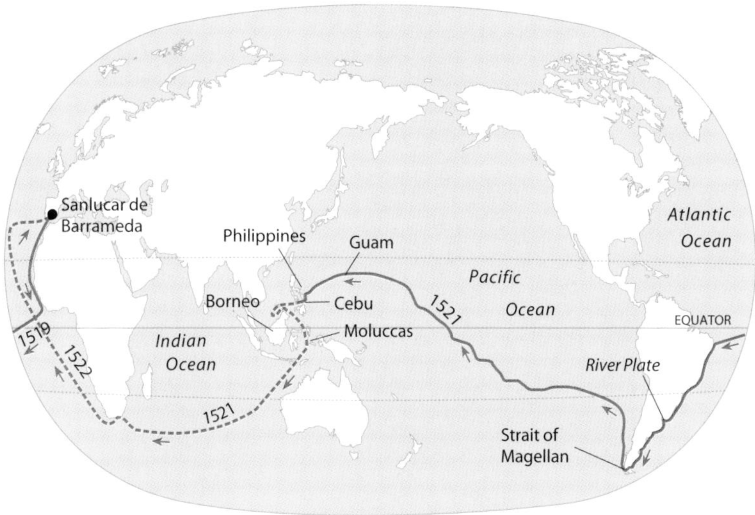

Map to show the route taken by Magellan's expedition around the world. Magellan himself was killed in Cebu, in the Philippines, and the expedition thereafter was led by Sebastian d'Elcano, and only one ship of the five that set out returned home. Technically, the expedition's Moluccan slave Enrique was the first man to go completely around the world.

maritime history. Magellan is memorialized by the Strait he discovered in South America, by the star-clouds in the sky that he saw from the heaving deck of his ship, and by the continuing regard he enjoys as a sailor-hero beyond all others.

Dividing the globe

It was indeed spices that lured Magellan and his men to sail their vessels across the bar outside the tiny south Spanish fishing-port of Sanlucar de Barrameda. Both he and the Spanish court well knew that the eastern islands called the Moluccas produced crops of cloves, nutmeg and mace in abundance, and so were generally known as the Spice Islands. But there was a problem – who had proper legal right to these islands: Spain, or her arch-rival, Portugal?

This question arose because of Pope Alexander VI and his infamous Treaty of Tordesillas in 1494, a decree which stated that all unclaimed territories to the east of an imaginary line drawn 370 leagues west of Cape Verde would henceforth be Portuguese (hence Brazil), while all to the line's west (such as Mexico, Colombia and Chile) would be given to Spain. By the curious maritime logic of the day, the papal decree was taken by some to mean that the Moluccas – which were reached by Europeans sailing *east*, round Africa and India – were Portuguese. This the Spaniards regarded as impertinent nonsense – and insisted that if they could reach these same islands by going westabout, across Balboa's newly seen (and soon to be named) Pacific Ocean, then Spain would have equal claim on these islands and the immense wealth they provided.

The 'Armada de Moluccas'

So the king of Spain pledged money for the expedition; Magellan was appointed Captain-General and in 1519 the five tiny vessels ('I would not care to sail to the Canaries in such crates' wrote the Portuguese consul in Seville, 'since their ribs are soft as butter') set off, hoisting their sails under the flag of Castile, for the west. Among the members of the expedition – the Armada de Moluccas, as Magellan grandly titled it – was a Moluccan slave named Enrique, as well as a leisured Venetian diarist, tourist and probable spy, Antonio Pigafetta, and an Englishman, a conscript matelot from Bristol, Master Andrew.

The key problem ahead for them all was going to be the bulk of the great continent that everyone knew lay between them and Balboa's Mar del Sur, as the Pacific's discoverer had called what he had seen as he stood, six years before, 'silent, on a peak in Darien'. Few other than the conquistadors had ever even visited the land; none had charted it; no one had any idea if the continent stretched, as some suspected, all the way to the South Pole, thus blocking any sea-route west. And Magellan had access to just one map, which showed, optimistically, a huge coastal indentation of the Atlantic at the site of the River Plate – of any other possible passageways cartography was silent.

It took well over a year of sailing – and a terrible mutiny, a number of maroonings and executions, the foundering of one ship (the *Santiago*), the discoveries of penguins and seals and of big-footed native South Americans who came to be called Patagones – before the sailors spotted a headland to their starboard, and noted that the land beyond it turned westward, and that there seemed a passageway ahead, a route through the continent and its snow-covered mountains. And so it turned out to be: this was the exceptionally trying, visually fugitive, cunningly twisting, navigationally difficult and ever wind-cursed Strait of Magellan, which divided the continent from the island of Tierra del Fuego, and still provides to this day a shortcut between the heaving grey waters of the Atlantic into the calm blue waters beyond.

The remaining three Spanish ships (the *San Antonio* had turned back, with vital stores, at the demand of its fearful crew) made it through this waterway in 38 testing and exhausting days: on 28 November 1520, the *Trinidad*, *Victoria* and *Concepción* passed out of the western end of the Strait and into a serene and golden sunset. Magellan broke down and wept, and then declared that the ocean ahead he would call the Pacific. All that remained now was merely to sail across it. It would take, he thought, three days, maybe four, to reach the Spice Islands.

He was horribly, tragically wrong. The journey across this immense and unknown body of water went on for week after week after week. Food and water ran out, the sailors' bodies were racked by scurvy (the Patagonian giants captured and put on board died too) and mutinous feelings welled up. It was only in the nick of time – after a trip in which the expedition missed almost every Pacific island close by which it sailed – they made it, head-on, to the islands of Guam. They reached them not after three days, but after three-and-a-half *months* – coming to a place where they could be watered and victualled and where, it turned out, the locals spoke a language of which Enrique, the slave, could understand some words.

From there it was but a short hop – by previous standards – to the Philippines. Ten days later they had arrived on Samar, and made contact with the islanders, who at first seemed friendly enough. And then they arrived on an island named Limasawa, and the Moluccan slave hailed the boats that came to greet them – and in a moment that should have been frozen in time, it became rapidly apparent that the boatmen understood *every word* that the slave was shouting to them. Linguistically, the world had now been circum-

Antonio Pigafetta's impression of the Ladrones, today known as the Mariana Islands, near Guam. Magellan was hugely impressed with the sailing abilities of the locals in their lateen-sailed outriggers.

Left *Warriors in the Mariana islands carried enormous ceremonial shields, decorated with bolts of human hair. Scores of them boarded Magellan's ships, engaging in a riot of looting. This human-hair shield is from Borneo, where the expedition also called and were frightened by a fleet of dugout outrigger canoes.*

The Cebuano islanders – tattooed, turbanned and terrifying – proved, under the leadership of their chief Lapu-Lapu, to be Magellan's downfall. He was killed in a fight on 26 April 1521.

navigated: Enrique, this most humble slave, had been the first of humankind ever to circle the world – albeit undertaking the journey in several stages and not of his own choosing, to accomplish his unintended feat.

But a month later, Ferdinand Magellan was dead, killed in a skirmish on the Philippine island of Cebu. Each year today they memorialize his killing, at the hand of local leader named Lapu-Lapu. On a monument erected on the site, at a place called Mactan beach, one side records the stalwart and foolhardy courage of the victim, the other the nationalist heroics of his killer.

Grief-stricken, the remnants of the fleet tried to make their way home, sailing westward along the conventional and (to Portuguese mariners) familiar route, crossing the Indian Ocean to the Cape of Good Hope and the Atlantic again, losing another ship along the way. Finally, on 6 September 1522 – almost exactly three years after the armada set out – the 85-ton *Victoria*, now commanded by Sebastian d'Elcano, crossed the bar of the Guadalquivir again, bringing home 18 men and a cargo of cloves for the King of Spain.

His Majesty presented Captain d'Elcano with a jeweled globe inscribed *Primus Circumdedisti Me* – whereupon the weather-worn sailor slipped into an oblivion for all but the most dedicated historians of the sea.

And although the mournful memorial on the seashore in Cebu, a great statue on the northern side of his eponymous Strait in Punta Arenas, and a patch of distant nebulae are all that remain as fixed remembrances to Magellan, it is an undeniable truth that the man who led this plucky little expedition, the outcomes of which determined that both nations had an absolute right to trade with the faraway skerries of the Spice Islands, remains one of the greatest and most revered of all mariners of all time. The slave Enrique may have been the first to go round the world; Sebastian d'Elcano may have been the first to do so in a single expedition; and yet it is to Magellan, the man who never did it at all, that the spoils remain. History, some will say, has a quirky injustice to it, like life itself.

Sebastian d'Elcano, the Basque captain of the Victoria*, managed to limp back to Cadiz – thus becoming the first true single-voyage circumnavigator.*

BRIAN M. FAGAN

Hernán Cortés

24

1519–21

These great towns ... and buildings rising from the water, all made of stone, seemed like an enchanted vision. ... Indeed some of our soldiers asked whether it was not all a dream.

BERNAL DIAZ DEL CASTILLO, 1519

In November 1519, Spanish conquistador Hernán Cortés and a motley band of soldiers stood atop a mountain pass and gazed down into the Valley of Mexico. They saw a great city of glistening buildings, canals and brightly coloured pyramids shimmering in the sunlight. Even the most hardened Spaniard was astonished.

Cortés and his companions confronted a society so alien to European eyes that it almost defied understanding. Over five million people lived in an orderly, highly organized civilization, ruled by a supreme monarch, Motecuzoma. 'The mode of life of [Tenochtitlán's] people was about the same as in Spain, with just as much harmony and order,' wrote Cortés to the King of Spain. 'Considering that these people were barbarians, so cut off from the knowledge of God, it is wonderful what they have attained in every respect.'

History has painted Hernán Cortés in many guises – as a great general, as a consummate statesman and as a gold-hungry robber. That he was a man of immense cunning and shrewdness is unquestionable, for his dealings with the Aztecs show how well he understood their weaknesses and preoccupations. He was a charismatic leader, who commanded the loyalty of his random band of soldiers, freebooters, friars and minor artisans. Above all, Cortés was his own master, defiant of authority and decisive in command, qualities that carried him to Tenochtitlán.

The journey to the New World

Born in 1485 in Medellin, Extremadura, Spain, Cortés studied law at the University of Salamanca. In 1501 he abandoned his legal studies and decided to find his fortune in the Indies, a popular escape for ambitious young men of the day. He sailed for Santo Domingo (now the Dominican Republic) in 1504, joining the soldier and administrator Diego Velázquez in the conquest of Cuba in 1511, and subsequently became mayor of Santiago de Cuba.

When Cortés heard of the sighting of the American mainland to the west by Juan de Grijalva, a nephew of Velázquez, in 1517, he

Hernán Cortés depicted in a contemporary portrait by the German artist Christophe Weiditz (c. 1500–59). Cortés holds his family arms, those of the Marqués del Valle de Oaxaca.

Cortés is greeted with gifts by Motecuzoma's envoys, as shown in the Dominican friar Diego Durán's account of the Spanish Conquest. Durán was an important chronicler of Aztec life and history.

persuaded the governor to give him command of an expedition of 11 ships to search for gold and 'any other kind of wealth'. Velázquez soon realized that his new commander might become a powerful rival; he tried to prevent him from sailing and cancelled his commission. Cortés ignored the governor's messages and sailed west with about 600 men, fewer than 20 horses and 10 crude field cannon.

The expedition first landed on the island of Cozumel on the eastern coast of the Yucatán, where Cortés found a marooned Spaniard, Jeronimo de Aguilar, who had travelled for eight years among the Maya and learned their language. He was pressed into service as an interpreter. So, too, was an Indian woman named Malinche (or Marina), who was given to Cortés after a fierce battle with the local inhabitants along the coast in Tabasco. He made an uneasy peace with the people and sailed to Veracruz, where he landed on Holy Thursday, 1519. There he encountered envoys from the Aztec ruler Motecuzoma.

Motecuzoma Xocoyotzin (1468–1520) was consolidating his predecessors' conquests when he heard of 'mountains' moving on the eastern sea, then tales of strangers who had come from the east. There was no precedent for such arrivals, only an ancient legend of the Feathered Serpent god Quetzalcoatl, who, centuries before, had been expelled from the revered Toltec city, Tula. He had fled to the Gulf of Mexico, where he had built a raft of serpents and sailed over the horizon, vowing to return in the Aztec year One Reed. By grotesque historical coincidence, Cortés arrived at Veracruz in that very year.

Motecuzoma, whether or not he believed that the newcomer was indeed the returned Quetzalcoatl, diplomatically sent five emissaries to meet Cortés, bearing rich gifts and divine regalia. The messengers greeted Cortés as they would a god, and bedecked him with the mask, feather headdress and necklace of Quetzalcoatl. Cortés had them cast in irons and fired a large cannon. He then challenged them to a fight with iron weapons. The emissaries retreated in confusion to Tenochtitlán. Motecuzoma ordered the local people to treat the visitors generously and sent more gifts, including a golden sun disk 'as big as a cartwheel'. Instead of deterring Cortés, the lavish gifts made him even more determined to explore Aztec domains.

The march to Tenochtitlán

Ignoring recall instructions from Velázquez, Cortés left a garrison at Veracruz and sent a ship directly to Spain promising the king a fifth share of all the gold he found. He then burnt his remaining ships to prevent desertions. On 16 August 1519, he set out for Tenochtitlán at the head of a tiny army of under 350 men.

Motecuzoma watched indecisively as the Spaniards marched steadily inland. Cortés zealously courted the chiefs along his route, who complained about the predatory Aztec tax collectors, and acquired an increasingly large army for his efforts. He was unopposed until he reached Tlaxcala, 2,100 m (7,000 ft) above sea level.

The Tlaxcalans fought two major battles with the Spaniards, who found themselves confronted with thousands of brightly costumed Indian warriors. By keeping their ranks tightly knit and making effective use of their horses and ordnance, the conquistadors weathered their mass attacks and won the day. Cortés was generous in victory, accepting modest tribute and wives for his captains. He then moved rapidly on Cholula, the ancient centre of Quetzalcoatl worship and a loyal Aztec ally. He entered the town without resistance, then slaughtered the assembled nobles in the temple precinct, killing about 5,000 people, looting the city and rewarding the Tlaxcalans with cloth and salt.

Motecuzoma and his people watched stoically as the conquistadors descended on Tenochtitlán from the mountains. The fateful first meeting of Hernán Cortés and Motecuzoma Xocoyotzin took place on a causeway on the outskirts of the capital on 8 November 1519.

Aztec warriors wore elaborate feathered uniforms; the second from the left is an Eagle Knight, the foremost rank in Aztec armies.

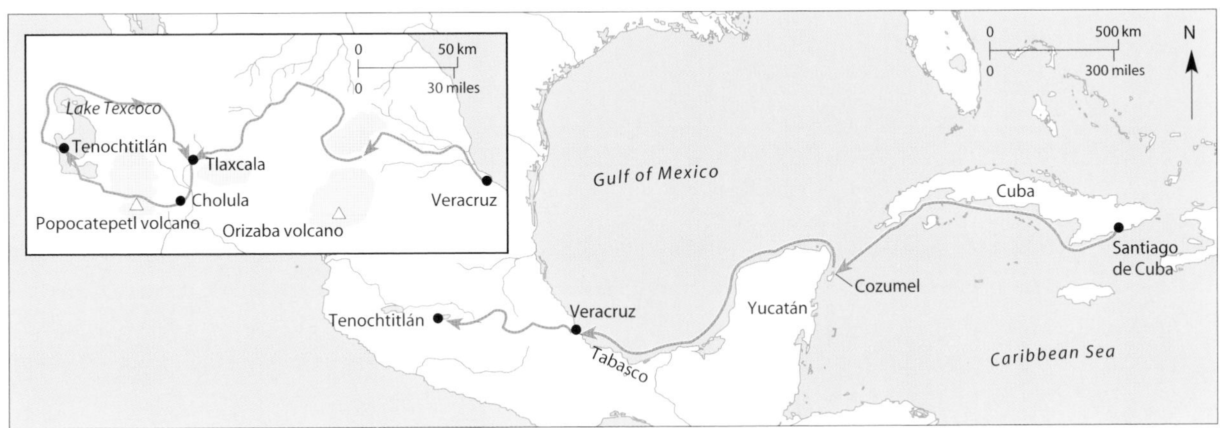

Map of Cortés's journey from Santiago de Cuba to the Valley of Mexico and the heart of the Aztec empire.

Cortés and his men explored the great city in astonishment. They climbed the pyramid of the sun god Huitzilopochtli, reeking with blood and the scent of human sacrifice, wandered through the great market, attended by 20,000 people daily. But above all, they lusted for gold. When rumours of unrest in Veracruz reached Cortés, he took Motecuzoma hostage. The ruler handed over more and more gifts.

When Cortés then learned of treachery by his deputy on the Gulf Coast, he took some men there to settle matters, leaving Pedro Alvarado in charge. A tough soldier with few diplomatic skills, Alvarado slaughtered hundreds of nobles at a festival, only to be besieged by thousands of furious Indians. Cortés returned to an ominous calm, but was soon blockaded in his garrison. Motecuzoma, no longer having the support of his people, was replaced as ruler and killed.

Cortés decided to abandon the city at night and fought his way out, back to Tlaxcala, reaching there with only a quarter of his force still alive. Shrewdly, he spent some time travelling the countryside, exploiting Aztec policies of terror and ruthless tribute gathering to recruit a new army. He then advanced along Tenochtitlán's causeways while a fleet of specially constructed galleys protected his flanks on the lake.

The siege

The siege of Tenochtitlán lasted 93 brutal days in the face of a stubborn defence. The conquistadors fought their way block by block, and watched with horror as priests sacrificed their captured comrades. Cortés blockaded the city. Many people died of starvation or from hunger-related diseases. The city finally fell on 13 August 1521. Only 60,000 of the original 300,000 defenders survived.

Hernán Cortés utterly destroyed Aztec civilization and the largest city in the Americas less than two years after he first arrived in the Valley of Mexico. He owed this victory to carefully formulated long-term strategies and to vastly superior war technology, including iron swords that could slice through wooden shields and past stone-bladed clubs. Horses provided mobility; savage war dogs struck fear into the bravest warriors.

Cortés founded Mexico City on the ruins of the ancient capital and consolidated his control over the countryside with great cruelty. He was appointed governor and captain general of New Spain in 1523, but was relieved of his post three years later and ordered to face investigations in Spain. After numerous vicissitudes, he lost much of his huge fortune and died on a small estate near Seville in 1547.

Scenes from the Codex Azcatitlan, late 16th century: on the left Cortés, accompanied by his mistress and interpreter Malinche and conquistadors and Indian porters, has dismounted from his horse. He advances to greet the emperor Motecuzoma. On the right, the last Aztec ruler, Cuauhtemoc, dies at the foot of the Tlalelolco pyramid in the heart of Tenochtitlan, in 1521.

JOHN HEMMING

Francisco Pizarro

1524–25, 1526–28, 1531–33

Truly, it was not accomplished by our own forces for there were so few of us. It was by the grace of God.

CRISTÓBAL DE MENA, ONE OF PIZARRO'S OFFICERS, 16TH CENTURY

Francisco Pizarro's great journey took him from Panama to Cuzco, the capital of Inca Peru, 2,500 km (1,550 miles) to the south-east. It was not done in one great sweep, but in a succession of expeditions over nine years. And, although it was into the unknown, its motive was military conquest rather than pure exploration.

Pizarro was a strange man, full of contradictions. Born in about 1477 in Spain's rugged Extremadura, he was the illegitimate son of a professional soldier and a serving girl in a convent. So he received no education and went through life illiterate and without mastering horsemanship or swordplay. But something drove this taciturn man to make a series of extraordinary decisions that propelled him into history as the discoverer, conqueror and destroyer of the last great empire unknown to the rest of humanity.

A contemporary portrait thought to be of Pizarro, wearing insignia of a Knight of Calatrava. Although illegitimate and illiterate, his conquest of Peru made him a marquis and one of the richest men of his day.

Obsession

Pizarro's first major decision was to sail to the New World, which he reached in 1502, aged about 25. For the next 20 years, he fought in ugly campaigns against indigenous peoples on Caribbean islands and the mainland. He became a reliable officer: in 1513 when Vasco Núñez de Balboa crossed the Isthmus of Panama and sighted the Pacific Ocean, Pizarro was his lieutenant and put his mark on the document claiming it for Spain.

The Spaniards founded the town of Panama on the Pacific. As a reward for his fighting, Francisco Pizarro received a small allocation of Indians, had an interest in a ranch breeding horses and became an *alcalde* of the new town. Now in his late forties, Pizarro should have settled down to a well-earned retirement. But he heard a rumour of a rich land known as Viru or Peru; and he determined to explore southwards down the coast of South America to find it, becoming obsessed with the idea.

Pizarro and his partner acquired one of the few ships that had been built on the Pacific side of the new continent, and embarked in November 1524 with 80 men and four horses. The voyage was a disaster. Anyone who has seen the mangrove

Francisco Pizarro's third expedition spent months struggling down the coast of Ecuador, through tough terrain such as this buriti-palm swamp.

swamps, mudflats and jungles of that coast of what is now Colombia will understand why. Their various landfalls had evocative names such as 'Port of Hunger' or 'Burned Village'.

Back in Panama, with nothing to show for their hardships, they determined to risk all in another attempt. The second voyage lasted from December 1526 to early 1528. The first breakthrough came when they captured an ocean-going Inca trading raft. This was carrying plentiful evidence of an advanced civilization: gold and silver ornaments, embroidered cloths, jewels and pottery.

Pizarro inexplicably removed his expedition to an uninhabited island they knew as Gorgona, the 'gate of hell'. Men began dying of disease and starvation and in desperation they smuggled a message to the Governor of Panama, begging to be rescued from 'a crazed slaughterer'. When the ship returned to the island, the Governor's reply gave any man permission to leave. Pizarro's response was to draw a line in the sand of a beach and challenge his men to cross it and join him. He offered hardship, danger – and riches – to those who followed him to Peru. His eloquence had little effect: only 13 men crossed. The rest returned to Panama.

The determined remaining few now sailed down the Pacific coasts of modern Ecuador and Peru in a voyage of discovery. They saw coastal towns and were dazzled by the prosperity and sophistication of these outposts of the Inca empire. Pizarro's men were not equipped for fighting, but anyway they encountered only hospitality.

Pizarro went back to Spain to obtain from King Charles the all-important *Capitulación* authorizing the projected conquest. He returned with more men and money, and left Panama on his third expedition in December 1530. The ships sailed directly for northern Ecuador. Pizarro now made a mistake: he landed near the equator instead of sailing on to the open shores of Peru that he had seen three years previously. This meant over a year spent hacking through coastal jungles, skirmishing with natives, and then wasting months on an island north of Peru.

Invasion

The expedition crossed to the Inca mainland on balsa rafts in May 1532, advancing cautiously down the coast with only 168 men, including 62 horsemen. The invaders immediately saw that they had arrived in the midst of a bloody civil war. This was between two sons of the last paramount

Left *Pizarro made several voyages in his conquest of the Inca empire.*

Above *A brightly coloured royal tunic or poncho, such as would have been worn by the emperor and as seen in the drawing (right).*

Above *The Inca emperor surrounded by his officials and courtiers in a drawing by Guaman Poma. The emperor wears a poncho tunic, the patterns of which are similar to those of the poncho shown above; these may be a form of writing or symbols of parts of the empire.*

Inca emperor – who had died of smallpox or measles brought to the New World in explorers' ships. One of the sons, Atahualpa, had just won, and was marching down the mountain highway to his coronation in the capital city Cuzco.

Pizarro made another audacious decision. He left the coast road and plunged inland to meet the mighty new Inca – thus abandoning any maritime line of communication or escape. The small column was apprehensive as it climbed into the Andes, but on the Inca's orders there was no resistance. They entered the town of Cajamarca and were lodged in buildings around a large square. The Spaniards were terrified by Atahualpa's enormous army, whose camp fires shone 'like a brilliantly star-studded sky'.

Check-mate and stalemate

On the following afternoon, 16 November 1532, the Inca went to meet the strangers. It was a ceremonial parade with thousands of unarmed retainers in elaborate uniforms, chanting as they advanced. Atahualpa was resplendent in gold and jewels, seated in a litter borne by 80 lords. Masses of Peruvians crowded into the square.

Pizarro now took his most reckless decision: to launch a surprise attack on his host. His few men charged out and slaughtered the Peruvians with

A beaker of solid gold with the face of a chief. Very few objects of precious metals survived being melted down by the conquistadors.

razor-sharp metal swords. 'In the space of two hours, all that remained of daylight … six or seven thousand Indians lay dead on the plain.' Pizarro fought on foot, and helped to topple Atahualpa from his litter. The conquest of the Incas started with check-mate: the capture of their king.

The astute Inca noted that his captors were obsessed with precious metals. Atahualpa therefore offered to fill a chamber with gold and silver, as ransom for his own release. An eight-month stalemate ensued, while trains of llamas brought the ransom treasure. Pizarro's men melted down 15 tons of gold and silver artifacts. But the adventurers reneged on their agreement to free Atahualpa. On 26 July 1533 the Inca was (wrongly) accused of organizing an army for his own rescue, given a summary trial and garrotted.

The prize, Cuzco

The conquistadors were now free to advance to the capital, Cuzco. It took three months to march 1,100 km (700 miles) along the royal Inca road through the Andes. Apart from four skirmishes against Atahualpa's armies, they were welcomed by supporters of the rival brother whom Atahualpa had defeated. Pizarro's men entered their goal in triumph on 15 November 1533, describing Cuzco to their king as 'the greatest and finest [city] … anywhere in the Indies.… It is so beautiful and with such fine buildings that it would be remarkable even in Spain!'

The aftermath of Pizarro's great journey was terrible for Peru. Cuzco was ransacked, with more gold and silver melted down than in Cajamarca. For 20 years, the conquerors fought one another in civil wars. Inca royalty attempted a great uprising, but this was defeated and many leaders were executed. The Inca system of good governance was destroyed, storehouses were emptied, herds slaughtered, terraces and buildings left to fall into decay. Ordinary Peruvians lapsed into semi-servitude to Spanish masters, and were massively depopulated by their diseases.

The sun temple Coricancha in Cuzco was the holiest shrine of the Incas. After the conquest, the Spaniards built the Baroque convent of Santo Domingo on top of its walls and terraces of magnificent masonry.

Francisco de Orellana 26

1541–42

Far greater than a shipwreck, more a miraculous event.
GONZALO FERNÁNDEZ DE OVIEDO, 1547

In late 1540, seven years after conquering Peru, Governor Francisco Pizarro sent his youngest brother Gonzalo to be lieutenant-governor of the Inca's northern capital Quito (in modern Ecuador). Gonzalo, aged about 30, was the most dashing of the four Pizarro brothers. When he reached Quito, he found its Spaniards abuzz about fabulously rich lands to the east. These Amazon forests were said to contain valuable cinnamon trees, *canela* in Spanish. More excitingly, beyond them lay a land so rich in gold that its chief anointed himself with gold dust – this was the 'Gilded Man', El Dorado. Gonzalo Pizarro immediately decided to conquer 'La Canela and El Dorado'.

Greed, hardship and betrayal

Pizarro set off early in 1541 with 220 Spaniards supported by hundreds of Indian porters and great herds of livestock. His second-in-command was his friend Francisco de Orellana, also aged 30 and an equally experienced soldier. Young Spaniards were the finest fighting men in Europe, but as soon as they descended into Amazon forests they became helpless incompetents. Pizarro's quest continued for 10 terrible months. All the Andean Indian porters perished or deserted; the 'cinnamon' trees were not real spices; and El Dorado was a chimera. The Spaniards were starving, wretched in the rains and lost in interminable forests.

In their despair they decided to build a boat to carry their supplies while most men hacked through the vegetation. There was no shortage of timber, lianas for cordage, or resin for pitch. Every emaciated man helped build this brig – a large open boat. Pizarro heard about a village with manioc fields, two days downstream; Orellana was to set sail down the River Napo with 57 men and return with looted food. Everything went wrong. There was no village or manioc. Orellana pressed ahead, always hoping to find habitations he could pillage. His men were reduced to eating their shoes cooked with herbs: seven died of starvation. The river led them on enticingly. It rained incessantly, a time when Amazon rivers are very powerful. Drifting with the flow was all that the exhausted men could do. They reckoned they advanced 1,200 km (750 miles) in eight days. They could not possibly return upstream.

It remains a question in the annals of exploration: was this treachery, a foreseen eventuality or unavoidable force of circumstance? On 4 January 1542, Orellana got his men to sign a document begging him not to try to battle back upriver. Pizarro, however, was convinced that it was dastardly betrayal. He turned homewards with 140 men, but it was nine months before

A golden Muisca model of a raft with priests, possibly depicting a ritual involving the Gilded Man – El Dorado – on Lake Guatavita near Bogotá in modern Colombia. In the 16th century, the Spaniards all sought for El Dorado in the rainforests of the Amazon.

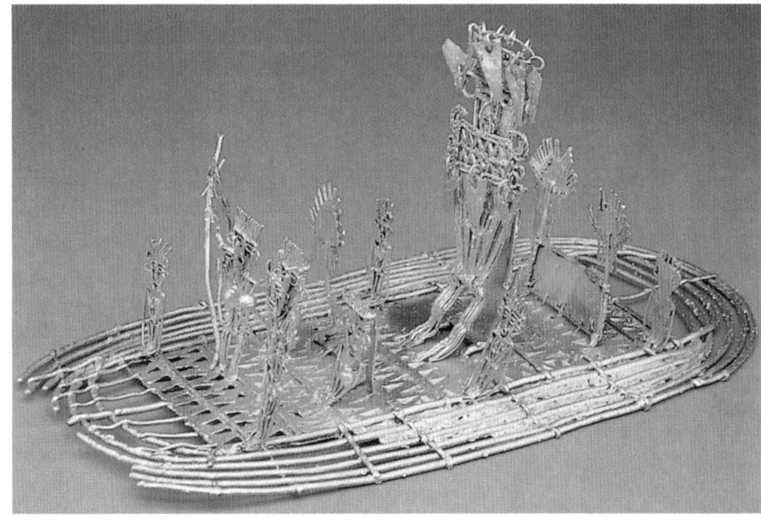

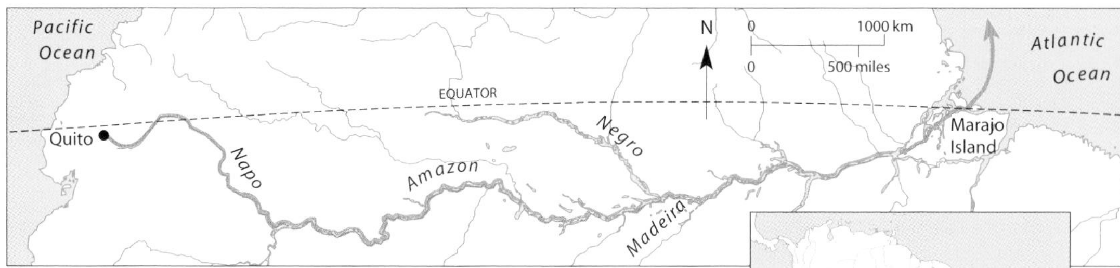

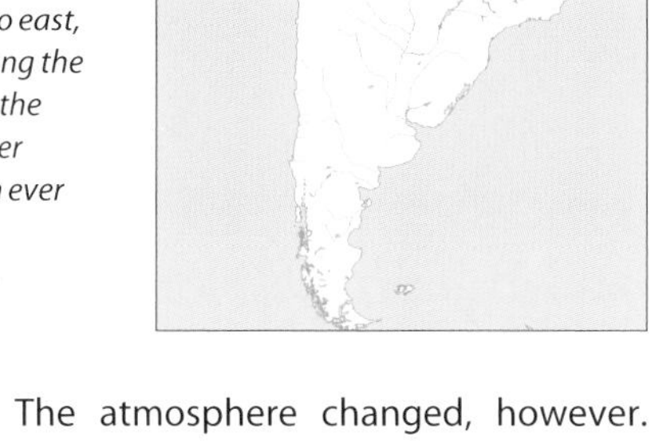

It took Orellana's men eight months in 1542 to descend the world's mightiest river, from west to east, roughly along the Equator, in the greatest river exploration ever made by Europeans.

battered survivors staggered into Quito using rusting swords as crutches. Pizarro denounced Orellana to the King: 'the greatest cruelty that faithless men have ever shown.... He carried off all the expedition's [food], arquebuses, crossbows, munitions and iron.'

Descending the world's mightiest river

Orellana was a remarkable linguist, who picked up enough words to persuade tribes along the river to barter food for beads and trinkets. In mid-February the boat and canoes sailed from the Napo on to the main Amazon. The men had no idea that they were descending the world's largest river; they had no option but to drift with the all-powerful current. After a long stretch of empty river-banks, the explorers entered the lands of the rich chief Aparia the Great. His 20 villages averaged 50 large huts and were separated by extensive farms of maize and manioc.

Orellana's strangers were so well received by Aparia's people that he decided to build a second boat. For 35 days his men felled and transported trees, cut planks, caulked their '19-ribbed' ship with local gum and made ropes and sails. They called her *Victoria*. The Spaniards were Aparia's guests until late April; they were never again to enjoy such hospitality.

They soon suffered from hunger because, as the expedition's chronicler, Friar Gaspar de Carvajal, wrote: 'Forest succeeded forest on the banks, so that we could find no place to camp at night, still less anywhere to fish.' Then came the great tribe of Chief Machiparo. There were days of fighting against decorated war canoes filled with warriors. The atmosphere changed, however. They were invited to visit Chief Machiparo himself, and he was awed by their beards and dress. The tribe had plenty of food, particularly farmed freshwater turtles. This was too much for the hungry Spaniards, who ran amok and started to pillage huts and turtle tanks. The Indians retaliated, and Orellana's men suffered two dead and 16 wounded before fleeing down the Amazon.

Beyond lay a nation with huts on stilts, whose pottery was 'the finest seen in the world ... all glazed and enamelled in every colour, amazingly vividly'. So it continued, for week after week. Two successive tribes were so hostile that the Spaniards never learned their names. They simply raced on, passing populous villages that stretched along the banks, occasionally landing to seize food, and frequently fending off war canoes.

Centre *Orellana's explorers passed great chiefdoms along the banks of the Amazon. Some of these made lovely pottery, of which this funerary urn from the island of Marajo in the river's mouth is a fine example. It dates from about* AD *500, a thousand years before the arrival of Europeans.*

Amazons

Below the confluences of the Negro and Madeira tributaries they were passing gleaming white villages, and a captive Indian girl said that this was 'the excellent land of the Amazons'. The intruders rowed their brigs against one of these settlements, defended by masses of warriors. There was savage fighting, in which so many arrows hit the boats that they looked like porcupines. Friar Gaspar was struck and 'had it not been for the thickness of my habit, that would have been the end of me'. The Spaniards slashed into the warriors, but these were led by a dozen Amazons 'fighting there as female captains in front of all the Indian men.... They killed any who turned back, with their clubs, right there in front of us.... These women are very pale and tall, with very long braided hair wound about their heads. They are very robust and go naked with their private parts covered, bows and arrows in their hands, fighting as much as ten Indian men.'

One printed book in Spain at that time was a compendium of Classical legends, and the Amazon story was a favourite. Conquistadors were therefore on the lookout for such curiosities in a New World brimming with marvels. So the world's largest river came to be called after the legendary tribe of sexually liberated women. One explanation for the tall warriors with hair piled on their heads is that they were Parikotó or Wai Wai *men*. These Carib-speaking peoples now occupy rivers where the Amazons were reported to have lived. The men's long hair is held on their heads in tubes; and both sexes hide their genitals with small aprons.

Orellana's veterans survived more skirmishes as they descended the seemingly interminable river. By late July they became aware of tides and salt water, and spent weeks refitting their boats for an ocean voyage. They had no compass, anchors, maps or qualified sailors, and pathetically little food and water. Despite this, and against all odds, light winds and currents carried the brigs past the Guianas. On 11 September 1542 the second boat reached Margarita Island off Venezuela.

In eight months they had completed one of the greatest explorations of all time. They descended, reported on, and named the world's mightiest river – three centuries before other Europeans 'discovered' Africa's rivers.

Above *The French cosmographer André Thevet imagined Amazons shooting and roasting men who intruded into their female realm.*

Left *Indigenous warriors of Amazonia were considered to be the world's finest archers. These Yanomami use extremely powerful bows and 2-m (6.6-ft) long arrows.*

BRIAN M. FAGAN

27 Early Explorers of North America

1528–36, 1540–42, 1539–42

The houses are all alike, four storeys high. One can go over the top of the whole village without there being a street to hinder. . . . [There are] corridors going all around it at the first two storeys, by which one can go around the whole village.

PEDRO DE CASTAÑEDA AT PECOS PUEBLO, NEW MEXICO, 1541

The European discovery of America unleashed a frenzied hunt for gold, not only in Mexico and Peru, but in lands to the north, where the Fountain of Youth and the gold-laden Seven Cities of Cibola were said to lie. Early probes northward yielded no gold. In 1528, Pánfilo de Narváez marched westwards from Tampa Bay, Florida. He lost contact with his ships and had to build makeshift rafts to sail west. Three sank, Narváez perished, but 80 survivors landed at Galveston Island. The following year, 15 survivors under the expedition treasurer, Alvar Núñez Cabeza de Vaca, travelled west by land. By 1533, only four men survived: Cabeza de Vaca, two conquistadors and a Moroccan slave, Estevanico.

The four continued westwards, sometimes close to shore, at others further inland. They found no golden cities, just scattered Indian bands subsisting in harsh desert environments. The party were the first Europeans to see buffalo; de Vaca described them as cows, 'the size of those in Spain. Their horns are small ... the hair is very long, like fine wool and like a pea jacket.'

Cabeza de Vaca arrived in Mexico in 1536, where he told officials of the exotic land to the north. But they waved aside his stories of buffalo and dozens of Indian tribes living in the arid lands. He could tell them nothing of gold. All he could report were rumours of large towns, crowded with people, which he had not visited – in reality Zuni pueblos.

The Seven Cities of Cibola

Did Cibola actually exist? Mexico City buzzed with excited tales. To find out, the Viceroy of New Spain sent an expedition north, headed by a Franciscan, Fray Marcos de Niza and Estevanico, the now-freed slave who had travelled with de Vaca. The venture was a disaster. Estevanico was killed

A Zuni man seated in the heart of Zuni pueblo, in a photograph taken in 1879. The pueblo was still little changed from Coronado's day.

Dutch artist Jan Mostaert painted this imaginary evocation of an attack by Spaniards on a pueblo such as Hawikuh (c. 1540).

by angry Zuni when he approached their pueblo. Marcos came up from the rear and gazed at the settlement from a distance, 'a faire citie' with many flat-roofed houses inhabited by 'light skinned people', who used gold and silver dishes. The friar's report caused a sensation in Mexico City. Angry officials accused Marcos of cowardice for not entering the 'city'. In fact, he may have fabricated the entire story and never travelled further north than the Gila River in southern Arizona. The Viceroy quickly appointed Francisco Vázquez de Coronado as leader of a new expedition. Coronado was a *hidalgo* of noble birth and a courtier to King Charles V of Spain before entering the viceroy's service in 1535, rising to become a military governor. In April 1540 he left with 220 horsemen and 60 foot soldiers, as well as numerous slaves, Fray Marcos and four other friars.

The expedition suffered horribly during the crossing of the southern Arizona desert and traversing the harsh ravines of the Colorado plateau along Indian trade routes. Word of Coronado's approach reached the Zuni long before he did. On 7 July 1540, the Spaniards sighted Hawikuh pueblo, 'a crowded little village looking as if it had been crumpled all up together'. Marcos's 'faire citie' turned out to be nothing more than a large village. The conquistadors quickly took the pueblo after fierce Indian resistance, raiding the storehouses for food, but found no gold. Coronado and his men investigated other pueblos and visited Hopi villages, guided by the Zuni. Again, there was no gold, only grain, textiles and turquoise.

Pecos Pueblo, dominated by the 18th-century Spanish mission church. The pueblo itself was founded in about AD 1300 and grew to more than 700 rooms.

Meanwhile other conquistadors ranged far over pueblo country – as far north as the Grand Canyon, where the soldiers gazed down at the river far below, and to Pecos Pueblo in the east, a town 'situated on a rock with a large court or yard in the middle containing the steam rooms'. A few days east, the Spaniards found themselves among vast herds of buffalo. In 1541, Coronado travelled eastward across the Plains for 37 days in search of that elusive dream, gold. His men encountered nomadic groups and learned how to hunt buffalo on horseback. Eventually, some of the party reached Great Bend, Kansas, where they found Wichita Indians living in grass lodges – but still no precious metals.

In 1542, Coronado led his dispirited conquistadors back to Mexico. Barely a hundred men of the original party returned, their booty consisting of some turquoises, some blankets and a wealth of new geographical knowledge about gold-less country. Half a century passed before attempts were made to settle the Southwest.

Expedition to the Mississippi

A year after Cabeza de Vaca had staggered back into Mexico City, Hernando de Soto returned home to Spain after serving with Francisco Pizarro in Peru. In 1537, the Spanish king appointed him governor of Cuba, with rights to conquer Florida. De Soto raised a force of 622 men and 200 horses. He landed in Tampa Bay in May 1539, where he found a small village. Having ravaged the settlement, he marched north through endless swamps, then came to higher ground where the soldiers harvested ripe maize for food. They took hostages at each village, raiding store houses to provide fodder for their horses.

De Soto was a ruthless and inflexible task master. He divided his party into smaller groups

Hernando de Soto was a ruthless and unbending explorer, hungry for gold and other wealth.

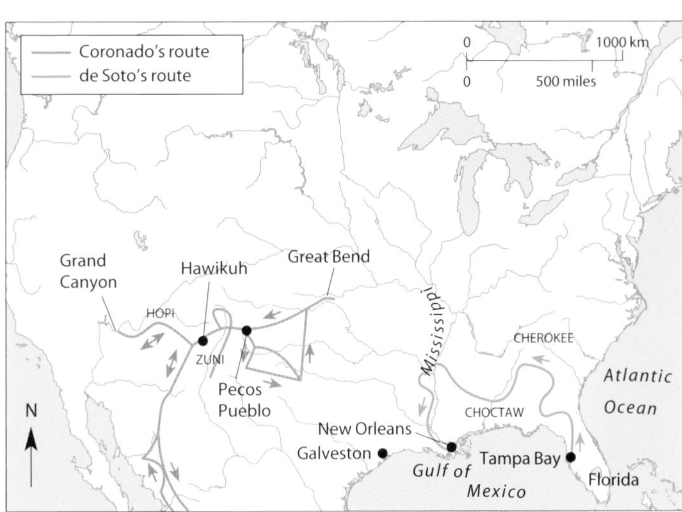

Above *Map of early European journeys in southwestern and southeastern North America (de Vaca's route is not known).*

so they could feed their horses, pressing on until he reached Cherokee country. A female chieftain presented him with lavish gifts of clothing, shawls and skins. The country, on the banks of the Savannah River, was fertile and densely cultivated, but there was no gold, the chieftain explaining that her people obtained metals through long-distance trade. She ordered the surrender of all copper and brass in her kingdom, even sheets of glittering mica, allowing the visitors to loot a nearby charnel house for freshwater pearls buried with her ancestors. These turned out to be worthless.

The expedition now moved into drier country, where Choctaw warriors ambushed the column. De Soto's porters stole his baggage train; he was forced to attack a Choctaw stronghold to recover it. Over 150 men were killed or wounded. The crippled expedition wintered near the Yazoo River, where they encountered 'fine looking' Indians in a fleet of canoes that 'appeared like a famous armada of galleys'. De Soto and his men wandered far to the west in search of gold, through the Ozarks and to the edge of the Plains, where they heard stories of 'many cattle', but never encountered buffalo in the flesh.

Finally, Hernando de Soto accepted that the gold-laden kingdoms to the west did not exist, except in his imagination. He gave up the search and headed toward the Gulf of Mexico, dying of fever by the Mississippi. Luís de Moscoso, one of his most competent lieutenants, then guided the party back to Cuba. Amazingly, half of the 622 men who had set out survived. The Indian slaves taken by the expedition were abandoned by the Mississippi.

De Soto's expedition disproved tales of gold-rich civilizations to the north of the Gulf of Mexico. Apart from two abortive French expeditions, the Mississippi Valley and Southeast were left in peace for another century; with no gold to lure rapacious conquistadors, there was no interest in a land of swamp, river and desert.

Below *A stone palette with incised decoration of the Middle Mississippian culture, typical of the ornaments worn by the Indians with whom de Soto came into contact.*

DAVID LOADES

Francis Drake

1577–80

Francis Drake told me, that having shot the Strait [of Magellan] a storm took him at first northwest, and after veered about to the southwest, which continued with him many days with that extremity that he could not open any sail.

JOHN WYNTER, 1622

Francis Drake was an adventurer. His father Edmund was a priest, and while he considered himself married, clerical marriage was unlawful at the time and so Francis may have been technically illegitimate. Some colourful (not to say criminal) escapades forced Edmund to leave Devon in 1548. Francis remained and was brought up and educated in the household of his wealthy relative William Hawkins, with his cousin, William's son, John. As soon as he was old enough, Francis was apprenticed to the sea, sailing in Hawkins' ships. In the middle of the 16th century the career best open to his kind of talent lay in a combination of trade and piracy.

By the time Drake commanded the pinnace *Judith* in John Hawkins' third slaving voyage of 1568, Hawkins was a well-known figure, patronized by Sir Christopher Hatton and in favour with Queen Elizabeth I. Francis's alleged behaviour on that expedition caused a rift between the cousins, but by then Drake had his own favour and connections, and was well known as a bold and enterprising captain.

In 1572–73, he consolidated that reputation with a successful raid on Panama. In spite of setbacks, and the death of his two brothers, he returned a rich man – and a notorious pirate in the eyes of the Spanish colonial authorities, to whose complaints Elizabeth paid not the slightest attention. In 1575 Drake served in that other place of desperate opportunity, Ireland, attracting the favourable notice of the Earl of Essex. Consequently, when a new maritime enterprise was being planned in 1576, he was seen as the obvious man to lead it.

The mysterious mission

There are a number of accounts of the venture, written by contemporaries with specific agendas, and none is particularly reliable. We do not know

Portrait of Sir Francis Drake (artist unknown), painted soon after his voyage around the globe.

where the idea came from: it may have been the Earl of Essex, Hatton or even Elizabeth. The queen was certainly involved from the very beginning, but did not want the fact to be known. Nor do we know what instructions were given for this voyage, which turned into a circumnavigation of the globe. It seems clear that trade in the ordinary sense was never part of the purpose, but that there was always an intention to 'annoy the King of Spain'. This would explain the choice of Drake as commander, and also the fact that the instructions seem never to have been written down.

The ostensible purpose was exploration, but information about any particular objective is vague. It may have been the western seaboard of South America, the 'Terra Australis incognita' which was believed to lie northwest of the Strait of Magellan, or perhaps the western end of the fabled 'Strait of Anian', which was supposed to offer a northwest passage to the East. All are mentioned in the contextual correspondence. The sponsors were significantly similar to those who had backed Hawkins in 1568: the Lord Admiral, the Earl of Leicester, Sir Francis Walsingham, Sir Christopher Hatton, the Admiralty officers William and George Winter, and (in spite of their differences) John Hawkins.

The Queen contributed her own ship, the *Swallow*, and insisted that the flagship, which Drake himself owned, should be renamed the *Pelican*. This was a symbolic indication of her support, because the pelican in her piety was one of her favourite images.

Rivalry with Thomas Doughty

Drake himself seems to have played little part in the logistics of preparation, but was seriously annoyed when the expedition almost came to grief within days of setting off from Plymouth on 15 November 1577. The five storm-battered ships were driven into Falmouth, and Drake blamed those who had been responsible for loading for this near disaster. After repairs they finally departed in mid-December. At first the voyage continued to be unpropitious. A landing on the African coast, which may have been intended to acquire slaves, produced nothing, and a raid on the Cape Verde Islands was equally unproductive. They took a Portuguese ship and looted the cargo, but retained the ship itself only briefly. They then headed for South America, and during

A compendium of different scientific instruments made by Humphrey Cole of London and reputedly owned by Drake.

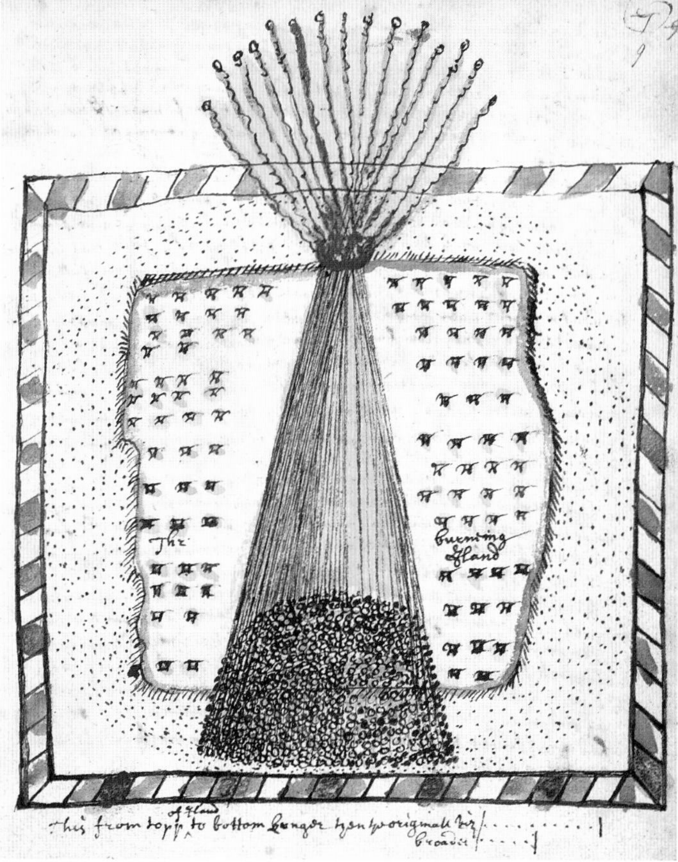

Sketch by Francis Fletcher, chaplain on the Golden Hind, *of Fogo, one of the Cape Verde Islands.*

the long Atlantic crossing Drake fell out disastrously with Thomas Doughty, the gentleman who was nominally his second-in-command.

The surviving accounts contain copious details of this quarrel, not entirely consistent, and neither party emerges with much credit. As Drake struggled to keep the small fleet of ships together, he became convinced that Doughty was not only a mutineer but also a necromancer – on no better evidence, apparently, than that he kept a diary in Latin. A ship which Doughty had commanded was abandoned, ostensibly because of its bad condition, but really, it would seem, because Drake believed that his colleague had cursed it.

After this crisis in relations had gone on for several weeks, Drake had Doughty framed on charges of mutiny and conspiracy, and executed him at Port St Julian. In spite of his claims to the contrary, he probably did not have the authority to do this, but if the expedition was to continue, it was the only solution. On 17 August 1578 the remaining ships set out again, and passed through the Strait of Magellan, where Drake renamed his ship the *Golden Hind*. In the course of that passage, storms again divided them. The *Marigold* was lost and the *Elizabeth*, driven back into the Atlantic, gave up and returned home. Only the *Golden Hind*, with about 90 men on board, continued into the southern ocean, where Drake made the important discovery that Tierra del Fuego was not joined to the supposed southern continent, as had been believed.

Undeterred, Drake turned north, raiding the small Spanish settlements on the coast of Chile, and causing panic as he went. English pirates had never been seen on that side of the continent

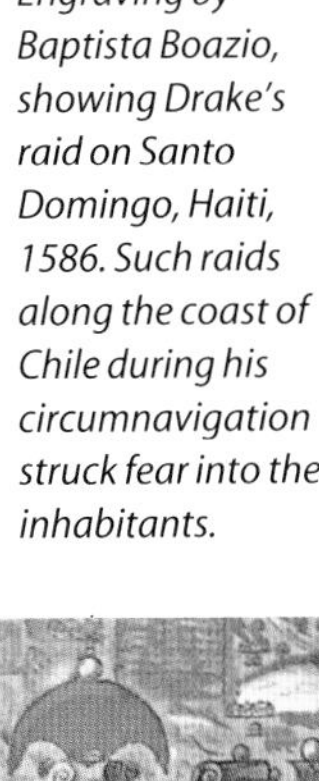

Engraving by Baptista Boazio, showing Drake's raid on Santo Domingo, Haiti, 1586. Such raids along the coast of Chile during his circumnavigation struck fear into the inhabitants.

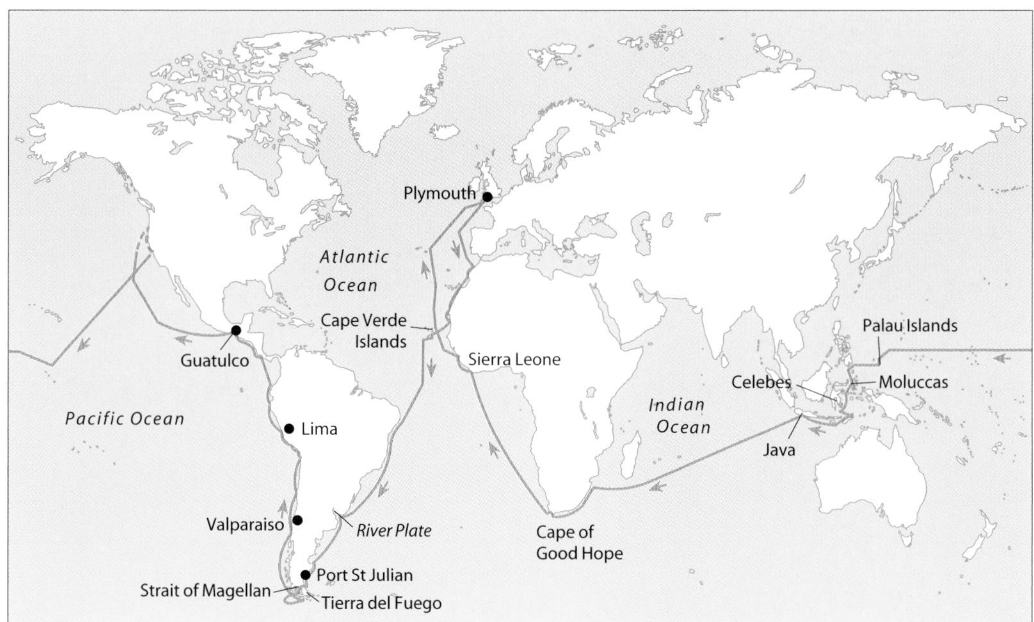

Drake's was the second expedition to complete a circumnavigation of the world. It is still not known how far north he reached up the coast of North America.

before, and Drake's depredations were lavishly recorded in local records. On his way north he captured his greatest prize, a Spanish treasure ship. Eventually he reached what is now Lower California, beyond the end of the Spanish settlements, and a subsequent story claims that he landed and claimed it for the queen. Unfortunately, no contemporary record confirms this.

Drake's intentions at this point, in early 1579, are unclear and confused by numerous contemporary Spanish guesses. He may have been looking for 'the Strait of Anian' as a way home, but if so he inevitably failed to find it.

The voyage home

It is uncertain how far north Drake actually ventured, but he seems to have made no landfall north of California. It was July 1579 before he finally quitted the coast of America and headed southwest, making his next landfall on one of the Palau Islands, east of the Philippines at the end of September. From there he threaded his way through the Moluccas and Celebes, meeting (on the whole) a friendly reception from the natives, but wandering in unknown waters and at least once getting stuck on a reef.

Unsubdued by adversity, Drake then picked a quarrel with his chaplain, Francis Fletcher, whom he subjected to public humiliation, not, apparently, valuing his intercessions. At this point, in February 1580, they were still in the East Indies. Thereafter their fortunes improved, and they had a fair and uninterrupted passage across the Indian Ocean and round the Cape of Good Hope. So well had they finally provisioned themselves, and serviced the ship, that they did not stop again until reaching Sierra Leone on 22 July 1580. From there a fair wind brought them back to Plymouth on 26 September.

Elizabeth was delighted. She had become so concerned about the fate of her 'favourite pirate' that there had been talk of her sending a search party. When news of his return reached her, she summoned him to London, and knighted him on the deck of his ship. He had brought back useful plunder, most of which ended in the royal coffers, but had opened no new trade routes and added only a little to geographical knowledge.

His circumnavigation of the globe had been a magnificent feat of seamanship and sheer bloody-mindedness, and Philip of Spain was seriously annoyed. Most importantly, however, he had stated an intention. England now had the technology, the seamanship and the will to establish global reach. Nowhere in the world was now safe from the English.

CONRAD E. HEIDENREICH

Samuel de Champlain

1603–16

It would be a matter of great toil and labour to be able to see and do by ship what a man might propose, except at great cost ... besides the risk of labouring in vain. But with the canoes of the savages one may travel freely and quickly throughout the country.... So that by directing one's course with the help of the savages and their canoes, a man may see all that is to be seen.

SAMUEL DE CHAMPLAIN, 2 JULY 1603

Samuel de Champlain was born about 1570 to a sea-going family in the small port of Brouage, near Rochefort, France, and died at Québec on Christmas Day 1635. From 1593 to 1598 he was a non-commissioned officer in the quartermaster's service of Henri IV's army, also performing 'important and confidential' work for the king. In 1598, when Henri's war against the Catholic League was over, Champlain set sail for the next two and a half years on a French ship hired by Spain for service in the Caribbean. It is probable that he gained his knowledge of surveying and navigation through these activities.

In 1603 Aymar de Chaste, holder of the fur trade monopoly for Canada, invited Champlain to determine if the lands along the St Lawrence River were habitable, and also whether there was a way across the Lachine Rapids towards China. Based on the earlier expeditions of Jacques Cartier (see box, p. 122) there was considerable doubt that either aim could be accomplished.

Canoes and maps

On 26 May, Champlain arrived at Tadoussac where he witnessed a treaty between the local Montagnais and Henri IV, the first of its kind in North America. By the terms of this treaty, French settlement was permitted adjacent to the St Lawrence in return for French military aid against the ancient foes of the Montagnais – the Iroquois. On his way up the St Lawrence, Champlain tried to explore the lower reaches of the Richelieu River, but was stopped by the first set of rapids. Impressed by the ability of the Montagnais to navigate in their canoes and portage around the rapids, he asked to be taken for a paddle across the river.

Later, upon arrival at Montréal Island, Champlain's men tested a skiff constructed specifically for navigating across the Lachine Rapids. When it failed, Champlain became the first European to recognize that their transportation technology was useless in the

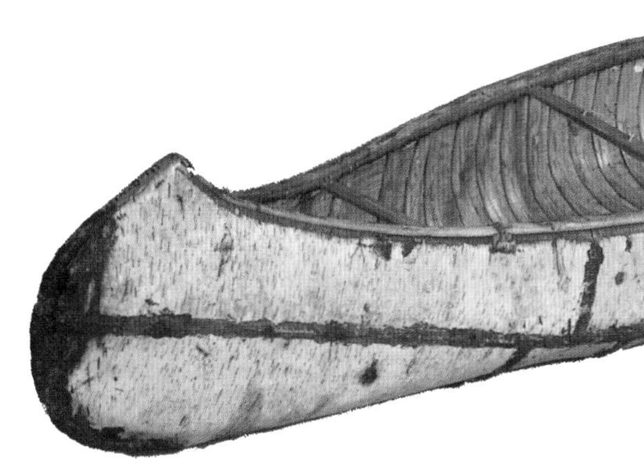

A modern Ojibwa birchbark canoe. The early 17th-century eastern Algonquin canoe described by Champlain was up to nine paces (c. 7 m/23 ft) long, and 1–1.2 m (3–4 ft) wide, with a capacity of about 455 kg (1,000 lb).

Canadian wilderness, but with canoes and helpful Native guides the interior could be opened up to exploration. On this voyage he also discovered that the Natives could draw maps and render good geographical descriptions. From the Montagnais he learned of Hudson Bay seven years before Hudson got there and the route up the Richelieu River to the Hudson River and the Atlantic coast. From the Algonquins he obtained maps and descriptions of the western Great Lakes.

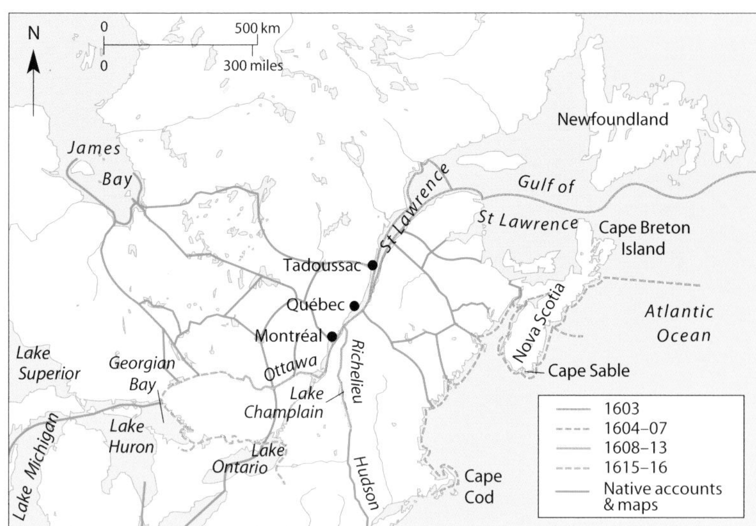

Above
Champlain made several exploratory voyages of the St Lawrence seaway and beyond, but also gathered a large amount of his geographical information from native accounts and maps; it was a method that was followed by other explorers after him.

Exploring inland

Between 1604 and 1607, Champlain explored and charted the Atlantic coast from Cape Breton to Cape Cod, developing his observational skills and gathering Native geographical information. In 1608 he was back on the St Lawrence to build a settlement at Québec and begin preparations for exploration out of the St Lawrence valley. He got his first chance in 1609, when he joined a Montagnais war party with two French volunteers to engage the Iroquois, in fulfilment of Henri IV's 1603 promises to the Montagnais. Entering the Richelieu River, the expedition paddled to the southern end of Lake Champlain where they raided a Mohawk fishing village;

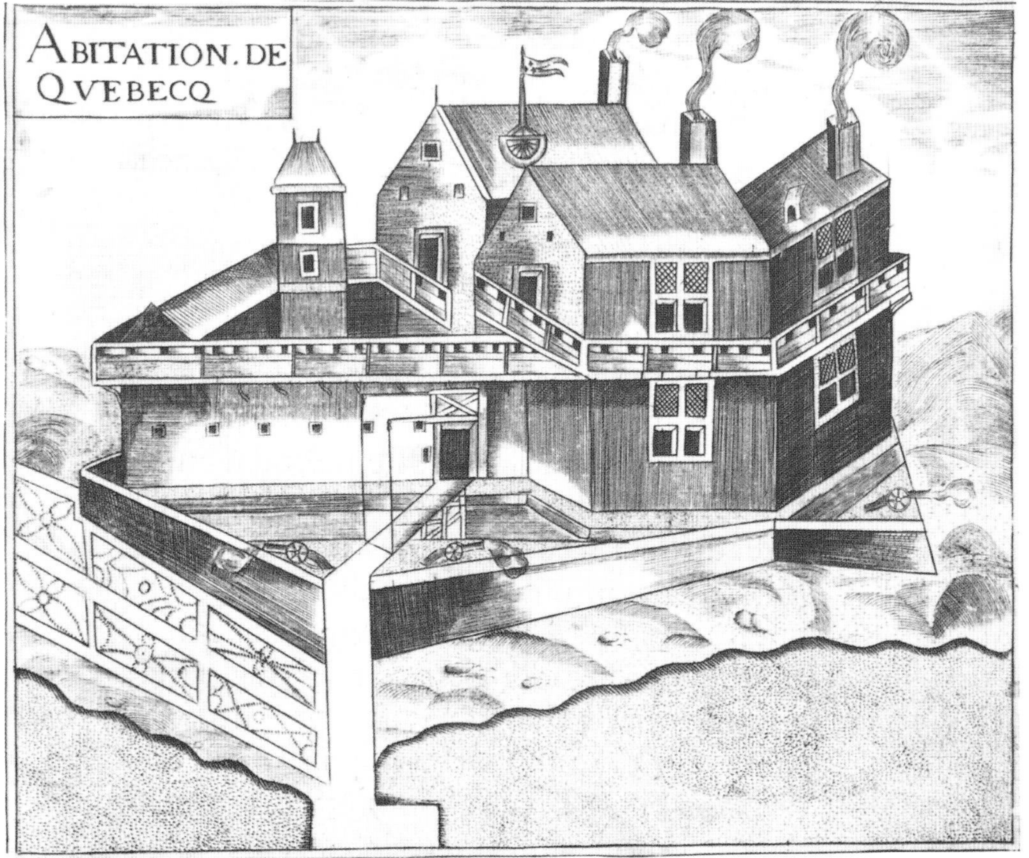

An engraving from a sketch made by Champlain for his book Les Voyages *(1613) of the 'Habitation' he built with his men at Québec in 1608. The erection of this building marked the beginning of the permanent settlement of Canada by Europeans.*

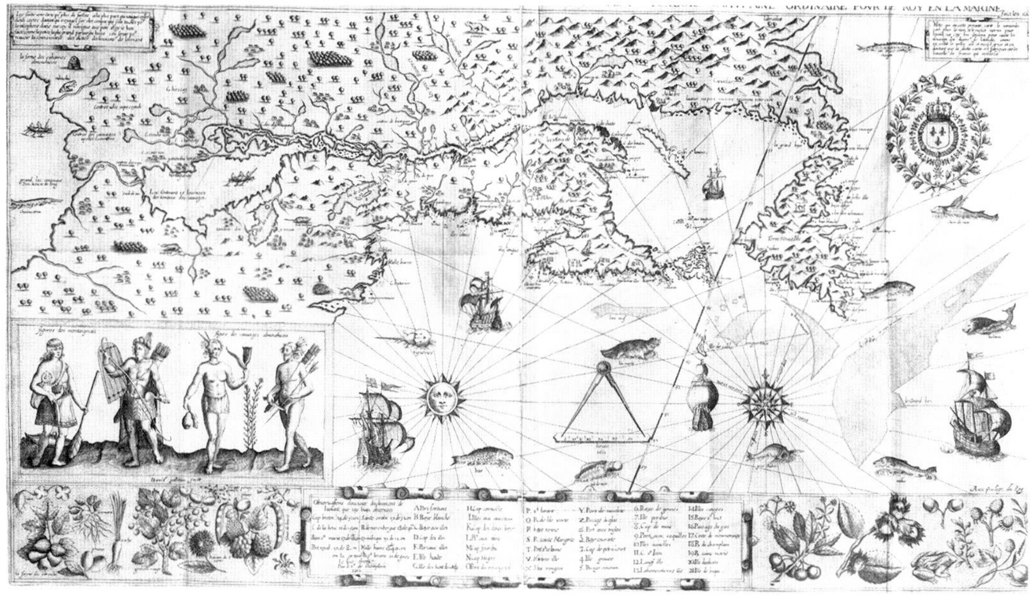

Champlain's 'Carte Geographiqve de la Novvelle Franse, 1612' includes his explorations and mapping of the coasts from present-day Cape Cod to Montréal to the end of 1611. The river and lakes system west of Montréal, including Niagara Falls, are here mapped for the first time, based on Algonquin maps and verbal accounts obtained by Champlain in 1603.

Champlain became the first European to explore inland.

Following this raid, he brought other Native groups into the alliance and began to exchange young Frenchmen with the Huron, Montagnais and Algonquins, to learn each other's languages and cultures. In 1613 he paddled north up the Ottawa River hoping to reach James Bay. Fearing that these inexperienced Frenchmen would come to grief, the Algonquin turned them back just north of the present city of Ottawa.

In 1615 he got the chance to explore westwards again by agreeing to join his Huron allies on another raid against the Iroquois. When he reached Georgian Bay on Lake Huron, he learned about Lake Michigan from an Odawa chief. Four years later he heard about Lake Superior from his interpreter Étienne Brûlé. Proceeding south, Champlain explored the Huron country and became the first European to travel through southern Ontario across the eastern reaches of Lake Ontario into the Iroquois country.

Late in life Champlain wrote that of his accomplishments those that pleased him most were his maps and also the fact that he had shown others how Canada could be explored. His four books and 29 charts, maps and picture plans were the first detailed descriptions of northeastern North America. His ability to gain the trust of Natives and learn from them how to travel and live in Canada made it possible for French explorers after him to explore and control the interior of North America until the English conquest in 1760.

JACQUES CARTIER

Jacques Cartier made three expeditions to Canada. In 1534 he circumnavigated the Gulf of St Lawrence in two ships, with 61 men, hoping to find a passage westward. After spotting an opening on the north side of Anticosti Island he returned the following year with three ships and 110 men. Reaching the mighty Lachine Rapids south of Montréal Island, he realized that the St Lawrence River was not a passage but a cul-de-sac. His persistent questioning of the Natives about possible locations of gold and precious stones, led them to fabricate stories of a fabulously wealthy 'Kingdom of Saguenay' far to the north of the St Lawrence River. After experiencing a dreadful winter of scurvy and bitter cold the French visitors, who were no longer welcome, set sail to France with 10 kidnapped Natives who were to repeat their stories to King François I. Hoping this 'Kingdom' would be like those encountered by Spain in Mexico and Peru, the French organized new expeditions under Cartier with five ships and perhaps 500 men (1541) and Jean-François de La Rocque de Roberval with three ships and 200 men and women (1542) to conquer the 'Kingdom of Saguenay'. Defeated by an inhospitable winter, the rough terrain adjacent to the St Lawrence valley and a Native population that had become hostile, and with no prospect of quick riches, the French returned home. Although the St Lawrence was roughly mapped through these expeditions, Canada received a reputation as an area unsuitable for settlement and with no useful resources except fish.

GLYN WILLIAMS

Early Searchers for the Northwest Passage

30

1576–1632

Many of our men complained of infirmities; some of sore mouthes, all the teeth in their heads being loose, their gums swollen, with blacke rotten flesh, which every day must be cut away.

CAPTAIN THOMAS JAMES, 1633

The quest for a sea route through or around America began as soon as the successors of Columbus recognized the vast continental dimensions of the new lands across the Atlantic. Seamen sailed along thousands of miles of coastline looking for a gap through which they could reach the lands of the East, but they found only the tortuous Strait of Magellan far to the south (p. 97). Across the North Atlantic, as the French probed the St Lawrence for a way through to the Pacific (p. 120), English seamen searched farther north for the sea route they called the Northwest Passage.

It was a name that soon carried emotive undertones of men and ships battling against hopeless odds. In the late Tudor and early Stuart period, explorers took their small wooden sailing ships into the eastern fringes of the Arctic archipelago in quest of an open strait, and the great geographical features of this frozen world are still named after them: Frobisher Bay, Davis Strait, Baffin Island and Baffin Bay, Hudson Strait and Hudson Bay, Foxe Basin, James Bay.

Portrait of the soldier and adventurer Sir Martin Frobisher, by Cornelius Ketel (1577).

Martin Frobisher and John Davis

The search began in earnest with the first voyage of the soldier and adventurer Martin Frobisher in 1576 in the service of the Company of Cathay (China) – the name an indication of the expedition's objective. In the tiny *Gabriel*, with a crew of 18, Frobisher reached the southeast coast of Baffin Island where he found an opening (later

John White, who may have been on the expedition, painted this scene depicting a skirmish between Frobisher's men and Inuit at Bloody Point, Frobisher Bay, on Frobisher's second voyage.

named Frobisher Bay) out of which surged a strong tide. In England, speculation about whether this was the entrance to a passage was overshadowed by excitement over reports that the mineral ore picked up by Frobisher's men at their landing place on Kodlunarn Island contained gold. Frobisher's next two voyages in 1577 and 1578 were directed more towards mining than exploration.

The first and second voyages were marked by hostilities with the local Inuit; five of Frobisher's men disappeared, while several Inuit were kidnapped and others killed. The third voyage in 1578 was made with 15 ships – an enormous fleet for the period. Hindered by fog, driving snow and ice, Frobisher entered an opening south of Frobisher Bay which he ruefully named 'Mistaken Strait'. It was in fact Hudson Strait, the great waterway into the heart of the Canadian North. Back at Kodlunarn Island, the ships were loaded with ore, while a small stone house filled with goods for the Inuit was the first permanent building erected by Englishmen in the New World. On the expedition's return to England the ore was found to be worthless iron pyrites, or 'fool's gold', and the Company of Cathay collapsed

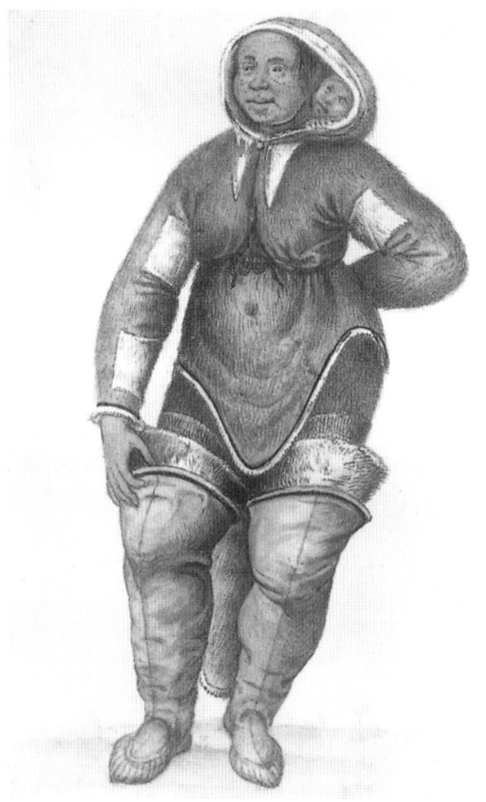

A painting by John White of an Inuit woman and child (in her hood), captured by Frobisher on his second voyage in 1577 and brought back to England, where they both died soon after.

amid financial loss, mutual recriminations and legal proceedings.

The next decade saw three further northern voyages under the outstanding navigator John Davis, who added much to Europe's knowledge of northern waters. On the first, in 1585, Davis crossed the southern part of the strait soon to be named after him and entered Cumberland Sound on the east coast of Baffin Island. When he returned home he insisted that 'The northwest passage is a matter nothing doubtful, but at any tyme almost to be passed'; but on the follow-up voyage the next year he was surprised to find pack ice blocking his way. It was a warning sign of the unpredictable seasonal variation of ice in Arctic waters.

On his third voyage in 1587 Davis planned to follow Davis Strait north, and by the end of June he reached latitude 73°N before crossing Baffin Bay and coasting back southwards along its western shores. Cumberland Sound was entered once more and followed to its head. Disappointed, Davis headed south, keeping clear of 'a very great gulfe' where the waters whirled and roared. Like Frobisher, he had reached Hudson Strait, and failed to realize its significance. Despite Davis's optimism that his finding of open sea in far northern latitudes meant that 'the passage is most probable, the execution easie', this was the last of his Arctic voyages, for war with Spain diverted ships and resources elsewhere.

Henry Hudson and William Baffin

After the signing of peace with Spain in 1604, English navigators resumed the search for a

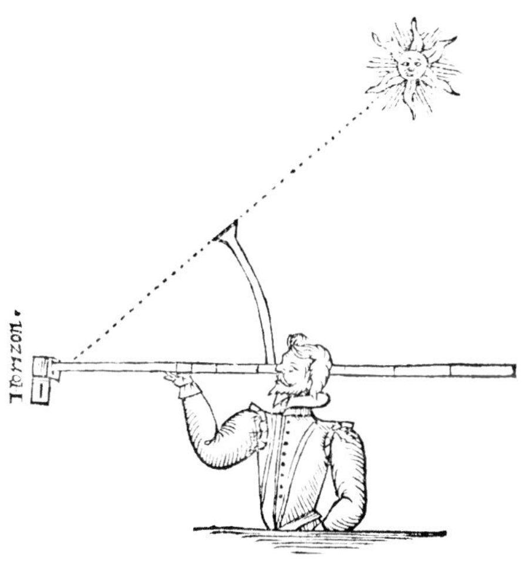

Far left *John Davis invented the backstaff for observing latitude. Its use is shown here in his navigation manual,* The Seaman's Secret *(1595).*

Left *An engraved portrait of Henry Hudson, (English School, undated).*

Right *William Baffin's chart of Hudson Strait, 1615. The red dotted line shows Baffin's track along the north shore of the Strait, and north into Foxe Channel, with flags marking the places where he landed to measure the tides. The great expanse of Hudson Bay lies to the west.*

passage, although no major discovery was made until 1610 when Henry Hudson, discoverer of the Hudson River the year before, sailed in the *Discovery* through Hudson Strait and into the huge bay that was soon to bear his name. The ship reached 'the bottom of the bay' (later James Bay), where the crew spent a miserable winter. When the ice broke up in the spring, most opposed Hudson's intention of renewing the quest for a passage. In one of the classic tragedies of Arctic exploration Hudson, his young son and seven crew members were cast adrift in a small boat, and were never seen again.

Reports from the survivors of the 'spacious sea' that they had entered kept alive hopes of a Northwest Passage. Encouraged by royal patronage almost 400 investors financed a series of expeditions, on which the pilot William Baffin was a key figure. In 1615 he and Robert Bylot (a member of Hudson's ill-fated voyage) explored much of the west coast of Hudson Bay without finding a passage, and the search shifted farther north. In 1616 Baffin and Bylot pushed through heavy ice in Davis Strait until they reached open water, the 'North Water' of the whalers who later sailed to Baffin Bay, named after the man who was the first to navigate it.

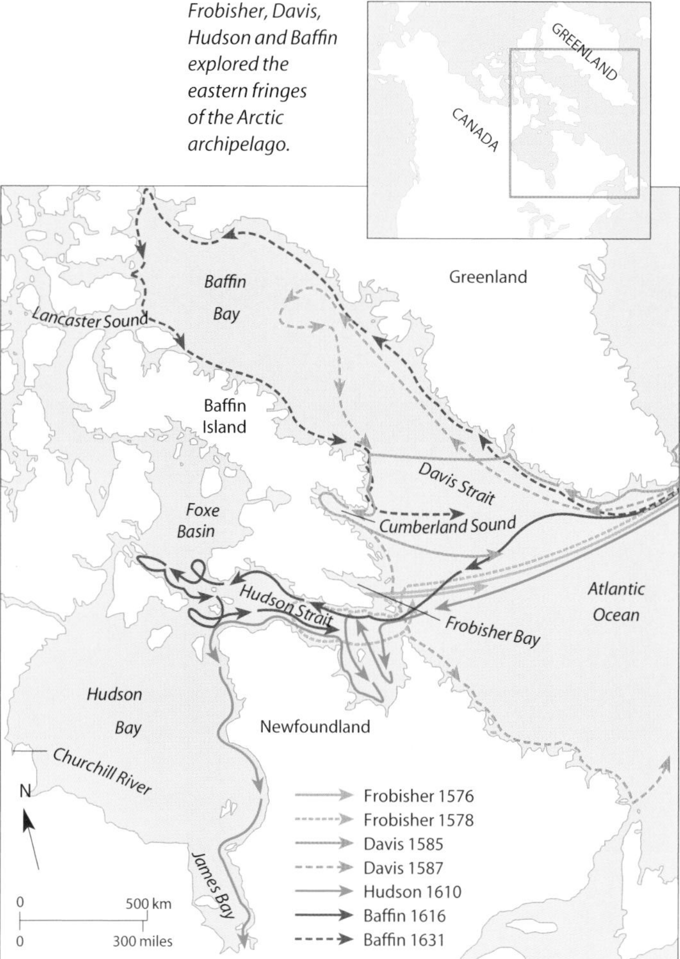

Frobisher, Davis, Hudson and Baffin explored the eastern fringes of the Arctic archipelago.

At the expedition's farthest north the ship was in latitude 78°N, not reached again for more than 200 years, and as it sailed south along the west coast of Baffin Bay it passed the entrance of Lancaster Sound. In the 19th century this proved to be the entrance of the Northwest Passage, but Baffin observed that it was blocked by ice, and sailed away. There was, he concluded, 'no passage nor hope of passage in the north of Davis Streights'.

Wintering in the North

In 1619 Jens Munk commanded a Danish discovery expedition to Hudson Bay, but it was notable less for its discoveries than for its experiences, which long stood as a warning of the perils of a northern wintering. Struck down by scurvy at Churchill River, out of a crew of 64 only Munk and

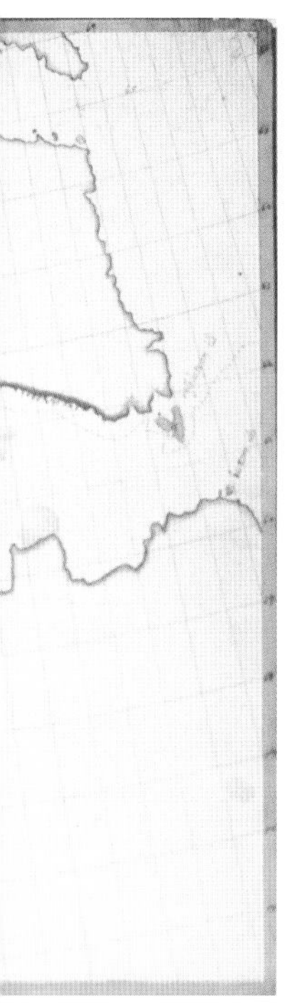

Left *Jens Munk's wintering place at Churchill, 1619–20. Most of his crews died in the ships, where, Munk wrote, 'I could not any more stand the bad smel and stench from the dead bodies'. This woodcut is taken from Munk's account of the voyage published in 1624. The original was clearly not drawn on the spot since trees of the size shown do not grow this far north.*

two others survived to sail their ship home in a remarkable feat of endurance.

The final voyages in this stage of the search for a Northwest Passage, those of Luke Foxe and Thomas James, both left England in 1631. Foxe explored and named much of the coastline of Hudson Bay without finding an opening to the west, and returned home with his crew intact. James, by contrast, decided to winter in the southern extension of Hudson Bay, later named after him. The men suffered from cold, hunger and frost-bite, and four of them died before the ship struggled back to England in 1632. James had made few discoveries, but his account, *The Strange and Dangerous Voyage of Capt. Thomas James*, became a classic of northern endurance and survival, which more than 150 years later Coleridge called on for his land of ice in 'The Rime of the Ancient Mariner'.

A halt in the search

The hardships and disappointments experienced by Foxe and James marked a halt in the search for a Northwest Passage. The explorers' narratives described what the crews had endured, and the risks that they had run. Mountainous icebergs towered above the tiny vessels, and pack ice bore down on them. Wooden hulls could be crushed, pierced or overturned as heavy floes smashed into them until, as Baffin wrote of one moment, 'unless the Lord himselfe had been on our side we had shurely perished'.

Nor was ice the only danger, for the tides were so violent that they spun ships round as in a whirlpool. The unpredictable variation of the compass added to the difficulties of navigation, while fog and snow often prevented the taking of sun-sights to establish latitude. And always there was the cold, so extreme that even in summer sails and rigging froze solid, and in winter men lost fingers and toes, and sometimes their lives, through frost-bite.

Yet the voyages from Frobisher's time onwards were not without result, for amid the hazards lessons were learned. A tradition of Arctic navigation was established, and seamen discovered how to deal with problems of navigating through ice, compass variation and the phenomenal rise and fall of the tides. These skills would prove profitable in the future, as later venturers exploited the resources in cod, whales and furs found in the northern regions.

17th & 18th Centuries

After the excitement, and rapacity, aroused by the discovery of a 'new world', the focus of travel turned back once more to the East. The Dutchman Abel Tasman led the way in the search for the great 'Southern Continent', claiming Tasmania (named then Van Diemen's Land) for the Netherlands and making the first, unsatisfactory, encounter with the Maori people of New Zealand.

By now the shape of the world had been ascertained, even if there were still blanks on the map. It was not yet known, for instance, whether the East and West were joined in the far north of the Pacific. Vitus Bering finally proved that the strait named after him divided Siberia from Alaska, although he did not catch sight of the American coast. His second voyage was a massive, multi-disciplinary enterprise. Bering succeeded in producing detailed maps of this frozen, inhospitable region of the globe, but died on the way home from scurvy, the scourge of many maritime expeditions at this period.

Cook, the English naval captain, filled in many of the gaps left by Tasman, charting meticulously, discovering the new inhabited islands of Hawai'i and sailing vast distances with phenomenal navigational accuracy. He also went further south than anyone before and, by circumnavigating Antarctica without ever actually seeing it, proved that there was no habitable continent there.

For the French, Lapérouse led a major scientific expedition in two ships to the Pacific, which lasted almost three years before he and both crews vanished without trace as they sailed from Australia towards Tonga. Bougainville gained the

Lapérouse receives his instructions from Louis XVI (seated), before setting out on his voyage to the Pacific in 1785, from which he never returned; painting by Nicolas André Monsiau.

honour of being the first of his nation to go round the world, discovering his eponymous island in the Solomon Islands on the way.

Meanwhile, an intrepid Dutchwoman was making a great journey in the Americas, on a smaller scale perhaps than the great circumnavigators, but remarkable in its own way. Maria Sibylla Merian was an outstanding naturalist and one of the finest artists of her age. Breaking every convention, she travelled through Surinam as a middle-aged divorcee, recording and painting everything she saw. Unlike her contemporaries, she illustrated nature holistically, noting symbiotic relationships between the innumerable species in the teeming rainforests.

At much the same time, Ippolito Desideri, an Italian Jesuit missionary, was travelling across the Himalaya to Tibet, eventually reaching Lhasa, where he stayed for six years, studying in a monastery. Unfortunately for Desideri, his account of his achievements was lost for 250 years and his great journey forgotten.

The first of the major explorers of Africa now makes a dramatic appearance. James Bruce was a big, strong man and also a doctor, which helped him to penetrate the sometimes hostile lands he encountered in his search for the source of the Nile. The fantastic stories of his adventures titillated the public but were derided by his contemporaries, and it was not until nearly 100 years later that he was vindicated.

Mungo Park, whose West African journeys followed some 25 years later, explored the Niger rather than the Nile. He was more fortunate in his reception by the establishment and also achieved instant immortality by dying on his second great journey: he was ambushed and killed when close to achieving his aim of descending the river to its mouth.

Across the Atlantic, Alexander Mackenzie demonstrated that the hostile northern wastes of America could be crossed by river, although the way was so hard that this did not prove to be the long sought-after trade route to the East.

Encounters: a Maori and an English officer are depicted in the process of bartering a lobster for a piece of linen, in a watercolour possibly by Joseph Banks, during Cook's first voyage around the world.

JOHN ROSS

Abel Tasman

31

1642–43

It is impossible to conceive a country that promises fairer from its situation than this of Terra Australis.

Abel Tasman, 1642–43

In the early 1600s captains of the Dutch East India Company ships encountered what one of them, Jan Carstenz, described as 'the driest, poorest area to be found in the world'. These men had mostly seen the forbidding coasts of northern Western Australia and the Great Australian Bight. Another, Frederik de Houtman, had made landfall in 1619 near today's Perth and reported: 'It seems to be a fine country'. He did not go ashore, however, and his comments were lost in the general lack of interest from a company which was motivated by trade.

A fresh impetus came with the appointment in 1636 of Antony van Diemen as Governor-General of the East Indies, based at its capital Batavia (as Jakarta was then called), on the island of Java. He was a former sailor in the 1619 expeditionary ship *Mauritius*, and was fired with ambition to add the unknown continent to the domains of the vigorous maritime nation of the Netherlands.

Portrait of Abel Tasman with his wife and daughter, c. 1637, attributed to Jacob Gerritz Cuyp. Such a portrait painted before his expedition is a measure of Tasman's standing within the Dutch East India Company.

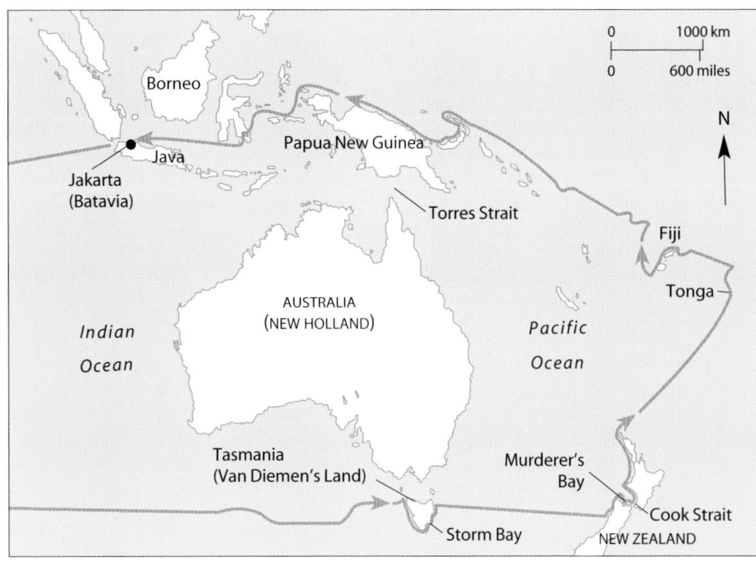

Map showing the route of Tasman's voyage of 1642–43: he initially sailed westwards from Jakarta to Mauritius to pick up favourable winds. Although he explored the western coasts of New Zealand, he did not realize that there were two separate islands.

His grand plan for a voyage of discovery was to send two ships as far south and east as possible to attempt to outline more of the supposed continent, known as New Holland. Such a voyage might also affirm whether or not it was connected with Antarctica and find 'many excellent and fertile regions' or, even, 'rich mines of precious and other metals'.

In 1642 van Diemen commissioned the 39-year-old Abel Janszoon Tasman to lead the expedition in the ship *Heemskerck*, accompanied by the transport ship *Zeehaen*. His instructions to Tasman stated that if he were to find a civilization he should 'parley with its rulers and subjects, letting them know that you have landed there for the sake of commerce'.

Tasman had been an ordinary seaman and had proved himself both adventurous and resourceful as he rose through the ranks. He sailed from Jakarta on 14 August 1642 and called at Mauritius to pick up his supplies and favourable winds, taking his ships south, down to the extremities of the easterly airstream, later known by English skippers as the Roaring Forties. Huge following seas and howling winds created weeks of extreme hardship for the crews, beset as they already were by fears of disaster in these uncharted waters. The necessity for kinder conditions forced Tasman to veer northwards in his easterly course.

Opposite above
The encounter at Murderer's Bay, when seven Maori canoes surrounded Tasman's ships, and one rammed a ship's boat (visible between the Heemskerck *and the* Zeehaen*), causing the deaths of four Dutch seamen.*

High mountains to the east

On 24 November 1642, Tasman was fortunate with clear weather as he headed towards a coast that would later claim thousands of lives through shipwreck in storms and fog. He sighted high mountains to the east and wrote: 'As this land has not before been known to any European we called it Antony van Diemen's Land' (now Tasmania). They began their sighting and charting of the coast, but a renewal of fierce winds drove the ships to shelter in a bay, which Tasman named Stoorm Bay (now Adventure Bay, renamed in 1774, on the east coast of South Bruny Island).

Crewmen rowed ashore on 2 and 3 December and gathered wild celery, which would aid in the constant fight against scurvy. They reported that they heard voices and the sound of a trumpet or gong, but could see nobody. They noted 7-m (23-ft) high 'steps' cut into trees, giving rise to thoughts of gigantic inhabitants, and the 'claw marks of a tiger' on the ground.

In another small bay the ship's carpenter swam ashore and set up a Dutch flag to take possession of Van Diemen's Land. Tasman later wrote, on a map of his voyage, his high opinion of this land (quoted at the beginning), and noted that it was 'no longer incognita as this Map demonstrates, but the Southern Continent discovered. It lies Precisely in the richest Climates of the World.' Tasman resolved with his Council of officers to continue eastwards. Perhaps they were beset by unfavourable weather, but for some reason he did not follow the coast of Tasmania (renamed after him in 1855). If he had done so, he might have found it was an island and also then sailed north to establish the Dutch on Australia's east coast.

Sailing eastwards he made another landfall on 16 December, sighting 'a large high land with mountain tops covered in dark clouds'. He called it Staaten Landt as he thought he might have reached the western edge of the land discovered and so-named in the Southern Atlantic Ocean in 1616 by his fellow countrymen Willem Schouten and Isaac Le Maire. Only a matter of months afterwards it was proved that Tasman's discovery was not connected with that Staaten Landt (South America), and the name New Zealand (Nieuw

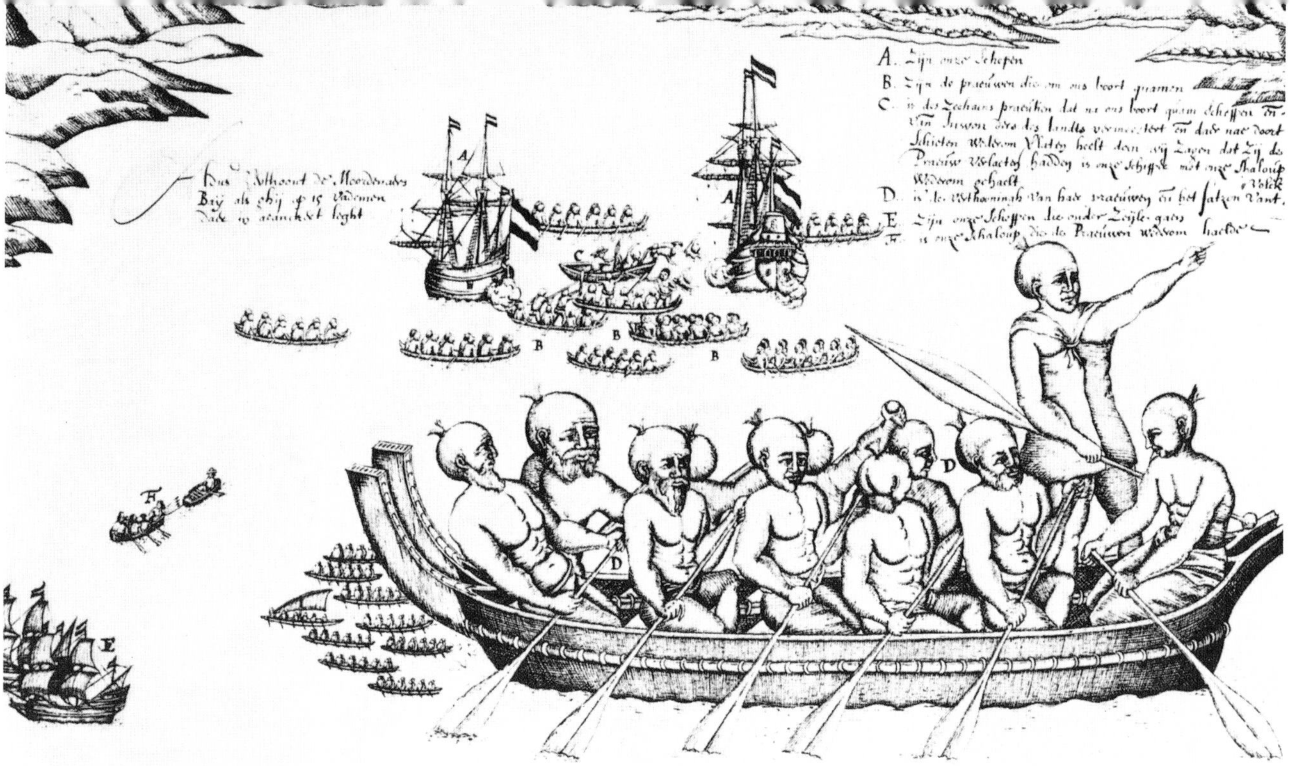

Zeeland) was adopted. His landfall was near today's town of Hokitika, on South Island.

Encounters with the Maori

On 18 December the ships were seeking a safe harbour from which to go ashore to find drinking water and edible wild vegetables. Lights were seen on land and eventually seven canoes surrounded the ships, crewed by men 'with black hair tied right to the top of the heads … naked from shoulder to waist'.

The Maori appeared friendly, but a ship's boat was sent from the *Heemskerck* to the *Zeehaen* to warn the officers aboard to be on their guard. This was suddenly rushed and rammed by a Maori canoe, killing three sailors and mortally wounding a fourth. The Dutch ships plucked the survivors from the sea and set sail, pursued by 22 canoes. Tasman named the place Murderer's Bay.

Tasman and his geographer Frans Visscher mapped the west coast of New Zealand as they sailed northwards (they missed Cook Strait and did not realize there were two islands). Tasman then continued northeast, reaching both Tonga and the Fiji islands. Turning west to make for home he sighted the entrance to the Torres Strait between Australia and New Guinea (navigated by the Spanish captain Luiz Vaez de Torres in 1606), but did not enter, opting for a more certain route. He coasted safely around the northern shore of Papua New Guinea and threaded his way through the Indonesian islands, providing a balmy respite for his crews after their hardships in the southern oceans, before returning to Jakarta, arriving in June 1643.

A further southern expedition by Tasman was planned in 1644, but war with the Portuguese intervened and he was restricted to a survey of the coast of northern Australia and southern New Guinea. As his voyages had returned nothing for the stockholders of the Dutch East India Company, his efforts were not regarded highly, and Dutch interest in the area waned.

Below *Tongan canoes welcoming Tasman's ships. Tasman noted in his journal that the bodies of the Tongan warriors were 'painted black' below the waist, referring to the Tongan custom of tattooing.*

32 Maria Sibylla Merian

1699–1701

And no one would so easily undertake such a hard and costly journey for such things. And the heat in this country is staggering, so that one can do no work at all without great difficulty, and I myself nearly paid for that with my death, which is why I could not stay there longer.

FROM A LETTER TO MR JOHAN GEORG VOLKAMMER OF NÜRNBERG, 1708

Right *In this detail from one of Merian's paintings the butterfly* Morpho menelaus *is rendered using a fine brush and bright colours.*

Maria Sibylla Merian is an overlooked figure. In an age when women virtually never did such things, she became a leading scientist and a great painter of flowers and insects. The high point of her astounding life was undoubtedly the two years she spent travelling in the remote rainforests of the Dutch colony of Surinam, in South America.

Born and brought up in Germany, Maria's father was a well-known Swiss publisher, who died when she was three. Her mother, who was Dutch, remarried a year later and Maria's stepfather, the Flemish flower painter Jacob Marell, became a major influence in her life. By the time she was 40 she was well established as an entomological illustrator and had published two illustrated books on insects and flowers. At this point, she divorced her husband and, with her mother and her two daughters, joined a Dutch sect known as the Labadists, named after Jean de Labadie, a renegade French priest and professor of theology. With them she was able to continue her work on insects and other creatures, such as frogs, which she dissected and drew meticulously.

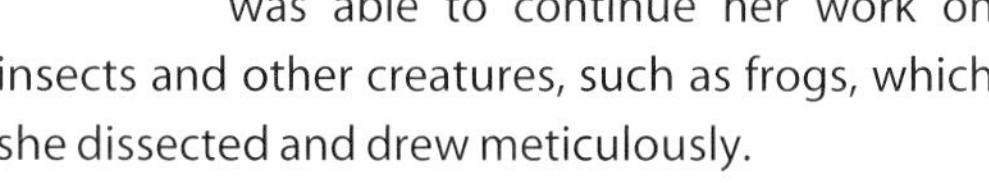

A modern portrait of Maria Sibylla Merian in later life, surrounded by natural history specimens, based on an early 18th century engraving.

Into the rainforest

In 1699, at the age of 52, Merian set off with her daughter Dorothea Maria on a long and dangerous journey to Surinam, a Dutch colony. Staying first in Paramaribo, they then based themselves on the many sugar plantations up the Surinam River, including the Labadist community at 'Providentia'. In this way the two women explored the interior and survived many perils. The rainforest was almost impenetrable and she wrote that her slaves were forced to hack their way through with axes.

It was unheard of for women to make such journeys without a male companion and they were dangerous times in Surinam. The French were threatening to invade from Cayenne and the Amerindians were constantly on the verge of revolting against their peace treaties. What made her travels even more remarkable, however, was not simply her exceptional fortitude but also the nature of her research. She was the first naturalist to go to Surinam and the first scientist to relate her studies of plants and insects to the cultural traditions of the people among whom she collected: the Amerindians and the slaves who had been brought there from West Africa. From them she gathered ethnographic nuggets of information about which plants, fruit, insects and animals could be eaten, and how they were prepared.

She sometimes tried out the taste of unknown plants and fruit herself, and one of her constant campaigns was to try to get the planters to recognize their medicinal use and to grow some of the indigenous crops rather than just the sugar with which they were obsessed. For this she was attacked, and some of her pictures were regarded as flights of female fancy. Her remarkable painting of a bird-eating spider was ridiculed until an English naturalist made the same observation nearly 100 years later.

Merian noted for the first time how each butterfly and insect depended on a particular plant. She collected assiduously, breeding insects in little boxes, recording their life cycles and revealing the mystery of metamorphosis: how eggs become larvae and then pupae and these in turn become adult insects.

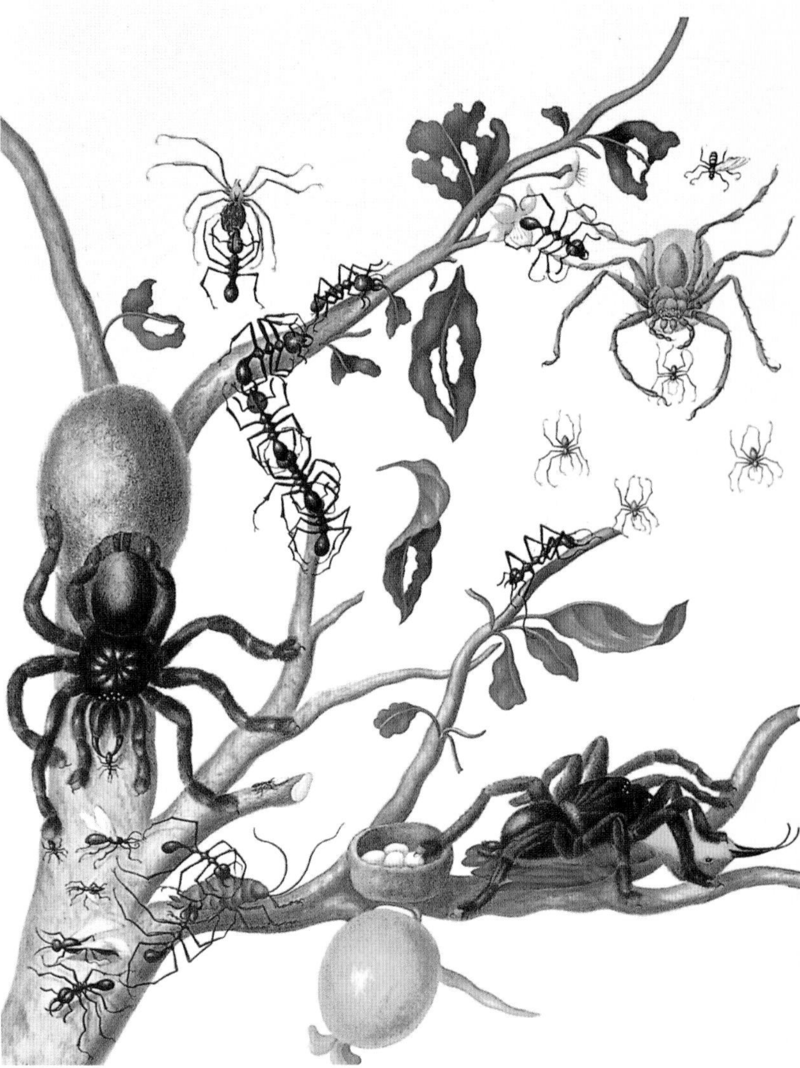

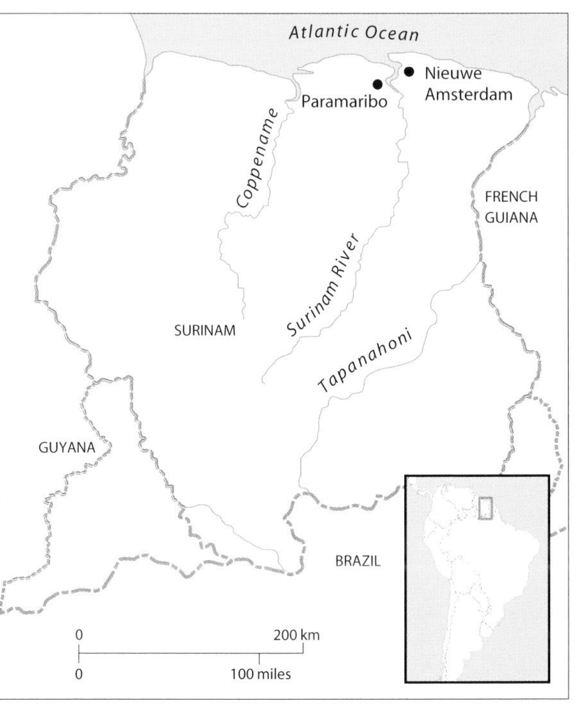

Unlike other scientists and artists of her time, she ordered her specimens in each picture according to their natural behaviour rather than by conventional classification. Thus she might have lizards, frogs and snakes side by side with butterflies on a flowering plant of which all made some use. This was revolutionary stuff and caused a stir in the scientific community. But it is what makes her pictures so marvellous. Her inspired eye recorded everything she saw, so that her illustrated books have been described as the most beautiful work ever painted in America.

Above *In her paintings Merian grouped together plants and insects that would be found together in nature. Here, various spiders include, at bottom right, the bird-eating spider* Avicularia avicularia, *with a hummingbird.*

Left *Merian made intrepid journeys through Surinam, a Dutch colony.*

CHARLES ALLEN

Ippolito Desideri

1715–21

For three whole months the traveller finds no village nor any living creature; he must therefore take with him all provisions.... Your bed at night is the earth, off which you have to scrape the snow, and your roof is the sky.

IPPOLITO DESIDERI, ON HIS JOURNEY FROM LADAKH TO LHASA

Above *A 17th-century illustration of Tibetan Buddhism by Athanasius Kircher.*

Below *Map of the route taken by Desideri and Freyre.*

There can surely be no greater tragedy for an explorer than to have journeyed to an unknown land, spent years studying its culture, written the first comprehensive account and then to be forgotten. Such a fate befell Ippolito Desideri. Born in Pistoia in Italy in 1684, he became a Jesuit missionary and, at 27, sailed to India. Inspired by the Portuguese missionaries who had crossed into Western Tibet a century earlier in search of Christians, he determined to do the same. He found a wealthy sponsor but was required to take with him a brother-Jesuit, Emanoel Freyre, 20 years his senior.

In autumn1714 these two set off in the wrong direction: for Srinagar in Kashmir rather than Srinagar in the Garhwal Himalaya. They wintered in Kashmir and then pressed on into what was then known as First and Little Tibet, Baltistan and Ladakh, overcoming snowblindness as they crossed the treacherous Zoji Pass. They found Ladakh 'altogether horrible', but its Buddhist inhabitants were 'kindly, cheerful and courteous', so much so that Desideri was all for staying on. Freyre, however, was desperate to return to India – but not over the fearsome Zoji Pass. They compromised by agreeing to return through Grand Tibet, Tibet proper.

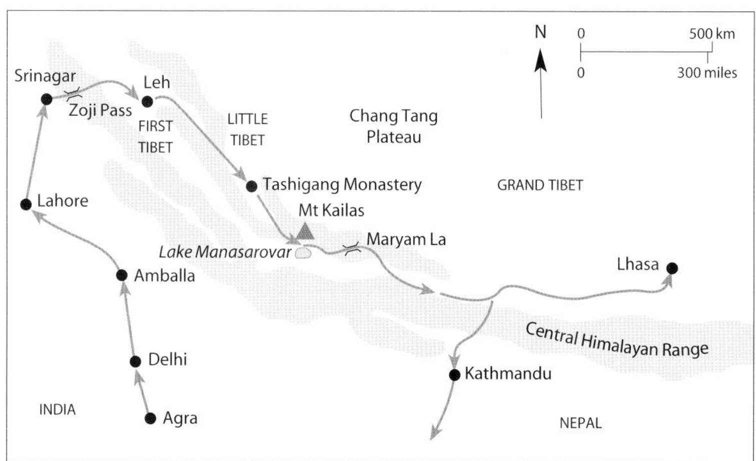

Three weeks of travelling brought them to the monastery of Tashigang, beyond which lay a 'vast, sterile and terrible desert': the Chang Tang plateau. Warned that they faced certain death without an escort, they resorted to prayer – answered in the form a Tartar princess about to set out for Lhasa with a yak caravan and a cavalry escort. She allowed the Jesuits to accompany her as 'well-meaning pilgrims'.

The cavalcade set out in October 1715. Governed by the pace of their yaks, which grazed as they went, they made slow progress across the great plateau, their linen tent no match for the Tibetan winter: 'The night was rather a cessation of fatigue than real repose,' noted Freyre, 'the intense cold and the intolerable annoyance of the insects harboured in our clothes prevented any real sleep.' When the opportunity arose they stripped to delouse themselves: 'We were saved the trouble of picking the lice off one by one, for we would simply sweep them off.'

Six weeks into their journey they entered a region held sacred, 'on account of a certain Urghien [Padmasambhava] who is the founder of the religion professed in Tibet', passing a high snow mountain 'hidden among the clouds' [Kailas] and camping beside a great lake 'held in high veneration by the superstitious people [Manasarovar]'.

In Lhasa

Ten months after leaving Kashmir they reached Lhasa, dominated by the great rock upon the summit of which stood the Potala: 'a sumptuous palace five storeys high'. The Seventh Dalai Lama was at this time a prisoner of the Mongols but the visitors were welcomed and questioned about their beliefs. To Desideri's regret, their benefactress princess then left them to enter a nunnery.

Freyre was desperate to reach warmer climes and left for India. Desideri, however, was determined to stay on, to 'explain our faith and to refute their false religion', and was given permission to study at the monastery of Sera, outside Lhasa. 'From that day until I left Tibet', recorded Desideri, 'I made it a rule to study from early morning to sundown, and for nearly six years took nothing during the day save tea to drink.'

Finally ordered to leave by Rome, Desideri left Tibet in 1721. After five years' mission work in India he returned to Rome to write a four-volume account of Tibet, but died suddenly before it could be published, aged 48. His great work was lost – until rediscovered in a private library in Pistoia in 1875. Freyre's lesser work was also lost, and only resurfaced in 1924. By this double misfortune these pioneers became a footnote in the annals of discovery.

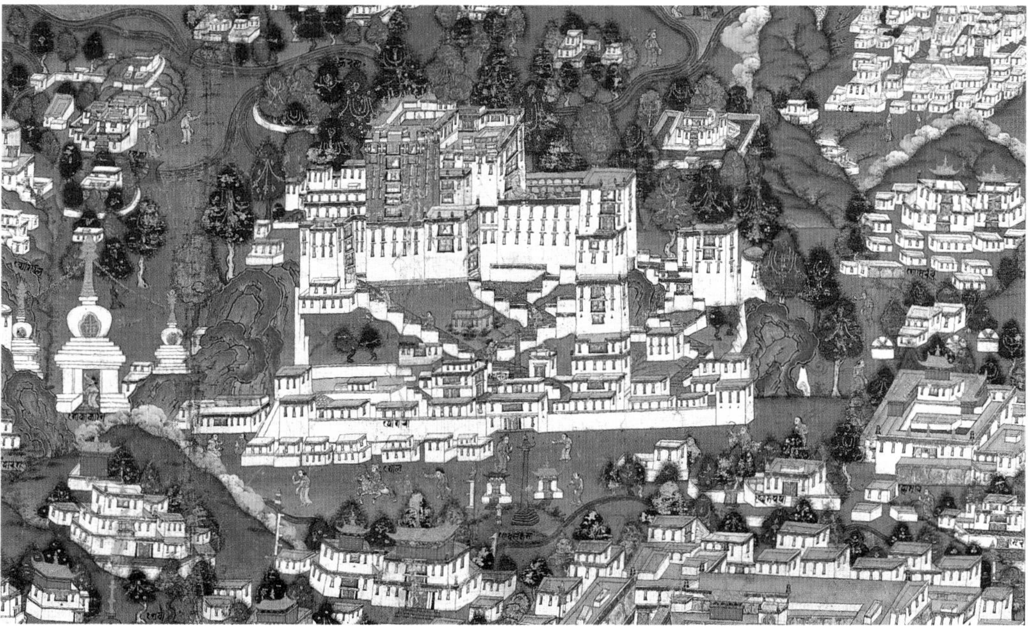

Above *Desideri began his studies of Tibetan Buddhism at Sera monastery soon after arriving in Lhasa. This photograph of the monastery was taken by C. G. Rawling in 1904 at the time of the British invasion of Tibet led by Colonel Younghusband* *(see p. 224).*

Left *Painting of the Potala Palace, Lhasa: a detail from a 19th-century Tibetan thangka.*

WILLIAM BARR

34

Vitus Bering

1733–43

July 17, 1741. At 12.30 we sighted high snow-covered mountains and among them a high volcano N by W [Mt St Elias] ... 8 o'clock.... A point of the sighted shore which we named St Aphinogena ... the mountains on it are lower than those we had sighted before.

BERING'S FIRST SIGHTING OF NORTH AMERICA, LOG OF *ST PETER*, 1741

Born in Denmark in 1681, Vitus Johansen Bering was recruited into the Russian navy in 1704. Twenty years later he commanded the First Kamchatka Expedition, the objective of which was to determine whether Siberia was connected to North America – which was unknown at the time. Sailing in July 1728, Bering ran north through the Strait now named after him as far as 67° 18'N in the Chukchi Sea before turning back. Bering had in fact sailed between the two continents, but at no point did he catch sight of the American coast and hence could not state positively that a strait separated them.

A portrait bust of Bering modelled on his skull, which was discovered when six skeletons were exhumed on Bering Island in 1991. Bering's body was the only one found in a coffin.

The Second Kamchatka Expedition

Bering's next project, the Great Northern, or Second Kamchatka Expedition was even more ambitious. It would consist of seven detachments, five of which would explore sections of the Arctic coast of Russia, while the sixth would explore the Kurile Islands. The seventh, under Bering's personal command, was to head east, and locate and map the coast of America. The expedition included numerous scientists and their support staff, plus hundreds of men involved in transporting supplies and equipment across the continent to the port of departure.

Bering left St Petersburg in 1733, but spent years supervising the overland transport of materials. It was not until 29 May 1741 that he sailed from Petropavlovsk with two ships, *St Peter*, under his own command, and *St Paul* under Captain-Commander Aleksey Il'yich Chirikov. The 77 men on board *St Peter* included the young German naturalist and surgeon, Georg Wilhelm Steller.

Separated in a gale on 20 June, the two ships never made contact again. On the afternoon of 17 July 1741, Bering and his men sighted and named Mt St Elias in Alaska. Sailing north and northwest, Bering landed on Kayak Island to fill his water casks. Steller went ashore and in a 6-hour foray (which he felt was much too short) made an impressive collection of plants and found a native food-cache.

St Peter then coasted northwest, west and southwest around the Gulf of Alaska, but by August scurvy had broken out: 21 men, including Bering, were seriously afflicted. On 30 August they reached the Shumagin Islands, where the water casks were again filled; on that date, the first death from scurvy occurred. Steller collected antiscorbutic plants ashore to try to counter the disease, initially with some success, but it reappeared and deaths became almost daily events.

On 5 November land was sighted, and was assumed to be Kamchatka but was in fact Bering Island, one of the Commander Islands. By then 21 men (28 per cent of the crew) had died. Next day *St Peter* was beached, having been damaged on a reef. The sick men were moved ashore and camp was set up. Again Steller collected antiscorbutic plants. Sea otters, foxes, sea lions and sea cows

Georg Steller, the naturalist and surgeon on the voyage, measuring a sea cow on Bering Island, in a drawing by L. Stejneger. This animal, named Steller's sea cow, was hunted to extinction within three decades. Steller was one of the first to treat scurvy successfully.

were killed and helped to save many lives, although deaths continued. The group settled down for the winter in semi-subterranean huts. Bering died on 8 December and was buried in a coffin, the only person to receive such treatment.

After a tough winter, constantly struggling for food and firewood, the survivors dismantled their damaged ship and built a smaller vessel from its timbers. Under the command of Lieutenant Sven Waxell they put to sea on 13 August and reached Petropavlovsk and safety on 26 August 1742.

In August 1991 a group of Danish and Russian archaeologists exhumed six skeletons at the site of the camp on Bering Island, including a tall man in the only coffin found – Vitus Bering. After thorough examination in Moscow, all six skeletons were reburied, after an appropriate ceremony, on Bering Island.

Despite the tragedy of loss of life, one important result of the expedition was the first fairly detailed map showing the trend of the coast of the Gulf of Alaska and of the Aleutian chain.

Below left *A drawing from Sven Waxell's journal of an Aleut in a canoe (baidarka). It was Waxell who led the survivors of the expedition back to Petropavlovsk.*

Below right *Map to show Bering's sea voyage, to his death on Bering Island. This was in fact only one part of the huge expedition which began with the transport of materials from St Petersburg.*

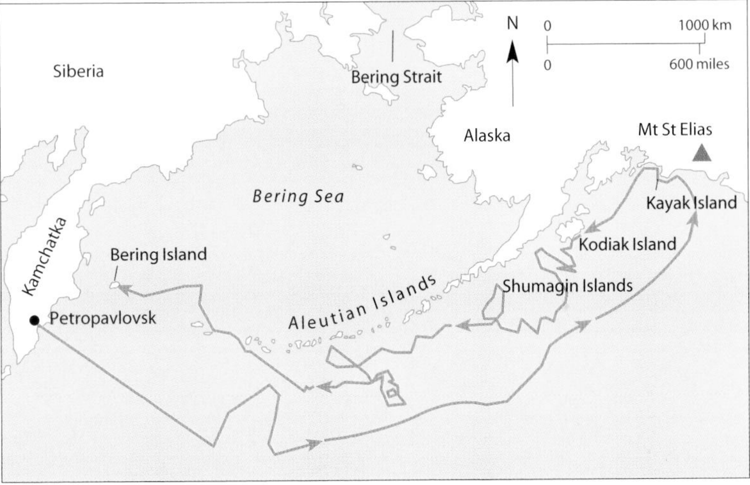

JOHN URE

James Bruce

1768–73

Africa is indeed coming into fashion. There is just returned a Mr Bruce, who had lived three years in the Court of Abyssinia, and breakfasted every morning with the maids of honour on live oxen.

HORACE WALPOLE, 1774

James Bruce was an explorer whose remarkable achievements were dictated to an extraordinary degree by his physique, personality and background. Born in 1730 in Scotland to a family who upheld the Stuart claim to the British throne, he was educated in England as a supporter of the ruling Hanoverian monarchy. At 1.93 m (6 ft 4 in) tall he was a giant by the standards of the time; he was also auburn haired, short-tempered and acutely conscious of his aristocratic (or royal – he claimed) ancestry.

After schooling at Harrow and a brief return to Scotland and Edinburgh University at the age of 16, Bruce rejected a career in law and came south again, where he married the daughter of an affluent London wine merchant. She died a few months later, leaving Bruce at the age of 24 footloose and uncertain of his aim in life. Predictably, he took off on the Grand Tour, developed an interest in languages – notably Arabic – and picked quarrels and fought duels as his irascible nature directed. He eventually decided his destiny was in Africa.

Pompeo Battoni's portrait of James Bruce of Kinnaird (1762), painted while Bruce was visiting Rome during his Grand Tour.

Seeking the source of the Nile

Bruce's first and only serious job was as Consul in Algiers, which he viewed as a jumping off point for the exploration of the African interior. However, the Bey of Algiers – a despot and patron of pirates – made life virtually intolerable for him, and after two years he was glad to be relieved of his post and resolved to seek out the long-elusive source of the Nile – the objective that had intrigued Herodotus (p. 33) and other explorers ever since.

Bruce was convinced that the source lay in Abyssinia (Ethiopia), then an unknown vacuum on the map. Having survived various North African adventures – bandits and shipwrecks – he proceeded to Cairo to prepare for his great expedition, hiring among others an Italian painter, Luigi Balugani, to record his discoveries. Eventually he crossed and re-crossed the Red Sea, making his entry into Ethiopia via the port of Massawa. Having previously equipped himself with letters and laissez-passers to enable him to pass through French territory on his earlier travels, he now set off for the Ethiopian capital. He also used his great facility for learning languages to acquire a working knowledge of all those spoken in the regions through which he passed.

Into the unknown interior

His route inland from Massawa was venturing into a perilous land from which no visitors (with the exception of one French doctor) had ever returned since two Portuguese Jesuit priests were expelled in 1632. Everything he observed, and subsequently reported, was therefore of enormous potential interest. But from the beginning Bruce's observations – like Marco Polo's (p. 75) – omitted much that he might have been expected to see and note, such as the Tabotats (representations of the Ark of the Covenant) in Ethiopian churches, and the celebrated antiquities of Axum. On the other hand, he recorded many facts and activities which positively strained credibility, such as the local practice of cutting steaks out of the flanks of living animals.

Apart from his credentials and languages, Bruce had other assets to facilitate his progress through this unknown and hostile terrain. He brought rich gifts; he was a self-taught medical practitioner and cured many ailments among his hosts; he was heavily armed and not afraid of

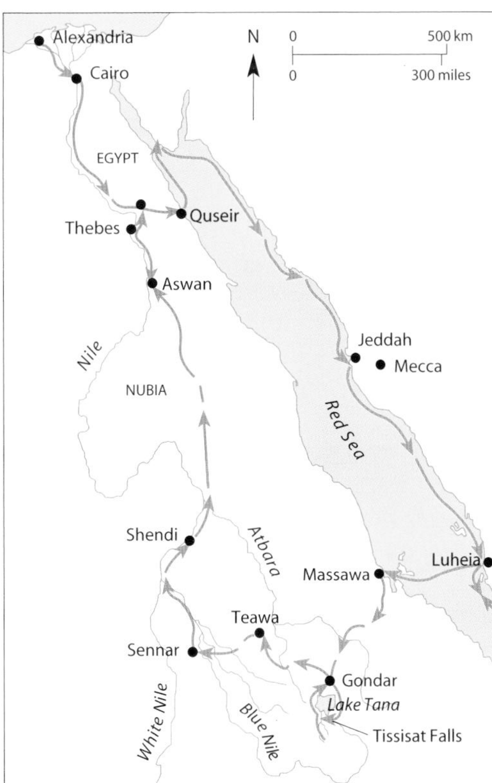

Above *A cartoon by Isaac Cruikshank (1791) ridiculing Bruce's claim that he had joined in the Ethiopians' practice of cutting steaks from living animals.*

Bruce's route from Alexandria to the source of the Blue Nile took him via the Red Sea and through what is now Ethiopia. His return from Gondar through Sudan and Nubia and back down the Nile was perhaps even more difficult.

'Bruce at the Source of the Nile', by Balugani, or Bruce, who was suspected of having claimed some of the former's works as his own after Balugani died on their expedition.

using his fire-power; and he had navigational equipment. But above all he had a stature, presence and personality that stamped him as a man of authority and a natural companion of kings and princes. He also clearly had a sexual magnetism which ensured that Ethiopian maidens – including a royal princess – fell under his spell. He needed all these assets when his quarrelsome nature involved him in a brawl in the palace – a crime which could have cost him his life.

When he reached the capital Gondar in 1770 he found the country in a state of civil war. He allied himself with the king and his ruthless general – Ras (Prince) Michael. Never one to stand back from a fray, he became heavily involved in local intrigues, campaigns and even battles.

It was with difficulty that Bruce detached himself from Gondar to seek out his main objective – the fountains which constituted the source of the Blue Nile and the spectacular Tissisat Falls. He was able to chart these features for the first time accurately on a map. He discounted the previous discovery by the Portuguese Jesuits, just as he played down the significance of the White Nile when, on his return journey, he witnessed its confluence with the Blue Nile – his 'true' Nile.

Returning from Ethiopia was possibly more difficult than reaching the source of the Blue Nile. Balugani, his artist companion, had died in Gondar, and is hardly mentioned by Bruce in his book, possibly because it is generally accepted that Bruce passed off many of Balugani's paintings as his own. He left Ethiopia through the Sudan and the Nubian desert, where he nearly died of thirst, and eventually reached Aswan and Cairo. He stopped off in Italy and France on his return, being received by the Pope and Louis XV, and being fêted as a hero.

Returning home: a mixed reception

When he eventually reached London in 1774, after 12 years away, his reception was less warm. The hauteur which had won him respect in Ethiopia raised hackles and resentment in London: his exploits were doubted and derided. King George III was unenthusiastic about his pictures, and William Pitt the Younger (much later) declined to respond to his request for a baronetcy. Fanny Burney was unimpressed, and Dr Johnson declared that although he had originally been inclined to believe his stories, 'he had afterwards altered his opinion'. Bruce retreated to his seat in Scotland and did not complete his account of his journeys for a further 17 years. When he did – in five handsome volumes – he was lampooned by the cartoonist Cruikshank and others.

Only after his death in 1794 (caused by falling down stairs, grossly over-weight and aged 64) did later travellers and research confirm that Bruce's accounts were fundamentally accurate and his journey among the most courageous and remarkable ever accomplished. It was another great Africa explorer – Dr Livingstone – who eventually set the record straight when he wrote of Bruce that he was 'a greater traveller than any of us'.

Watercolour of a hyena by Balugani or Bruce.

VANESSA COLLINGRIDGE

James Cook

1768–71

Ambition leads me not only farther than any other man has been before me, but as far as I think it is possible for a man to go.

JAMES COOK, 30 JANUARY 1774

In three epic journeys, equivalent in distance to sailing to the moon, James Cook discovered more of the earth's surface than any other person in history. He also helped to conquer the fatal disease of scurvy and pioneered the art of scientific navigation with maps so accurate that some were still used right up to the 20th century. Furthermore, he exploded the greatest myth of his day: the existence of a 'Great Southern Continent' – a *provincea aurea* or 'golden land' – that would make the country that discovered it the richest nation on earth.

In 1768 the British Admiralty and the Royal Society mounted a scientific voyage of discovery in order to observe the Transit of Venus. This was a rare astronomical event, when the disc of Venus would pass over the face of the sun. From the length of time it took to do this, astronomers could calculate the distance between the earth and the sun, which in turn would help to gauge the size and scale of the universe. This was no mere academic exercise: as the Royal Society wrote to King George III when petitioning him for funds, it would also 'contribute greatly to the improvement of Astronomy, on which Navigation so depends'.

To achieve this, however, they needed somewhere in the Southern Ocean from which to view the event – and they also needed a captain who could be relied upon to do the job properly. The first problem was resolved with news of the discovery of Tahiti – perfectly positioned in the Southern Ocean for the Transit observations.

Equally fortuitous was the Admiralty's choice of captain: James Cook, the son of a Scottish farm labourer. Born in Marton, Cleveland, in 1728, Cook trained with the merchant navy at Whitby before transferring to the Royal Navy in 1755, where he won much praise for his 'genius and capacity'. When given command of Her Majesty's Bark, *Endeavour*, in 1768, he was not even a lieutenant, let alone a captain, but he was renowned within the Admiralty for his navigational skills and for his work in Canada, meticulously charting Britain's newly won lands. He was also an able astronomer, determining longitude from the stars and even publishing a brief paper on a solar eclipse in the *Transactions* of the Royal Society. James Cook was therefore the perfect balance of seaman and scientist to lead the expedition.

Portrait of Cook by John Webber (1776). Cook was the right man at the right time: a true son of the 18th-century Enlightenment, he died just as the Age of Romance was beginning, ensuring he became a heroic icon for the 19th century.

These cramped conditions were home for a hundred sailors for almost three years. This reconstruction of HM Bark Endeavour *was built using mainly 18th-century methods but with some modern materials for added safety.*

The Voyage of HM Bark *Endeavour*

On 26 August 1768, Cook sailed a specially adapted former coalship, *Endeavour*, out of Plymouth on what was to become one of the greatest voyages in history. On board were some '94 persons including Officers Seamen Gentlemen and their servants', most famously the hugely wealthy and influential Joseph Banks. Banks – later Sir Joseph, baronet, and honorary director of Kew Gardens and President of the Royal Society – was a larger-than-life aristocrat with a very genuine passion for natural history. His knowledge and expertise would transform natural history and, upon his return, his collections increased by a quarter the number of known plants in the world.

Cook's orders were to sail to Tahiti for the Transit observations on 3 June 1769, and he wasted little time tracking south from the English Channel via Madeira to Rio de Janeiro and then down the coast of Latin America to Cape Horn. Two-and-a-half long months were to follow as the *Endeavour* traversed the vast open waters of the Pacific, from the icy storms of 60° South – two-thirds of the way to the Pole – to the tropical sun of Tahiti, without ever touching land.

At last, on 10 April 1769, Cook saw the volcanic peaks of land and two days later anchored in the broad sweep of Tahiti's Matavai or 'Royal Bay', welcomed by the locals who had paddled out to greet them in their canoes. With just seven weeks until the Transit, he immediately set up camp at 'Fort Venus', while Banks began his botanizing and ethnographic studies. The day of 3 June dawned with a 'favourable' sky – but the Transit observations proved disappointing: a blurred outline of Venus called the *penumbra* made it impossible to determine the exact moment when the two planets coincided. With all their results showing different times, Cook and his fellow observers agreed a compromise and said no more about it. He used his remaining time on the

island to conduct a survey of stunning exactitude – a work of science and art that was used by navigators for the next 100 years.

'To the Southwards'

As Cook sailed from Tahiti after his three-month stay, he opened a second, sealed packet of secret orders given to him by the Admiralty: he was to sail to 40° South in search of the Great Southern Continent – the Holy Grail of exploration.

Leaving behind the Society Islands, Cook set his course due south but any 'land' that came into view was soon revealed as cloud. As they pushed further south, the weather grew colder until the men's hands were freezing to the rigging – and still no continent appeared, nor any indication that there was land nearby. On reaching their target of 40° South without sighting land, Cook once again stood northward and then headed westwards towards the snatches of coastline charted by Dutch explorer, Abel Tasman (p. 131) over a hundred years before.

At 2 p.m. on 6 October 1769, land was finally sighted – so was this the sought-after 'Great Southern Continent'? Banks was convinced; Cook was sceptical but, following his orders, made a thorough survey of what turned out to be the two large islands of New Zealand, which he claimed

Fort Venus, Tahiti: Cook set up an observatory using some of the best equipment of his day – the astronomical quadrant and clock and the reflecting telescope.

The voyage of the Endeavour*: this and his two later voyages made Cook the most famous navigator of his day.*

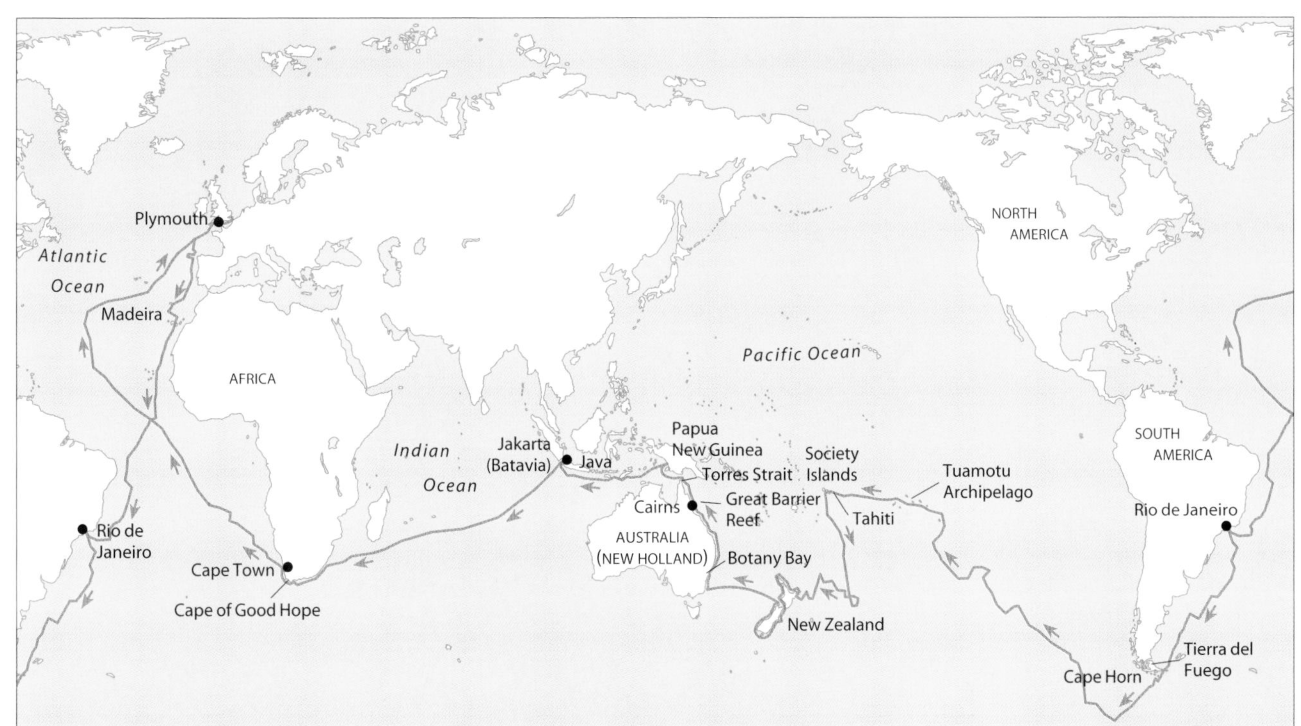

Above *Maori war canoe 'bidding defiance to the ship', by Sidney Parkinson. After a rocky start to relations with the Maori, Cook developed a close and mutually respectful relationship with the New Zealand inhabitants.*

for King George III. By the time he departed its shores on 31 March 1770, James Cook had established a life-long friendship with the local Maori, destroyed the hopes of even the most fervent 'Continentalists' and completed one of the most remarkable works in the history of cartography: some 3,860 km (2,400 miles) of coastline surveyed and charted in under three months of sailing, with landings at just eight sites.

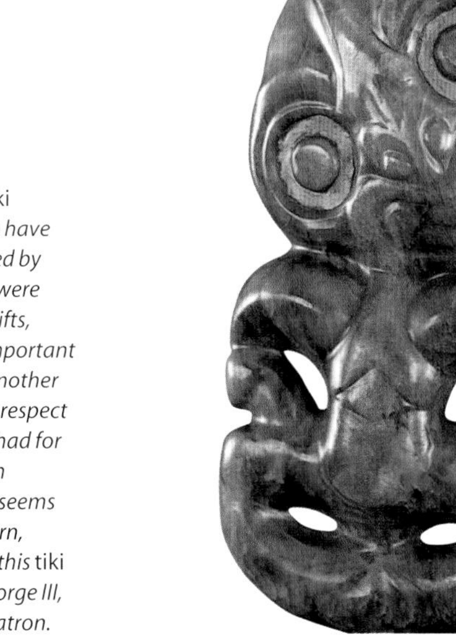

A Maori tiki *thought to have been owned by Cook. Tiki were valuable gifts, given to important people – another sign of the respect the Maori had for this foreign captain. It seems Cook, in turn, presented this* tiki *to King George III, his royal patron.*

His Admiralty orders fulfilled, his remaining task was to get home by the safest route possible. Rejecting a direct route via Cape Horn, he chose instead to sail via the uncharted east coast of 'New Holland' (Australia) to Batavia (Jakarta) where he could get the *Endeavour* repaired before the long journey back to Britain. Three weeks after leaving New Zealand, land was again sighted on 19 April 1770, and nine days later the ship dropped anchor in a bay, watched suspiciously by the Gwiyagal Aborigines.

While Banks did his botanizing that gave the site its name, Botany Bay, Cook and his men made detailed surveys of the coastline and interior before pushing northwards up towards modern-day Cairns and 'Cape Tribulation' – for 'here began all our troubles'. Smashing into the deadly coral of the Great Barrier Reef, the *Endeavour* was stuck for almost 24 hours before she was finally re-floated, leaking badly. Limping up the coast with emergency repairs, they found refuge near modern Cooktown.

Cook's men spent seven weeks repairing the ship and befriending the Gogo-Yimidir Aborigines who told them the name of the strange jumping creature they had so often seen – 'Kanguru'. Cook left 'Endeavour River' on 4 August 1770 and began one of the most impressive feats of navigation in Pacific history: weaving his way through the deadly reef in a leaking ship and then proving the existence of the legendary Torres Strait on his way to Batavia (Jakarta).

A kangaroo painted for Joseph Banks by George Stubbs, who based it on the skin of an animal shot on Cook's first voyage by one of the officers. Cook's men were bemused by this animal 'about the size of a greyhound, slender, mouse-coloured, swift, with a long tail, jumping like a hare.'

A 'Compleat' voyage

Three months of repairs were followed by the devastation of Cook's crew by malaria and dysentery, but the *Endeavour* struggled home via the Cape of Good Hope to a rapturous welcome, though with Banks cast as the hero of the voyage. However, it was Cook's discoveries in New Zealand and what he named 'New South Wales' that transformed the British Empire, opening up a new world for colonization.

Two further ground-breaking voyages followed, which both finally destroyed the myth of the Great Southern Continent and also challenged the idea of an ice-free Northwest Passage. When he was tragically killed in Hawai'i on 14 February 1779, Cook was the most famous navigator of his day – and he has remained a legend ever since.

Left Overseeing the *Endeavour's* watering at the Bay of Good Success in Tierra del Fuego, *1769, by Alexander Buchan. The native peoples of Tierra del Fuego were one of the first of many indigenous peoples Cook and his men would encounter on this voyage. His orders were to treat them with respect and humanity.*

VANESSA COLLINGRIDGE

Jean-François de Lapérouse

1785–88

May they return to our shores, even though they die of joy in embracing this free land!
APPEAL BY FRANCE'S HISTORICAL SOCIETY TO THE NATIONAL ASSEMBLY

Jean-François de Galaup de Lapérouse was a French minor noble, born in 1741 in Albi in Languedoc, and a world-class sailor and navigator. Joining the navy at 15, his family had added the suffix 'La Pérouse' to his name to emphasize his social class and ensure prestigious promotions. It worked: he soon played an active part in battles against the English during the Seven Years War, and following the declaration of peace in 1763, was commissioned as an Ensign (Sub-Lieutenant), joining vessels that plied the French and Mediterranean coasts.

Etching by Thomas Woolnoth after a miniature of Lapérouse in the possession of his niece. Lapérouse sent sufficient material home for a narrative of his voyage, which was published in 1791.

Inspired by the achievements of James Cook and Louis Antoine de Bougainville's round-the-world voyage (see box, p. 150), Lapérouse sailed to the West Indies in 1771; the following years saw trips to India, the Seychelles and Madagascar from his base in Île de France (Mauritius). Here, he fell in love with Louise-Eléonore Broudou, but his family rejected the match as unsuitable. However, when he left Mauritius in December 1776, Eléonore followed him back to France.

More trips to the West Indies and North America ensued during the American Revolutionary War for independence from Britain, but with the peace of 1783 – and now a post-captain – he resolved to marry Eléonore, who was still patiently waiting for him in Paris. At last his bride won the approval of both his family and the Navy and buoyed up by this personal success and a yearning to follow Cook's achievements, Lapérouse joined a government team, supported by the king, Louis XVI, planning a great sweep of the Pacific. Two ships and crews were secretly selected for the scientific expedition, which would last three or four years, focusing on botany, ethnography, geology and astronomy, with a cartographer charting their progress – and Lapérouse as leader.

Lapérouse's voyage to the Pacific

The ships sailed from Brest on 1 August 1785, Lapérouse captaining the renamed *Boussole* and

his friend Paul-Antoine-Marie Fleuriot de Langle in charge of the *Astrolabe*. Rounding Cape Horn to Concepción in Chile, they visited the giant statues of Easter Island before sailing via Hawai'i to Alaska. Despite arriving in the summer of 1786, the weather was cold and foggy with treacherous swells which made exploring dangerous; 21 men drowned during a survey of Port de Français (now Lituya Bay). After a desultory search for a Northwest Passage he did not believe existed this far south, Lapérouse headed to Monterey in California where he spent a sociable fortnight before sailing in search of rumoured lands to the southwest. None were discovered and they turned north, discovering the uninhabited Necker Island and almost foundering on a sudden coral reef (French Frigate Shoals) whose central rock is now called La Pérouse Pinnacle.

To China

It was now 18 months since Lapérouse had left home and he was keen to send reports and packages back to France via one of the frequent ships sailing from Macao. Here, he organized the sale of large numbers of Alaskan sea otter skins and restocked the ships with supplies and replacement men for those lost in the Lituya Bay disaster. Just over a month later they set sail for the Philippines and then onwards through rough seas and shoals via Taiwan, and between Korea and Japan to the Sea of Tartary. The Tartary and Sakhalin coasts were a place of mystery to most Europeans, but they were now accurately charted by the French, with welcome landings for the naturalists but unwelcome fog for the navigators.

With the summer of 1787 now waning, Lapérouse sailed towards the Kurile Islands and

Lapérouse anchored in Cook's Bay on the west coast of Easter Island on 9 April 1786, where the French were well received, trading with the locals and exchanging gifts. De Langle took a party of men to examine the clusters of large statues they had seen from the ships; from an engraving by Duché de Vancy.

LOUIS ANTOINE DE BOUGAINVILLE

Bougainville (1729–1811) was one of the most dashing men in French and Pacific history – an intellectual, soldier and explorer. During the Seven Years War, he saw action in North America, in which his rival James Cook was also involved, but with France's defeat he switched from the army to the sea.

After an ill-fated attempt to establish a French colony in the Falkland Islands, he took up command of a great voyage of science and exploration. On 15 November 1766, Bougainville set sail from Nantes in *La Boudeuse* with orders first to hand the Falkland Islands back to Spain, before continuing on his voyage around the world. Handover achieved, he sailed north to Rio de Janeiro to meet up with his supply ship *L'Étoile*. Bougainville then passed through the Strait of Magellan and into the Pacific. The two ships weaved through the Tuamotus, before heading west to Tahiti, which Samuel Wallis had claimed for Britain the previous year. The French reports of Tahiti – and the Tahitian man, Ahu-toru, who returned with them to France – added weight to Jean-Jacques Rousseau's ideas of the 'Noble Savage'. From Tahiti and the Society Islands, Bougainville sailed on to Samoa and the New Hebrides (Vanuatu), being driven back from the east coast of New Holland (Australia) by the Great Barrier Reef, thus leaving its discovery to Cook (p. 143). Heading instead to southeastern New Guinea and the Louisiade Archipelago he at last discovered a new part of the Solomon Islands, where the largest of the islands still bears his name. Sailing north then westwards through the Dutch East Indies, Bougainville finally arrived at Île de France (Mauritius) before returning via Cape Town to St Malo, France, on 16 March the following year.

Bougainville received a hero's welcome. Despite lacking both naval training and experience, he was the only late 18th-century French explorer to survive a circumnavigation, whatever its paucity in actual discoveries and scientific data (though the expedition's botanist, Philibert Commerson, named hundreds of new species of plants). More significantly, his experiences renewed French interest in the Pacific and spurred successors like Lapérouse to go in search of further discoveries.

Tahitians presenting fruits to Bougainville, attended by his officers, in 1768. Bougainville managed to miss most of the Society Islands, which were discovered by Cook the following year.

back into the waters of the Pacific, finally anchoring near Petropavlovsk on the Kamchatka Peninsula. Here, after a two-year silence, the men at last received their mail from home. The letters included confirmation of Lapérouse's promotion to commodore and notification that the British had sent ships to Australia's Botany Bay. Lapérouse was ordered to investigate, so after enjoying the Russian hospitality they dispatched letters, journals and charts overland to France, and sailed south. By the time the documents arrived in France a year later, Lapérouse had already disappeared.

The South Pacific

In December 1787 the *Astrolabe* and *Boussole* arrived in the Samoan Islands to a friendly reception. However, a skirmish with 1,000 locals left 39 Samoans and 12 Frenchmen, including de Langle, dead. Rejecting revenge, Lapérouse sailed via Tonga to Botany Bay. He arrived on 24 January

The attack on French boats at Massacre Bay, Samoa. Having initially received a friendly welcome, on 11 December de Langle and a party of men went ashore and were involved in a skirmish in which de Langle was killed. Lapérouse was devastated by the death of his friend, but sailed away two days later without taking reprisals.

1788, and saw the British 'First Fleet' – ships carrying convicts from England to establish the first European colony in New South Wales – who had arrived on 19/20 January. Despite the surprise meeting, relations were warm between the crews of the two nations, with Lapérouse using his time to restock, make repairs and despatch more documents detailing his route and plans. On 10 March, the British watched the French ships sail from Frenchman Bay. They were never seen again.

Aftermath

Lapérouse had planned to visit Tonga, New Caledonia and the Santa Cruz Islands before passing through the Torres Strait en route to Mauritius, hoping to arrive in France by spring 1789. When the ships failed to return home, the government, navy and Eléonore grew increasingly worried. By 1791, the experienced navigator, d'Entrecasteaux was commissioned to lead an expedition to find Lapérouse.

Two ships sailed in September that year, circumnavigating Australia before heading to Tonga and New Caledonia in a fruitless search for their countrymen. D'Entrecasteaux little realized that a distant island in the Solomons that he sighted in spring 1793 was where Lapérouse's ships had been wrecked some five years before – and there may still have been survivors. It was not until 1826 that an Irish sea captain, Peter Dillon, learned that Vanikoro in the Santa Cruz group in the Solomon Islands was the probable final resting place of Lapérouse's two ships and some of the survivors. He visited Vanikoro in 1827 and found items that were later identified as belonging to the French expedition. In the following year the French captain, Dumont d'Urville, also found objects from a French ship and, like Dillon, was convinced they came from Lapérouse's expedition. In the 1960s two wrecks were located by a diver, and in 2005 the final confirmation came when another expedition discovered an 18th-century sextant from the *Boussole*.

Eléonore died childless in 1807, with no further news of her husband. Although his remarkable journey ended in tragedy, Lapérouse had contributed hugely to European knowledge of the Pacific and his journey well deserves its place amongst the greatest voyages of all time.

Lapérouse's ships travelled huge distances around the Pacific, making accurate charts of many areas, until their disappearance near Vanikoro in the Solomon Islands.

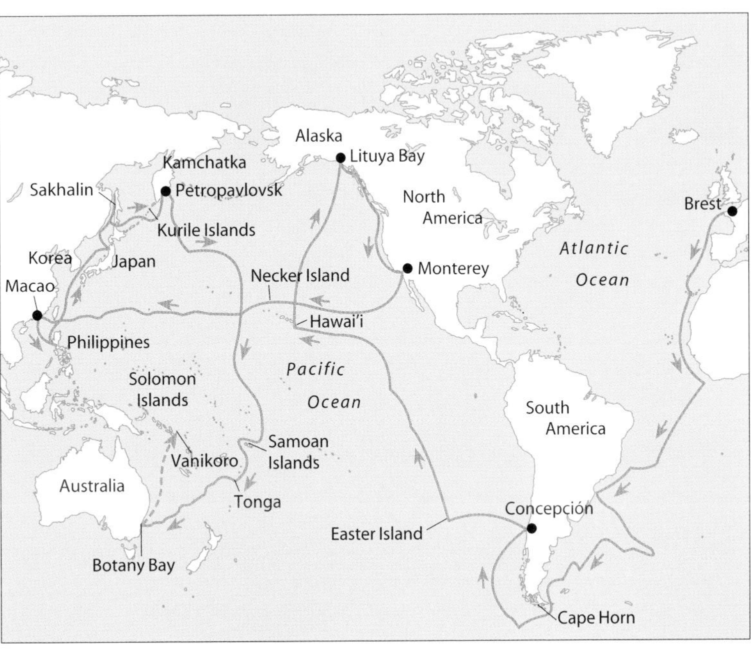

Alexander Mackenzie

1792–93

Here my voyages of discovery terminate. Their toils and their dangers, their solicitudes and sufferings, have not been exaggerated in my description. On the contrary, in many instances, language has failed me in the attempt to describe them. I received, however, the reward of my labours, for they were crowned with success.

ALEXANDER MACKENZIE, 1801

In the 18th century, apart from the narrow isthmus of Mexico, no one had linked up the two coasts of North America and crossed the entire continent. The impulse to cross America was not merely one of exploration. There was the possibility of great wealth to be made from fur, needed in Europe for the popular 'beaver' hats.

In 1793, 12 years before Lewis and Clark's expedition (p. 165) – often wrongly described as 'the first to cross America' – a Scotsman, Alexander Mackenzie, with nine companions in a 7.6-m (25-ft) birchbark canoe, became the first to cross North America.

This painting by Thomas Lawrence (c. 1800) is the only known portrait of the Scot Mackenzie.

A lad from the Outer Hebrides

Born between 1762 and 1764 in Stornoway, in Scotland's Outer Hebrides, Mackenzie grew up on a farm; his first language was probably Gaelic. His mother died while he was still a child, and aged 12 he emigrated with his family to New York and then to Montréal. At 16, he became a clerk in a fur warehouse. At 22 he was offered a partnership 'on condition that I would proceed to the Indian country in the following spring'.

He set off from Montréal on the first stage of his crossing of the continent, travelling over half way across Canada to the Athabasca River, in what is now northern Alberta. He arrived there in 1787 and spent the winter with Peter Pond, a fur

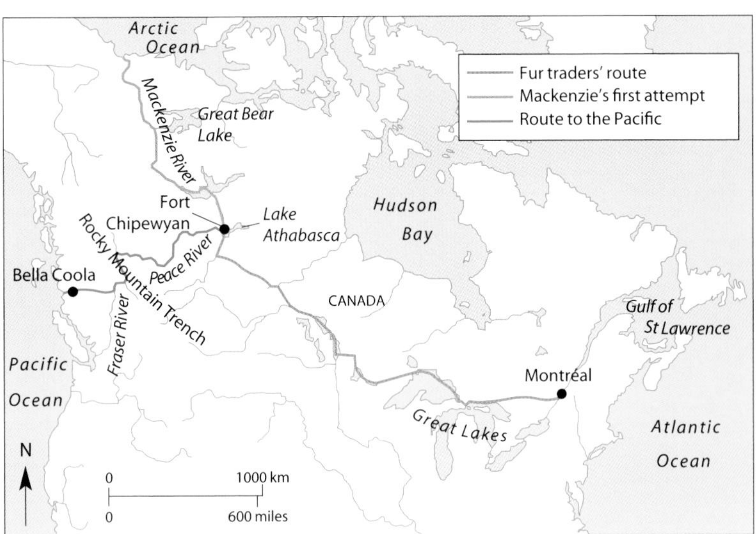

Above *From Montréal to Fort Chipewyan, Mackenzie followed the fur traders' route; he then made two attempts to reach the Pacific, and succeeded on the second. He constantly underestimated the distance involved in the journey as he wanted to attract investors in a new trade route.*

Retracing Mackenzie's voyage by canoe, going against the current of the Peace River, just as Mackenzie did.

trader who had killed a man in a duel in Detroit. Pond was notoriously tough and difficult, but he had a dream: to expand the fur business as far as the Pacific. Mackenzie learnt from Pond how to deal skilfully with native people. He also became inspired by Pond's dream.

First crossing of the continent

Mackenzie's first attempt ended in failure – he reached the Arctic Ocean rather than the Pacific. Two years later, in 1792, he set out again, this time with better native information. He took with him two Beaver Indians as interpreters, six French Canadian voyageurs – professional canoe paddlers – a Scottish assistant, Alexander Mackay, and a small dog. He left from the fur-trading base of Fort Chipewyan, close to Pond's original cabin, and ascended the Peace River for 1,000 km (620 miles). Here he overwintered. This was the furthest west any European had been.

The following summer he set out, always paddling against the current of the mile-wide Peace River. It was a physically gruelling task – day after day towing, wading and poling against a strong current. Slowly he clawed his way forward until he reached the Rockies. Here he wanted to turn right, but he was persuaded by an Indian guide to go left, again against the current. He entered the narrower confines of the Rocky Mountain Trench before reaching the dry land that separates the Arctic drainage system from the Pacific. It is a gap of only 817 paces, along a muddy undulating path. Crossing it, Mackenzie was now going downstream, down what he named Bad River.

Mackenzie was finally compelled to turn back at this rock on the Pacific coast, but he left an inscription to record his name and the date that he reached this point: 'From Canada by land 22nd July 1793'.

A street in Bella Coola, in a photograph taken in 1897. This was the end of the voyage and the first settlement on the Pacific Coast.

Here he wrecked the fragile canoe and almost drowned. His men spent four days gathering birchbark and pine resin to fix it. They cut a trail through boggy forest to meet a wide tributary of the Fraser River. For a while it was easy, until the boat was again wrecked in the terrible canyons. They rebuilt it and hid it for the return journey and set out to walk to the ocean.

Following a 'grease trail' walked by natives who traded oolikan fish oil with the Nuxhalk coastal Indians, in 17 days they walked 350 km (217 miles) to the Pacific coast. There Mackenzie borrowed dugouts to go a further 50 km (31 miles) up the fiord that leads from Bella Coola (in British Columbia). Here he finally ran into truly belligerent Indians and was forced to retreat.

On a rock that is still there today he left an inscription recording the date of his arrival. Retracing his way back, he returned to Fort Chipewyan in only six weeks. As a commercial route, his was a failure. But he was first, and for that he achieved glory, riches and a knighthood, though his health was ruined. He died in his native Scotland before he was 58.

Mungo Park

1795–97, 1805–06

... whatever difference there is between the Negro and European in the confirmation of the nose and the colour of the skin, there is none in the genuine sympathies and characteristic feelings of our common nature.
MUNGO PARK, 1795

Late in the 18th century, a 24-year-old Scotsman, with a restless heart and a memorable name, set off in search of the River Niger. It was to be the start of one of the most incredible journeys of exploration in West Africa. In many ways it was not surprising that Mungo Park ended up in Africa. Droves of other Scots were already making their mark overseas, most notably James Bruce (p. 140) and Alexander Mackenzie (p. 152).

Born to tenant farmers, Park's childhood in a remote cottage in the hills of the Scottish borders was ideal for a fledgling explorer. At first his father believed quiet, studious Mungo (the seventh of 13 children) would be suited to a career in the church. But soon his increasingly driven son had other ideas and chose instead to study medicine at Edinburgh University.

After graduating, Park's brother-in-law, James Dickson, introduced the 21-year-old Mungo to the influential statesman, Sir Joseph Banks. It proved a meeting that was to seal Park's destiny. On a recommendation from Banks – who had sailed the world as Captain Cook's botanist (p. 143) – the young adventurer was soon bound for Sumatra as surgeon's mate on an East India Company ship.

The three-month voyage was unremarkable, but Park earned his spurs and was soon recruited by the African Association, a recently formed group of affluent London movers and shakers, helmed by Banks, and intent on 'Promoting the Discovery of the Inland Parts of that Quarter of the world [Africa]'.

In search of the Niger

Park's instructions were to solve the mystery of the mythical Niger – the direction of this great river's flow having been a matter of conjecture for centuries. The African Association's last Niger-bound 'geographical missionary', Major Daniel Houghton, had recently perished in the African bush. Houghton's lonely death did little to dent Park's enthusiasm – if anything firing him up all the more. 'I had a passionate desire to examine ... a country so little known', he later wrote in his journal, 'and to become experimentally acquainted with the modes of life and characters of the natives.'

A portrait of Mungo Park in his mid-20s by an unknown artist (after Henry Edridge), c. 1797.

'The Dance of the Mombo-Jombo according to the travels of Mungo Park', by J. Ferrario (c. 1820). Park described this as 'an indecent and unmanly revel'.

Diagram of a timber bridge, from Park's Travels in the Interior Districts of Africa.

Park was certainly to succeed in this goal. One month after sailing out from Portsmouth on 22 May 1795, the excited explorer, still dressed in heavy European clothes, docked on the Gambia River. At the little outpost of Pisania he stayed with Dr Laidley, an English slave trader, who nursed Park through his first brush with malaria. Unlike so many Europeans in Africa at the time – quinine was still untried as a remedy – Park survived. Reinvigorated, he set off eastwards towards the Niger.

Park's first journey would last over two years. Some tribes believed the tall, pale explorer to be a cat-eyed devil who had been dipped in milk, while others welcomed him with open arms. One moment he was being taken in and fed by a good-hearted family, the next tormented by the Moors of Ludamar. The trip was not without comic moments. At one stage a group of fascinated women wanted to check whether Park, being a Christian, was circumcised or not. He jovially insisted only the youngest and prettiest girl should do the honours.

Although he never made it to Timbuktu, Park was able to confirm (near the river port of Ségou) categorically which way the River Niger flowed: a crusading discovery. 'I saw with infinite pleasure the great object of my mission,' wrote Park. 'the long-sought-for, majestic Niger, glittering in the morning sun, as broad as the Thames at Westminster, and flowing *slowly to the eastward*.'

Later, Park – half-starved and riddled with disease – latched on to a coffle (line) of slaves and staggered back to the Gambia coast. It was a near miracle he made it home alive. On his return to London on Christmas Day, 1797, the humble explorer was lionized, the Duchess of Devonshire even writing a poem in his honour. But Park soon tired of all the attention and, once settled back in

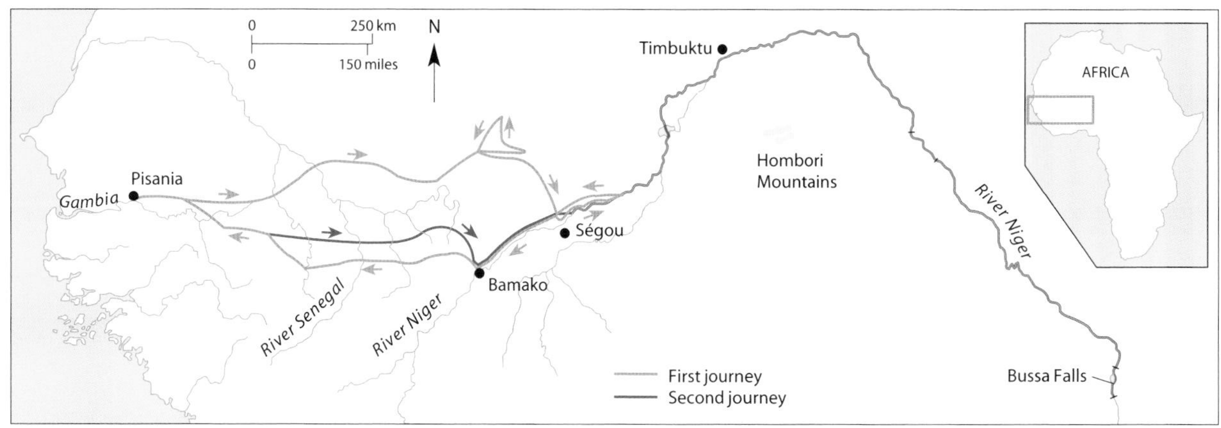

Park made two journeys exploring the River Niger; the second ended in his death in 1806 at Bussa Falls in northern Nigeria.

Scotland, he completed his diary, *Travels into the Interior of Africa*. It became an instant bestseller and is still in print today.

To Africa again

Park married his childhood sweetheart, Ailie Anderson, and set up a doctor's practice in the little town of Peebles. But it was not long before the Niger's Sirens called to him again. He admitted to his friend the novelist, Walter Scott, that he 'would rather brave Africa and all its horrors than wear out his life in long and toilsome rides over cold and lonely heaths and gloomy hills'.

In 1805, leaving Ailie pregnant with their fourth child, he headed once more towards the Niger. This time he was not alone, but travelling with a caravan of over 40 white men, mostly soldiers and a few carpenters. Plagued by rains and fever, the bulk of them died before even reaching the river. Park later drowned – probably having been ambushed in early 1806 – at Bussa Falls in north Nigeria, some 480 km (300 miles) from the point where the river segues into the Atlantic.

After the shining achievement of his initial expedition to Africa, Mungo Park's return was little more than a tragic and vainglorious foray. The explorer's courage and stamina remained intact, but he had lost the humility that had served him so well a decade before. Mungo Park, the legendary traveller, had believed himself unstoppable.

Now, 200 years since his death, Mungo Park is still remembered as one of the world's great explorers. The diary of the modest but lion-hearted young Scot not only inspired figures as diverse as Dr David Livingstone, Joseph Conrad and Ernest Hemingway, but continues to spark the imagination of readers across the world.

The port of Ségou, in Mali, where Mungo Park first caught sight of the River Niger. For centuries the 4,025-km (2,500-mile) long river, which runs from the hills of Sierra Leone to the Nigerian coast, had been shrouded in mystery. It was not until Park reached the river on 20 July 1795 that the secret of the Niger's flow – eastwards – was revealed to the outside world.

19th Century

Scientific investigation explodes in the 19th century, when intrepid explorers penetrate pristine regions to apply Linnaean principles of classification to the welter of unknown plants and animals they find. Some began also to recognize and record the experience and wisdom of the people they met. This is the great era of exploration, when most of the remaining blanks on the maps of Africa, South America and Central Asia are filled in. The search for fame and glory spurs many, while others are driven by religious or patriotic fervour. National pride in simply being the first begins to play a major role, and this is evident wherever flags are proudly raised, but behind this nearly always lay the global scramble for power and influence.

In the 19th century travel enjoyed its finest hour. These were true 'Renaissance Men' – fearless and brave, they were scientists, linguists, archaeologists and naturalists. They spent years in often desperately harsh conditions, plagued by diseases such as malaria and surrounded by hostile locals – many died on their travels – but they were determined to succeed. They began the massive task of unravelling how the world worked, and named and labelled everything they encountered.

Humboldt epitomized this attitude. A rich German nobleman, he took huge amounts of equipment with him and recorded absolutely everything he could get his hands on. The breadth of his travels throughout South America still dazzle and his scientific output remains of interest and value. Darwin was cast in the same mould. Although his journeys were less arduous, his con-

Humboldt and Bonpland by the Orinoco River, in a painting by Eduard Ender (c. 1850). The two explorers are surrounded by their specimens and equipment, which had to be carried with them for their entire journey.

clusions resulted in the theory of evolution, which he propounded in *On the Origin of Species*, and changed our view of the world for ever.

Other scientists began to examine the traces of vanished civilizations, travelling into remote parts of the known and still unknown world to do so. Burckhardt, travelling in disguise, was the first westerner to visit Petra, as well as many of the legendary Egyptian temples, such as Abu Simbel, some of which Belzoni was soon to excavate. Stephens and Catherwood were revealing similar treasures in the jungles of Central America, where huge Maya temples had lain hidden for hundreds of years.

Back in Africa, Barth finally crossed the Sahara and demonstrated that the legendary empires to its south and the fabled city of Timbuktu were not as great as had been thought. The search for the source of the Nile gathered pace, sending Burton, Speke and many others to compete for the prize of finding it. Livingstone's colossal journeys through the continent revealed more of its geography, followed by Stanley, who crossed it from side to side. The Frenchman Garnier, hailed at that time with Livingstone as one of the two greatest explorers of the age, set off up another major unknown river, the Mekong in Southeast Asia. His journey was to lay the foundations of an empire, the French colonies of Indo-China.

Burke and Wills successfully crossed Australia for the first time, but perished in the attempt. Doughty and Palgrave penetrated the wastes of Arabia Deserta, to be followed by others fascinated by the purity of these arid regions and the hard people who lived there. Przhevalsky and Younghusband competed to unravel the mysteries of remote parts of Central Asia, and began the Great Game for economic and strategic advantage between their Russian and British masters. In places where westerners could not go, however clever their disguise, the exploration was done by courageous Pundits, Indian servants of the British Raj, who risked their lives to survey the Himalaya.

In America, the urge to occupy all the lands to the west was given a major boost by the successful crossing of the continent by Lewis and Clark. They were helped by the many Indian tribes they met along their route; this, however, did not prevent their lands being taken from them. Some 10,000 Cherokee people were forced to march from their ancestral homelands along what became known as the Trail of Tears, with many dying on the way. This was only one shameful example of American oppression of its native people at that time.

The search for the Northwest Passage continued, still unsuccessfully and resulting in terrible suffering and loss of life. The attempt by Franklin and his disappearance sparked searches for survivors which continued for a decade, and the route was not successfully negotiated until the next century. By contrast, the Northeast Passage, around the top of Russia, was completed in 1879 by the Swedish naval officer, Nordenskïold. Neither passage fulfilled the hopes of centuries that they would provide fast routes around the continents, but perhaps with global warming that will change.

A pair of boots worn – and mended – by Henry Morton Stanley while on expedition in Africa in 1867–69.

GHILLEAN PRANCE

Alexander von Humboldt

40

1799–1804

I shall collect plants and fossils and make astronomical observations. But that's not the main purpose of my expedition – I shall try to find out how the forces of nature interact upon one another and how the geographic environment influences plant and animal life. I must find out about the unity of nature.

VON HUMBOLDT, 3 JUNE 1799

Alexander von Humboldt was a true polymath who could unite the different sciences of geography, meteorology, magnetism, heat distribution, botany, zoology, anthropology, politics and agriculture. A glance at the list of the equipment he took with him on his expedition shows its broad scientific aims: it includes books, barometers, a rain gauge, chronometers, hygrometers, electrometers, telescopes, sextants, theodolites, quadrants, a dipping needle, compasses, a magnetometer, a pendulum, eudiometers to measure atmospheric oxygen, a cynometer to measure the blueness of the sky, and chemical reagents for analyses. Everything was carted on oxen and mules through the plains of Venezuela and over the Andes of Colombia and Ecuador, and by boat on long trips at sea and along rivers. It is evident that it was all put to good use – everything that could possibly be measured was indeed measured.

Portrait of Baron Alexander von Humboldt engaged in botanical work, by Friedrich Georg Weitsch, 1806.

An epic journey

A journey that started in 1799 and climbed the highest peak in the Canary Isles, crossed the mountains and plains of Venezuela, ascended the Orinoco to its meeting with the Amazon, briefly visited Cuba, travelled 55 days up the Magdalena River valley, to the great cordilleras and volcanoes around Quito in Ecuador, navigated the margin of the Pacific Ocean, wandered over extensive areas of Mexico and then returned to Europe via the United States in 1804, must certainly rank as one of the great journeys of history.

Humboldt and his travelling companion, the French botanist Aimé Bonpland, set sail from La Coruña in Spain on 15 June 1799 in the ship *Pizarro*. The ship's captain was instructed to stop in Tenerife long enough for them to ascend Tiede peak, which they determined to be 12,182 ft (3,713 m) high. Humboldt also defined five different zones of vegetation as he ascended the mountain. Already, while waiting for permission from the governor to land, they had measured the longitude of Santa Cruz harbour with their Berthoud's Chronometer; their figure differed from that of Captain Cook, but was later found to be accurate. From then on measurements, observations and the collecting of specimens never ceased throughout their journey.

The travellers landed at Cumaná on the northern coast of what is now Venezuela on 16 July. During their stay of several months they made excursions to the Araya Peninsula, Chaima Indian missions and to the caves of the guácharo oil birds. Since there had been earthquakes in Cumaná in 1776 and 1797 Humboldt wrote extensively about them in his *Personal Narrative* of the expedition. On 11–12 November he observed a spectacular meteor shower of the Leonids. Shortly thereafter the party left for Caracas where they stayed until 7 February 1800, when they set out to explore the Orinoco region.

This remarkable trip crossed the llanos to the Apure River, ascended many cataracts and arrived at San Fernando de Atabapo on 24 April. The Orinoco section of the expedition alone lasted four months and covered 2,760 km (1,725 miles) of wild country, inhabited by many different tribal peoples and with numerous hazardous rapids and plagues of insects. The most important result was establishing the existence of a communication between the water-systems of the Orinoco and the Amazon through the Río Casiquiare. They then drifted downstream to Angostura (now Ciudad Bolívar), from where, after recovering from malaria, they made their way back to Cumaná. Of this part of the expedition Humboldt wrote:

> *How hard it is to express the pleasure of arriving in Angostura.... The discomforts felt in small boats cannot be compared to those felt under a burning sky, surrounded by swarms of mosquitoes, cramped for months on end in a pirogue that does not let you budge an inch because of its delicate balance.*

They next sailed to Cuba on 24 November. During their three-month stay there, Humboldt and Bonpland made several excursions around Havana and then sailed back to the mainland town of Cartagena on 5 March 1801. During the next four months they ascended the swollen Magdalena River to reach Bogotá, where they met the great Spanish botanist José Celestino Mutis. Proceeding south along the Andes they crossed frozen ridges and deep valleys to reach Quito, in Ecuador, on 6 January 1802. During their six months around Quito they ascended the vol-

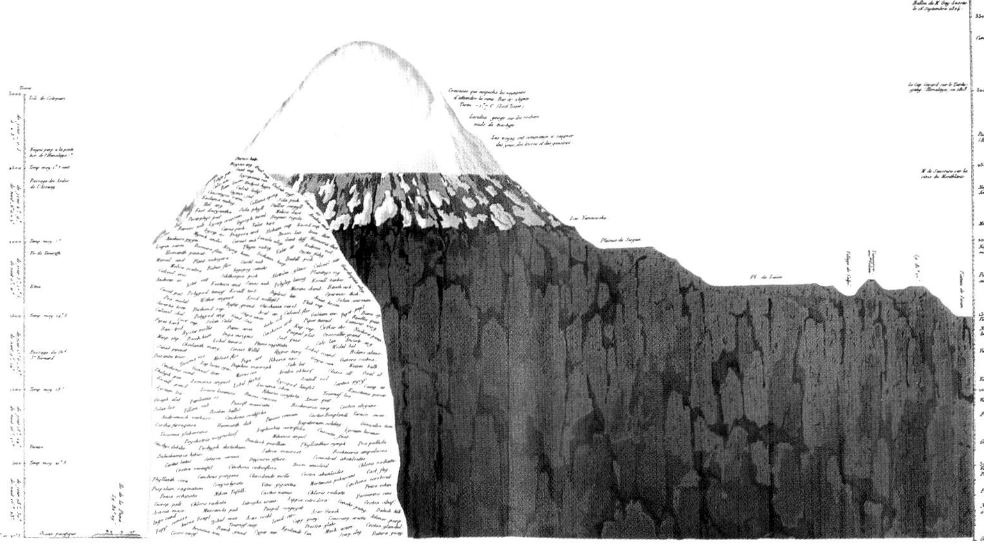

Humboldt's drawing of the peak of Chimborazo volcano in Ecuador showing the zonation of plants at different altitudes. This diagram formed the basis for future ecological studies of the distribution of mountain plants along elevational gradients.

canoes Pichincha and Chimborazo. Although they did not reach the summit of the latter, then believed to be the world's highest mountain, their climb to 6,005 m (19,700 ft) was a world altitude record at the time.

From Quito they made their way to Lima via the sources of the Amazon, arriving on 2 September. At Callao, Humboldt observed the Transit of Mercury and while on the coast he studied the fertilizing properties of guano, which led to its introduction to Europe. On 3 January 1803 they left Guayaquil for Mexico and after a tempestuous sea journey arrived in Acapulco in mid-February. It is appropriate that the ocean current that flows up the western coast of South America is named after Humboldt.

Humboldt and Bonpland reached Mexico City on 11 March and explored the country until early in 1804, including a climb up Jorulla volcano. They then began the return journey home via the United States, first visiting Cuba, where they had left part of their specimens. The purpose of the two-month visit to the United States was to study its political constitution and commercial relations, but Humboldt also befriended president Thomas Jefferson, who asked the German's advice about the impending expedition by Lewis and Clark (p. 165). The great journey finally ended when Humboldt and Bonpland arrived in Bordeaux on 3 August 1804.

Humboldt's account of his expedition dwells relatively little on the hardships, illnesses and adventures, yet these were numerous. Instead, he wrote extensively about the geology, astronomy, natural history, the measurements of altitudes and longitude, the peoples of the many different cultures he encountered, and the hospitality of many missionaries in Venezuela. We just get a few glimpses of the hazards, such as: 'The descent [of Cerro Imposible] is very dangerous for the pack-animals; the path is only some 15 inches wide, with precipices on either side', and he does admit to fright when encountering a large jaguar alone on a beach. Humboldt's attitude to the indigenous peoples is also commendable. He says that he uses the terms 'wild' or 'savage' with regret because they imply a difference of cultivation which does not always exist. He provided many

Humboldt and his companions stride out towards Cajambe volcano in Ecuador, in an illustration from the 30-volume account of the expedition published in 1814.

Painting of the orchid Catasetum macrocarpum, *from* Nova Genera et Species Plantarum VII.

useful details about cultures that have long been extinct and became quite concerned about slavery after visiting a slave market in Cumaná.

Scientific results

One of the most remarkable outcomes of Humboldt and Bonpland's voyage is the huge scientific output they published after their return to Europe. It was so great that only a few publications can be mentioned here. The seven-volume folio *Nova Genera et Species Plantarum* described and illustrated many new genera and about 4,500 species of plants. This was backed up by a herbarium collection of over 6,000 dried and pressed specimens, and Bonpland's botanical journal describing 4,000 species. Perhaps the greatest contribution to botany was Humboldt's *Essai sur la Géographie des Plantes*, that forms the basis for modern plant geography and ecology. Much light was shed on the migrations and relations of the indigenous tribes of the Americas, their origin, languages and behaviour, in *Vues des Cordillères et monumens des peuples indigènes de l'Amérique*, published in 1811.

Humboldt also published two volumes on the animals he had encountered, and a geological comparison between the rocks of Europe and South America. His astronomical observations were brought together in *Recueil d'observations astronomiques, d'opérations trigonométriques et des mesures barométriques...*, which includes a table of almost 700 geographical positions. His map of the Orinoco, presented to the Académie des Sciences in 1817, showed definitively that the Amazon and the Orinoco rivers are joined by the Casiquiare Channel. His 1817 delineation of isothermal lines enabled the comparison of climate conditions between different regions. In his five-volume work *Kosmos*, Humboldt attempted a physical description of the entire world.

It is no wonder then that Charles Darwin described Humboldt as 'the greatest scientific traveller who ever lived'. Darwin prepared himself for his own voyage (p. 174) by avidly reading Humboldt, and of his preconceived impressions he said 'all mine were taken from the vivid descriptions in the *Personal Narrative* of Humboldt, which exceed in merit anything I have read on the subject.'

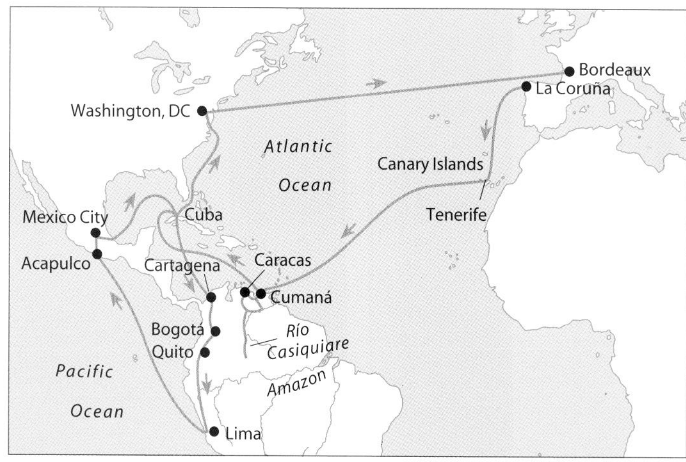

Map of Humboldt and Bonpland's journey to the equinoctial regions of the New Continent.

A black saki monkey, Simia satanas, *from* Recueil d'Observations de Zoologie et d'Anatomie Comparée, *by Humboldt and Bonpland.*

Lewis & Clark

41

1804–06

Our vessels consisted of six small canoes, and two large pirogues. This little fleet altho' not quite so respectable as those of Columbus or Capt. Cook were still viewed by us with as much pleasure as those deservedly famed adventurers ever beheld theirs ...

MERIWETHER LEWIS, 1805

With these words, written in his journal on 7 April 1805, Meriwether Lewis deliberately placed himself and William Clark, his co-commander, in the grand tradition of exploration. Lewis and Clark would carry the flag of empire to vast unexplored lands, proclaim a new reality to the unsuspecting native peoples who lived there, and return bearing hundreds of scientific specimens and written descriptions of the wonders they had seen.

Their quest originated with President Thomas Jefferson, who had long sought to send a quasi-scientific expedition across the continent of North America. He first proposed such a journey in 1783 to George Rogers Clark, the older brother of William. Later, he discussed with the adventurer John Ledyard the idea of a west-to-east exploration from Europe across the Bering Strait to North America. (Ledyard embarked on his journey but was arrested in Siberia by soldiers dispatched by Catherine the Great.)

Then, in the summer of 1802, Jefferson was galvanized by reading Alexander Mackenzie's *Voyages from Montreal ...*, the Scottish explorer's account of his 1793 journey across Canada to the Pacific, the first overland crossing by a European (p. 152). Alarmed by Mackenzie's assertion of British sovereignty over the Pacific Northwest, Jefferson ordered his Virginia neighbour and personal secretary Meriwether Lewis to organize a military expedition to find 'the direct water communication from sea to sea'. Within a year, Jefferson's diplomats in Paris had negotiated with Napoleon the purchase of the Louisiana Territory, a vast area drained by the western watersheds of the Mississippi and Missouri rivers. What had begun as a furtive mission with murky geopolitical and scientific objectives had now become a fully fledged military exploration of America's newest possessions.

Lewis, born in 1774 and just 29, turned for help to a far more experienced military man. After an American military campaign against the Ohio

Captain Meriwether Lewis in Shoshone costume, 1807, by Charles B. J. F. de Saint-Ménin. A year after the expedition, Meriwether Lewis posed in Philadelphia wearing the mantle of 140 ermine skins given to him by the Shoshone chief Cameahwait. The garment, Lewis wrote, 'is the most elegant piece of Indian dress I ever saw'.

Four years older and more experienced than Lewis, William Clark (this portrait of 1810 is attributed to John Wesley Jarvis) emerged as the de facto *commander of the expedition. He later served as territorial governor and chief Indian agent in the western United States for three decades.*

Valley tribes in 1795, Lewis had served in William Clark's elite rifle company. Clark, four years older than Lewis, had won distinction leading soldiers in combat and in river expeditions. To attract Clark to the mission, Lewis made an unorthodox proposal: they would be equal co-captains, sharing command 'in all respects'.

Preparations in Philadelphia

Jefferson sent Lewis to Philadelphia to be trained in botany, mineralogy, navigation and medicine by the most eminent scientists of the day. Clark began recruiting the frontiersmen and soldiers who would eventually comprise the permanent party of 33. The two captains joined in Louisville, Kentucky, and proceeded down the Ohio River and up the Mississippi to a camp opposite St Louis, where they spent the winter of 1803–04.

The following spring, the Corps of Discovery, as they called it, headed up the Missouri River, poling and pulling a 17-m (55-ft) keelboat and two smaller wooden pirogues against the current. A division of responsibilities between the captains was decided upon – Lewis would handle the scientific objectives, often walking on the shore and measuring everything, from the height of an anthill (10 in/25 cm) to the distance between the eyes of an enormous catfish (18 in/46 cm). Clark

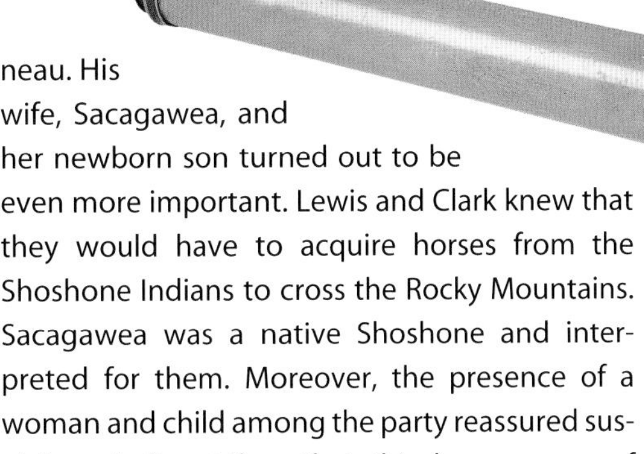

would take charge of everything else: the men, the maps and the meals. They both would keep journals, as would four sergeants. In the end, their combined journals totalled more than one million words, offering a richness of detail without parallel in the history of exploration.

A second, frigid winter was spent at Fort Mandan, a palisaded fort on the banks of the Missouri River near present-day Bismarck, North Dakota, 2,575 km (1,600 miles) upriver from St Louis. Up till now, the explorers had travelled through lands already familiar to early traders and trappers. In the spring of 1805, however, they would be heading west into uncharted territory. Their primary goal was to find the elusive Northwest Passage, a water route to the Pacific that would give fur traders access to markets in the East. Reasoning that the western part of the continent was a mirror-image of the east, Jefferson and the captains expected no more than a short half-day portage across the continental divide.

At Fort Mandan, Lewis and Clark hired a French-Canadian interpreter, Toussaint Charbonneau. His wife, Sacagawea, and her newborn son turned out to be even more important. Lewis and Clark knew that they would have to acquire horses from the Shoshone Indians to cross the Rocky Mountains. Sacagawea was a native Shoshone and interpreted for them. Moreover, the presence of a woman and child among the party reassured suspicious Indian tribes that this large group of strangers was not a war party.

Into an uncharted wilderness

After leaving Fort Mandan, the men dragged their boats against the Missouri current for another 1,610 km (1,000 miles), including one 27-km (17-mile) portage on the rugged high prairie around the Great Falls. They encountered no fewer than 62 grizzly bears – one of the dozens of species they described to science for the first time.

The explorers found a busy wilderness. Dozens of indigenous Indian tribes controlled the land, rivers and trade throughout the west. The British and French Canadians were competing for the burgeoning empire of fur, as were the Spanish in Mexico. When the Spanish learned of Lewis and Clark's journey, they were so alarmed that they sent out three mounted parties to intercept the explorers, all unsuccessfully.

After great difficulty they located the Shoshone, who provided horses and a guide. But trapped in deep snows crossing the Bitterroot Mountains, the explorers ran out of food and were forced to eat the horses. They survived only after Clark and several men pushed on ahead and located another hospitable tribe, the Nez Perce. The explorers constructed dugout canoes and floated down the Clearwater, Snake and Columbia rivers, shooting rapids and passing dozens of tribes assembled along the region's great salmon fisheries. On 7 November 1805, Clark wrote in his elkskin journal, 'Ocian in view! O! the joy'.

The explorers wintered at the mouth of the Columbia at what they named Fort Clatsop, after the local tribe. In March 1806, they departed on

Above *This 'spy-glass', said to have been carried by Lewis on the expedition, was made by the Englishman William Cary. Its five brass draw-tubes extended to almost 1.5 m (5 ft) long, but collapsed to just 38 cm (15 in).*

Above left *Lewis and Clark amplified their daily journal entries with drawings of flora and fauna. Lewis's drawing of the eulachon, or candlefish, was the first scientific description of this species. After roasting them in their own fat, Lewis pronounced them 'superior to any fish I ever tasted'.*

Opposite below Lewis and Clark, 1804, *by L. Edward Fisher. Lewis and Clark's 1804 party was the first large expedition to proceed up the Missouri River. The armed keelboat was rigged with sails to help overcome the river's powerful currents.*

Above *Native peoples assisted Lewis and Clark throughout the expedition, but were later displaced by American expansion. These relocated Nez Perce and Yakima chiefs gathered in 1910 at the mouth of the Columbia River, near the explorers' encampment of winter 1805–06.*

Below *The 28-month journey was largely by water, along the Missouri, Clearwater, Snake, and Columbia rivers.*

the return trip. After crossing the Bitterroots, Lewis divided the expedition into several smaller parties. He intended to explore the northern watershed of the Missouri River, near Canada, while Clark would descend the Yellowstone River. The result was a near-fiasco. Undermanned, Lewis fell into a confrontation with several young Blackfeet warriors. One or possibly two Blackfeet were killed in the only violent incident of the entire journey. Lewis and his companions fled on horseback for 145 km (90 miles) across the prairie to rejoin their comrades.

Safe return

When they arrived back in St Louis in September 1806, the explorers were hailed as returning heroes. They had travelled more than 14,485 km (9,000 miles) by river and land in 28 months, with the loss of only a single member (a sergeant who died of suspected appendicitis). While not establishing a permanent post in the Pacific Northwest, they had at least parried Britain's ambitions – and defined the aspirations of a westering republic to stretch from 'from sea to shining sea'.

But just as notable was what they had *not* achieved. They had found no easy water route to the Pacific – future American settlers would travel on the Oregon Trail. Fur traders would soon open the trans-Mississippi trade regardless of Lewis and Clark – the captains had already passed boat after boat moving up the Missouri on their return trip. Their written account, including Clark's magnificent map of the inner continent, was not published until 1814, when the expedition was passing into history.

Unable to adjust to civilian life, Lewis died in what was almost certainly a suicide in 1809, three years after the expedition. Clark married twice and carried on in government service for another 30 years. When he died in 1838 at the age of 68, he was the most powerful federal official west of the Mississippi. Several years later, one of Clark's friends wrote to Sir Roderick Murchison, President of the Royal Geographical Society in London, to inform him of the explorer's death. Clark, he said, 'was a man of strong and vigorous mind and commanding character.... He (with Mr. Lewis) opened the career of geographical discovery in the vast area of the Mississippi valley, where cities and states are now rapidly rising to cover the wilderness.'

ANTHONY SATTIN

Jean Louis Burckhardt

42

1812–15

The dangers that await me are not so innumerable as the name Africa may perhaps already seem to you to imply … countries such as these are the subject of many stories.

JEAN LOUIS BURCKHARDT IN A LETTER TO HIS FAMILY

In March 1809 a young merchant, Shaykh Ibrahim ibn Abdallah, arrived in the harbour of Valletta, Malta. He said he was returning home to India. In fact he was a Swiss gentleman, Jean Louis Burckhardt, and was on his way to Aleppo in Syria. But his ultimate goal lay across the Sahara, in northern Africa – the fabled city of Timbuktu.

Burckhardt was the latest traveller to be set in motion by the African Association, the world's first geographical society. The Association was made up of some of the most powerful and influential people in Britain, and their stated motives were scientific – to fill in the blanks on the map – and humanitarian, for they hoped exploration would help bring an end to the slave trade. They were also patriotic, reasoning that discoveries in Africa would bring benefits to Britain. Their sights were set on the River Niger, and on Timbuktu in particular, which they believed was the key to the markets of central Africa.

In the 21 years of its existence, the Association had sent out seven previous travellers – Burckhardt, who had studied Arabic at Cambridge University, was the eighth. Twelve years earlier, Mungo Park (p. 155) had returned to London having reached the Niger, but without seeing Timbuktu. Park and several others had since died attempting to reach it. Burckhardt was going the long way in, not via the Gambia River, but by crossing the Sahara from Cairo with a caravan of West African Muslims. Caravan traders were known to be fanatical Muslims: Burckhardt would only make it across the desert if he could pass as one of them.

To perfect his disguise, he intended to spend two years in Syria, but once there he realized there was no need to hurry to reach Cairo: trouble in the Hejaz (modern Saudi Arabia) had brought the trans-Saharan caravans to a temporary halt. In the end, he stayed three years in Syria, studying Arabic and travelling widely in the region, making particularly impressive journeys to Palmyra and to the Jebel Druse. Then, on 18 June 1812, he left Damascus for Cairo.

Portrait of Burckhardt as he appeared at the end of his life. Henry Salt, the British Consul in Egypt, who made this portrait, described him as 'the perfect Arab'.

Right *Burckhardt's travels in preparation for the Saharan crossing took him to some of the most remote places in the region.*

Centre *Painting by David Roberts of a conference of Arabs at Petra. The Bedu jealously guarded the ruins at Petra, convinced that the tombs contained buried treasure.*

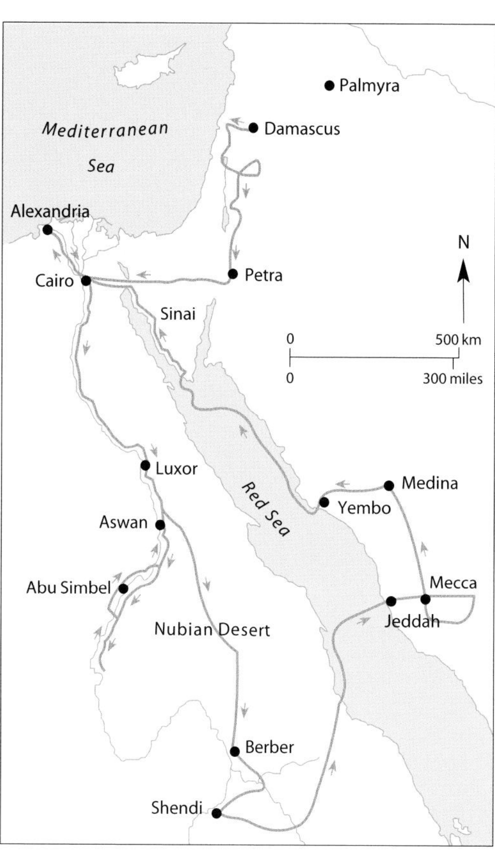

The Holy Land

'I put up every time in the dirtiest of caravanserai,' Burckhardt wrote of his travels through Palestine, 'take my cloak for a blanket, the earth for a mattress, eat with camel drivers, groom my own horse – but see and hear things those who travel in comfort will never know.' This plan produced rewards: in Kerak (modern Jordan) he heard mention of ruins in the Wadi Musa. Hiring a guide, and taking a goat on the pretext of wanting to make a sacrifice to Aaron, whose tomb was nearby, he came to a narrow cleft in the rock, which he followed down through a long gully until he emerged in front of a massive rock-cut monument. Others lay nearby, 'several hundred large and eloquent sepulchres,' as he wrote to a friend in England, as well as 'temples and palaces, an aqueduct, an amphitheatre cut entirely out of the rock'.

He knew he couldn't inspect the site further – his curiosity had already made the guide suspicious – so the goat was sacrificed and they moved on. 'Whether or not I have discovered the remains of the capital of Arabia Petraea,' he wrote home, 'I leave to the decision of the Greek scholars.' The scholars agreed: Petra, the 'rose-red' Nabataean capital not seen by a European since the Crusades, had been rediscovered.

Opposite *The first glimpse of Petra: the Treasury at the end of the Siq. Burckhardt was the first European since the Crusades to see this ancient site.*

Nile journeys

When he reached Cairo, his disguise was so perfect that he had difficulty entering the British Consulate. But still there was no caravan. Burckhardt now decided to travel up the Nile, assuring his masters in London he would undertake nothing hazardous. At the beginning of 1813, he set off south for Aswan and beyond into Nubia, where he had heard about a small temple, which he visited on 22 March 1813.

'Having, as I supposed, seen all the antiquities of Ebsambal, I was about to ascend the sandy side of the mountain by the same way I had descended; when having luckily turned more to the southward, I fell in with what is yet visible of

four immense colossal statues cut out of the rock.' He had just become the first known European since antiquity to see the Great Temple of Ramesses II at Abu Simbel.

A year after visiting Abu Simbel, Burckhardt joined a caravan to cross Nubia into Sudan. He reached Shendi, one of the major crossroads for Saharan caravans and further up the Nile than any known European had penetrated. In Shendi souk he found goods originating from across northern Africa, as well as from Germany, Venice and India, but no trans-Saharan caravans.

Continuing south was not an option – he was assured he would die – so he joined a group crossing the Red Sea to Mecca. Before leaving Shendi, he wrote a stunningly perceptive letter to his employers, insisting that 'Europe will have done but little for the Blacks, if the abolition of the Atlantic slave-trade ... is not followed up by ... the education of the sons of Africa in their own country, and by their own countrymen.'

Pilgrimages

Burckhardt was not the first European to visit the holy cities of Mecca and Medina, forbidden to non-Muslims, but his was the first full description of the *Hajj*. In January 1815 he contracted dysentery, which laid him up for three months. As soon as he was well enough, he took a boat up the Red Sea to Sinai, where he recuperated in a hillside Bedu village. By the time he finally reached Cairo in June, riding in with the khedive's wife and her caravan, he had been away for two and a half years and had completed one of the great journeys of the age.

For the next two years, Burckhardt stayed in Egypt, writing about his travels and collecting manuscripts. A celebrity both in the Middle East and in Europe, he was described by Henry Salt, the British Consul in Cairo, as 'the perfect Arab'. And there was good news – caravans were beginning to move again and Burckhardt arranged to travel to Fezzan and on to Timbuktu with one that would leave Cairo at the end of the year. But when the caravan left, he was not with it: he had suffered a relapse of dysentery and died on 15 October 1817.

He is best remembered now for the rediscovery of Petra and Abu Simbel, but Burckhardt's legacy was more significant, including leaving his Arabic manuscripts to Cambridge University and publishing brilliantly perceptive accounts of the Holy Land, Nubia, the Bedouin and the *Hajj*. And although he never finally managed to set out for Timbuktu, he provided inspiration to future travellers, among them Richard Burton (p. 195).

'Excavation of the Great Temple of Ramesses II at Abu Simbel' (1819), by Linant de Bellefonds. Belzoni had found a passage into the temple the previous year, but Linant de Bellefonds was among the party that went to clear the façade of sand.

GIOVANNI BELZONI

Above *Belzoni: detail of a memorial engraving commissioned by his wife Sarah.*

Below *Dragging the massive bust of Rammesses II towards the Nile at Thebes.*

The most unlikely of adventurers, Giovanni Belzoni (1778–1823) was a circus-strongman from Padua, Italy, who designed an ox-drawn hydraulic pump for the modernizing Egyptian ruler, Muhammad Ali. His machine failed the test, but while in Cairo Belzoni met Burckhardt, who had a project for him. In Luxor, Burckhardt had seen what he thought was the most perfect piece of Egyptian sculpture – the massive bust of 'Memnon', actually of the pharaoh Ramesses II. Burckhardt suggested that it should be donated to the British Museum. The British Consul, Henry Salt, helped arrange permission and agreed to share the costs, while Belzoni, with his energy, determination and resourcefulness, was engaged to move it. Belzoni described the bust as 'smiling at me, at the thought of being taken to England', although the Italian found little to smile at in the 17 days it took to drag the statue across the plain to the Nile.

Ramesses awakened Belzoni's curiosity, and from there he wrote his name large in the records of Egyptology. He opened the tomb of Seti I, one of the most remarkable and beautifully decorated in the Valley of the Kings. Then, while Burckhardt lay dying in Cairo, Belzoni moved to Abu Simbel, where he cleared a passage into the temple the Swiss traveller had found – Belzoni admitted he was astounded to discover 'it was one of the most magnificent temples'. Back in Cairo the following year, 1818, Belzoni forced a way into the pyramid of Khafre (Chephren), the 'second' of the Giza pyramids. When he finally returned to London, he was a celebrity: 2,000 people attended the opening day of his exhibition at the Egyptian Hall, Piccadilly.

However famous he had become, Belzoni was not finished with Burckhardt, and from London he sailed to West Africa, hoping to complete the Swiss traveller's mission of reaching Timbuktu. But, like Burckhardt, he went down with dysentery and died in Benin in December 1823.

43 Charles Darwin & the Beagle

1831–36

The voyage on the Beagle *has been by far the most important event in my life and has determined my whole career.*
CHARLES DARWIN, 1887

Few naturalists have ever been given such an opportunity as Charles Darwin was when he was invited to be the companion of Captain Robert FitzRoy on a two-year surveying voyage to the east coast of South America. And few people, if any, have made such good use of the results of an expedition that turned into a five-year circumnavigation of the globe. Usually thought of as primarily a sea voyage, in fact Darwin was only at sea 533 days of the five years. FitzRoy spent much more time on board as his ship travelled up and down the coasts while surveying. It was perhaps just as well for Darwin that it worked out this way, given his sea-sickness and his opinion of travel in the ship:

'If a person suffer much from sea-sickness. Let him weigh it heavily in the balance. I speak from experience.... But it must be borne in mind, how large a proportion of the time during a long voyage is spent on the water, as compared to days in the harbour.'

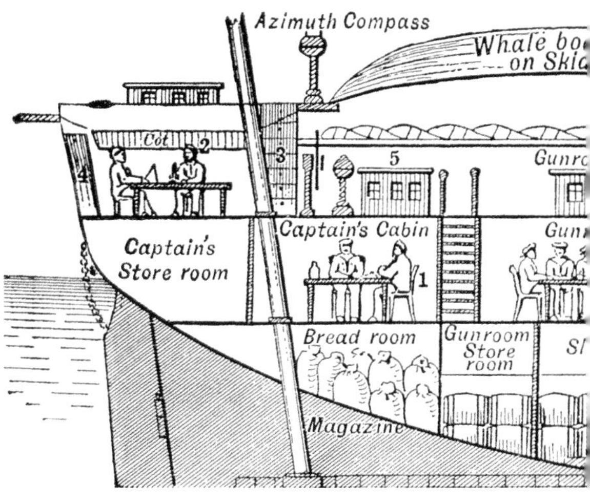

Right *Watercolour portrait of Darwin aged 31, by George Richmond (1840).*

Centre *A side elevation diagram of the* Beagle*, showing how the different areas of the ship were arranged.*

A sketch of two Patagonian Indians at Gregory Bay, Argentina, by Conrad Martens, artist on part of the voyage of HMS Beagle.

Darwin prepared himself for the journey by reading of Humboldt's voyage (p. 161), and quoted him and compared experiences in his account of the voyage of the *Beagle*. FitzRoy crammed 22 chronometers and many other instruments into his small cabin to carry out his assigned task.

The journey

After setting out and being forced back twice by storms, the *Beagle* finally left Plymouth on 27 December 1831. Brief visits were made to the Cape Verde Islands and then Fernando Noronha off the coast of Brazil. During their stay in Rio de Janeiro Darwin nearly left the ship over an argument with FitzRoy about slavery, which Darwin detested, but on the whole they were good companions and remained friends at the end of the journey. At Rio, Darwin rented a cottage on Botafogo Bay for three months, and participated in carnival.

From April 1832 until July 1835, the *Beagle* travelled around the east and west coasts of South America, including a visit to the Falklands. Many of Darwin's inland journeys were made in Argentina, including a 1,125-km (700-mile) trek from Bahia Blanca, via Buenos Aires, to Santa Fe. An entire year was spent along the west coast of South America at Chiloé, Valparaiso and Lima. At Chiloé, Darwin watched an eruption of Mount Osorno. While near Valdivia he experienced an earthquake, subsequently visiting the ruins of Concepción, a town completely

Charles Darwin's pocket sextant from his voyage on HMS Beagle.

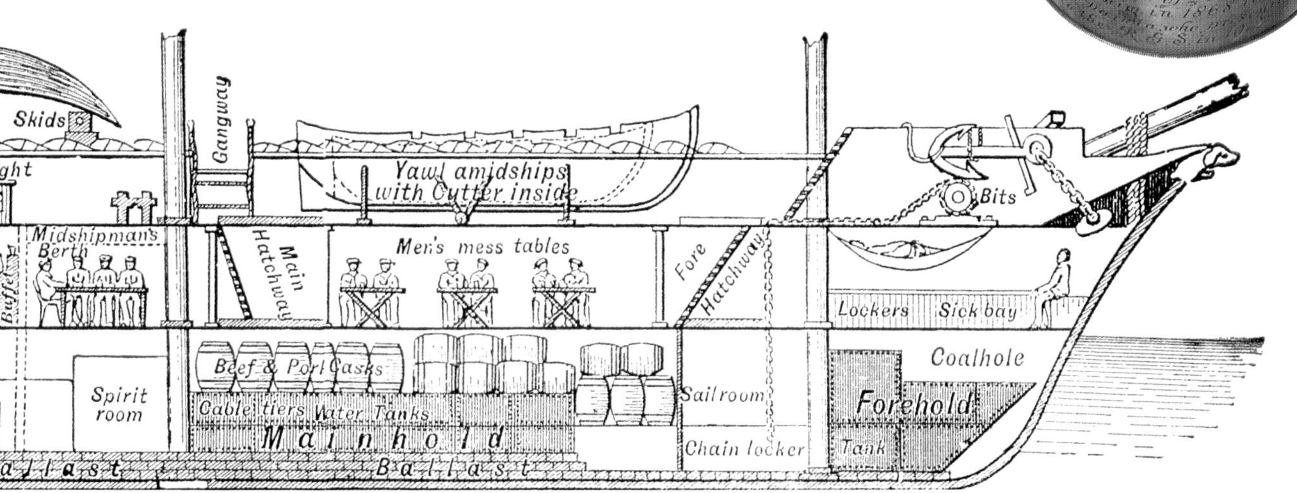

HMS Beagle *sailing through the Murray Narrow, Beagle Channel, in Tierra del Fuego, by Conrad Martens.*

destroyed by the tremors. Darwin set out from Valparaiso on one of his extensive inland journeys to explore the Andes, crossing the Portillo Pass and reaching Mendoza in Argentina. In Valparaiso Darwin suffered from a severe fever and was nursed back to health by his old school friend, Richard Corfield, who fortunately had settled there.

Darwin witnessed revolutions in both Montevideo and in Lima and met with the revolutionary General Rosas in Argentina in August 1833. The famous visit to the Galápagos Islands was made in September and October 1835. In November he was in Tahiti. Darwin wrote much about the friendly people of Tahiti and liked them more than the natives of New Zealand, where they were in December. While he describes most indigenous people as savages, he also gives alarming descriptions of seeing the gauchos exterminating the indigenous peoples of the pampas, which he did not condone.

From New Zealand the *Beagle* sailed to Australia, reaching Sydney in January 1836, Tasmania in February and King George's Sound in March. From Sydney Darwin made one of his many land journeys, 195 km (120 miles) inland over the Blue Mountains to Bathhurst. Continuing on the return journey, the *Beagle* stopped at the Cocos Islands, Mauritius, Cape Town and St Helena, reaching Ascension in July. Darwin maintained his enthusiasm for land-based excursions right to the end of the voyage, climbing the hills in St Helena and the 865-m (2,840-ft) high Green Hill in Ascension. Finally, on 2 October 1836, the *Beagle* arrived back at Falmouth, with both FitzRoy and Darwin in good shape.

Scientific results

Darwin returned from the voyage decided to remain a full-time naturalist rather than a clergyman. He concluded that 'nothing can be more improving for a young naturalist, than a journey in distant countries'. By far the most important result of his journey was the fact that the observations made and the specimens collected contributed greatly to his realization of the muta-

A cactus finch (Geospiza scandens) *from the Galápagos Islands, painted by John Gould.*

bility of species and the survival of the fittest, and consequently to the theory of evolution, which was formulated after rather than during the voyage.

His interest in geology, stimulated by Adam Sedgwick at Cambridge and through reading Charles Lyell's *Principles of Geology* during the voyage, led to many interesting observations and to his increasing awareness of the age of the Earth. Wherever he went Darwin made extensive observations on geology, and he was particularly interested in the uplift of the Andes. The many fossils of large beasts he found in Argentina confirmed that extinction was part of a natural process and he was impressed by their obvious relationship to living animals.

Darwin's scientific collections were distributed among leading specialists in each field and the results were promptly published. The five-part *The zoology of the voyage of HMS* Beagle was edited by Darwin, with the fossil mammals described by Richard Owen, the birds by John Gould and the mammals by George Waterhouse. Today, herbarium specimens are kept at Cambridge, the Natural History Museum, London, and Kew.

The scientific results were by no means confined to Darwin himself. FitzRoy made good use of the many instruments the ship was equipped with to measure longitude and accurately survey many places. FitzRoy's own collections of birds in the Galápagos were better labelled than Darwin's and were invaluable to Darwin as he studied the variation between islands. After their shared voyage on the *Beagle,* FitzRoy and Darwin, men of very different personalities, drifted apart; FitzRoy later took his own life.

Specimen of a caterpillar-hunting ground beetle collected by Darwin in Patagonia. Beetles were always a favourite insect of Darwin.

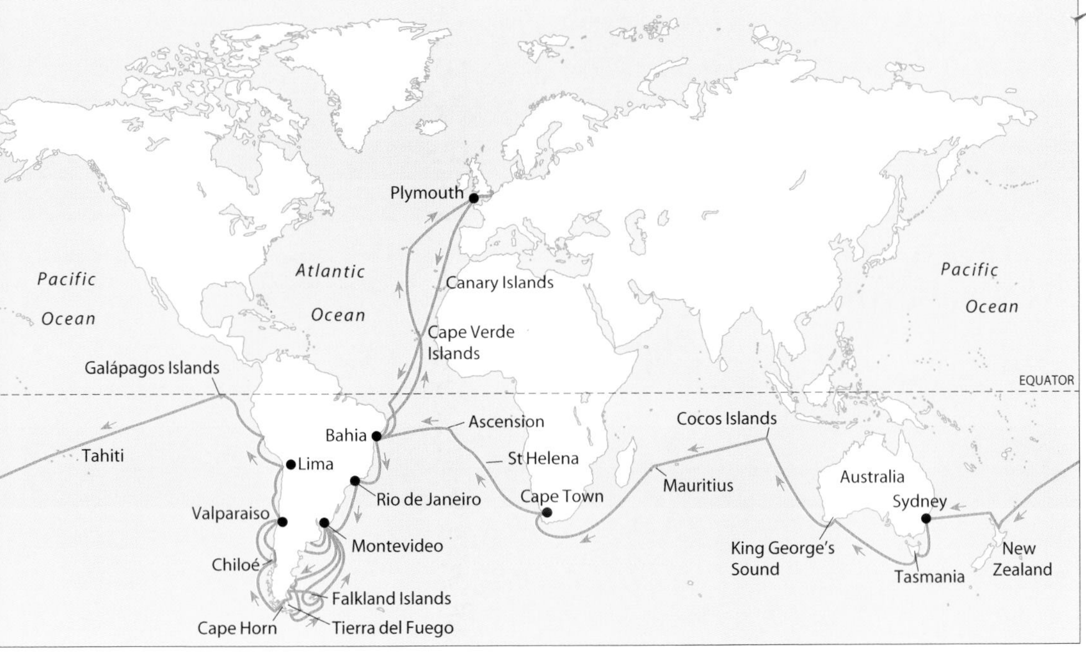

Map showing the route of the circumnavigation of HMS Beagle. *Darwin was in fact at sea only 533 days in the five years that the voyage took.*

DUANE KING

44

The Trail of Tears

1838–39

We have now been on our road to Arkansas seventy-five days and have travelled five hundred and twenty-nine miles ... I am afraid that, with all the care that can be exercised ... there will be an immense amount of suffering and loss of life attending the removal.... And the fact that the removal is effected by coertion [sic] makes it the more galling to the feelings of the survivors.

REVD EVAN JONES, 30 DECEMBER 1838

In 1838, virtually all the Cherokee people living in their ancestral homeland of the South Appalachian mountains were forced by the United States government to embark on an arduous 1,610-km (1,000-mile) journey to the Indian Territory, now Oklahoma. The number of deaths and the immense human suffering that occurred during the forced removal were so great that the route has become popularly known as the 'Trail of Tears'.

Unable to conclude an agreement with the duly authorized leaders of the Cherokee Nation, the United States government signed a treaty with a minority faction willing to cede the last remaining portion of the original Cherokee homeland on 29 December 1835. Despite the protests of the overwhelming majority of Cherokee people, the 'Treaty of New Echota' was ratified by US Senate vote on 23 May 1836. The Cherokees were given two years from that date to remove to the Indian Territory. When the time had expired only 2,000 of the more than 17,000 Cherokee in the east had voluntarily emigrated.

The Arkansas River, seen from Stout's Point. Two of the detachments of Cherokees travelling by boat were stranded by low water near here in the summer of 1838.

Military round-up

In May 1838, Brigadier General Winfield Scott and 7,000 federal and state troops arrived in the Cherokee Nation to enforce the removal. The military round-up began in Georgia on 25 May. Within two weeks, two regiments of Georgia militia had apprehended more than 3,600 Cherokee. Soon, throughout the Cherokee Nation, families were forced from comfortable homes into 31 stockades and open military stations strategically located in southeast Tennessee, western North Carolina, northwest Georgia and northeast Alabama. From the stockades the prisoners were then sent to three principal emigrating depots. Two were in Tennessee – near Ross's Landing at Chattanooga, and Fort Cass near Calhoun – while a third was situated 13 km (8 miles) south of Fort Payne, Alabama.

Removal of the Five Civilized Tribes, *a mural by Elizabeth James. The Five Civilized Tribes were a loose confederation of tribes, including the Cherokee, who were deported from their ancestral lands and forced to settle in Indian Territory (present-day Oklahoma).*

Water route

Between 6 June and 5 December 1838, 17 detachments of Cherokees numbering more than 15,000 began the journey that changed the destiny of the Cherokee people. The first three detachments captured by the Georgia Guard were forced to depart from Ross's Landing. One group, consisting of 489 individuals, departed on 6 June on the Steamboat *George Guess*, escorted by Lt Edward Deas. On 12 June, another detachment of 776 people under Lt R. H. K. Whiteley also departed by boat from Ross's Landing. Both had to travel a 96-km (60-mile) section – between Decatur and Tuscumbia, Alabama – by rail, to avoid the Tennessee River's most treacherous shoals. A member of Whiteley's detachment became one of the first recorded fatalities of a railway accident in the US.

On 17 June 1838, the third detachment of Cherokee prisoners, conducted under military escort by Captain Gus Drane, departed Ross's Landing. All three detachments consisted of Georgia Cherokees who were still wearing the clothes they had on at the time of their capture several weeks earlier. Most were not allowed to gather even meagre belongings before being herded off to stockades and then marched to the emigrating depot.

Hardships of travel

Unlike the first two detachments, the third group, consisting of 1,072 Cherokees, was forced to march overland for the first 322 km (200 miles) to Waterloo, Alabama. By the end of June, more than a dozen were dead and 293 had escaped to make their way back to the concentration camps in east Tennessee, only to be sent west again with other detachments later in the same year.

On the Arkansas River, the steamboats carrying the Whiteley and Drane detachments were stranded by low water just below Lewisburg (present-day Morrilton), in Arkansas. The groups thus had to travel overland through western Arkansas during the peak of the summer. In the hot, dry, dusty conditions, both detachments suffered from excessive sickness along the way. Towards the end of the journey, Whiteley had to halt the detachment because more than half the members were sick. Whiteley reached the head of Lee's Creek in the Flint District on 2 August 1838 and reported 72 deaths on the 2,500-km (1,554-mile) journey.

The Drane Detachment disbanded at Mrs Webber's Plantation (present-day Stilwell in Oklahoma) in the Indian Territory on 5 September 1838; only 635 individuals were still with the detachment, including two born on the way.

John Drew, a Cherokee merchant who conducted the final group of Cherokee to the Indian Territory. Drew had been a colonel of the 1st Cherokee Mounted Rifles in the American Civil War.

With 146 deaths en route, this detachment had the highest mortality rate of any of the Cherokee detachments during the forced removal. Early reports of the suffering by the Drane and Whiteley detachments caused the military and the Cherokee leaders to re-think their strategy. Soon, General Scott gave permission both to delay the removal of the other groups until autumn, and for Cherokee leaders to superintend them.

Overland routes

The remainder of the Cherokees thus began the overland journey to the west. A fourth detachment with a military conductor comprised about 660 supporters of the Treaty and left the Cherokee agency near Calhoun on 11 October 1838, disbanding at Vinyard Post Office (present-day Evansville, Arkansas) on 7 January 1839. This detachment travelled 1,138 km (707 miles) overland via Memphis and Little Rock.

The remaining 13 detachments, averaging 1,000 people in each, were under the supervision of John Ross; all had Cherokee conductors. Of these, 12 went overland and one, consisting primarily of the aged and invalids, journeyed by water. One of the land detachments, conducted by John Benge, started near Fort Payne, Alabama, crossed the Tennessee River at Gunter's Landing, crossed again at Reynoldsburg, Tennessee, crossed the Mississippi River at the Iron Banks, near Columbia, Kentucky, took the military road into Arkansas, then travelled up the White River, stopping at Fayetteville before entering the Indian Territory on a journey of more than 1,236 km (768 miles). The other 11 began the journey in East Tennessee and travelled the preferred route via Nashville, Golconda and Springfield – approximately 1,610 km (1,000 miles).

Different detachments of Cherokees travelled by water and overland by various routes on their forced removal from their homeland.

A story of survival

After the forced march during an extremely severe winter, the detachments arrived in the Indian Territory in the first few months of 1839. It has been estimated that between 2,000 and 4,000 Cherokees died as a result of the journey and the oppression surrounding it. For the Cherokee people themselves, the true story of the forced removal is one of survival. In spite of their hardships, they adapted and rebuilt their homes and government. Today, the Cherokee Nation, centred in 14 counties of northeastern Oklahoma with its capital at Tahlequah, is thriving – more numerous and more prosperous than at any time in its history.

MICHAEL D. COE

Journeys into the Mexican Jungle

1839–40

Of the moral effect of the monuments themselves, standing as they do in the depths of a tropical rainforest, silent and solemn, strange in design, excellent in sculpture, rich in ornament, different from the works of any other people, their uses and their purposes, their whole history so entirely unknown, with hieroglyphics explaining all, but perfectly unintelligible, I shall not pretend to convey any idea.

JOHN LLOYD STEPHENS, 1841

Maya archaeology began on 3 October 1839, when the brig *Mary Ann* sailed out of New York harbour, bound for Belize, the British Empire's remote Central American colony. Aboard were the 33-year old American lawyer and diplomat John Lloyd Stephens, and the English architect and topographical artist Frederick Catherwood, six years older than Stephens. Already a seasoned traveller, Stephens' published accounts of his journeys to Arabia Petraea, Egypt and the Holy Land, and subsequently to Greece, Russia and Poland, had met with huge popular and critical success. The classically trained Catherwood had drawn ruins on many trips to the Mediterranean, the Levant and Egypt. The two had met in London in 1835 and had become friends; both were superbly prepared for their first journey to the land of the Maya.

A portrait of John Lloyd Stephens (by an unknown artist): Stephens was a lawyer and diplomat, but also a dedicated explorer and traveller.

The ostensible reason for this voyage was diplomatic: Stephens had been commissioned by US president Martin Van Buren to find a legitimate head of government in war-torn Central America, then in a state of total chaos, and to present his credentials to this figure. But Stephens had additional plans of his own. While in London he had read a report by a Spanish-Irish captain of dragoons named Juan Galindo on an ancient city called 'Palenque' in Chiapas (Mexico); this had been published in 1822 and illustrated with somewhat inaccurate engravings by the colourful Frenchman Jean Frédéric Waldeck. Stephens also knew about Galindo's later exploration of another ruined city in Honduras named 'Copán'. Having earned the then-enormous sum of $15,000 from the royalties on his *Arabia Petraea* travel book, he had ample funds to explore, with Catherwood, the strange places described by Galindo.

Into the Maya jungle

After a brief stopover in Belize, the two men went by a small steamboat up Guatemala's narrow Río Dulce, while above them rose on both sides 'a

On their expeditions into the Mexican jungle Catherwood and Stephens often had to negotiate dangerous and difficult trails with their mules.

wall of living green ... a fairy scene of Titan land, combining exquisite beauty with colossal grandeur'. From there they passed by horrendously difficult trails over high mountains down into the valley of the Río Motagua. Proceeding on muleback (and cursed with a surly, offensive muleteer), they finally reached Copán after a series of delays, including their temporary detention by a band of armed insurgents.

The ruins of this great Classic Maya city were completely shrouded in dense tropical forest, inhabited only by troupes of monkeys that chattered overhead. Taken by a local guide wielding a machete, they uncovered monument after monument, that 'gave us the assurance that the objects we were in search of were interesting, not only as the remains of an unknown people, but as works of art, proving, like newly discovered historical records that the people who once occupied the Continent of America were not savages.' This being the season of heavy rains, the overlying forest could not be cut down and burned, so they cleared their way by machete from one spot to another.

With the aid of his *camera lucida*, Catherwood began to draw the numerous standing stone stelae, 'altars' and various fallen monuments, beset by so many mosquitoes that he was forced to work with gloved hands. At first he found the style of the monuments and the writing on them alien and bewildering, but by trial and error he at last began to comprehend the baroque, involved nature of Maya art. In their fidelity, his renderings comprise the first accurate visual records ever made of Maya antiquities. At the same time, he and Stephens prepared a map of the ruins by theodolite and tape. During their stay in the area, the two explorers had to cope with the unrelenting hostility of an ignorant local tyrant who lorded it over a miserable village of six huts, and they ended up by buying the entire ancient city for the grand sum of $50.

After 13 days in Copán, Stephens left for Guatemala City on a hunt for his elusive head of

government. Catherwood stayed on to complete his drawings; once he had finished, he returned over the mountains to the lower valley of the Motagua, and there he discovered the small Classic city of Quiriguá, a site distinguished by the enormous height and magnificence of its sandstone stelae. In the meantime, Stephens had been granted an interview with the man who was to be the long-time dictator of Guatemala, Rafael Carrera, but who had not yet assumed total power. This led Stephens on a search for the real president, Carrera's enemy, General Francisco Morazán, who had fled to Costa Rica. His successful quest took Stephens by boat to Costa Rica and back to Guatemala.

Palenque

Stephens and Catherwood were now free to pursue their ultimate goal, an exploration of Palenque, in the Mexican state of Chiapas. Crossing the highlands of Guatemala, they briefly explored the ruins of cities that had been laid

Above *View of the cracked and fallen Stela C at Copán in a storm, from a lithograph by Catherwood, published in 1844.*

Left *Drawing of Stela N at Copán. Catherwood's drawings of such monuments were the first accurate visual records ever made of Maya antiquities.*

The palace at Palenque today: Catherwood and Stephens set up an uncomfortable camp inside the ruins while they explored them.

waste by the Spaniards, down past the Classic city of Toniná in Chiapas, and to Palenque itself. Accompanied by a young expatriate American named Henry Pawling, they spent most of the month of May 1840 in that most beautiful of Maya sites, located in the foothills of the Sierra de Chiapas, overlooking the broad Gulf Coast plains.

At Palenque they set up their sleeping quarters in one of the corbel-arched corridors of the Palace, but they were far from comfortable. On beds of sticks set on stones, they were beset by hordes of mosquitoes which 'were beyond all endurance; the slightest part of the body, the tip end of a finger, exposed, was bitten. With heads covered the heat was suffocating, and in the morning our faces were all in blotches'. Every day the local Chol Maya Indians came from the nearby villages with tortillas and other provisions.

In the ruins they rediscovered the delicate carved panels, stucco reliefs and airy architecture that that had been seen by a few earlier travellers (such as Galindo), but Catherwood's magnificent views far surpassed anything that had been done by less competent artists. Previous versions of the art and hieroglyphic texts had been crude, or in the case of those of Waldeck (trained in the studio of David), fanciful and misleading. The two explorers were enormously impressed with Palenque, in spite of the heat and insects, and they recreated in their minds the lives of the people who would have lived there.

For the last leg of their first journey into the Maya jungle, the two left by sailing vessel from the fishing village of Carmen to Sisal, then the main port of Yucatán, concluding their expedition with a visit to Uxmal, the splendid Terminal Classic site to the south of Mérida, the Yucatecan capital. Having braved the dangers of the road, revolutions and recurring fevers and other maladies, Catherwood now fell seriously ill. This left no recourse but to return to America; they left the Maya area for New York on 24 June 1840. They vowed to return as soon as possible to complete their exploration. They fulfilled this vow the following year, concentrating on the Yucatán peninsula, including its sites of Uxmal, Tulum and the great city of Chichén Itzá.

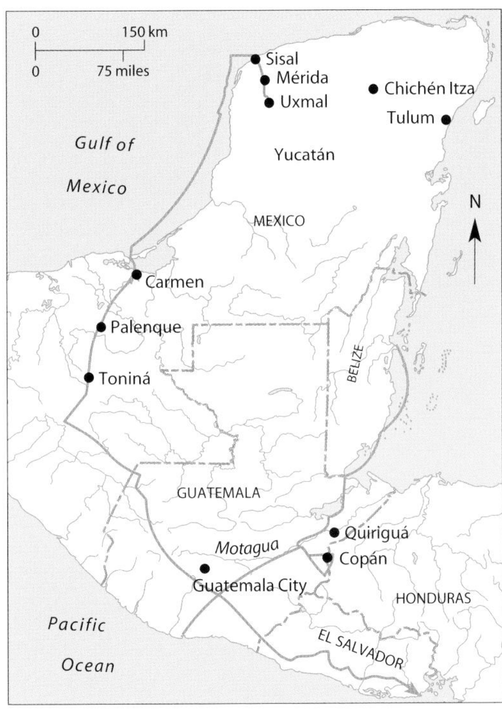

On their first journey in Central America, Catherwood and Stephens spent some time at Copán, buying the entire ancient city for $50. They then went on to visit several other Maya sites, notably Palenque.

Founders of Maya archaeology

On his homecoming, Stephens immediately got to work on an account of the wonders they had seen, and his two-volume *Incidents of Travel in Central America, Chiapas, and Yucatan* was published in May 1841 (his *Incidents of Travel in Yucatan* was published in 1843). Fully and beautifully illustrated by engraved reproductions of Catherwood's drawings, it was an instant best-seller. For the very first time the reading public, and the world of scholarship, could see that a great civilization had flourished in the Central American jungles, and they could read about it in the unpretentious, commonsensical, slightly ironic prose of one of history's greatest travel writers. Stephens had made it abundantly clear that Copán and Palenque were created not by emigrants from Palestine, or any other Old World place, but by the ancestors of the living Maya.

Small wonder that all Mayanists consider Stephens and Catherwood to be the founding fathers of Maya scholarship.

A view of Uxmal, a Maya site in the Yucatán peninsula that Catherwood and Stephens visited at the end of their first voyage, and explored more fully during their second.

ANN SAVOURS

46 Later Searchers for the Northwest Passage

1845–48

I have an excellent set of officers and men who have embarked with the best spirit in the cause. It will be my study to keep them united and happy, and to encourage them while they put forth their own strenuous endeavours, to commit the issue of their safety to God.

LETTER FROM SIR JOHN FRANKLIN, 7 JULY 1845, HMS *EREBUS*

By the time the two ships *Erebus* and *Terror* departed in 1845 on the last of the naval expeditions to seek the elusive Northwest Passage, this blank space on globes and charts had shrunk considerably. Following the earlier searches by men such as Frobisher, Davis, Hudson and Baffin (p. 123), the year 1670 saw the foundation by royal charter of a northern fur trading company – the Hudson's Bay Company. The company acquired a large part of what is now modern Canada, establishing posts or 'factories' on the coast of Hudson Bay and subsequently along the great northern rivers and through the Rocky Mountains.

In 1744, the British government offered a substantial amount of money to whoever discovered the Northwest Passage, but a hundred years later it was still unclaimed. The journeys of Samuel Hearne and Alexander MacKenzie (p. 152) down the northern rivers to the Arctic Ocean, and Captain Cook's and Vancouver's voyages, demonstrated that no sea route between the Atlantic and Pacific oceans could exist in temperate latitudes. The search had to be pursued further north.

In the 19th century, whalers operating in Davis Strait and beyond were a presence varying with the extent of the sea ice during the Arctic summer. It was also during the 19th century that the fur-trading companies in the persons of Messrs Dease and Simpson and Dr John Rae added substantial pieces to the jigsaw of the Canadian Arctic archipelago, thus contributing to the charting of the Northwest Passage.

Parry and Franklin

After the end of the Napoleonic wars with France in 1815, which left Great Britain supreme at sea, the Admiralty despatched a number of ships in different years to resume the search. The most notable expeditions were commanded by William Edward Parry. His vessels sailed beyond 110° West along the great channel later named after him, which divides the Canadian Arctic islands, thus qualifying for a huge official award.

An engraved portrait of Franklin by F. C. Lewis, with a compass and a theodolite. It appeared in Franklin's Narrative of a Journey to the Shores of the Polar Sea, *published in 1823.*

Birch bark canoes buffeted by a strong wind and a heavy sea while making a dangerous traverse along the north coast of America on 23 August 1821; a plate from Franklin's Narrative of a Journey to the Shores of the Polar Sea.

Besides accomplishing a great deal in charting the complicated geography and in scientific observations, Parry organized the first successful wintering in the ice, keeping boredom and depression at bay during the sunless months.

These sea-borne expeditions were complemented by two overland journeys, in 1819–21 and 1825–27, across northern Canada to the 'Canadian shores of the Polar Sea', by the naval officer John Franklin. Consisting of a small number of officers and men, accompanied by Indians, Voyageurs and Esquimaux interpreters, these surveyed much of the northern coastline of North America, though the first expedition almost ended in tragedy.

As a very young man Franklin had taken part in Matthew Flinders' voyage to chart Australia, and he later commanded HMS *Trent* during an attempt to sail to the North Pole. Although nearly 59 years old in 1845, he was thus well qualified to lead what was expected to be a successful voyage to discover a sea route linking the Parry Channel with the north coast of America.

In the event, it proved to be the last of the British naval Northwest Passage expeditions. Franklin's ships, *Erebus* and *Terror*, last seen by whalers off Greenland, disappeared into what we now know is the ice-bound maze of the Canadian Arctic archipelago.

The disappearance of the Franklin expedition was all the more surprising because it had been well prepared and provisioned. The ships, fitted for the first time with auxiliary engines, also had their bows reinforced with sheet iron to protect them from the ice. Sufficient supplies and equipment were taken to last those on board the two ships for three years.

The search for Franklin

When it was realized that these two well-built and ice-strengthened ships had not emerged triumphantly into the North Pacific at the western exit from the Passage, numerous official and private expeditions searched for them from 1848 to 1855, all in vain. Among them was that of Robert McClure, in HMS *Investigator*. Travelling both by ship and by sledge, McClure in fact connected the western and eastern entrances of the Northwest Passage. He, his officers and men were given another huge Parliamentary award for this and credited with its discovery.

A further Parliamentary award was made to Dr John Rae, a chief factor of the Hudson's Bay Company and his men, for discovering the first news of the fate of Sir John Franklin. In 1854 this skilled and determined Orkneyman and Arctic traveller brought to London some relics of the lost expedition, obtained from the Inuit (Eskimos). These people described how a party of hungry white men had been encountered travelling southwards over the ice, and how, later that season, some 30 bodies were discovered on the mainland, some buried, some in a tent and others under a boat.

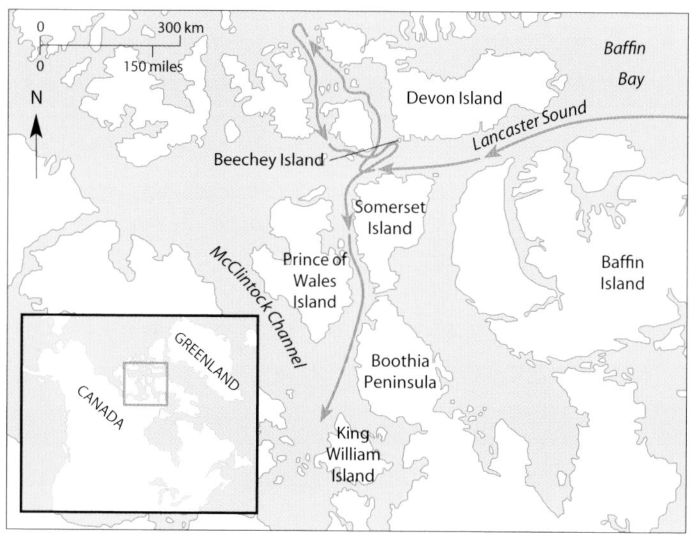

The final route of Erebus *and* Terror *was pieced together from evidence found later. After overwintering on Beechey Island, the ships were later beset by ice and finally abandoned off King William Island.*

'From the mutilated state of many of the corpses, and the contents of the kettles', reported Rae to the Admiralty, 'it is evident that our wretched countrymen had been driven to the last resource – cannibalism – as a means of prolonging existence.' These words created a sensation, even a furore, when published by the Admiralty in *The Times*.

Franklin's widow, Jane, was determined to find out more about the fate of the lost expedition, and in 1857 she and various well-wishers funded a search led by Leopold McClintock in the yacht *Fox*. Only two single-page written records were found in cairns, together with a boat, clothing and other items, on the bleak west coast of King William Island. In a few short lines, these related the tragic story of Franklin's expedition.

Erebus and *Terror* had wintered (as the search expeditions had already ascertained) at Beechey Island from 1845 to 1846. Later in that year the ships had been trapped in ice, and Franklin had died on 11 June 1847. The ships were finally abandoned on 22 April 1848, 'beset since 12th Sept 1846'. The loss of men at that date was recorded as nine officers and 15 men. The remaining officers and crews, 105 in all, were about to depart southwards for Back's Great Fish River (on the North American mainland).

The other record, written the year before, on 24 May 1847, reported 'All well'. The party of two officers and six men then said to have left the ships on that date were almost certainly the first to traverse another Northwest Passage, connecting King William Island (off which the ships were later abandoned) with the mainland to the south. In the belief of the valiant Lady Franklin

'Beechey Island: Franklin's first winter quarters', as discovered by the search expeditions of 1850 to 1851 and drawn by James Hamilton from the sketch by Dr Kane, surgeon of the first US Grinnell *expedition; the plate is from E. K. Kane's* Personal Narrative.

Left *Artist's impression of HMS* Erebus *and HMS* Terror *beset in the ice off King William Island, Canadian Arctic; from Sherard Osborn's article in* Once a Week, *October 1859.*

and in the words of Sir John Richardson, they and their starving shipmates 'forged the last link with their lives'.

The rest of the tragic story has been told from the skeletons, clothing and relics discovered by later travellers, such as C. F. Hall and Frederick Schwatka. The recollections of the Inuit as to the deaths of the officers and men have added pieces to what is still to some extent a mystery – the ships have never been located, and there are theories to this day about the causes of the tragedy. Scurvy, starvation and the relentless grip of the sea ice on the ships seem the most likely.

There are in fact eight possible Northwest Passages, navigable or not according to the thickness of the sea ice and the vessel concerned. Roald Amundsen was the first to sail through the Passage, in *Gjøa*, at the beginning of the 20th century. The wide western sea route across the top of the world to the Far East, so ardently sought in earlier centuries, has never been a viable alternative to the Panama Canal. Should global warming cause the ice to melt, shall we see the development of the international northern sea route, envisaged by Sir John Barrow of the Admiralty, in the early 19th century?

Below *The last record of Franklin's 1845–48 voyage: messages written a year apart on a multilingual form solved some of the mysteries of the lost expedition.*

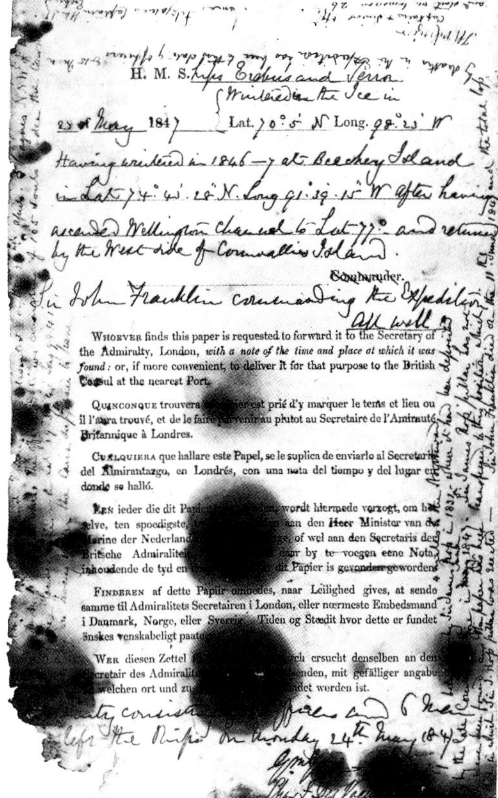

H. M. Ships Erebus and Terror
Wintered in the Ice in
28 of May 1847 Lat. 70°5' N Long. 98°23' W
Having wintered in 1846–7 at Beechey Island
in Lat 74°43'.28" N. Long 91°39'.15" W After having
ascended Wellington Channel to Lat 77° and returned
by the West side of Cornwallis Island.
Commander.
Sir John Franklin commanding the Expedition
All well

Whoever finds this paper is requested to forward it to the Secretary of the Admiralty, London, *with a note of the time and place at which it was found:* or, if more convenient, to deliver it for that purpose to the British Consul at the nearest Port.

Quinconque trouvera ... est prié d'y marquer le tems et lieu ou il l'aura trouvé, et de le faire parvenir au plutot au Secretaire de l'Amirauté Britannique à Londres.

Cualquiera que hallare este Papel, se le suplica de enviarlo al Secretario del Almirantazgo, en Londrés, con una nota del tiempo y del lugar en donde se halló.

Een ieder die dit Papier ... wordt hiermede verzogt, om het zelve, ten spoedigste, ... aan den Heer Minister van der Marine der Nederlanden ... of wel aan den Secretaris der Britsche Admiraliteit ... daar by te voegen eene Nota, inhoudende de tyd en ... dit Papier is gevonden geworden.

Finderen af dette Papir ombedes, naar Leilighed gives, at sende samme til Admiralitets Secretairen i London, eller nærmeste Embedsmand i Danmark, Norge, eller Sverrig. Tiden og Stædit hvor dette er fundet ønskes venskabeligt paateg...

Wer diesen Zettel ... ersucht denselben an den Secretair des Admiralit... senden, mit gefälliger angabe ... welchen ort und zu... det worden ist.

Party consisting of 2 Officers and 6 Men
left the Ships on Monday 24th May 1847
Gm. Gore
Chas. F. Des Voeux

Below *An Inuit snow knife, collected by McClintock from the Boothia Peninsula – he believed it to have been made from wood and metal abandoned by the Franklin expedition.*

JAMIE BRUCE LOCKHART

47 Heinrich Barth & the Central African Mission

1849–55

Lonely and companionless in these regions ... [but] nevertheless in good health and best spirits ... I have full confidence in my safe return and in my being able to lay the proceedings of this expedition in an elaborated form before the public.

HEINRICH BARTH, 26 SEPTEMBER 1852

Heinrich Barth was highly suited to exploration. Born in 1821, his upbringing in cosmopolitan Hamburg and a strict Lutheran family environment had instilled an interest in far away places and a strong sense of purpose. As a youth he learnt many foreign languages and trained himself to withstand physical hardship. Following post-graduate studies in Berlin, he undertook a two-year journey to review the culture and history of the countries of the Mediterranean basin. Barth thrived on intellectual stimulation, but found academic life tedious. The British discovered a ready recruit for their new mission.

Portrait of Heinrich Barth, appointed by the British to take part in the Central African Mission.

The Central African Mission

The aims proposed for the Central African Mission by James Richardson, its appointed leader, following initial reconnaissance of the hinterland of Tunis and Tripoli, were abolitionist and commercial. In addition, the British government required a geographical and scientific inventory of the central Sahara and Sudan (in Arabic: *bilad as-Sudan*, 'land of the blacks').

Barth's African journey would cover 16,000 km (10,000 miles), completing the work of previous European expeditions. Mungo Park (p. 155) had seen little of the Middle Niger region; Gordon Laing's information on Timbuktu hadn't reached home after his death; and Réné Caillié (see box, p. 192) spent just two weeks there. The trail blazed in Sudan in the 1820s had yet to be consolidated, and attempts to ascend the River Niger from the coast in the 1830s and 1840s had failed to penetrate very far inland.

Five years in the Sahara and Sudan

Richardson, Barth and Adolf Overweg, their 25-year-old assistant, left Tripoli (in Libya) in July 1849, travelling through western Fezzan and around the Ténéré to Aïr. Here Barth detoured to

'Songhay village', a colour plate from Barth's account of his journeys, the English title of which was Travels and Discoveries.

Agadez before the mission headed for Hausaland with a salt caravan. The extortionate demands of desert freebooters having exhausted their supply of trade goods, the three explorers parted company, planning to meet in Kukawa, capital of Borno, the following April. On arrival there, finding that Richardson had died on the journey, Barth took command; leaving Overweg to explore Lake Chad by boat, he set out to investigate the country to the south and east.

An expedition to the upper reaches of the River Benue confirmed the existence of a navigable water highway into the heart of Sudan; it was a moment of great personal satisfaction and of considerable significance for British policy. An attempt to explore to the east of Lake Chad had to be aborted in the lawless state of northern Kanem; but Barth's second sortie south of the lake constituted another important milestone in geographical discovery. A journey to the upper Logon river in the train of a military expedition – from whose brutal slave raids he did his best to dissociate himself – identified the watershed dividing the Niger and Lake Chad basins and established that the mountains of Mandara were not connected to the highlands of central Africa but were bordered to the east by a region of fertile plains.

Barth's third attempt to travel south was curtailed when he was detained in the state of Bagirmi on suspicion of espionage; he nevertheless obtained a wealth of information about this country, then unknown to Europeans. And while there he received long-awaited mail from England: plaudits for his valuable despatches, a much-needed supply of funds and orders requiring him to make for Timbuktu.

When Overweg died in Borno that summer, Barth headed west alone. He spent six months in the heartland of the Caliphate of Sokoto before

RÉNÉ CAILLIÉ AND TIMBUKTU

European fascination with Timbuktu (in Mali) originated in reports from medieval Arab travellers of the city's fabulous wealth and its reputation as a centre of learning. The legend was enhanced by the arrival in Cairo in 1350 of King Mansa Musa of Mali (p. 68) with so much gold that the commodity's price on the Mediterranean markets remained depressed for a decade. By the turn of the 19th century, public attention in Europe was focused on the geographical and commercial aspects of the fabled city's central position in the populous Middle Niger region. But Réné Caillié (1799–1838), the impecunious son of a Breton baker, just wanted to see Timbuktu for himself. He first journeyed to Africa at the age of 16 and spent a decade attempting to turn boyhood dreams of adventure into reality, making expeditions into the interior as opportunity arose. Ill health forced a temporary retreat, but in 1824 he returned to the west coast to try again.

Caillié taught himself Arabic and studied Islam in order to travel alone, posing as an Alexandrine captured by the French who was seeking to return home across the desert. The announcement of a 10,000-franc prize from the Geographical Society of Paris for the first European to reach Timbuktu provided added stimulus. Caillié set off inland from the River Nunez in April 1827.

He travelled in company with a handful of petty merchants to Kankan on the upper reaches of the Niger, where severe scurvy forced him to halt for five months before he continued east with a trade caravan to Djenné. In July 1828 he boarded a boat transporting kola nut traders down the Niger to Timbuktu, and six weeks later reached the city of his dreams.

He was disappointed, however, to find no grandeur or wealth, and to learn that Gordon Laing had arrived there two years before him. Despite the risks to his disguise, Caillié thoroughly explored the city, even attempting to ascertain the fate of the British explorer; but Timbuktu was in a state of unrest and Arab acquaintances urged him to leave. Two weeks after arrival, he joined a caravan of 1,200 camels taking slaves, gold and ivory to Morocco. Enduring considerable privations on the 3,220-km (2,000-mile) journey across the western desert, Caillié eventually reached Tangier.

On his return to France in September 1829, though he impressed the Geographical Society, not everyone believed Caillié's account. It was only after the British press (at a time of mounting Anglo-French rivalry) called his claims into question that Caillié received due credit at home. Created a chevalier of the Légion d'Honneur, he was awarded a gold medal and a pension.

Caillié's absorbing record reveals that he journeyed for purely personal reasons. His adventure had no scientific, evangelical or imperial purpose, but it was influential in the rise of French interest in the western Sahara and Sudan.

The lone traveller died in relative obscurity aged 39, saddened by the doubts cast on an extraordinary achievement.

'Mr Caillié meditating upon the Koran and taking notes'. Caillié taught himself Arabic and wore local costume.

Drawing of Timbuktu by Caillié.

crossing the Niger at Say to travel through Songhay to the Niger Bend. On arrival in Timbuktu in September 1853, however, he found the country in the throes of a Fulani *jihad* against Arab and Tuareg communities. Though, as a foreigner and Christian, Barth's own life was in danger, for six months he carried out his customary intensive researches under the protection of an influential Arab Sheikh, before being forced to seek shelter at his protector's camp outside the capital. It was another two months before he could safely slip away to travel alongside the Niger back to the Sokoto Caliphate and Borno.

'Entering Timbuktu', from Barth's account of his travels. This city in Mali had long fascinated Europeans; when Barth arrived the country was in turmoil and his life was in danger, but he stayed for six months to carry out his researches.

Meanwhile, in London, Barth had been given up for dead, his previous year's despatches having failed to arrive. Thus, in December 1854 on the road to Borno, he was astonished to meet Eduard Vogel, the leader of a mission to find him or discover his fate. Vogel himself embarked on further expeditions but, after five years' privation in Sudan, Barth was ready to return home. He joined a caravan bound for Fezzan, reaching Tripoli on 28 August 1855.

Personal achievement

Carrying his compass, watch and two pistols in his belt at all times, Barth was completely self-reliant and happiest travelling alone. He managed political difficulties, episodes of illness and constant

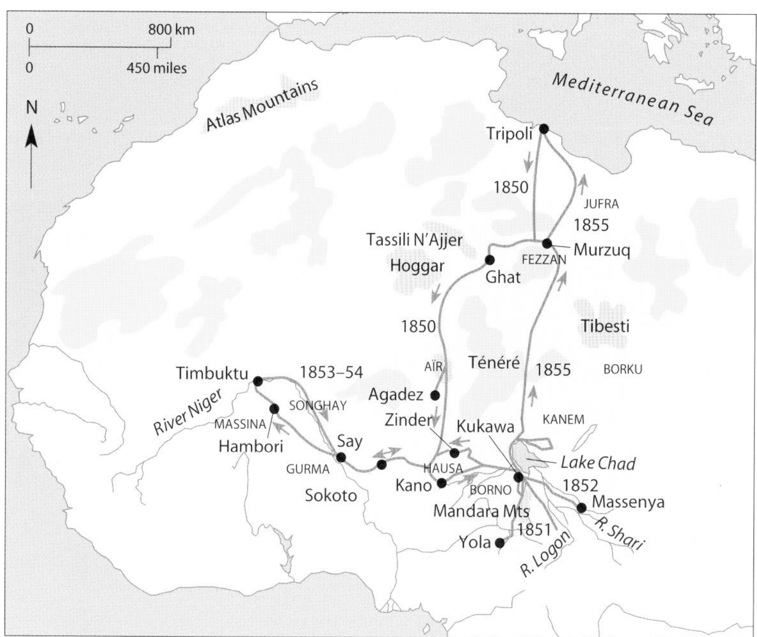

Map showing Barth's journey from Tripoli to Lake Chad and then to Timbuktu and back. The information he gathered is still of use to scholars today.

financial embarrassment with patience and skill, determined to complete a comprehensive account of the geography, history and politics, ethnography and languages of each country he visited. He interrogated everyone – his own employees, passers-by, pilgrims, travelling scholars, local officials and desert nomads – usually in their own language. (He became fluent in five African languages and drew up word lists of another half dozen.)

British engagement in the country which became Nigeria and withdrawal from the Sahara were direct results of the findings of the Central African Mission; and scholars of pre-colonial Sahara and Sudan still bow to Barth's comprehensive insights.

Public acclaim

In London, though applauded by the government, Barth's work received limited public acclaim. His researches were eclipsed by the discoveries of Burton (p. 195) and Livingstone (p. 203); and there was some displeasure in scientific circles that German geographers had been the first recipients of his reports. Commuting between Berlin and Hampstead, north London, Barth wrote up a five-volume narrative of his travels (in both English and German).

He was, however, a disappointed man. Though later officially honoured in both countries, he became increasingly introspective, longing only 'for a night camp in the desert, that immeasurable open space, without ambition and without cares for the thousand little things that torture men here; and for the utter enjoyment of the freedom that comes at the end of a day's march, stretched out on my mat, with my belongings, my camels and my horse around me.'

The mudbrick mosque in Agadez, Niger: Barth made a sketch of the same mosque.

CHRISTOPHER ONDAATJE

Search for the Source of the Nile

48

1857–63

18 July. Here at last I stood on the brink of the Nile; most beautiful was the scene, nothing could surpass it! ... a magnificent stream from 600 to 700 yards wide, dotted with islets and rocks ... flowing between fine high grassy banks, with rich trees and plantains in the background.

JOHN HANNING SPEKE, 1863

Richard Burton's search for the source of the Nile with John Hanning Speke contributed to his being the best-known traveller of the 19th century. Burton was an outstanding orientalist, archaeologist, linguist, anthropologist and a controversial diplomat. He wrote over 50 books covering an amazing diversity of subjects, and his translation of the Arabian Nights remains the most famous ever published. The startling drama of Richard Burton's existence continued after his death. His remaining papers were burnt by his widow, perhaps one of the most destructive crimes ever perpetrated on the literary world.

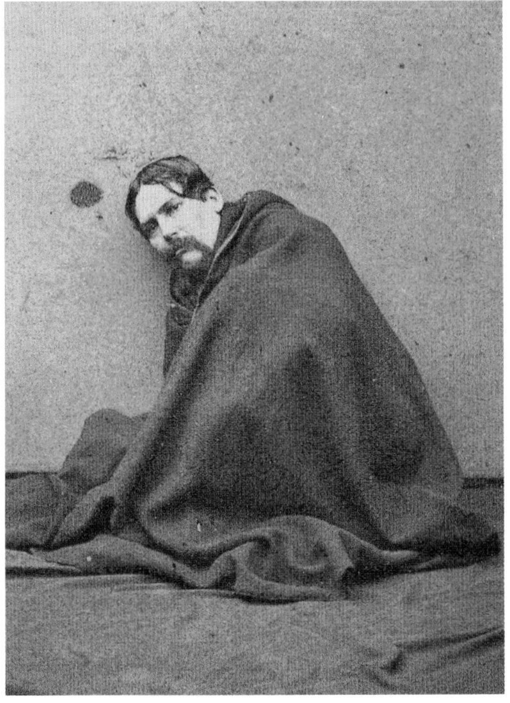

Captain Richard F. Burton, wrapped in a blanket after pilgrimage to Mecca, around 1855 – before his journey with Speke in search of the source of the Nile.

Two Niles

The Nile is the world's longest river, stretching for 6,695 km (4,160 miles). The fact that it flowed through a desert, and that it flooded annually, fascinated people. The single river that flows from Khartoum into the Mediterranean Sea combines the waters from two rivers: the Blue Nile, which rises in Ethiopia, and the White Nile, which rises in the lake region of Central Africa. The Blue Nile, the Nile's main tributary, is a shorter, less complicated river, and was first explored by Francisco Alvarez and Pedro Paez in the 16th and 17th centuries, and later by James Bruce in the late 1760s (p. 140). The White Nile, however, was still regarded as a great mystery. Where did all this water come from? Europeans still knew little about Africa. In the early 19th century, missionaries arrived; then came explorers who paved the way for colonization until, 100 years later, the enormous continent was ruled by European powers.

In the 1850s Great Britain, seeking tighter control over the east coast of Africa and increasing its interest in the exploration of Central Africa, encouraged the Royal Geographical Society to sponsor an expedition to search for the source of the Nile. They chose Richard Burton and John Hanning Speke, two officers in the Indian Army, to lead the journey, and on 16 June 1857 the two men set out from Zanzibar.

Below
'Navigation of the Tanganyika Lake' from The Lake Regions of Central Africa, *by Burton. Burton and Speke were the first Europeans to reach Lake Tanganyika but were disappointed to discover that it was not the source of the White Nile.*

Opposite left
Portrait of Speke by James Watney Wilson. Speke was the discoverer of Lake Victoria, one of the Nile's two great reservoirs.

Learning from Arab caravans, the two explorers recruited over 200 porters, as well as an armed escort of 30 men and an Arab guide. However, the financial backing of the Royal Geographical Society proved woefully inadequate to pay the men. There were arguments and desertions, but after 134 tortuous days in appalling conditions the party reached Kazeh – a key meeting centre of the Arab slave and ivory route.

The two explorers and their intrepid band crossed desert, marshes and mountains, and were afflicted with malaria, sickness and exhaustion. For much of their journey they were carried on litters. The expedition continued west, and on 13 February 1858 the two men finally reached the eastern shores of Lake Tanganyika. They were the first Europeans to set eyes on it; though Speke, suffering from ophthalmia, is unlikely to have seen this first glimpse of the mighty lake. Burton, luckier in this respect, was almost totally paralysed and still had to be carried. Nevertheless, the two explored the northern end of Lake Tanganyika in dugout canoes, discovering that part of the lake was surrounded by a circle of densely vegetated mountains and that the Ruzizi River flowed into rather than out of the lake. Disappointed, they realized that Lake Tanganyika could not be the source of the White Nile. Surviving a hazardous lake storm, they recuperated in Ujiji for nearly three months, after which they continued their journey north and east and arrived again at Kazeh.

There, left to regain his health, Burton mistakenly allowed Speke to lead a small expedition north from Kazeh (now Tabora), which changed history. On 3 August 1858, Speke reached the summit of Isamiro hill near present-day Mwanza and wrote 'I no longer felt any doubt that the lake

at my feet gave birth to that interesting river [the Nile], the source of which has been the subject of so much speculation, and the object of so many explorers.'

He christened this lake Victoria, in honour of his queen, returned to Kazeh and arrogantly proclaimed that he had found the source of the Nile. Burton, still clinging to the hope that Lake Tanganyika might possibly be the true source of the Nile, denounced Speke's claim with ridicule. A suggestion by Speke that Burton should return with him to explore the great lake further was also rejected. It was a final terrible mistake by Burton, who threw away his last claim to the discovery of the Nile's source.

The source discovered?

Sick, and in worsening health, the two weary travellers endured a painful four-month journey back

to Zanzibar. Relations between the two now deteriorated significantly. They sailed together to Aden but then parted company. Speke returned to England ahead of Burton, where, ignoring a prior agreement, he announced his discovery and claimed that he alone had discovered the source of the Nile. But was Speke right?

In 1860, flushed with success, and spurred on by adulation, Speke convinced the Royal

A page from Speke's sketchbook with watercolour drawings of the palace of Mtesa, king of Buganda, and a Uganda cow. The king ordered Speke to shoot four cows – which he promptly did.

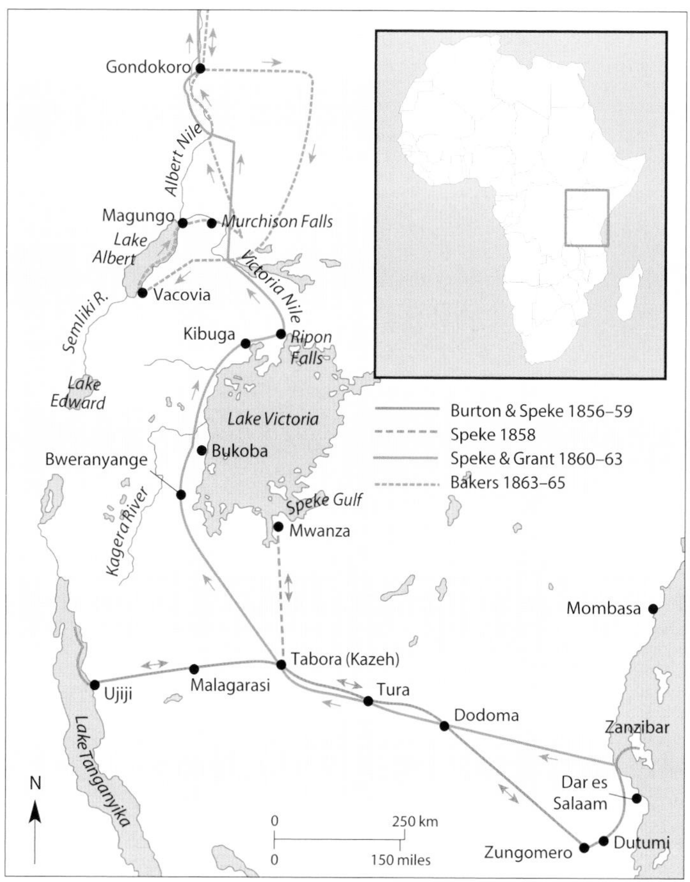

In the mid-19th century the source of the River Nile was still a great mystery. Burton and Speke set out from Zanzibar and first explored Lake Tanganyika, before Speke came upon and named Lake Victoria, which he thought was the only source. In reality the situation is more complex.

Geographical Society to sponsor him on a second expedition to verify his discovery. Speke chose James Augustus Grant, another Indian Army officer, to accompany him. Again setting out from Zanzibar in 1860, Speke and Grant travelled westwards through Kazeh (clockwise) around Lake Victoria to the northeast corner. Here, at a spot he named Ripon Falls, Speke confirmed that Lake Victoria did indeed give birth to the Victoria Nile River. Although accepted by the Royal Geographical Society, Speke's claim was eventually found to be a gross overstatement. His discovery solved only part of the riddle. The Kagera River which fed Lake Victoria had yet to be explored.

Anxious to return to a jubilant England from Gondokoro in 1863, Speke then tipped off another RGS sponsored explorer, Samuel Baker, and his young companion Florence von Sass (whom he had recently bought out of a slave market in Turkey) that there were rumours of yet another great lake – the Luta Nzige – further west. Enduring incredible hardships, and virtual imprisonment by the ruler of Bunyoro, the Bakers eventually reached the shores of a second great lake that they named Albert, after Queen Victoria's husband. Baker rightfully claimed his discovery to be a second source of the Nile, but failed to realize that Lake Albert, like Lake Victoria, was only a second great reservoir and that it was in turn fed by the important Semliki River which drained the Ruwenzori Mountains – the famed Mountains of the Moon.

Speke, on his return to England, was both fêted and questioned, and eventually challenged to a debate on the Nile's source with his former leader, Richard Burton, in Bath in September 1864. Tragically, on the afternoon before the debate, Speke killed himself in a shooting accident which many suspected to be suicide.

The riddle of the Nile

Over millions of years, rift valleys formed in Africa as land sank between parallel geological faults, pushing the edges up into escarpments. Lakes formed in the bottom of the rift valleys, collecting the waters that previously drained away to the west. The rifts also formed a shallow bowl around today's Lake Victoria. Rivers that had flowed west, notably the Katonga and the Kagera, now flowed east, filling the depression. Then, only about 12,500 years ago, the waters of Lake Victoria found a low point at the northern edge of the basin and finally established, at Ripon Falls, a permanent outlet down to the western rift valley at the north end of Lake Albert – and a connection to the Nile.

Speke's claim that Lake Victoria is the only source of the Nile is, to say the least, optimistic. It is not. But it is one of the Nile's two great reservoirs – the other being Lake Albert. And the rivers – the Kagera feeding Lake Victoria, and the Semliki feeding Lake Albert – are the two main sources – draining the watershed of the Burundi Highlands and the Ruwenzori Mountains, the Mountains of the Moon. Although he did not solve the puzzle completely, Speke did succeed in unravelling some of the mysteries of this great African river.

JOHN ROSS

Crossing Australia

1860–61

I hope we shall be done justice to. We fulfilled our task, but were not followed up as I expected. The depot party abandoned their post.

R. O'Hara Burke, 29 June 1861

By the middle of the 19th century most of the geographical puzzles of the Australian interior had been resolved by means of slogging exploration, but there still remained a great unknown area in the centre and north. Many lives had been expended in exploring it, including those of expedition leaders Ludwig Leichhardt, somewhere in that northern inland, and Edmund Kennedy, in the jungles of the tropical northeast, both in 1848.

In 1859 a new expedition was being mounted. In the colony of Victoria the rush of wealth from gold made the time ripe for a grand gesture, and what finer project than to be the first to cross Australia from south to north and unlock the secrets of that region? The plan came from the Victoria branch of the Royal Society, but was endorsed by the citizenry, who contributed £9,000 to a funding appeal. Robert O'Hara Burke, a dashing police superintendent, was selected by the Society as leader, with William Landells, commissioned to bring 25 camels and their handlers from Karachi (then in India), as second-in-command.

An official party of 15, with various other travellers, the camels, horses, 20 tonnes of baggage – including 450 litres of lime juice and rum to combat scurvy – left Royal Park, Melbourne, on 20 August 1860, bid farewell by a crowd of 15,000. The Society instructed Burke to establish a camp at Cooper Creek, situated about half way

Below left *A posthumous portrait of Robert O'Hara Burke, by William Strutt (1862). Burke was a Superintendent of Police before his selection, aged 38, for the expedition.*

Below *The expedition in Royal Park, Melbourne, on the eve of departure, 19 August 1860; some 15,000 people came to see them off the next day.*

Above *William John Wills, 26, the expedition surveyor and astronomer, was promoted to second-in-command when Landells resigned after an argument with Burke.*

Opposite above *Burke and Wills reached the mangrove swamps of the north coastal region before turning back. They returned to Cooper Creek and then tried to reach Mount Hopeless.*

between the south and north coasts. From there he should proceed north, making for Leichhardt's track near the Gulf of Carpentaria on the north coast. If his progress became impossible he was to turn westwards and attempt to link up with other explorers' paths to make a safe return.

Trouble started soon enough. Landells resigned after a shouting match over his habit of giving rum to both camels and drivers. Burke promoted William John Wills, a 26-year-old surveyor and astronomer. By October Burke was in Menindee, 650 km (400 miles) from Melbourne. He established a base camp on the Darling River, and pushed on with a party of nine. On 20 November the party camped at Cooper Creek, a series of waterholes in wooded, grassy country.

Burke and Wills each scouted north, but encountered wastelands and searing heat. If they stayed at Cooper Creek over summer they would be safe, but Burke wanted quick glory. He and the committee were aware that John McDouall Stuart was also making an attempt to cross Australia from the south to the north (see box, opposite). The committee had sent a message: 'The honour of Victoria is in your hands'.

A dash for the north

Burke decided to make a dash for the north with three others: Wills, ex-soldier John King and a former seaman, Charlie Gray. They took six camels, Burke's horse Billy and provisions for three months. Left in charge at Cooper Creek was stockman William Brahe, instructed by Burke to wait three months and then take his group back to Menindee.

The party struck north on 16 December, following the waterholes noted by Charles Sturt on his expedition in 1845. They were soon in unknown country, skirting the edge of Sturt's Stony Desert, but finding pockets of pastureland, and creeks and rivers to keep up their water supplies. The route took them past today's settlements of Birdsville, Bedourie and Boulia as they reached the Tropic of Capricorn. They proceeded through land described by Burke in his diary as 'everything green and luxuriant'. But he also wrote, 'the frame of man was never so sorely taxed.'

They passed over stony ground and then found themselves in the stifling humidity of the tropical north. Burke and Wills decided to make a dash for the sea. They floundered through 'soft and rotten' country, until, on 11 February, they

Right *'Portrait of Dick, the brave and gallant native guide, 21 December 1860', by Ludwig Becker. Dick saved two expeditioners who became lost while bringing letters from Menindee to Burke's advance party on its way north to establish the Cooper Creek depot.*

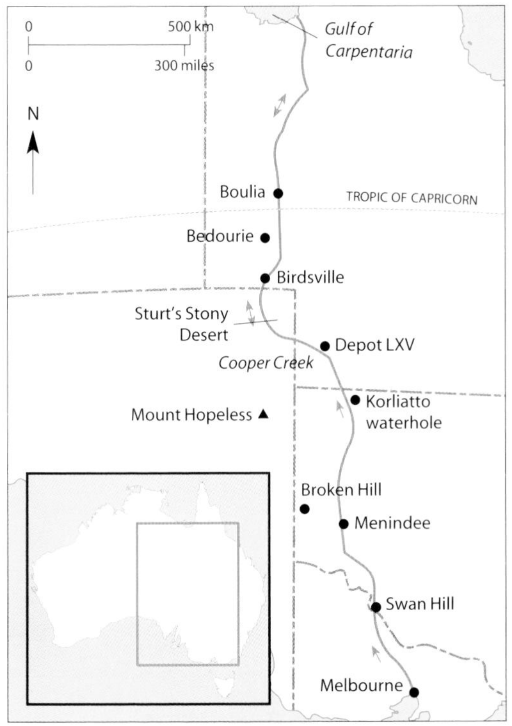

came to a tidal river, salt marshes and mangroves, but could not see open sea. Without a boat, they could go no further.

Without ceremony they turned back to find their companions. Their task was to get back to Cooper Creek before their meagre provisions ran out – and before the three-month deadline expired on 16 March. Trouble came again in the form of storms which made the ground boggy and impassable, then stifling humidity. Wills wrote of 'a helpless feeling of lassitude'.

With the deadline long passed the men were still well short of their goal, and physically spent. Burke discovered Gray pilfering from their supplies and gave him what Wills described as 'a good thrashing'. They were still 500 km (310 miles) from Cooper Creek.

They shot and killed the camel Boocha and ate as much as they could. It was the horse Billy's turn 10 days later and his 'healthy and tender meat' gave them the strength to face the Stony Desert. This crossing proved too much for Gray. He died in his bedroll on 16 April. The survivors made a final effort and arrived at Cooper Creek with the two remaining camels on 21 April with, as Wills wrote,

STUART FINALLY BREAKS THROUGH

When John McDouall Stuart mounted an expedition in 1859, sponsored by the South Australian Government, to cross Australia from south to north, he was well experienced in the trials of exploration – he had been a member of Charles Sturt's expedition of 1844, which had sought to find an inland sea.

Captain Charles Sturt had struck inland in 1827 to discover that the Lachlan and Macquarie rivers ended in swamps. He then went on to the southwest to discover the Darling and Murrumbidgee rivers, and the 'broad and noble' Murray, which flowed to the southern ocean.

In 1844 Sturt was still determined to unlock the mystery of the rivers which flowed inland. His party struck north from Menindee, but became marooned by drought for five months at a permanent waterhole at Depot Glen, north of today's Broken Hill. Rain finally fell and the party ventured north. They came upon the Stony Desert 'as lonely as a ship at sea'. Retreating from this barrier Sturt, unable to walk with scurvy, was wheeled in a cart. His dreams of an inland sea had evaporated.

In his own expedition McDouall Stuart traced a route further west. He left Chambers Creek, north of Adelaide on 2 March 1860, with the aim of making the crossing to the Gulf of Carpentaria on Australia's north coast. By 22 April he had reached, to his reckoning, the geographical centre of Australia, now named Central Mount Stuart. The journey came to an abrupt halt near today's Tennant Creek after his party was attacked and pursued by Aborigines.

Stuart went north again in November 1860, bolstered by £2,500 from the South Australian Government. Finding dry country on his preferred shorter route to the Gulf he kept straight to the north and came across the wide Roper River, named by Leichhardt in 1845. 'I must go where the water leads me', Stuart had written, and that principle guided him to the sea on 24 July 1862.

John McDouall Stuart, photographed on expedition, date unknown.

Above *A photo of the Dig Tree, taken around 1911, with the blaze which carried the vital message visible.*

'legs almost paralysed'. The depot was deserted, but they saw letters cut into a Coolibah tree:

DIG
3FT. N.W.
APR. 21 1861

They found the supplies and the 'pleasing information' that Brahe and his party had left that very morning for Menindee. Brahe, to his credit, had waited four months, rather than three, and his men were ill with scurvy.

A tragic twist of fate

Burke's party was in no condition to try and catch Brahe, however. Resting and taking stock, Burke decided to follow Cooper Creek west and south to make for a police post, Mount Hopeless, 140 km (87 miles) away. They buried a message beneath the 'Dig Tree', advising of their intentions, but in a tragic twist of fate they failed to add a new blaze to the tree itself.

Brahe and the other expeditioners had met up at Korliatto waterhole, 139 km (86 miles) from Cooper Creek, and Brahe was having second thoughts about his departure. He and William Wright made a dramatic dash back to Cooper Creek, but the place seemed undisturbed and they left again.

Burke, Wills and King failed in their attempt to break out, again reaching waterless country, and were left to try and sustain themselves on flour made from the husks of the Nardoo plant, and

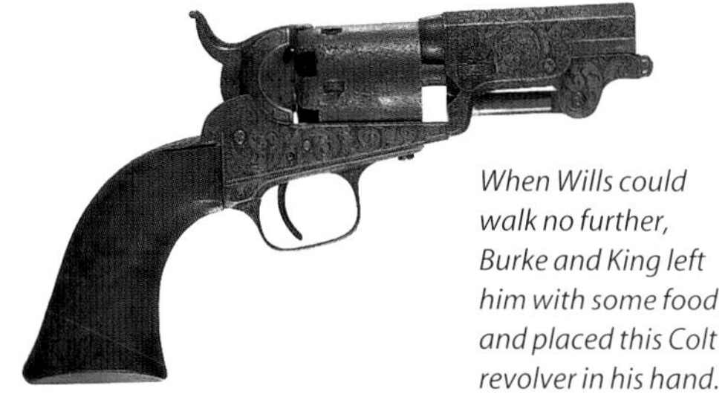

When Wills could walk no further, Burke and King left him with some food and placed this Colt revolver in his hand.

such game as they could catch. Assistance from Aboriginals sustained them until Burke fired his pistol at a pilfering tribesman and the whole tribe vanished.

When Wills could no longer walk, Burke and King left him with some food, but Burke soon succumbed. He scrawled his final bitter note (quoted at the beginning), in his diary on 29 June and died at about 8 a.m. the next day. King wandered on, and was lucky enough to shoot four birds to sustain him. He then lived with Aborigines, who cared for him and fed him well, before a rescue party found him two months later.

The deaths of Burke and Wills caused a sensation in Melbourne, and their state funeral in 1863 attracted a crowd of 40,000 people, the largest assembly in Australia up to that time. A bronze statue was erected and now stands in the City Square, Melbourne. Technically, they had achieved the first crossing of Australia south to north, as the mangrove swamps in which they foundered were tidal, but the 'achievement' was overshadowed by the tragedy and all the acclaim went to John McDouall Stuart.

Below Border of the mud-desert near Desolation Camp, March 9, 1861, *by Ludwig Becker. He died at Menindee from malnutrition and scurvy.*

SIMON WILSON STEPHENS

Into the Heart of Africa

50

1853–56, 1871–72, 1874–77

We came to a ridge and I looked back and watched his grey figure fading dimmer in the distance for a presentiment or suggestion stole in my mind that I was looking for the last time at him. I gulped down my great grief, and turned away to follow the receding caravan.

H. M. Stanley, 14 March 1872

In the early afternoon of 10 November 1871 two of Africa's greatest explorers met for the first time at Ujiji on the shores of Lake Tanganyika. This meeting has been recorded in history as the moment when a little-known Welshman, Henry Morton Stanley, greeted the respected Scottish missionary with the words 'Dr Livingstone, I presume'.

In 1871 David Livingstone was coming to the end of his life as an explorer, having travelled in Africa since 1841. Stanley's career as a journalist and explorer was just beginning. Having found Livingstone, Stanley returned to Britain and was to become a household name. This famous encounter, under the shade of a mango tree in the heart of Africa, could be seen as the moment when the mantle of African exploration was handed from one generation to the next.

Livingstone and Stanley met at a time when Britain was still heavily involved with solving many of Africa's remaining geographical mysteries. The two men spent three months together exploring the northern half of Lake Tanganyika,

A sextant used by David Livingstone on his travels in Africa. It was later given to Stanley by Livingstone's daughter.

'Dr Livingstone, I presume': Stanley's famous greeting to Livingstone when the pair met at Ujiji, Lake Tanganyika, on 10 November 1871. Livingstone had been thought lost until Stanley located him.

Town of Tete from the north shore of the Zambezi, *by Thomas Baines. Baines was an artist and explorer who accompanied Livingstone on his Zambezi expedition of 1858–59.*

to see if any river left the lake that might be a tributary of the River Nile. The descriptions in their diaries show the deep and lasting impressions they made on each other. Both were from humble Celtic origins and had experienced tough childhoods. Both completed extraordinary journeys, walking through unexplored Africa from one side of the continent to the other.

Livingstone's Coast to Coast Expedition

Raised as a Presbyterian in the town of Blantyre, outside Glasgow, Livingstone's childhood was marked by purpose and doggedness. As one of seven children he realized to succeed in life he would have to learn quickly and work hard. At the age of ten he worked in the cotton mills from 6 a.m. to 8 p.m., six days a week, returning to the small family house each evening to read and study until midnight. This determination paid off as he qualified as a doctor and was accepted by the London Missionary Society. Arriving in Africa for the first time in 1840, he joined Robert Moffat's Kuruman mission in South Africa.

In 1853, when he embarked on his Coast to Coast Expedition, Livingstone had already been mauled by a lion (1844), crossed the Kalahari to find Lake Ngama (1849) and discovered the lower Zambezi (1851). Livingstone was frustrated that there were few places near the Zambezi River free from disease where he could settle with his wife and family. His main goal was to 'open a path into the interior'.

Setting off from Cape Town he walked north to find a suitable location for a missionary station. He was also eager to find out if there was a passage to the sea on the west coast of Africa. With only 27 Makololo men loaned to him by a friend, Chief Sekeletu, he headed west through swamps and thick forests. After six months and 2,415 km (1,500 miles) of jungle, sickness, hunger and hostile tribes they arrived at Luanda on the Atlantic Ocean. Broken in health, Livingstone was invited by a British naval captain to take passage back to England. Most people in his physical state would have accepted, but Livingstone realized that having become such an outspoken campaigner against the slave trade he could not abandon his men at this point.

Livingstone turned round and headed back into the interior through the swamps towards Sesheke. Contending with wet weather, they could find few dry places to sleep. He was nearly blinded as a result of being hit in the eye by a branch and nearly went deaf because of rheumatic fever. Crocodiles, hippopotami and javelins of hostile tribes were further perils to be faced.

Eventually Chief Sekeletu came to his rescue, providing him with supplies and 120 men to accompany him down the Zambezi River. In November 1855 he continued east and after only 80 km (50 miles) came across a magnificent waterfall, known by the local people as 'Mosi Oa Tunya' or the 'Smoke that Thunders'. Livingstone called them Victoria Falls. Buoyed by this geographical discovery he continued down the Zambezi, arriving at Quilimane on the Indian Ocean coast in May 1856. Leaving his Makololo tribesmen in good hands at Tete, he sailed back to Britain. On his arrival in London the Royal Geographical Society honoured him with the Gold Medal for crossing the entire African continent from west to east – a feat no one else had achieved before him.

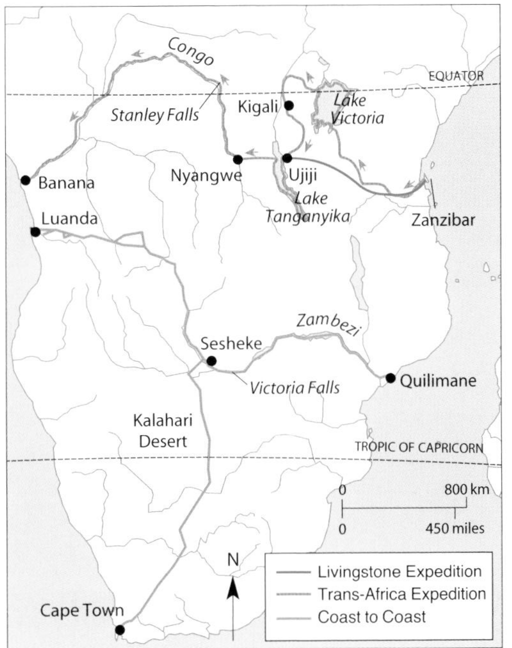

Livingstone was the first person to cross Africa, from west to east, on his Coast to Coast Expedition. He was later thought lost, until Stanley went in search of him. Stanley then completed his own crossing of the African continent.

Below *The Victoria Falls, named by Livingstone in 1855. To the local people they were known as the 'Smoke that Thunders'.*

MARY KINGSLEY

Mary Henrietta Kingsley was a British explorer who made two pioneering trips to West and Central Africa. Born in Cambridge, England, on 13 October 1862, she never received a formal education and was taught to read at home. She stayed there, caring for her invalid mother until both her parents died in 1892, when she was 30 years old.

In 1893, Kingsley went to West Africa to study religion. She intended to write about her adventures and complete the studies on religious fetishes that her father, George Henry Kingsley, had begun. Although a woman travelling alone was almost unheard of at this time, Kingsley was not deterred.

Travelling on a cargo ship from Britain she sailed along the west African coast from Freetown, Sierra Leone, as far as Luanda in Angola. She then journeyed inland from Guinea to Nigeria, collecting many scientific specimens, including insects and fresh-water fishes, for the British Museum. She was one of the first people to study flora and fauna in the lower Congo River.

On her second journey, Kingsley left Liverpool in December 1894, on the ship *Batanga*. From Sierra Leone she went on to Gabon, travelling up the Ogooué River initially by steamboat and then by canoe. She was the first European to visit remote parts of Gabon and the French Congo. Kingsley visited the Fang tribe, who had a reputation for fierceness and cannibalism, and she climbed the southeast face of Mount Cameroon, the tallest mountain in West Africa, at 4,500m (14,435 ft). During this trip, she traded British cloth for ivory and rubber, thus funding her expedition.

After returning to England in 1895 Kingsley wrote the controversial book entitled *Travels in West Africa*. In this she wrote of her opposition to many of the common European practices in Africa and of her sympathy for African natives.

Her final trip was to South Africa in 1899, during the Boer War. Working as both a journalist and a nurse in Cape Town, South Africa, she tended Boer prisoners of war. Following this she wrote her book *West African Studies*. Kingsley died of typhoid fever on 3 June 1900 – she was only 38 years old.

Above right *Photograph of Mary Kingsley.*

Left *Fang warriors of the Congo: a photo taken by Kingsley. The Fang had a fearsome reputation.*

Right *Kingsley collected this power figure, or 'nkisi', from the Congo.*

Stanley's Trans-Africa Expedition

Stanley could not have had a harder start in life. Born John Rowlands in Denbigh, north Wales, on 28 January 1841, he was disowned by his mother at birth. He never knew who his father was. His grandfather looked after him until he died when Stanley was five years old. For the next 11 years he lived at St Asaph's Workhouse, a typical Victorian establishment with harsh living conditions.

In a similar way to Livingstone, Stanley realized that if he studied hard he could put his impoverished background behind him. Aged 16, he sailed across the Atlantic to the United States where he re-invented himself. He worked for a cotton trader called Henry Stanley, whom he was to rename himself after.

After several years, and various occupations, James Gordon Bennett, owner of the *New York Herald* newspaper, presented Stanley with a great opportunity to make a name for himself as a journalist. Bennett instructed him to go to Africa and find David Livingstone. Stanley did just that, returning to Britain with the news that the explorer was still alive, contrary to popular belief.

Stanley's taste for success and African exploration was now ignited. A year after Livingstone's death in 1873, Stanley decided to continue his unfinished exploration work. Livingstone had died thinking that the Congo River was a tributary of the Nile. Stanley also wanted to solve the problem of whether Lake Victoria was one body of water or not and also to find the mysterious 'Mountains of the Moon'.

On 17 November 1874, Stanley's Trans-Africa Expedition departed from Zanzibar – the most expensive expedition to leave the shores of Africa for the interior. With three European officers, 8 tons of supplies divided amongst 300 porters and a 12-m (40-ft) wooden boat called the *Lady Alice* cut into six sections, Stanley headed west towards Lake Victoria. After 100 days of marching through dry savannah plains he reached the shores of the lake where he assembled the *Lady Alice* and became the first man to circumnavigate the second largest freshwater lake in the world. Continuing by foot to Lake Tanganyika he sailed down the western side of the lake to its southernmost point and returned up the western side to Ujiji, where he had last seen Livingstone.

Above *A brass-cased sighting compass used by Stanley on his Trans-Africa Expedition.*

Centre *Portrait of Henry Morton Stanley by E. M. Merrick.*

The Congo was the next challenge. Having reached its banks he obtained several canoes for his porters and supplies and took to the river. Despite constant battles with local tribes and several powerful rapids, Stanley persevered. However, he began to realize that Livingstone was wrong – the river was heading west and could not be a tributary of the Nile. His views were confirmed when the river headed southwest, back into the southern hemisphere. Having travelled for 999 days and 11,265 km (7,000 miles), Stanley and his depleted expedition reached Banana on the Atlantic coast. All three of his European officers perished along the way and only a few of the porters that set off from Zanzibar with him survived. Nonetheless, in the same vein as Livingstone before him, he accompanied them back to Zanzibar by boat before sailing back to Britain.

Two extraordinary men

Livingstone and Stanley are the only two explorers in the 19th century to have crossed the African continent successfully, as well as discovering important geographical places along their journeys. Despite the short period of time that they spent together, a rare relationship between two extraordinary men was formed. Stanley was the 'son' that Livingstone wished he'd known, whilst Livingstone was the father Stanley never had.

The Mekong River Expedition

1866–68

Each meander of the river added to my map was an important geographical discovery. This constant preoccupation, from which nothing could distract me, amounted to an obsession. I was mad about the Mekong.

FRANCIS GARNIER, 1885

One of the greatest expeditions of the 19th century was mounted not in Africa or Australia but in Asia. In 1866 the six officers of the Mekong Exploration Commission (MEC) disappeared into the Southeast Asian rainforest only to emerge – those who did – two years later. Through Cambodia, Laos, Thailand, Burma and Yunnan they navigated one of the wildest of the world's major rivers, explored the upper reaches of another, the Yangtze, mapped some 17,500 km (11,000 miles) of unknown terrain, and outlined an empire – the future Indo-China. The Royal Geographical Society called the expedition 'one of the most remarkable and successful of the century', and the International Geographical Congress chose as the two greatest explorers of the age Francis Garnier of the MEC and Dr Livingstone. Yet, unlike Livingstone, Garnier and the MEC are now largely forgotten.

Members of the Mekong Exploration Commission assembled at Angkor Wat in June 1866. Seated on the extreme right is Commander Doudart de Lagrée and on the extreme left is his obsessive deputy and eventual successor, Francis Garnier.

One reason is that they were French. With France's imperial ambitions frustrated by the British in both India and China, Paris disparaged Asian exploration. When in 1859 a French naval squadron seized Saigon in southern Vietnam, the government of Louis Napoleon was unenthusiastic and favoured withdrawal from what soon proved a liability. But in the colony itself, enthusiasts led by the diminutive Francis Garnier looked to the vast Mekong delta on Saigon's doorstep. Crediting rumours that the river originated in Tibet, they determined to save the colony by demonstrating the Mekong's navigability as a waterway into China. Saigon and the Mekong could be like New Orleans and the Mississippi – a backdoor into the heart of a continent.

In Cambodia

Accompanied by an escort of 20 and with about 5 tons of supplies (including a generous 1,000 litres/220 gallons of liquor), the expedition steamed up the delta from Saigon by gunboat to Angkor Wat, arriving in June 1866. Angkor, then under Thai rule, was surveyed, and its restoration to Cambodia, over whom France already claimed protectoral status, strongly urged.

With the rains beginning and the river rising, on 7 July they cast off from Phnom Penh, heading north against a stiff current. 'A few moments later

In Cambodia, to avoid the ferocious current, the expedition poled their pirogues through flooded forest on the river's margins.

we sailed alone on the vast river,' wrote Garnier. Deemed too headstrong for command, Garnier acted as surveyor and deputy to le Commandant Ernest Marc Louis de Gonzagues Doudart de Lagrée. Lagrée was aloof, old enough to be Garnier's father, and suffering from an acute laryngitis that obliged him to whisper. Doubts over the extent to which le Commandant actually commanded, plus his premature death, would spark a controversy that further obscured the expedition's achievements.

Only two days out from Phnom Penh, the gunboat was defeated by the current. They transferred to pirogues – long dugout canoes made from single tree-trunks – and entered the first rapids. Whether they were aware of the horrors ahead is doubtful. But they certainly expected rough water. The boats had been modified so that they could be punted rather than paddled, the poles having a hooked spike for purchase on trees and rocks protruding from the raging waters. Hugging the east bank, they forged ahead through inundated forest. Leeches and mosquitoes tormented them. All six Frenchmen suffered from malaria; Garnier slipped into a coma.

To Laos

Garnier therefore missed the most sensational water-feature of the entire river. The great Khon Falls on the Cambodian-Lao border thunder over a wall of rock and jungle 16 km (10 miles) wide with a discharge greater than that of Victoria and

Dry season on the Mekong below Luang Prabang. Hereabouts the expedition put ashore to bathe and dress for their grand entry into the capital of upper Laos.

Having set out from Saigon to explore the Mekong, at Jinhong the expedition found further progress impossible and abandoned the river. They then travelled overland to reach the Yangtze and sailed down it to Hankow.

Niagara combined. Though not as high, they are utterly unnavigable. The expedition climbed round them and commandeered new pirogues at the top. Only the comatose Garnier remained oblivious to this obstacle.

He also managed to miss the next hazard. Louis Delaporte, the expedition's artist, alone braved the Kemarat rapids and recorded the whirlpools that would later swallow up a small steamer. The others were exploring the river's tributaries and searching for gold deposits.

Wat Mai in Luang Prabang, as depicted by Louis Delaporte, the Commission's artist; the temple has scarcely changed to this day. Much reproduced, Delaporte's drawings remain the most familiar legacy of the expedition.

Garnier, now recovered, was chased by a leopard; meat was scavenged from the kills of tigers; only peacocks were actually shot. In a party mainly of naval officers, jungle skills were in short supply .

Vientiane, the Lao capital, was reached after six months' boating. It turned out to be as ruinous as Angkor. Luang Prabang promised real comforts, including a roof; but they had barely tasted them when Garnier insisted they press on for China. Funds were running low and physiques cracking. Their liquor supplies had drained away, the barrels punctured by termites, and their second monsoon was breaking.

Burma and Yunnan

From the gorges above Luang Prabang they emerged into the sodden wilderness of the Shan States. Each state in turn held them to ransom; for food they sucked alligator eggs and bartered their clothing. The 160-km (100-mile) Tang-ho rapids convinced even Garnier that the Mekong was not meant for ships, and at Jinghong, now in China, they abandoned the quest.

For Lagrée, it was too late. Le Commandant died north of Kunming, the Yunnan capital. His political officer was also critically ill and would barely survive the trek to the Yangtze. Garnier nevertheless ordered a final bid to regain the Mekong. It failed. Captured and sent packing by the rebel sultan of Ta-ly (Dali), they retraced their steps to the upper Yangtze and sailed down through the famous gorges to Hankow and an incredulous reception.

But in France the expedition's achievement barely registered. First the 1871 Franco-Prussian War intervened, then Garnier himself was discredited when killed during a mad-cap bid to capture Hanoi and claim its Red River as another waterway into China. Not until the 1880s did France act on his recommendations and challenge the British in Southeast Asia by creating French Indo-China. This empire consisted of a resentful Vietnam, a reconstituted Cambodia, and a reinvented Laos, all linked by the hopelessly unnavigable Mekong. Instead of a highway to China, the river had been relegated to the status of an imperial, and later ideological, barrier.

JOHN URE

Travels in Arabia Deserta

52

1876–78

I passed one good day in Arabia, and all the rest were evil.
CHARLES DOUGHTY, 1888

Of all the 19th-century travellers in Arabia, Charles Doughty was perhaps the most improbable, and he was certainly uniquely ill-equipped to integrate into Islamic life: he was a militant Christian; he was a tall, red-headed, full-bearded European; he was continuously hard up, unlike such affluent travellers as Hester Stanhope, Jane Digby or the Blunts, and reduced to begging from his Arab hosts; and he had a cantankerous and impatient personality. While others, like Richard Burton, relished the strange and dangerous nature of travel in Arabia and the Islamic way of life, Doughty rejected the latter and described it as 'the most dangerous grown confederacy and secret conspiracy, surely, in the whole world'.

Doughty had learnt Arabic and an urge for travel and adventure saw him set out in 1876 from Damascus with a pilgrim caravan to Mecca. Curiosity about the desert nomads he encountered soon diverted him from the route, however. He spent many months with the Bedouin graziers, undergoing a succession of daunting experiences: at different times he was robbed, abandoned in the desert, on the verge of starvation, taken prisoner and even threatened with death by his captors. He armed himself, not with a sabre or a sword, but with a pen-knife (a fact that drew derision from Burton) and latterly felt obliged to keep a revolver concealed under his shirt. On the one occasion he felt so threatened that he drew the revolver, he found that in the event he could not bring himself to use it. It was no wonder his enthusiasm for life in Arabia was less than total.

But despite all these setbacks, Doughty, by dint of dogged determination, explored the terrain and familiarized himself with the day-to-day life of the Bedouin to a greater degree than any of his predecessors. In the two years he spent with them he recorded in minute detail the practical aspects of Bedouin life: the pitching and striking of camps, the loading and unloading of camels, the relationships within and without the immediate family or tribe. Although he would not have described himself as an anthropologist, in fact he was the originator of much work in that field. One of

Charles Doughty (in a photograph used as the frontispiece to his Travels in Arabia Deserta*) was tall, red-headed, full-bearded and always distinctively European in appearance.*

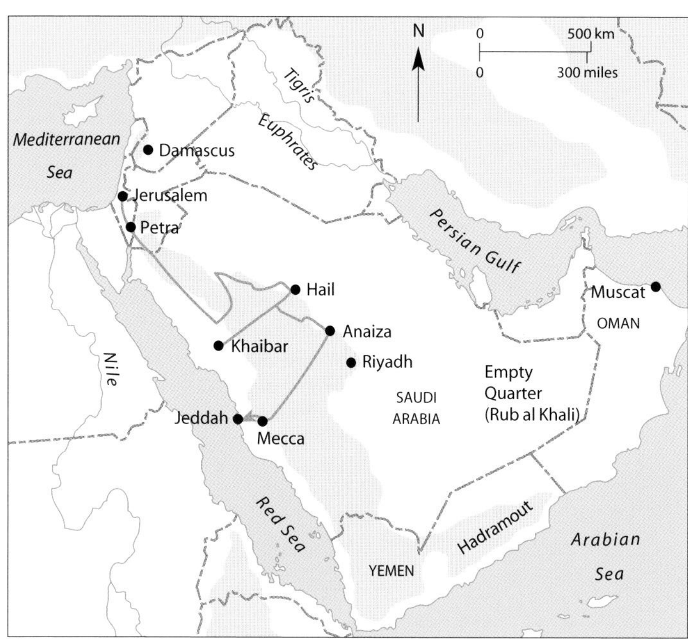

Charles Doughty set out with a pilgrim caravan to Mecca, but soon left it to spend many months with nomadic Bedouin graziers, moving around the Arabian Peninsula. He did eventually reach Mecca.

Doughty's recurring themes is that the 'pure' nomad, who lives in and off the desert, is a nobler being than the Bedouin who live on the fringe of the desert and are infected by the corruption of the wicked cities of the Levant; those tribesmen 'smelling of settled countries' were, in his view, tainted with the pernicious influence of Sodom and Gomorrah. There is a touch of the Old Testament prophet about Doughty.

After he left his original pilgrim caravan to pursue his contact with the Bedouin graziers, he was continually being moved on by his hosts: at different times he was expelled by the Rashid tribesmen and also by the Turkish Ottoman authorities. Undaunted, he later returned to the pilgrim route to Mecca, though this did not prevent him being robbed again and harassed at every turn. When eventually he emerged from his protracted travels at Jeddah he was destitute and exhausted.

Doughty is best remembered for the book he wrote about his journey, called *Travels in Arabia Deserta*. The book is as strange as its author, being written in a curious mixture of medieval and Renaissance English. Because the text has a certain resonance, in the same way as the King James version of the English Bible, and because it also gratified a certain curiosity about the world of the Arabian Nights, it appealed to a wide readership in Victorian England, despite an obscurity of language which renders some passages almost incomprehensible. However, in an introduction to a later edition of *Travels in Arabia Deserta* T. E. Lawrence wrote: 'I do not think that any traveller in Arabia before or after Mr Doughty has qualified himself to praise the book – much less to blame it'.

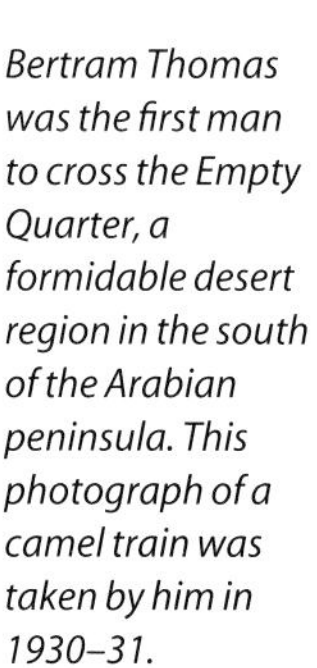
Bertram Thomas was the first man to cross the Empty Quarter, a formidable desert region in the south of the Arabian peninsula. This photograph of a camel train was taken by him in 1930–31.

The Empty Quarter

Although he covered much ground in Arabia and recorded much new information, Doughty never attempted to cross the most formidable desert region in the south of that peninsula, the so-called Empty Quarter or Rub al Khali. That achievement is forever associated with three other English explorers: Bertram Thomas (1892–1950), St John Philby (1885–1960) and Wilfred Thesiger (1910–2003).

Thomas and Philby were single-mindedly determined to be the first to make the epic

A photograph of William Palgrave by Julia Margaret Cameron, 1868. Palgrave crossed northern Arabia, though his motive for the journey is still a mystery.

WILLIAM PALGRAVE

William Giffard Palgrave was a man with a mission, but what that mission was remained an enigma both during his life and after. He was born in 1826 into a Jewish family, but his father had renounced the name of Cohen in favour of Palgrave and had gone on to become an establishment figure in Victorian England, as had his other sons. William was different. Although he started conventionally enough – a scholar at Oxford and a hard-hunting young officer in the East India Company's regiment – he then broke the mould by becoming a Jesuit priest, a missionary and an explorer.

In 1857 he had arrived in the Lebanon and busied himself converting followers of Islam to Christianity. He took to travelling in disguise in Arab robes, but even so was forced to retire in the face of anti-Christian demonstrations and massacres. It was while in retreat at a Jesuit college in France that he first embraced the idea of making a major journey across northern Arabia from west to east – effectively from the Levant to the Persian Gulf.

His motivation for the journey was – and still is – a mystery. He was later to write that 'the men of the land, rather than the land of the men, were my main objective of research and principal study'; this would have been consistent with his previous missionary activities and interest in nomads. But there was another more intriguing possible motive: while he was in France, Palgrave accepted an invitation to meet the emperor, Napoleon III, and it seems possible the emperor (who was known for his ambitions to extend French commercial and colonial interests into the Gulf region) may have recruited Palgrave as a clandestine agent of his expansionist plans. The fact that Palgrave changed his name back to Cohen at this point further suggests a weakening of his English ties.

Whatever his motives, he made a first and spectacularly dangerous crossing of the Nafud Desert, 'an immense ocean of loose reddish sand'. He had adopted the disguise of a Syrian doctor and when he reached Riyadh – 'the lion's den' – the Emir's son tried to obtain strychnine from him to poison a rival brother. Palgrave had to make a rapid and secret escape during the unguarded hour of evening prayer.

Palgrave wrote a two-volume account of his travels, but his descriptions of many aspects of the desert – population, height of sand-dunes, Arab horses – were so full of inaccuracies that some rival explorers questioned whether he had ever really made the journey. There now seems little doubt he did, but still much doubt as to why.

journey, and in the event Thomas achieved this in 1930, crossing the Empty Quarter from south to north. Philby crossed from north to south by a longer route the following year and claimed that his was the first true crossing. Thomas was accompanied by Rashid tribal guides who steered him from one well to another; but he had the disadvantage that the Rashid had many enemies and his expedition was continually under threat from other local Bedouin tribes.

Philby obtained (albeit belatedly) the blessing of the King of Saudi Arabia for his project, which gave him a greater measure of security. Not only was he fluent in Arabic, but had also converted to Islam, which further helped to protect him from some of the hazards facing Thomas; indeed, Philby was a man of few fixed loyalties, being arrested at one point during the Second World War for anti-British activities, and being singularly detached from his companions on his Arabian travels. (His son Kim Philby, the notorious Communist spy and traitor, seemed to inherit this trait to a much greater degree.)

Below left *A curved Arabian dagger and its sheath, which belonged to Wilfred Thesiger.*

Right *Photograph by Thesiger of bin Kabina and bin Ghabaisha, who were his companions in the Oman desert.*

Wilfred Thesiger, the last of these Empty Quarter pioneers, made his journeys in the 1950s. He too was guided by the Rashid and his interest was always as much in the ways and practices of the Bedouin as in the competitive achievement of crossing the Empty Quarter for its own sake. It is to him we owe a more sympathetic presentation of the Bedouin (notably in his book *Arabian Sands*) than to almost any of his predecessors.

Unlike Doughty he had a real empathy with the Arabs and describes the paradoxes of their way of life with humour and understanding: while generous with hospitality, they were also great scroungers; while seeking the silent open spaces of the desert, they noisily crowded in on each other in camp; while fond of poetry, they were oblivious to the beauty of landscape or even the architecture of mosques. Thesiger sees no 'dangerous confederacy and secret conspiracy' in their ways.

But all these later explorers had read Doughty's book and studied his observations about the life and hazards of the Arabian deserts. Without his 19th-century travels and commentaries, the British commitment to and obsession with Arabia might never have developed in the way which resulted in some of the most remarkable journeys of that century and the 20th.

WILLIAM BARR

The Northeast Passage

53

1878–79

By 11a.m. [on 20 July 1879] we were in the middle of the sound which unites the North Polar Sea with the Pacific, and from this point the Vega *greeted the old and new worlds by a display of flags and the firing of a Swedish salute. Thus finally was reached the goal towards which so many nations had struggled...*

A. E. NORDENSKIÖLD, 1881

Born in 1832 into a prominent family in Finland, then a Grand Duchy of Russia, Adolf Erik Nordenskiöld obtained a degree in geology from the University of Helsingfors (Helsinki). He fell foul of the Russian authorities, however, and was obliged to flee to Sweden in 1857. Having participated as geologist on several expeditions to Svalbard and to West Greenland, in 1872 his attempt to reach the North Pole from Svalbard using reindeer was foiled when the reindeer escaped. Nonetheless, Nordenskiöld achieved the first crossing of the ice cap on Nordaustlandet.

With the support of Göteborg businessman Oscar Dickson, Nordenskiöld next turned his attention to trying to develop a regular commercial sea route to Western Siberia via the Kara Sea, but with little success. Then, in 1878, hoping to combine a further attempt at developing a shipping route to the Yenisey River with an attempt at the first transit of the Northeast Passage he bought the steam whaler *Vega*. Attempts had been made before to find a commercial sea route to the Far East around the northern coast of Europe and Russia, from the Atlantic to the Pacific – including by Willem Barents (see box, p. 217) – but none had so far succeeded.

The expedition

Vega was a barque-rigged vessel of 299 registered tons, with an engine of 60 h.p., built in 1872–73. In

Previous page A. E. Nordenskiöld and the *Vega* in the Ice, by Georg von Rosen.

Right *Engraving of* The *Vega* and *Lena* saluting Cape Chelyuskin – *the northernmost point on the Eurasian mainland and perhaps the crux of the Northeast Passage (after a drawing by A. Hovgaard).*

There had been previous attempts to make a transit of the Northeast Passage around the north coast of Europe and Russia, but Nordenskiöld was the first to succeed, returning to Sweden via Japan, Sri Lanka, through the Suez Canal and the Mediterranean.

command of the ship was Captain Louis Palander of the Swedish Navy. A team of scientists included a botanist, a zoologist, a lichenologist (also the ship's medical officer), a hydrographer (and ship's master), a meteorologist and a geomagnetist; there was also a zoologist and Russian interpreter, Lt Oscar Nordqvist, from the Russian Guards Regiment. The crew totalled 17 men, plus a scientific assistant and three Norwegian sealers.

Vega sailed from the Swedish naval base of Karlskrona on 22 June 1878; after calling at Copenhagen and Göteborg she reached Tromsø on 17 July. She sailed again four days later, accompanied now by *Lena*, a steamer of 100 tons, commanded by Captain Edvard Holm Johannessen, bound for the Lena River. The two ships reached the Nenets village of Khabarovo on Yugorskiy Shar on 30 July, where they made rendezvous with the steamer *Fraser* and the sailing vessel *Express*, which were bound for the Yenisey River to load grain to haul back to western Europe

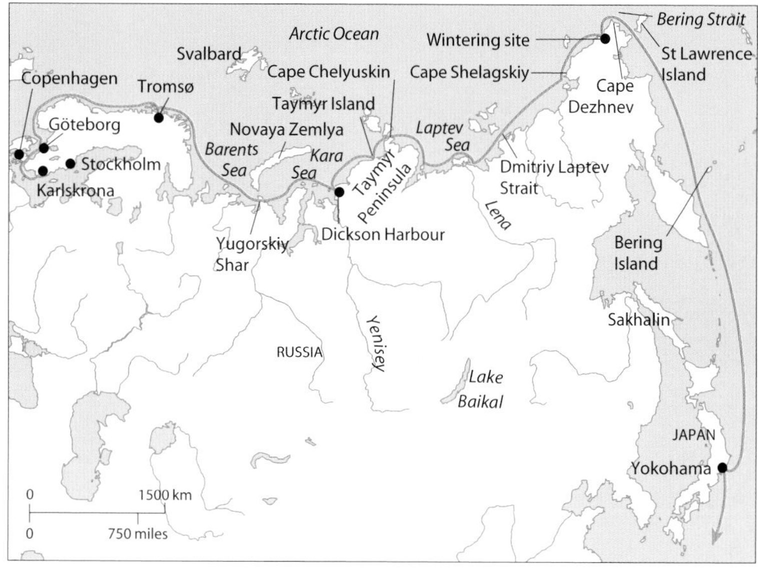

The small flotilla put to sea again on 1 August, heading east across the Kara Sea in ice-free waters and fair weather, reaching Dickson Harbour (now Dikson) on 6 August. Once *Vega* and *Lena* had resupplied from *Express*, the latter and *Fraser* headed up the Yenisey. *Vega* and *Lena* put to sea, eastward bound, on 10 August.

The passage

Some loose, broken ice was encountered, but a greater problem was posed by the persistent fog which forced the ships to lie for three days in Aktiniya Bay on Taymyr Island. On the evening of 19 August they reached Mys (Cape) Chelyuskin, the northernmost point of Eurasia. They were the first ships known to have reached this cape, in many ways the crux of the Northeast Passage.

A drawing from the journal of a survivor of the interior of the hut in which Barents and the crew spent a winter when their ship was beset by ice.

At noon next day the ships continued eastwards across the Laptev Sea. Encountering quite heavy ice and fog on 22 August, Nordenskiöld was forced to turn south along the east coast of the Taymyr Peninsula, to Preobrazheniye Island, where a brief landing was made. Nordenskiöld's surveys revealed that the entire east coast of this peninsula had previously been plotted much too far east – according to the available charts the ships had been steaming over land.

On 27 August, off the Lena Delta, the two ships parted company; *Lena* headed into one of the distributaries of the Lena River bound upriver to Yakutsk; *Vega* pushed on eastwards. On 31 August she ran through Dmitriy Laptev Strait and, despite ice which was quite close at times, by 3 September she was passing the Medvezh'i Islands. But eastwards from there the passage was confined to a relatively narrow ice-free channel along the coast, in places only 6–7 km (around 4 miles) wide. On the morning of 7 September, off Cape Shelagskiy, two umiaks

WILLEM BARENTS' EXPEDITIONS 1594–97

In 1594 the Dutch dispatched three ships, in an attempt to reach the Far East via the Northeast Passage. One of these, *Mercurius*, out of Amsterdam, was commanded by Willem Barents. Barents reached the coast of Novaya Zemlya and followed it northwards as far as Cape Zhelaniya, the northeasternmost tip of Novaya Zemlya, before being forced to turn back by ice.

In the following year the Dutch dispatched a fleet of seven vessels, one of them again commanded by Barents; on this occasion the entire fleet was blocked by ice in Yugorskiy Shar, the southernmost strait leading to the Kara Sea, and was forced to retreat.

Nothing daunted, in 1596 the Amsterdam merchants dispatched two ships, one commanded by Jacob van Heemskerck, with Barents as chief pilot, the other by Jan Corneliszoon Riip. Attempting a more northerly route, they first discovered and landed on Bjørnøya, then pushed on north to Amsterdamøya off the northwest tip of Spitsbergen (Svalbard). Thereafter they headed back south to Bjørnøya, where they separated. Riip returned north to explore Svalbard further, but Barents and van Heemskerck headed due east. Rounding the northern tip of Novaya Zemlya they were blocked by ice at 'Yshaven' (Ledyanaya Gavan). The ship was beset and damaged, but the crew built a house on shore and spent quite a comfortable winter – although two men died of scurvy. In the spring they started back south in two boats. On 20 June, Barents died and was buried on Novaya Zemlya. The rest of the party reached the mainland coast in late August where, by a coincidence, they were rescued by a ship commanded by Riip. On the basis of his voyages, Barents produced a surprisingly accurate map of the west coasts of Novaya Zemlya, pointing the way for later seafarers who attempted the Northeast Passage, including Nordenskiöld, who finally succeeded.

manned by Chukchi put off from shore; thereafter encounters with Chukchi were quite frequent.

Overwintering in the ice

Having been detained by ice for a week off Cape Severnyy (now Cape Shmidt) *Vega* passed Cape Vankarem and Cape Onman, but on 29 September rapidly forming new ice halted progress. The ship was forced to winter, moored to a grounded floe, just inside the northeast cape at the entrance to Kolyuchin Gulf, off the Chukchi settlement of Pitlekay, about 225 km (140 miles) from the Bering Strait.

Scientists, officers and men settled down for what would turn out to be a fairly comfortable and scientifically productive winter. They pursued a programme of meteorological, tidal and geomagnetic observations, the latter from a special observatory set up on shore. Numbers of Chukchi visited the ship almost daily, and Nordqvist soon acquired a fluent command of their language; he and others visited various of the nearby villages and the expedition obtained an impressive collection of tools, weapons and clothing.

Returning home

The melt began in mid-June 1879 and on 18 July *Vega* got under way again. At 11.00 a.m. on 20 July she passed Cape Dezhnev, the first vessel to complete the Northeast Passage from Atlantic to Pacific. With stops at Zaliv Lavrentiya, Port Clarence (now Teller), Alaska, Bukhta Konam, St Lawrence and Bering islands, *Vega* headed south, reaching Yokohama in Japan on 2 September.

Nordenskiöld and his companions were given an extremely warm welcome in Japan and travelled quite widely while *Vega* was being overhauled and having copper sheathing fitted. They resumed their homeward voyage from Nagasaki on 27 October. Returning via Hong Kong, Singapore, Galle (Sri Lanka), Aden, the Suez Canal, Naples, Lisbon, Falmouth, Vlissingen and Copenhagen, they reached Stockholm on 24 April 1880. Scientists, officers and men were fêted at every port-of-call. King Oscar made Nordenskiöld a Baron and presented him with the Great Cross of the North Star; Palander was knighted and was awarded the Knight's Cross of the North Star. Today, 24 April is still celebrated as '*Vega* Day' in Sweden.

The crew of the Vega *photographed at Naples, in February 1880, homeward bound to Stockholm after the transit of the Northeast Passage.*

PETER HOPKIRK

The Pundits Explore Tibet

54

1865–85

When I was in Ladakh I noticed the natives of India passed freely backwards and forwards between Ladakh and Yarkand in Chinese Turkestan, and it consequently occurred to me that it might be possible to make the exploration by that means.
CAPTAIN THOMAS MONTGOMERIE, 1862

At the height of the Great Game, that shadowy struggle between Victorian Britain and Tsarist Russia across Central Asia, much of this wild and lawless no-man's-land remained a mysterious blank on British military maps. This lack of detailed knowledge of what lay beyond India's northern frontiers soon became a matter of growing concern to Raj military strategists. For it was no secret that Russian troops were advancing there at an alarming rate. Indeed, some British strategists became convinced that the Russians would not halt until India, the richest of the world's imperial prizes, was theirs too.

The main obstacle to mapping the vulnerable passes and other strategic routes into India lay in the fact that the region was officially judged too dangerous for British officers and military surveyors to venture into. But then, in 1862, Captain Thomas Montgomerie, a young Bengal Engineers officer attached to the Survey of India in Dehra Dun, suddenly hit upon a brilliant solution. Why not, he put it to his chiefs, send in native Indian explorers, hand-picked for their intelligence and resourcefulness, and trained in clandestine surveying techniques? For he had noticed, when in Ladakh, that Indians could pass unhindered into Chinese Turkestan and back (as quoted above).

Montgomerie's superiors were impressed by the idea, confident that a non-European could always be disowned if caught, and that reprisals would not be called for in the event of their death. And so began an extraordinary chapter in the history of Central Asian exploration. Montgomerie's 'Pundits' – as they became known – would set out on a series of top-secret journeys from their base in Dehra Dun after months of training in the covert use of cunningly designed hidden instruments, cover stories and disguise as holy-men or traders.

Captain Thomas Montgomerie, whose ingenuity gave birth to the Pundits.

The Dehra Dun spy school

Montgomerie first taught his men, through exhaustive practice, to take a pace of known length which would remain constant whether walking uphill, downhill or on the level, and be maintained over huge distances. He next devised ways whereby they could keep a precise but furtive count of the total number of such measured paces taken during each day's march.

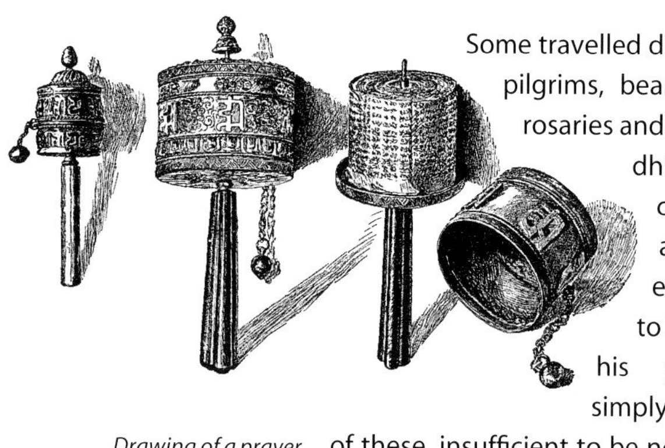

Drawing of a prayer wheel, with its cover removed to show the prayer scroll – the prayer wheel could be adapted by inserting a roll of blank paper for making notes instead of the scroll.

Some travelled disguised as Buddhist pilgrims, bearing the customary rosaries and prayer-wheels. Buddhist rosaries normally consist of 108 beads, a sacred number, enabling the owner to keep a daily count of his prayers. However, simply by removing eight of these, insufficient to be noticeable, the rosary was left with a mathematically convenient 100. At every 100th pace the Pundit would slip one bead, enabling him to clock up 10,000 measured strides with each complete circuit of the rosary. At the end of each day, he would record the distance he had thus covered, together with other discreet observations. This he would do with the aid of his doctored prayer-wheel, with its copper cylinder. Instead of the usual scroll of prayers this contained a roll of blank paper, on which the Pundit noted down his day's total. Other secret devices included small compasses hidden in the prayer-wheel tops, thermometers concealed in their pilgrims' staves, for working out altitudes, and mercury hidden in cowrie shells for setting artificial horizons.

The only known portrait of the Pundit Nain Singh, who secretly explored the forbidden city of Lhasa and beyond.

Tibet – into the Forbidden Land

There were a dozen of these explorer-spies in all; their travels covered many hundreds, sometimes thousands, of miles, always on foot, often lasting many months, even years, and together spanning some three decades. One at least, sadly, never returned. Two of the most memorable went into Tibet, then the least-known corner of Central Asia, whose mountainous borders were jealously guarded by the Tibetans.

One was Nain Singh, code-named 'Number One', who finally reached Lhasa in 1865, a full year after leaving Dehra Dun. He had to change his disguise twice after coming under suspicion, but none the less meticulously counted every single pace of the way, as well as taking innumerable secret compass bearings and other observations. He remained undetected in the Tibetans' holy city for three months, endeavouring to establish its

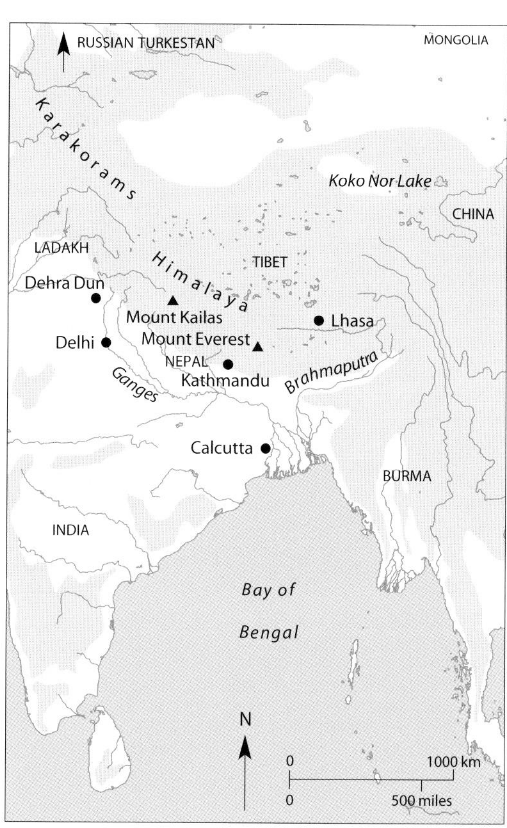

precise geographical co-ordinates and altitude, while also compiling a detailed description of the capital and its surroundings. His calculations, on his return, showed that Lhasa stood at 29 degrees, 39 minutes and 17 seconds. This compares most impressively with today's atlases, which show him to be less than 2 minutes out. His boiling-point thermometer readings showed the city to stand at 11,700 ft (3,566 m) above sea level, comparing favourably with the 12,000 ft (3,658 m) generally given as Lhasa's altitude today.

After many adventures and near disasters en route, Nain Singh returned safely to Dehra Dun, having walked some 1,200 miles and counted and logged 2.5 million individual paces. In all, he had been away 18 months, but he was not allowed to rest long. Within six months of his return he was despatched on another secret mission – this time to the legendary Tibetan gold-fields of Thok Jalung. Nain Singh was eventually awarded the Gold Medal of the Royal Geographical Society for his remarkable feats.

The Pundits commemorated

Our second Pundit, Kishen Singh – code-named 'A.K.' – had already completed two earlier missions when, in 1878, he was despatched on what proved to be a marathon route-survey of nearly 3,000 miles, taking him some four years. His destination was the then-unknown northeastern corner of Tibet around Koko Nor lake, towards the Chinese and Mongolian frontiers. He reached Lhasa without incident, but was marooned there for many months while seeking a caravan bound for this barren wasteland. The Pundit discreetly used this time, however, to prepare by far the most detailed map of the Tibetan capital yet seen. He also learned Mongolian, which was to prove invaluable when he finally joined a north-bound caravan of Mongolians, well armed against attack. In fact, they were attacked by some 200 bandits in Tibet's great northern desert. But although heavily outnumbered they managed to drive them off.

Left *Pundit Kishen Singh in old age. His last secret journey took him four years.*

It was the first of many such misadventures which Kishen Singh faced on that journey, including arrest by the suspicious Chinese, who held him prisoner for seven months. Ragged and emaciated, but with his maps and secret surveying instruments intact, having counted 5.5 million paces, he finally reached Dehra Dun, where they had all but written him off.

Other British-trained pundits had similar tales to tell of their hazardous exploits and escapes, but these are the two most memorable of such heroes. They, and others, are still honoured to this day in India, in the Survey of India's museum in Dehra Dun. Here also is the room where Colonel Montgomerie gave his final instructions to these intrepid men, whom he knew he might well be sending to their deaths.

Above *The 1,000-room Potala Palace, Lhasa, whose measurements were secretly taken by Nain Singh.*

Opposite above right *The once-mysterious Tibet was at the eastern end of the Great Game battlefield. The Pundits covertly surveyed huge areas of this region, all setting out from Dehra Dun.*

JOHN URE

Exploring Central & East Asia

1871–88

Here you can penetrate anywhere, only not with the Gospels under your arm, but with money in your pocket, a carbine in one hand and a whip in the other … a thousand Russian soldiers would be enough to subdue all Asia from Lake Baykal to the Himalayas.

COLONEL PRZHEVALSKY, PRIVATE LETTER TO GENERAL TIKHMENOV, 1873

Nikolai Przhevalsky was a man with an obsession: to explore Central Asia, and if possible to reach Lhasa, the forbidden capital of Tibet. His whole life was devoted to these objectives, at the expense of his military career – though he attained the rank of major-general never having commanded a serious military unit; at the expense of his private life – he never married; and at the expense of his personality – which became increasingly intolerant.

Nikolai Przhevalsky, a Russian officer who devoted his military career to reconnoitring Central Asia in the interests of Russian expansion.

Each of his expeditions into Central Asia from the fringes of the Tsarist Russian empire followed hard on the heels of the one before: 1871–73, 1876–78, 1879–80, 1883–85, and finally he died on his last expedition, which set out in 1888. Collectively, these form one of the great journeys of history, since they were all part of an on-going campaign which traced and retraced its own lines of advance into the heart of Chinese-dominated Central Asia.

In the course of these journeys he reached from Siberian Amur to Mongolia, the Gobi Desert, Xinjiang and Tibet; he crossed the Tien Shan mountains between modern Kyrgyzstan and China; he mapped and named the Humboldt Mountains; he skirted the Taklamakan Desert; he surveyed the Lop Nor region for the first time; he revealed the Caves of a Thousand Buddhas at Dunhuang; and he recorded the hitherto blank areas on the map of the Altyn Tagh and Tsaidam regions of western China.

Until his expeditions, all this hinterland of the upper Oxus river, east and south of the Pamirs and the Karakorams, was an unknown wilderness of desert, mountains, fast-flowing and often frozen rivers: this was to be Przhevalsky's virgin domain, a land where food and sustenance were so short that his camels not infrequently tore open their own saddles to eat the straw stuffing. But despite all this achievement to his credit, he is often best remembered for his failure to reach his self-appointed goal of Lhasa, which he saw as the centre of a Buddhist spiritual power stretching from Ceylon to Japan, and therefore the prime target for Russian diplomacy and influence.

A passionate sportsman

Przhevalsky had a wide variety of talents to bring to the task of exploration: he was a serious botanist who collected plants wherever he went (897 specimens on one trip alone); he was an anthropologist who brought back important comments on the ethnology of the inhabitants round Lop Nor; he was a zoologist who memorably discovered and gave his name to the Przhevalsky horse (also spelled Przewalksi), with its short, erect mane, enormous teeth and truncated legs; and he was both a geographer and geologist, with a keen instinct to map and record rock formations.

But to his companions, and to the readers of his numerous books, he was – more obviously than any of the above – a passionate sportsman. He shot everything that moved on the Central Asian steppes, and everything that flew over them. He would crawl from his Mongolian *ger* holding the tripod of his gun above his head to persuade a short-sighted elk that he was a potential mate. He would empty cartridges (always kept in his cap) at any approaching yak. He shot wolves at every opportunity (on one occasion frustrated by the fact that a wolf had carried off and eaten his cartridges). New Year's Day 1885 was celebrated by shooting 23 orongo antelope, while 60 deer were shot near the source of the Huang Ho. It was no wonder that wherever he went, Przhevalksy was followed by flights of vultures looking to feed on his prey.

Unfortunately, Przhevalsky's penchant for shooting did not confine itself to game. He was regularly provided with a Cossack escort and they were equally trigger-happy. On one occasion on the shores of the Oring Nor near the Tibetan frontier he provoked an attack by the Ngolok tribesmen and his Cossacks killed 30 of them.

Colour plate made by the Russian Imperial Geographical Society from specimens collected by Przhevalsky.

Imperial ambitions

This attitude was never clearer than during what was probably his greatest as well as his longest single venture: the expedition of 1879–80 through the Mongolian Altai Desert, across China and the Humboldt Mountains, deeply into Tibet and approaching Lhasa, and finally home through Ulan Batur. When preparing for this expedition he and his men spent three weeks on fire-arms drill – 'the best of all Chinese passports' as he called it. It was also on this trip that he first encountered the Przhevalsky horse, 'but not within shooting distance'; and that one of his Cossack escorts was abandoned for dead on a yak hunt, only to be found after six days wandering alone in the mountains. The trip was to prove the

Reed huts at Lop Nor, whose inhabitants were studied by Przhevalsky.

FRANCIS YOUNGHUSBAND

Francis Younghusband (1863–1942) was a British protagonist in the Great Game, operating in a similar area and at a similar time to Przhevalsky. The heartland of Younghusband's early exploration and military reconnaissance was the Pamirs, the Karakorams and the passes through the unclaimed corridor between Afghanistan and China, which, he rightly suspected, the Russians were trying to penetrate with a view to claiming sovereignty.

In the 1880s Younghusband was a young officer in the King's Dragoon Guards who was seconded to the Political Service of the British Raj in India. One purpose of his extended and often solitary journeys – frequently disguised as 'shooting leave' – was to reconnoitre those mountain passes which might be used by the Russians as an invasion route into India, and at the same time to detect and report any evidence of Russian activity there.

On one occasion in 1891 Younghusband encountered a Russian Colonel Yanov, accompanied by some 40 Cossacks, in this remote, unclaimed and disputed area. It was clear to Younghusband that they were in the process of staking out a claim, and this became even more apparent when Yanov returned with instructions to escort Younghusband out of the region. When the latter reported this to the Viceroy and the British government, the challenge to British authority in this strategically vulnerable frontier area nearly resulted in war between Imperial Russia and Britain. Eventually the Russian nerve gave way and they withdrew.

With his reputation as a fearless explorer, gallant soldier and skilful diplomat, it was not surprising that when the Viceroy of India, Lord Curzon, decided in 1904 that the only way of preventing Russian influence and armaments dominating Tibet was to send a military force to Lhasa, it was Younghusband who was chosen to lead the expedition. Although Younghusband – who (unlike Przhevalsky) was always in favour of using minimal force – defeated the Tibetans and occupied Lhasa, the campaign was not a glorious one and the reasons for it (Russian arms) were revealed as unfounded.

Younghusband's active life was over, but as a later president of the Royal Geographical Society he was remembered for his daring and original journeys in Central Asia.

Above *Francis Younghusband, an Edwardian who played the Great Game in Central Asia with panache.*

Below *British troops entering Lhasa, during the British Mission to Tibet, 1903–04.*

Two Przhevalsky's horses today: it was fortunate that the first one Przhevalsky saw was out of rifle range.

most arduous as well as the longest in distance; little wonder that when he regained Russia he found he had been given up for dead.

As a military man he was very conscious of the strategic importance of his forays into Central Asia. Imperial Russia was extending its territory and its influence into the whole region in a manner which gave rise to acute anxiety in the British Raj in India at a crucial point in the Great Game struggle for dominance. He tried to build diplomatic bridges to Yakub Bey, the Muslim despot who had carved out an independent emirate of Kashgaria, but received only limited assistance on his route to Lop Nor as Yakub Bey correctly suspected that his motives included military reconnaissance.

His imperial aspirations were one reason why Przhevalsky, in intervals between his expeditions, was widely acclaimed and fêted in St Petersburg. He was invited to give tutorials to the Tsarevich (the future Tsar Nicholas II) about Central Asia and to encourage his ambitions of expansion into the region. But Przhevalsky himself hated the claustrophobic glitter of the capital, and was always anxious to return to his country estate, shoot more game and plan his next venture. He liked to keep his own team of explorer-adventurers with him and developed an emotional attachment to them which substituted for any family life. And despite his failure to reach Lhasa (the Chinese always headed him off with firm notes and threats of irresistible force) and his overtly chauvinistic approach to exploration, his services to discovery and geography were widely recognized, including in the United Kingdom where the Royal Geographical Society applauded him for having shed more light on Central Asia than anyone since Marco Polo. They were probably right.

Map of the route of Przhevalsky's longest journey, in 1879–80: this was just one of many expeditions he undertook in the region.

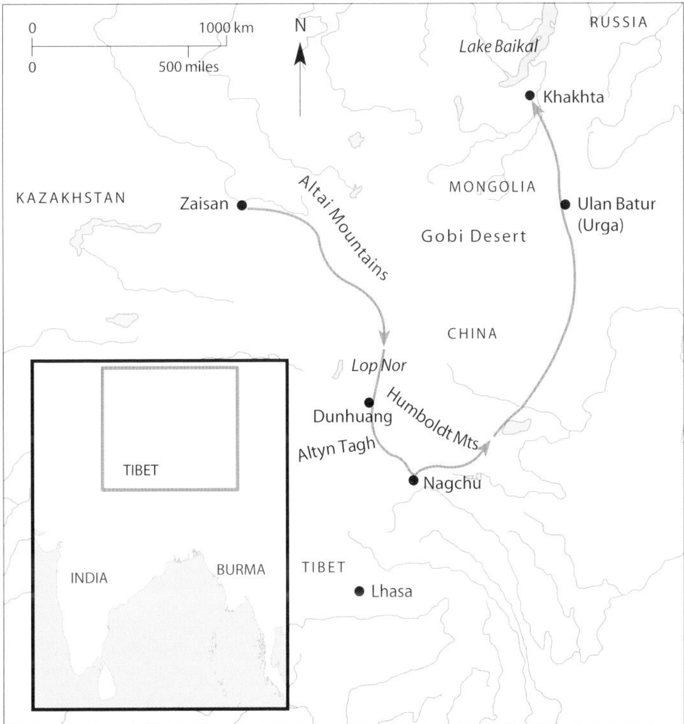

Modern Times

Today is the great age of travel. Never has it been easier, or cheaper, to arrive at a destination in a few hours that our ancestors would have taken months or even years to reach. In some ways, this means that the world is better known than ever before, although there are still parts that are untravelled. At the same time, however, we have become aware of how little we understand about the actual workings of life on earth. As a result, there are as many opportunities to make 'great' journeys of discovery as ever.

Times have moved on, and it would be hard now to repeat some of the significant and relatively recent journeys featured here. Some regions of the globe are changed irrevocably, or closed to travellers. For instance, the wastes of the Taklamakan Desert in China, crossed by Hedin and Stein, no longer contain the treasures emerging from the sands or the caches of Buddhist manuscripts in caves that they discovered (including texts brought back from India in the 7th century, which Stein in turn brought back to the British Museum). Nor could courageous women such as Gertrude Bell, Isabella Bird and Freya Stark inspire today the same admiration for their courage – even if the deserts in which they roamed were still open to single Christian women. Many social and political developments have brought this about, not least in China, where the Long March by Chinese communists was a great journey of a different sort.

Instead, in the modern era men and women have pioneered new fields and new technologies. Often with the invaluable help of the latest equipment, they have been able to triumph over conditions and circumstances which previously

Edmund Hillary and Tenzing Norgay approach Camp IX at around 8,535 m (28,000 ft), on the way to the summit in their successful ascent of Everest in 1953.

seemed insuperable. Since Hillary and Tenzing reached the summit of Everest, virtually every mountain has been climbed, and in many expeditions the human spirit has been tested to the limit time and again by spectacular feats of endurance.

Both Poles have been reached, each in a blaze of controversy and recrimination. There have been several who have claimed to be the first at 90° North. Peary's assertion is now questioned and remains scientifically unvalidated, while Herbert's epic traverse, the longest polar trek in history, met with undoubted success. Amundsen's defeat of Scott in the race to the South Pole, a harrowing story of duplicity on the one hand, and heroic courage and, perhaps not victory, but great scientific achievements, on the other, still raises strong emotions. Shackleton's journey, notwithstanding the fact that it was unplanned and that he never reached his intended destination, remains one of the greatest of all.

The brave pilots who conquered a new element and led the way in the air acquired a different sort of celebrity. Lindbergh survived the first solo crossing of the Atlantic and went on to even greater exploits. But the two legendary women fliers, Amelia Earhart and Amy Johnson, both perished mysteriously, thus adding to the mystique of exploration in the air. These early aviators risked their lives in tiny, fragile machines; now, men like Piccard, Jones and Fossett have circled the globe in balloons at the mercy of winds and air currents. Doubtless, challenges will continue to be overcome and records broken.

Great journeys by sea carry a special quality. Heyerdahl and his companions electrified both the scientific community and the general public when they crossed from South America to Polynesia on *Kon-Tiki*, a raft made from balsa logs. Knox-Johnston, who writes first-hand of his journey, epitomizes the courage of the lone yachtsman, single-handedly facing the forces of nature.

The oceans still present some of the remaining unexplored places, where no one has been before. Ballard's scientific expedition to the bottom of the deepest ocean was not only a great feat, it may also have overturned our understanding of evolution, through the discovery of life forms around thermal vents.

When man first set foot on the Moon, the human spirit of adventure crossed the next great boundary and took a great leap forward. At last we could conceive of travel beyond the Earth and into space – and now the scope is literally infinite.

The giant planet Saturn and its satellites photographed by Voyager 2. *Humans are now beginning to explore the outer planets of our solar system – though by remotely controlled space probes.*

JOHN URE

Journeys Across Asia

56

1890–91, 1893–97, 1899–1902, 1905–08, 1927–35

You can go in but you can't get out.

SAYING ABOUT THE TAKLAMAKAN DESERT, QUOTED BY SVEN HEDIN

Few explorers achieved such fame and celebrity as Sweden's Sven Hedin, and few ended their lives in such disrepute and ignominy. Hedin was an extraordinarily purposeful and courageous traveller who not only penetrated the dreaded and previously unexplored Taklamakan Desert in China's Sinkiang province, but also opened up this region to a generation of acquisitive scholars who raided the former staging posts of the Silk Road for Buddhist manuscripts and other treasures that cast fresh light on the earlier travellers through this inhospitable land.

Hedin started his exploring early: in 1890, at the age of 25, he first visited Kashgar in Central Asia and became known to that elite band of explorers and empire-builders that included the Russian consul Nikolai Petrovsky and his English counterpart George Macartney, as well as Younghushand (p. 224). Three years later he began a series of trips of exploration that were to spread over 40 years; but his first serious expedition nearly proved fatal.

In 1895 he set out from Kashgar and took on a full complement of men, camels and stores at Merket, on the Yarkand River. He planned to cross the Taklamakan Desert, mapping as he went, and pass on to Tibet. But he had only been in the desert for two weeks when he discovered that at the last well they had passed his men had not filled the water tanks on the camels with the required 10 days' supply, but only with enough

Digging for a well in despair, from Through Asia *by Hedin: thirst nearly killed Hedin on this, his first major expedition.*

Sven Hedin seated on a heavy Bactrian camel of the sort familiar in Central Asia and much used for transport and trade.

for two. He should have turned back, but he was persuaded that not far ahead they would encounter the Khotan River, so he cut the water ration for his men and went forward.

As the river failed to materialize, he abandoned the weaker camels and pressed on through sandstorms, steering by compass alone. However, he then made the terrible discovery that his meagre supply of water was even less than he had reckoned, as one of his guides had been stealing it. His diary entries in the next few days were as bleak and unhopeful as those of

Returning from the river with water in his boots, Hedin saved the life of his companion; from his book Through Asia.

Captain Scott on his attempted return from the South Pole some 17 years later (p. 239).

Some of his men passed out through fatigue and thirst, while others drank spirit from their primus stove, and yet others again drank the blood of sheep they had brought to eat. Eventually only Hedin and one other were able to continue, crawling on with swollen tongues and glazed eyes. When they finally reached the Khotan River, they found it had dried up; but a few more hours of crawling – following the sounds of a water bird – brought Hedin to a fresh-water pool. He drank all he could, and having filled his boots with water he carried them back to his companion. In the end only two of his party had perished, but it was enough to make Hedin return to Kashgar and adopt more prudent methods on his many subsequent trips. But this adventure was only a prelude for what was to follow.

Kashgar to Khotan

Hedin set out from Kashgar again later in 1895 and this time skirting the Taklamakan reached Khotan after three weeks. Here he became intrigued with the treasures that were emerging from the desert sands. His own interest (unlike the locals) was not in gold or silver objects, but manuscripts, coins and assorted antiquities. He made a series of excursions into the desert to locate and excavate these objects. On one of these forays, at sub-zero temperatures in mid-winter, he discovered a Buddhist staging post on the Silk Route described by travellers such as Fa Xian in the 4th century AD (p. 59).

Whenever his local helpers reported something of interest, such as part of a half-submerged primitive painting, Hedin was quick to follow it up in person and mark the spot for further, more detailed investigation. Hedin's contribution was finding and recording the location of these sites in a region which no Westerner had penetrated before; it was left to others – archaeologists and historians – to develop and exploit the sites.

After a month's rest and recoupment at Khotan, where he codified the results of these

The camp at Ala Kungler Busrugvar, in the course of Hedin's journey on the Tarim River using a locally constructed boat.

AUREL STEIN

While Sven Hedin was pre-eminently an explorer, Aurel Stein was additionally a scholar, an archaeologist and a field surveyor who brought an array of skills to the region Hedin had opened up. Born in 1862 into a Jewish family in Hungary, he adopted both Christianity and British nationality, being notably proud of both.

Stein's first major trip, and probably his greatest, was undertaken at the age of 37 in 1900. He started from Kashmir (in British India), with the backing of many influential people including the Viceroy, Lord Curzon, and travelled over the Karakoram Mountains into Chinese Turkestan. Having entered the Taklamakan Desert, like Hedin, he was surprised by the quantity of early manuscripts provided by a local dealer called Islam Akhun; investigation proved the man to be a fraud and a forger. Undeterred by this and convinced that genuine treasures were to be found, Stein set out into the desert in midwinter, when temperatures were consistently below freezing and conditions in marked contrast to the gruelling heat Hedin had often encountered. On this and later expeditions he discovered large numbers of Sanskrit Buddhist texts and most notably unearthed from a cave the so-called secret library at Dunhuang (Tun-Huang).

Stein's successes drew other explorers and treasure hunters to the region: Albert von Le Coq led German teams, and the Japanese were not far behind. Eventually the Chinese authorities began to resent the extent of foreign intrusion and the amount of 'national' treasures that were being exported to museums in the West and elsewhere; later expeditions were deliberately frustrated by officialdom.

Meanwhile, Stein had his own problems and rewards. Badly frost-bitten on one expedition, he had to have his toes amputated by a missionary, and was fortunate not to lose his leg. But on return to England he was knighted and received the gold medal of the Royal Geographical Society. Restless as ever, he was planning yet another expedition in Kabul when he died aged over 80 in 1943.

forays, Hedin then pressed on with the greatest of all his journeys, to Tibet, eventually returning to his native Sweden through Peking and by the Trans-Siberian railway.

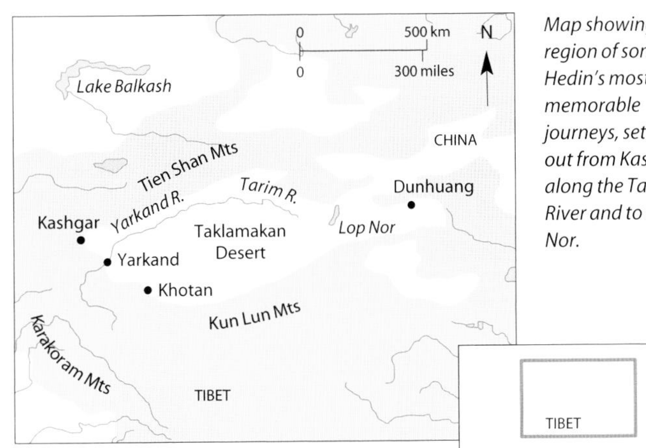

Map showing the region of some of Hedin's most memorable journeys, setting out from Kashgar, along the Tarim River and to Lop Nor.

Triumph and fall from grace

Hedin was greeted at home as a hero, and subsequent expeditions were to be financed by the King of Sweden and the industrialist Nobel among others. He did not disappoint his sponsors, discovering a formidable cache of ancient manuscripts at the Chinese garrison town of Lou Lan between the Taklamakan and Gobi deserts. At one point he travelled on a locally constructed boat down the Tarim River, and later found that the salt lake Lop Nor had shifted its positions since Przhevalsky had been there nearly two decades earlier (p. 222). This was a far longer trip than that of 1895, but it was his earlier encounter with the terrors of the Taklamakan for which he will be best remembered.

Hedin's life was to be long (he died aged 87 in 1952) but latterly sad and inglorious. Having in his heyday been friends with most of Europe's leaders – including the Tsar, the Kaiser, and Lords Kitchener and Curzon – he allowed himself to become involved in politics and ended up as a champion of Fascism (a strange affiliation, as Peter Hopkirk has observed, for one with Jewish blood). He was denounced by most of his former admirers. But nothing could detract from his achievements in exploration, and his successors, such as Aurel Stein, acknowledged this.

Top left *Stein with a plane table (and his dog Dash) at Yaka-yardang-bulak.*

Top right *An embroidery found by Stein on the floor of a cave at Dunhuang.*

Left *Cave 16 at Dunhuang, with bundles of manuscripts from Cave 17 that were added to the photograph by Stein.*

Right *The ruins at Lou Lan during excavation: a photograph from Hedin's published account.*

To the North Pole

1909, 1968–69

The discovery of the North Pole on the 6th of April 1909, by the last expedition of the Peary Arctic Club, means that the splendid frozen jewel of the North, for which through centuries men of every nation have struggled, and suffered and died, is won at last, and is to be worn for ever, by the Stars and Stripes.

REAR-ADMIRAL ROBERT E. PEARY, 1909

Only the North Geographic Pole, one of the three great challenges presented by the high Arctic, remained unattained by 1906. Nordenskiöld had made the first traverse of the Northeast Passage (p. 215) and Roald Amundsen had finally traversed the Northwest Passage (p. 186). Although the possibility of opening up an effective trade route to the Pacific over the Arctic Ocean via the North Pole was now assumed to be equally, if not more, unviable, that did not reduce the Pole's appeal to explorers. Whoever was the first to reach the North Pole would secure personal fame and national honour on a scale without precedent in polar exploration. Many expeditions had tried and failed; many explorers had died in the attempt. It had now become one of exploration's greatest icons and the contest to be the first claimant to 90° North – the top of the world – seemed to be between two American polar explorers: Dr Frederick A. Cook and Commander Robert E. Peary.

Map showing the route of Wally Herbert's crossing of the Arctic Ocean, 1968–69, and Peary's possible route.

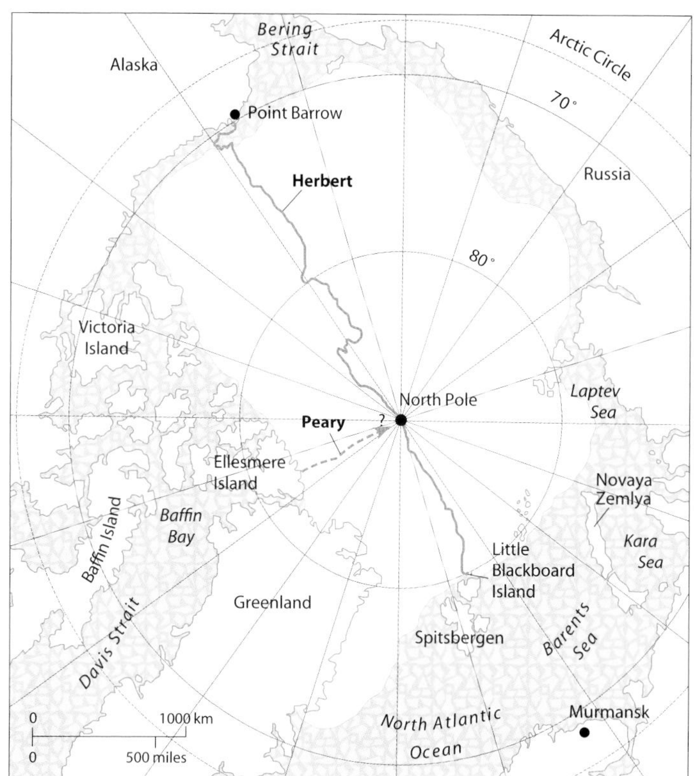

The Pole, located near the middle of the Arctic Ocean, is in a peculiarly inaccessible and inhospitable place. Much of the ocean's surface is covered in a crust of frozen sea water, currently averaging 2.75 m (9 ft) thick, with ever-changing areas of chaotically jumbled ice blocks and open water caused by the interaction of the tides, currents, winds and seasonally variable solar radiation. To sail a vessel into this polar pack ice was both difficult and hazardous – most ships were either rebuffed or crushed by its immense forces. The only option to reach the Pole was to abandon the notion of a ship-bound voyage and make a journey across the sea ice on foot. Such an undertaking was to commit to a logistical, physical and mental challenge so great that only the most exceptional explorer was likely to succeed.

Cook – the fraudulent claimant

Cook, an American, and once a surgeon on an expedition led by Peary in Greenland, had set sail from the United States without announcing his intention to attempt the Pole. Accompanied by just two Greenlandic Eskimo and 26 sledge-hauling dogs, he set off from Ellesmere Island on to the ocean's pack ice on 20 March 1908. He returned to civilization claiming he had reached the Pole on 21 April 1908, but by December 1909, US newspapers were denouncing him, following the conclusion of a scientific commission that '...the material transmitted for examination [by Cook] contains no proof whatsoever that Dr Cook reached the North Pole.' His claim was rarely taken seriously again. According to his Greenlandic companions, he had given up after two days.

Peary – the obsessive

Peary had made his first foray on to the pack ice in 1900, abandoning his attempt at 84°17' North. He had lost eight of his toes the previous year attempting to reach the start point. In 1906 he claimed a 'furthest north' at 87°06' (275 of the 475 statute mile total distance). Going beyond 87° North had put Peary definitively ahead of the previous 86th latitude records of the renowned Norwegian, Fridtjof Nansen (1893–96), and the Italian, Umberto Cagni (1899–1900). Peary became a national celebrity whose polar endeavours were held aloft by the US media, the august National Geographic Society, and even the American President.

Peary had developed a 'pyramid strategy', whereby pre-arranged teams within the overall team structure would peel off from the expedition's route and head back to land once their planned contribution to breaking the trail and moving the supplies forward for the remaining teams was complete. On 28 February 1909, Peary, Matthew Henson, Robert 'Bob' Bartlett, George Borup, John Goodsell, Ross Marvin and Donald MacMillan, together with 17 Eskimos, 19 sledges and 133 dogs, set off from Cape Columbia at 83°07' North on another attempt

Problems soon emerged. Two sledges were smashed beyond repair on the first day. Borup and Marvin then became separated from the main expedition and were not re-united for several days. McMillan, who had been ear-marked to continue to 86° North, next revealed a severely frost-bitten foot. Peary ordered him back immediately. The daily grind continued remorselessly in temperatures *c.* 15–45°C below zero (5 to -49°F).

Peary, wrapped in furs, searching the horizon through a telescope from the top of a pressure-ridge.

Peary and his team, supposedly at the North Pole, cheering the Stars and Stripes.

On 1 April the last sub-team peeled off under Bartlett, apparently at 87°47′ North. Only Peary, Henson, and four Greenlanders – Ootam, Egingwah, Seegloo and Ooqueah remained. The Pole team covered the closing 153 statute miles in an impressive five days, arriving at 89°57′ North (less than 3.5 statute miles short of the Pole) on 6 April. Much of 7 April was spent by Peary trying to establish his exact latitude and longitude. Disconcertingly he never felt able to confirm his exact position – even to his team on the day. Peary later recorded of his time 'furthest North': 'The Pole at last! ... The prize of 3 centuries, my dream and ambition for 23 years! Mine at last!' By 23 April the team had safely retraced its entire route across the sea ice to the relative safety of land.

However, recent expert examinations of his personal log-book, and accompanying evidence, including a rigorous, if contentious, assessment by Wally Herbert, have revealed a navigational record that is seriously compromised both by its extraordinary lack of rigour on positional information and by the enormity of the daily distances claimed on the return. Most notably he claimed that over four particular days in which he approached, travelled in the vicinity of, and subsequently departed 'the Pole', he covered 225 statute miles (excluding detours for terrain) representing a daily average of 56 statute miles – a speed no one has come close to before or since. Experts now regard the explorer's own evidence, ultimately upon which any claim must stand or fall in such circumstances, at best as 'inadequate' to validate his claim.

In the years that followed a small number of expeditions passed under, flew over or arrived at the Pole by a variety of means of transportation. But by as late as 1968 no one had yet undisputedly reached the Pole on foot without using motorized transport, and certainly, no one had made a surface crossing from one side of the Arctic Ocean to the other via the Pole – not even by icebreaker.

Self-portrait of Wally Herbert, using pencil and scalpel.

The longest polar trek in history

Wally Herbert, a dedicated and experienced British polar explorer, set himself this enormous task. His team-mates were to be Allan Gill, Ken Hedges and Roy 'Fritz' Koerner, and they left Point Barrow, Alaska, each with a team of dogs, on 21 February. It took a month to cross the dangerously mobile fracture zone of sea ice off-lying the

Herbert and his team crossing the polar ice with dog teams.

Herbert's team at the North Pole, 6 April 1969. Their epic journey, consisting of a surface crossing from one side of the Arctic Ocean to the other, via the Pole, has never been repeated, nor ever will be because of climate change.

Alaskan coast. Their daily distance rose rapidly to over 24 km (15 miles) as the surface conditions improved and warmer spring weather prevailed. All too soon the summer melt was upon them, however, and the frequency of encountering open water slowed them down again. With 1,900 km (1,180 miles) behind them they set up a temporary camp – dubbed Meltville – on a large pan of ice, to see out the watery summer conditions. On 4 September, with the dropping temperatures finally refreezing the waters, they set off again, expecting to travel until the gathering darkness of autumn prevented further travel that year.

But eight days later and just 10 km (6 miles) further north (and still 386 km/240 miles short of their planned over-wintering position), a sudden medical crisis shattered the plan. Gill, immobilized, probably with a slipped disc, could walk no more and the expedition was forced to abandon its autumn trek and sit out the winter, hoping his back would recover with the enforced rest. One of their several planned drops by aircraft brought materials and fresh supplies for their premature over-wintering camp. The four men endured five months and seven days without sight of the sun in temperatures routinely below -30°C (-22°F) outside, in a hut 4.6 m (15 ft) square. During this phase they had to relocate the entire camp in total darkness when their ice pan broke up.

Off again, with Gill's back recovered, on 24 February, they finally made it to the Pole, following weeks of extreme effort, on 6 April 1969 – 60 years to the day after Peary had claimed the Pole to be his. Herbert described the moment of his arrival thus: 'It had been an elusive spot to find and fix – the North Pole, where two separate sets of meridians meet and all directions are south. Trying to set foot upon it had been like trying to step on the shadow of a bird that was hovering overhead, for the surface across which we were moving was itself a moving surface on a planet that was spinning about an axis beneath our feet.'

On 29 May 1969, Herbert's team completed its epic 16-month crossing of the Arctic Ocean when Gill and Hedges landed briefly on Little Blackboard Island. Only a few weeks later US astronaut Neil Armstrong became the first person to land on another planet (p. 275).

RANULPH FIENNES

Race to the South Pole

1910–12

Great God! This is an awful place and terrible enough for us to have laboured to it without the reward of priority.
ROBERT FALCON SCOTT, 1912

In the short Antarctic summer of 1911–12 five Britons and five Norwegians raced each other to the bottom of the world. Only the Norwegians returned. What happened to the British?

First explorations

In 1910 very little was known about Antarctica. Nobody knew even whether it was a continent or a mass of floating ice, for it had been penetrated only once for any distance. In 1902, the British Royal Navy captain Robert Falcon Scott (together with his chosen team of merchant navy officer Ernest Shackleton and doctor Edward Wilson) had travelled 645 km (400 miles) southwards over the frozen Ross Sea ice shelf. This, a mainly scientific expedition, was the brainchild of the Royal Geographical Society.

Scott had been an obscure torpedo specialist with no expedition experience. After his 1902 Antarctic epic, however, he was accepted worldwide as the greatest of Britain's polar leaders. This changed in 1908, when Shackleton led his own four-man team. Using the lessons learnt and terrain discovered under Scott, he pushed further

Scott in his den in the expedition hut at Cape Evans; family photos line the wall behind him. The baby in his wife's arms was to become the famous wildlife artist and ecologist Sir Peter Scott.

Right *Roald Amundsen, seen here in front of his ship* Fram, *deceived everyone, including Scott, into thinking he was making an attempt on the North, not the South, Pole.*

south towards the Pole, only turning back because of dwindling supplies just 156 km (97 miles) short of his goal. In March 1909 Scott was walking past a news hoarding in London with an old polar friend and saw the news of Shackleton's narrow failure to make the Pole. 'I think', he remarked, 'we'd better have a shot next.'

Scott's plans

Just as Shackleton had used Scott's experience to plan his own polar attempt, so Scott sensibly based his second journey on studying Shackleton's near triumph. The latter had used sturdy ponies on the flat ice shelf and then men on foot to haul their sledges up the glacial valley to reach the 3,050-m (10,000-ft) high polar plateau.

Scott had nobody to learn from other than himself and Shackleton, since no other human had travelled extensively in the unique terrain of Antarctica. Why use dogs, which may or may not be able to cope with the terrible glaciers of Antarctica, when a proven system was available? Shackleton had almost reached the Pole with only manpower, four ponies, no skis and no dogs. What Scott clearly had to do was to reach the same point that Shackleton had at his furthest south, but with a stronger team and the crucial extra supplies needed to cope with a return trip over the last stretch that had defeated Shackleton.

In addition, Scott was determined to make his second expedition even more scientifically successful than his first. He crammed his team with the most accomplished scientists he could find, for he had a dual aim: priority at the Pole and the furtherance of scientific discoveries.

The secret rival

Scott knew of no rival and so did not anticipate having to move south any faster than seasonal travel limitations dictated. He would have to race the weather, but not human competitors, and he planned everything accordingly. He did not – and could not – know that Roald Amundsen, the most experienced Arctic traveller of the day was, by late 1909, plotting to beat Scott to the Pole.

Amundsen proved to be a master of deceit. At first he had intended to be the first to reach the North Pole, but when the American Robert Peary claimed to have reached it (p. 234), Amundsen secretly switched his focus to the South Pole. Not wishing to alert Scott to his new plans, for then Scott would have time to re-assess his own travel methods, Amundsen told nobody of his new aim except for his brother. He deceived the world that he was still aiming at the northern target. He was believed by his nation, whose ship he was borrowing, by his king and by his Patron, the great doyen of Norwegian polar endeavour, Fridtjof Nansen – and even by his own expedition team.

In March 1910, three months before his departure for Antarctica, Scott telephoned Amundsen

Centre *The British expedition hut at Cape Evans today, still full of supplies and equipment, preserved by the Antarctic cold.*

to request scientific co-operation between himself in the South and Amundsen in the North. The latter would not take the call, and Scott continued his plans with no thoughts of a race. He aimed to try out four methods of travel including experimental motorized sledges, but, since they were likely to break down, he did not mean to rely on them; all his calculations were based on the possibility of zero machine usage.

Scott had long since concluded that dogs could be counted upon to drag loads further than men provided you did not mind their very considerable suffering in the process. So he planned to use his dogs in 1911/12 only for so long as they could cope without ill usage; they would not be relied upon as the main haulage means. As it turned out, dogs would have been absolutely critical for the specific purpose of speed racing for the Pole. But Scott was not expecting to race. And as Tryggve Gran, a Norwegian soldier and the single ski expert Scott took with him, later wrote: 'Could Scott have beaten Amundsen? ... should he have had the possibility of competing fairly ... he would have had to know that Amundsen planned to be the South Pole conqueror well before the winter of 1910, for the battle is won at the preparation stage.'

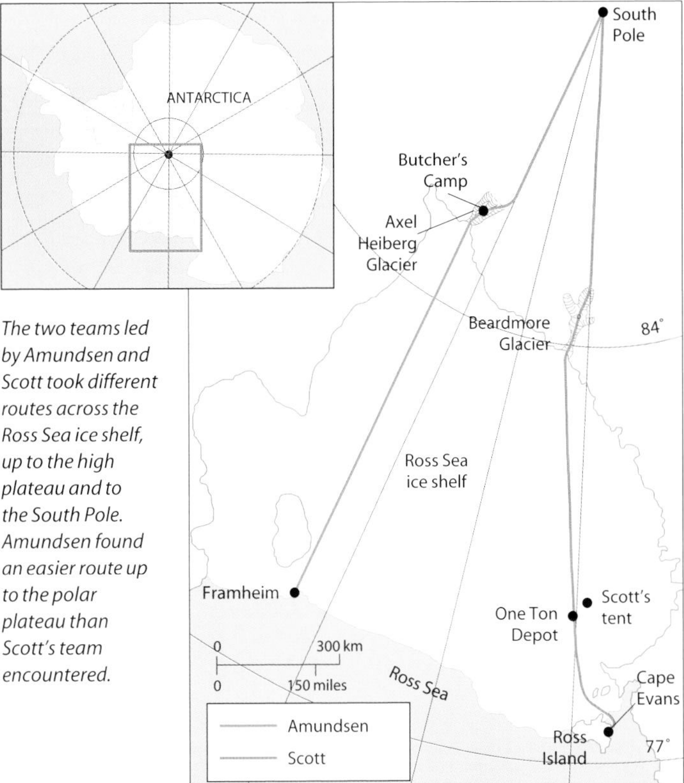

The two teams led by Amundsen and Scott took different routes across the Ross Sea ice shelf, up to the high plateau and to the South Pole. Amundsen found an easier route up to the polar plateau than Scott's team encountered.

Once Scott had left Britain on his way to Antarctica (with no chance of altering his team or of purchasing racing huskies) Amundsen sent him a cryptic message to await his arrival in Australia. The text merely offered:

'Beg leave to inform you *Fram* [his ship] proceeding Antarctic. Amundsen.'

Amundsen knew Scott was planning a major scientific programme involving many scientists and cumbersome instruments. There would be 65 men setting out with Scott. Amundsen would take no scientists and only a tight-knit group of travellers based around the world's best dog-sledgers and skiers – a total of 19 men.

To the Pole

After passing the winter of 1910 at separate polar bases on the edge of the Ross Sea, the two teams of five selected men set out for the Pole – Scott on 1 November and Amundsen, from a base (96.5 km (60 miles) closer to the Pole, 12 days earlier. By a stroke of sheer good fortune Amundsen reached the mountains that form the high barrier to the

The British team at the South Pole, already aware that Amundsen had reached it before them: (left to right) Oates, Bowers, Scott, Wilson, Evans. The photograph was taken using a remote-control device held by Bowers.

polar plateau at the exact point where a glacier offered a steep route to the top by which all crevasse fields could be avoided. Such a bonus was nowhere available on the Scott/Shackleton route.

Early in December, Scott's men shot the last of their ponies at the base of their glacial route while, at the top of theirs, the Norwegians shot 22 dogs at a site called the Butcher's Shop. The remaining dogs continued to tow their sledges as the British began their traditional manhauling.

On 14 December Amundsen's men reached the Pole; the British still had 580 km (360 miles) to cover. Despite the need to make distance, Scott's men surveyed with accuracy all their visible surroundings and made geological forays whenever interesting formations were passed.

By the end of December, on the high plateau, the British, with and without skis, were averaging 21 km (13 miles) a day compared with the average Norwegian rate of 24 km (15 miles) per day with dogs. Only when they reached the immediate vicinity of the Pole did they spot the Norwegians' tracks and realize that they had been beaten. Henry Bowers wrote in his diary 'We have got here and if ever a journey has been accomplished by honest sweat, ours has.'

On their return from the Pole, Scott's men manhauled 14 miles a day, only one mile less than the Norwegian dog teams could manage. Taff Evans, a long time sledge-mate of Scott, died of hypothermia on their way back down the glacier as they ran into a labyrinth of deep crevasses. The next to die, an army captain named Titus Oates, purposefully left the tent in a blizzard rather than continue to hold back the others due to a frostbitten leg.

Scott, with his two surviving colleagues, Bowers and the doctor Edward Wilson, suffered various problems including leaking fuel bottles and a failed resupply system. However, a careful study of their records and diaries, found later in their tent, prove conclusively that they would have successfully made it back to their base but for a single key factor – freak weather. What is now certain, since the publication in 2001 of *The Coldest March* by a US atmospheric scientist, is that Scott's group were unlucky enough to experience an extreme low temperature weather front akin to a rogue wave on an ocean.

One by one the three survivors died slowly in their lonely tent, unable to move further despite the knowledge that one of their supply dumps lay but 18 km (11 miles) further on. Scott was the last to die, his remarkable diaries testifying to his hardy spirit. For the last eight terrible days inside the dark, snow-drifted tent, Scott lived on without food or liquid, heat or light. His story, perhaps not one of victory, is certainly one of great courage in adversity.

Scott's men lost their race against dog-power, but their scientific aims were successfully carried out. By the time, in the 1960s, that the results of all their work was analyzed, it was clear that the results of Scott's two expeditions exceeded by far the total information garnered by all other international Antarctica expeditions in the first half of the 20th century.

As for Amundsen, he spent the rest of his life an aloof and embittered man constantly in search of new triumphs. He never forgave his Antarctic second-in-command who had briefly revolted against him, and humiliated him down the years, adding to the causes of his eventual suicide.

And what did the victorious Norwegian team think of their rival's feat? One of Amundsen's great Pole team, Helmer Hanssen, said:

It is no disparagement of Amundsen and the rest of us when I say that Scott's achievement far exceeded ours ... Just imagine what it meant for Scott and the others to drag their sleds themselves, with all their equipment and provisions to the Pole and back again. We started with 52 dogs and came back with eleven, and many of these wore themselves out on the journey. What shall we say of Scott and his comrades, who were their own dogs? Anyone with any experience will take off his hat to Scott's achievement. I do not believe men ever have shown such endurance at any time, nor do I believe there ever will be men to equal it.

we shall stick it out
to the end but we
are getting weaker of
course and the end
cannot be far
It seems a pity, but
I do not think I can
write more —
R. Scott
Last entry —
For God's sake look
after our people

Left *Scott's final diary entry, written as he lay in the tent, unable to move further, on 29 March 1912. It reads: 'We shall stick it out to the end, but we are getting weaker of course and the end cannot be far. It seems a pity, but I do not think I can write more ... For God's sake, look after our people.'*

Below *Scott's tent just as the relief party found it on 12 November 1912. Scott's diaries were retrieved, along with his body and those of Bowers and Wilson.*

DAVID McLEAN

Shackleton & the Endurance

1914–16

A picture haunts my mind – of three boats, crammed with frost-bitten, wet, and dreadfully thirsty men who have had no proper sleep for many days and nights. ... All night long [Shackleton] sits with his hand on the painter, which grows heavier and heavier with ice as the unseen seas surge by, and as the rope tightens and droops under his hand his thoughts are busy with future plans.

APSLEY CHERRY-GARRARD, *THE NATION*, 13 DECEMBER 1919

This journey is unique. It was not planned. It should never have happened. By the usual laws of nature and human endurance it should never have succeeded. Given the extreme circumstances, some or all of the participants should have died.

The Imperial Trans-Antarctic Expedition had sailed from South Georgia in December 1914 with hopes of making the first traverse across the Antarctic continent, the next big challenge of polar exploration after the reaching of the South Pole three years previously (p. 239). It was led by Sir Ernest Shackleton, already famous for almost reaching the South Pole in 1908. He was the rare kind that tough men would follow anywhere. He mingled with the crew, eschewed special treatment, but was also immensely firm, maintaining control of the situation, however bad. Crucially, he kept his own and others' spirits up.

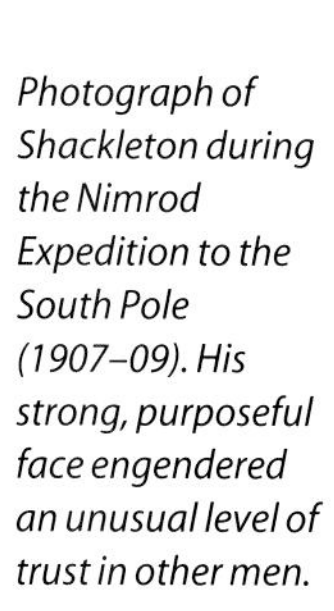

Photograph of Shackleton during the Nimrod Expedition to the South Pole (1907–09). His strong, purposeful face engendered an unusual level of trust in other men.

Beset by ice

In January 1915 the expedition ship, the *Endurance*, became beset by pack ice off Antarctica and drifted in the Weddell Sea for 10 months, until it was slowly crushed by great plates of ice and finally sank on 21 November 1915. In the meantime, the crew managed to salvage the dogs, the ship's three whaleboats and some provisions and equipment.

With their ship gone, the men were marooned on a frozen sea, far from help, in one of the most inhospitable places on earth. Without communication, no one in the world knew where they were. Where once the ship's walls protected them against the blizzards and cold, now they had only thin, flimsy tents. It was so cold they could hear the water freeze and the ice beneath them drifted, cracked and heaved with the ocean currents. Unable to drag the salvaged boats, they camped where they were, drifting northwards on the ice towards land and an uncertain fate.

The men drifted for four months until the ice broke up and they were able to launch the three boats. Sailing and rowing, they then threaded their way through the ice until they reached Elephant Island, an inhospitable place at the tip of the Antarctic peninsula – desolate, but at least solid land.

The desperate voyage

No rescue party would look for them here. Shackleton would have to take one of the boats and go for help, or they would all be doomed. The prevailing winds and currents meant that the only practical place to aim for was South Georgia, an island 1,400 km (870 miles) to the northeast, where there was a Norwegian whaling station. But crossing the world's roughest and coldest ocean in one of the open boats, just 7m (22ft) long, was surely impossible. If its wooden hull was not holed by floating ice, it would be swamped or blown over, or the men, weak and improperly clad, would die of exposure. Even if the boat was able to weather the seas, how could they navigate well enough to find such a small island with the primitive instruments they had? Everything pointed to the impossibility of making such a perilous journey in so inadequate a boat.

A few days later, however, the *James Caird* (as it was named by Shackleton) was on its way. For the voyage Shackleton took five companions: Frank Worsley, skipper and navigator; Tom Crean, for his formidable physical and mental strength – he was once described 'as close as one can come to being indestructible'; Harry McNeish for his shipwright skills; and Timothy McCarthy and George Vincent for their boat skills.

For equipment they took sails, oars, a sea anchor, compass, sextant, chronometer, charts, a bailer, a bilge pump, fishing line, a primus stove, candles, matches, a pair of binoculars – and food and water for a month. When the *James Caird* set off on 24 April (with the Antarctic winter coming on) neither the six on board nor the 22 waving them off from the shore ever thought they would see each other again – but all knew that the voyage had to be attempted.

During the voyage, one crew helmed, one trimmed the sails, one bailed, and all kept a

The Endurance, *in all her glory, butting the 2-m (6-ft) thick ice floes with engine and sails, in the days before anyone realized her predicament.*

'The End' as Shackleton later captioned this photograph by Frank Hurley. The Endurance *had been home to both men and dogs for over 12 months. Now the ice ground and split the sturdy hull timbers until the ship finally sank on 21 November 1915.*

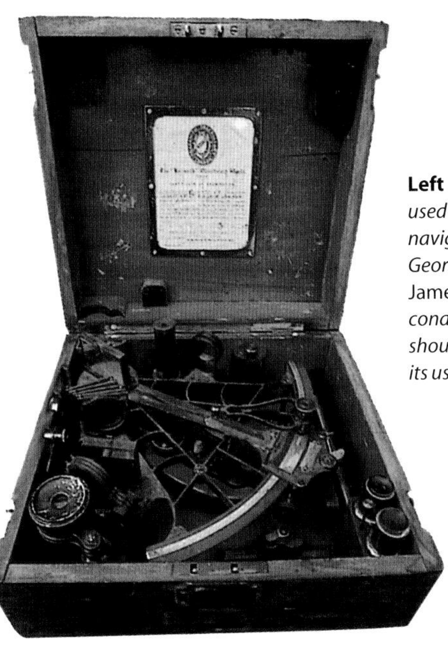

Left *The sextant used by Worsley to navigate to South Georgia in the* James Caird, *in conditions which should have made its use impossible.*

Above *Departure of the* James Caird *from Elephant Island, 24 April 1916.*

lookout. Their clothing – thick wool layers, gabardine overalls, woolly helmets – was designed for dry cold, not for the sea spray which soaked the men and often froze, causing frost-bite, blisters, and chapped skin. The oilskins had all gone down with their ship.

Deprived of warmth, the crew relied on food and Shackleton saw to it that hot 'hoosh' (bovril stew) was served at regular times interspersed with brews of hot milk. In the ever-pitching boat two men braced themselves against the sides and held the Primus stove between their feet while a third cooked. Unable to sit upright below the deck they ate their food cramped up in the darkness. Sleeping involved squeezing forward between the ballast and the thwarts in darkness until they reached damp sleeping bags in the bows. With the bow's rise and thumping fall, sleep was barely snatched.

Long before electronic navigation Frank Worsley used compass, sextant, chronometer and 'dead reckoning'. Due to poor weather only four sun-sights were obtained, with Worsley being held steady by two men while he measured angles. An error of half a degree would put them out by 48 km (30 miles) and South Georgia might be missed from 16 km (10 miles) away. At night course checks were made by striking a match near the compass. Otherwise it was the age-old method of watching the waves and feeling the wind on the back of the neck.

During heavy gales they had to turn the boat into the wind, riding to a sea anchor and by constant tacking. South Atlantic waves are the 'highest, broadest and longest swells in the world', blocking out the horizon as they approach. Riding them in a small boat took the

Below *The route of the* Endurance *until she sank, and the route of the men as they went in search of rescue.*

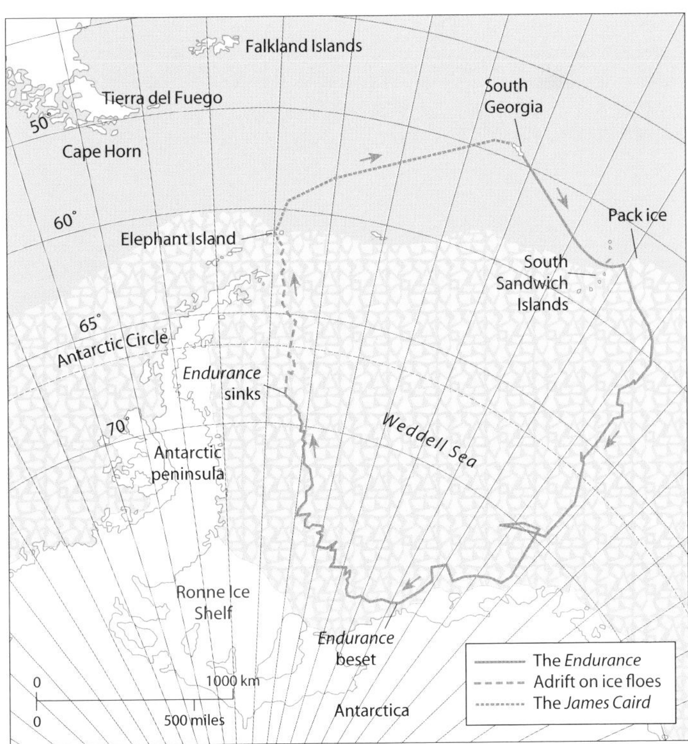

helmsman skill, strength and dogged seamanship. Shifting ballast and pumping out water were painstaking chores. When spray froze in lumps and made the boat top-heavy the men had to chip it away without falling overboard.

One night Shackleton, at the helm, noticed a slither of clear sky to the south and announced a break in the weather. On looking again he realized it was the crest of an enormous wave. 'For God's sake, hold on! It's got us' he yelled before the crest gathered the boat up and flung it forward in a maelstrom of tortured water – almost swamping it. The boat groaned under the blow and half rose full of water but, incredibly, still upright. For 10 minutes they bailed for their lives until the boat rose again. It took them two hours to straighten out. Despite such dangers, and sailing a lumbering seaboat across the world's most dangerous ocean, the men were cheerful, matter-of-fact and joked in understatements, confident they would make it.

On the 14th day, thanks to remarkable navigation, the mountains of South Georgia came into sight – but it was the uninhabited and precipitous west coast. With horrible misfortune hurricane-force winds struck the *James Caird* that very night and the crew, by now desperately tired and thirsty – their water was contaminated – had to tack all night away from the black cliffs and uncharted reefs. Worsley regretted that, if they were wrecked, no one would ever know just how nearly they had succeeded in getting rescue. His fears were well justified – during the same storm a 500-ton steamship foundered nearby.

The next morning in calmer weather they finally got ashore on a beach. It was 10 May; they had spent 16 days at sea.

Crossing South Georgia

The exhausted men slept under their upturned boat. Their journey was by no means over: it was 242 km (150 miles) by sea to the whaling station, but only 48 km (30 miles) by land. South Georgia resembles a slice of the Alps sticking up out of the ocean, with 2,743-m (9,000-ft) mountains, glaciers and steep slopes. There were no maps, indeed no one had ever before attempted to walk across it.

After a few days' rest Shackleton, Worsley and Crean were ready. They were tired and had no proper equipment or experience of winter mountains. But they were desperate, were assumed to be dead, and the lives of 25 other companions depended on them reaching help. With boat screws in their boots, 15 m (50 ft) of rope and a ship's adze, they set off. Without sleeping bags or shelter they dared not stop, apart from brief rests. In growing darkness Shackleton was cutting steps down a steep slope, but progress was too slow. Sitting on the coiled rope, they slid down at breakneck speed, shouting with joy when they survived a 274-m (900-ft) descent.

On the far side, after more trials, they descended towards Stromness Bay. At an early breakfast, they heard a faint steam-whistle, the call to work at the whaling station. Within hours they walked into the whaling station to the amazement of the Norwegians. That night Worsley was taken round in a whaler to collect the three men and the already famous *James Caird*. Because Elephant Island was so often cut off by ice, it took Shackleton four attempts before he finally rescued the remaining 22 men. Not a man was lost.

In terms of duration, distance travelled, obstacles overcome, this self-rescue is the most extraordinary in the annals of exploration. Their success owes much to the toughness of the men, good fortune, and the qualities of their remarkable leader, Ernest Shackleton.

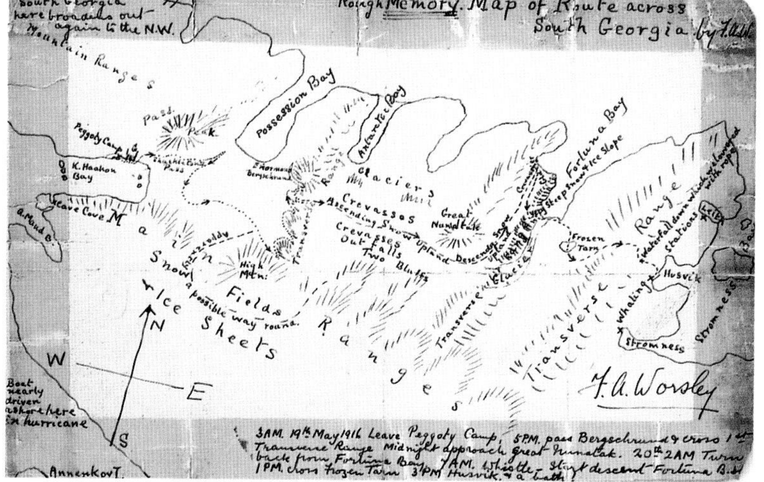

Frank Worsley's sketch map – from memory – of the route he, Crean and Shackleton took across South Georgia.

JANE ROBINSON

Women Travellers in Asia

1913–14

I fear, when I come to the end, I shall say: 'It was a waste of time.' It's done now, and there's no remedy, but I think I was a fool to come into these wastes.

GERTRUDE BELL, 1914

There was something about the desert regions of Western Asia that seemed to attract British women travellers in the late 19th and early 20th centuries. Three of the most remarkable – Gertrude Bell, Isabella Bird and Freya Stark – made journeys there which they considered to be the most significant of their careers. Each responded to the uncompromising desert landscape, contrasting so startlingly with its peoples' generous hospitality, with an intriguing mixture of despair and exultation. They described their journeys in some of the finest examples of travel-writing.

Gertrude Lowthian Bell was a restless romantic. Born in 1868, her precocious intelligence was recognized by her wealthy family. But even though she was allowed to attend Oxford University, becoming the first woman awarded a First Class Degree in modern history, she was then expected to devote herself to leisured domesticity. This changed in 1892 when she visited Tehran in Persia (Iran) with an aunt. Immediately Bell arrived in the East she was captivated, not just by the people and their history, but by the whole experience of travel. She had found her vocation.

Early expeditions

Armed with a working knowledge of archaeology and surveying, Bell spent the next decade excavating Byzantine and Roman remains in Syria, Turkey, Mesopotamia, and what is now Iraq, producing a number of successful books. She also, rather shockingly, earned a reputation as a skilled and fearless Alpine mountaineer.

Bell was genuinely interested in archaeology, but it masked another impulse. Her intelligence and keen political awareness made her a reliable witness to the shifting balance of power in the Middle East, where she acted as an unofficial roving spy for the British government. Reports resulting from her greatest journey, through Najd to Hail (now in Saudi Arabia) from 1913 to 1914, were invaluable in the build-up to the First World War. Displaying the same courage (or

Gertrude Bell photographed in the Lebanon in 1900, during one of her earliest archaeological expeditions. She rode astride, which was still a progressive approach for a Western woman, but eminently practical.

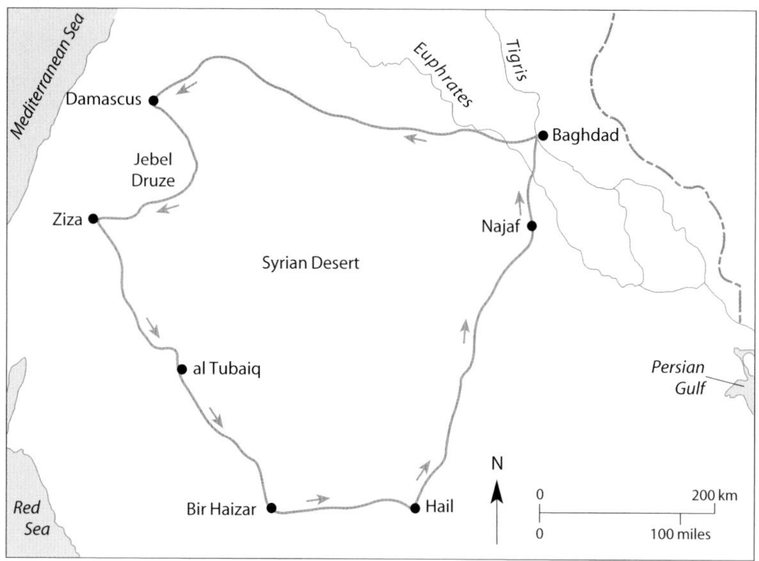

Bell's journey began and ended in Damascus. For 136 days she travelled through what is now Syria, Jordan, Saudi Arabia and Iraq.

recklessness) she showed as a mountaineer, she chose a dangerous route leading her through partly uncharted country, across a succession of fiercely held tribal territories, to the violent heartland of Arabia. No European had penetrated Hail for over 20 years.

Labour of love

The motives behind Bell's Hail expedition were further complicated by her being desperately in love. But Major Charles Doughty-Wylie, nephew of the Arabist Charles Doughty (p. 211), was married, with no prospect of divorce. Only when he was posted from London to Albania in the autumn of 1913 did Bell feel free to leave for Hail, and only because they were forced apart did she feel the need to lose herself – perhaps literally – in the fickle embrace of the desert, his only rival. The best account we have of her journey appears in a secret diary written for Doughty-Wylie; supplemented by her letters, it chronicles a paradoxical pilgrimage to find things out, and forget.

Bell's starting point for the journey to Hail was Damascus. Having engaged 17 camels there, a guide, servants, gifts for local leaders, and enough food and water to see her through the expanses between oases, she set out for the south on 16 December 1913. The journey was not without its difficulties, including brutal encounters with Jebel Druze tribesmen and a period of detention by over-zealous Turkish officials who, along with the Germans and British, were doing all they could in this immediate pre-War era to influence the various Arab peoples into allegiance. With no official sanction for the journey, Bell was content to travel as an unprotected outlaw, and reached Hail on 26 February 1914.

Hail

Hail was the headquarters of the Rashid family, opposed to the British-backed Sauds (based in Riyadh) and renowned for their treachery. Bell was aware, however, that as a woman she was uncategorizable as a threat, being more a curiosity. And as the supposed 'daughter of kings' (that is, proclaiming her high status in Britain and behaving with suitable authority) she was bound by Arabian custom to be honoured as a guest.

Indeed, she was conducted to the Rashids' summer palace immediately on arrival – and virtually imprisoned there for 11 days. Meanwhile

Right *Bell took several photographs in Hail, despite being imprisoned for most of her stay. It was an enchanting city she said: a place to 'widen the heart'.*

Isabella Bird (also known as Mrs Bishop) explored Manchuria on her way from Korea to the USSR during the Sino-Japanese war of 1894–95.

Below left *'West Gate at Chia-Ling Fu' (1896), photographed by Bird on a journey through China in her mid-60s.*

Below right *Bird's tent in the Bakhtiyari region of western Persia (Iran). She stands on the right; her companions are passing British missionaries.*

ISABELLA BIRD

In 1892, a controversial election took place in London. Fifteen 'well qualified ladies' were chosen to become the first female Fellows of the Royal Geographical Society, and among them – best qualified of all – was Isabella Bird. Bird had just completed the most arduous journey of her life, a winter trek from Baghdad to Tehran, and even though certain old salts might object to mere 'globe trotteresses' being honoured with Society Fellowship, it was hard to deny Bird's right to recognition.

The journey began in January 1890, when Bird was 58. She had been to Tibet, and while recovering in India, met a British Officer on his way to Tehran. Curiosity compelled Bird to ask if she could join him. This was a mysterious and challenging part of the world (as Gertrude Bell appreciated), and Bird relished a challenge.

It was a ghastly journey. Even though she was shielded against the icy glare of the winter sun by a cork hat, snow spectacles and a grey woollen face-mask, the weather soon froze Bird to her saddle by day and her blanket by night. She stayed in village caravanserai, or guest-houses, whenever possible; although these might sound grand they were invariably slimy with filth, and cold as the grave. She survived on a meagre diet of biscuits, dried soup, dates and goat's milk, losing nearly 12 kg (2 st) in the course of the journey.

When her mule staggered into Tehran 46 days after leaving Baghdad, so stiff and mud-caked was Bird that she could hardly dismount. But she never regretted the journey. It had revealed to her, if only in fleeting moments, something of what she called 'the congenial barbarism of the desert': a rare prize indeed.

Bird went on to travel in Kurdistan, Korea and China before her death in 1904, but the Persian journey remained one of the proudest achievements of this remarkable Victorian pioneer.

A photograph taken by Bell of a tribal harem. She wrote: 'some of the sheikhly women were very beautiful. They pass from hand to hand – the victor takes them; and think of it, his hands are red with the blood of their husbands and children!'

Bell's political acumen ensured she was taken seriously by both the British administration, for whom she acted as an unofficial spy, and by those amongst whom she travelled. This affectionate cartoon is by her brother-in-law, Sir Herbert Richmond.

she made astute observations of the political situation, gleaned from visiting officials; she became the first British traveller to detail life and attitudes in an Arabian harem from the inside, and took a series of documentary photographs she developed herself. Eventually negotiating her release, she left Hail for Najaf, Baghdad and finally Damascus again, reaching her starting-point 136 days after setting out.

After the journey

Bell was awarded the Royal Geographical Society's Gold Medal in recognition of her courage and resourcefulness during the journey. Modestly, she doubted her fitness for the honour; but it was well deserved. The British government showed its appreciation by appointing her Oriental Secretary to the Chief Political Officer in Iraq during the First World War. She became an advisor to King Faisal, helping to draw up the boundaries between Iraq, Kuwait and Saudi Arabia; she even founded Baghdad's National Museum. But in 1926, with Doughty-Wylie long dead and her physical and political powers diminishing, she took an overdose and died.

Bell may not have discovered vast treasures, or mapped blank tracts of Arabia, but in travelling as a lone woman, reflecting her outward journey in intense self-awareness, and writing about it with such exquisite passion and sensitivity, she trod new ground with every step.

FREYA STARK

Like Gertrude Bell, Dame Freya Stark was fascinated by blanks on the map. And despite both Bell's and Isabella Bird's best intentions, there were still plenty of them when Stark embarked in 1931, aged 38, on her travelling career in Luristan (an area on the western borders of what is now Iran) on her first great journey.

The valleys of Luristan cradled the stronghold of the infamous Assassins, a sinister and fanatical people whose culture was unimaginably alien to Stark's traditional Western femininity. They were named for their copious consumption of hashish, and had terrorized the region between the 11th and 13th centuries with absolute brutality. Their culture of secrecy remained, and Stark the archaeologist planned to expose their history at last. Meanwhile Stark the cartographer planned 'to disentangle the absolute wrongness of the map' thereabouts, which she did with aplomb. On her return she was hailed by the Royal Geographical Society as a serious and 'worth-while' explorer.

Far more valuable to Stark the traveller, however, was the intangible fruit of the journey. She contracted malaria in the Elburz Mountains soon after setting out from Baghdad, and chose to take her chance and stay there to recuperate, rather than scuttle back to friends in the city. That decision shaped the rest of her illustrious career. In entrusting herself to the local people, weak and delirious as she was, she showed them the ultimate degree of respect, and received in return real love and fellowship. For weeks she was tenderly nursed back to health by strangers, and continued with a new sensitivity, and an understanding of the emotional and cultural interdependence necessary between successful travellers and those amongst whom they travel, which enriched her life and writing ever after, until her death in 1993.

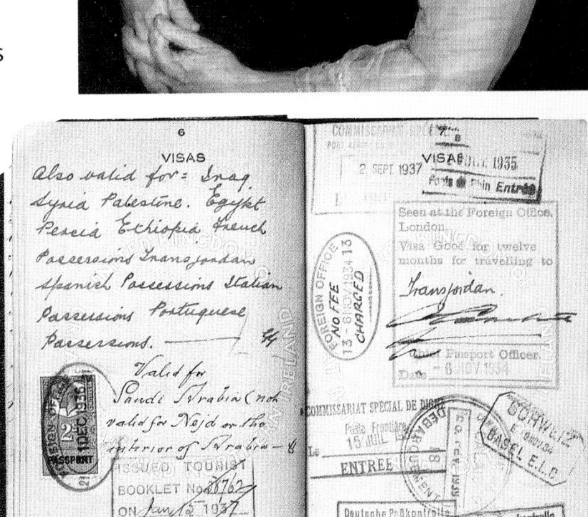

Top *A portrait of Freya Stark in her youth, by Herbert Olivier, 1923. Later, she advised women travellers to dress plainly, modestly and unobtrusively.*

Below *Qal'a Alishtar, Iran: a photograph taken by Freya Stark.*

Centre *Pages from one of Stark's passports, from 1934.*

FREDERICK ENGLE

First to Fly the Atlantic Solo

1927

What freedom lies in flying! What godlike power it gives to man! I'm independent of the seaman's coast lines, of the landsman's roads; I could as well have drawn that line north to the Arctic, or westward over the Pacific, or southeast to the jungles of the Amazon.

CHARLES LINDBERGH, 1953

Modern aviation began at the edge of the sea. In December 1903, the Wright Brothers flew above the sands of a barrier island on North Carolina's Outer Banks. Technically their achievement is described as the first powered and controlled flight by a piloted heavier-than-air aircraft. The Wright Brothers' first flight at Kitty Hawk lasted 12 seconds, not long enough to cross a small river.

In July 1909, another aviation milestone was reached: Louis Blériot was the first to fly across a major body of water, in this case the English Channel. Flying without a compass and over trackless water, Blériot's open cockpit had just two instruments – an oil pressure gauge and an engine tachometer. However, he successfully landed his model XI aircraft in a field just west of Dover after a flight lasting 36 minutes.

By the First World War, aircraft were patrolling coastal waters, and as the war ended the US Navy developed a seaplane that could carry enough fuel for a 16-hour flight. In May 1919 three four-engine NC model seaplanes set out from Long Island, New York, for Plymouth, England. Each seaplane had a crew of six and the aircraft made refuelling stops in Nova Scotia, Newfoundland, the Azores and Lisbon. Only one of the three aircraft, the NC4, completed the 23-day trip. In June 1919, two British fliers, John Alcock and Arthur Brown, took off from Newfoundland in a twin-engine Vickers land biplane and crash-landed in an Irish bog 16 hours later.

Louis Blériot poses with his wife and onlookers next to his open box-framed aircraft after flying from France to England. The first to cross a significant body of water in a heavier-than-air aircraft, Blériot reported being lost until Dover's white cliffs came into view.

The prize

As the NC4 was making its successful trans-Atlantic crossing, New York hotelier Raymond Orteig offered a prize of $25,000 for the first non-stop, heavier-than-air flight between Paris and New York. The 5,760-km (3,600-mile) flight would take approximately 40 hours. In September 1926, a three-engine biplane designed by Igor Sikorsky crashed on take-off for an attempt at the prize. Two of the Sikorsky's four-man crew were killed in the fire that engulfed the aircraft as the full load of fuel burned. The crash highlighted the basic problem, getting into the air with sufficient fuel for a 40-hour flight. The weight of gasoline was the limiting factor to non-stop trans-Atlantic flight.

Carrying the mail – making a plan

In the autumn of 1926, Charles Lindbergh mulled over the news of the Sikorsky's crash as he piloted a war-surplus de Havilland between St Louis and Chicago. The 25-year-old air mail pilot and former barnstormer gave thought to the problem of time, speed, distance and the weight of fuel. Lindbergh was frustrated by flying obsolete aircraft, having occasionally to bailout when an engine failed. He decided that he would make the first New York to Paris flight, that he would do it alone and that he would fly a single-engine aircraft. All he needed was the right aircraft, and the money to buy it.

Businessmen in St Louis agreed to support Lindbergh and provided funds for a single-engine aircraft. However, major aircraft builders turned Lindbergh down; they regarded his plan as too risky since conventional wisdom called for a multi-engine aircraft for flying over water. Lindbergh found an aircraft builder, Ryan Airlines, in San Diego, and he worked alongside the company's craftsmen and engineers to build a single-seat, single-engine monoplane. The aircraft had an extra large wing in order to lift the 1,026 kg (2,750 lb) of fuel carried in five tanks. The large main tank was directly forward of the enclosed cockpit so that the only view ahead was by a periscope fitted on the left side of the instrument panel.

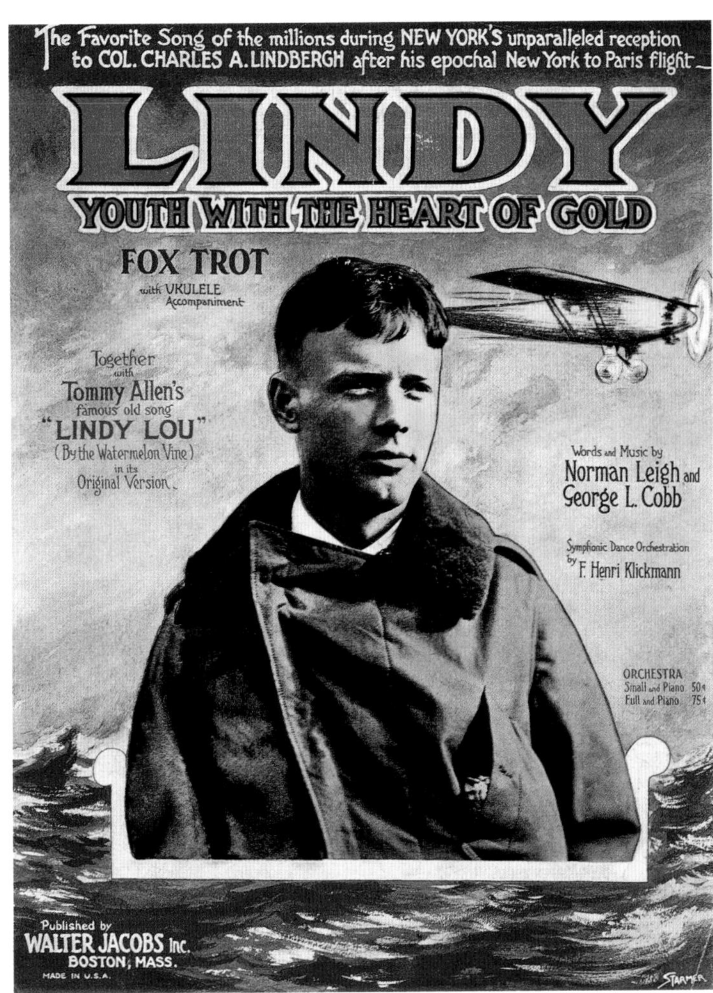

Overnight Lindbergh was idolized by the media and celebrated in song and dance. These lyrics ask 'Who's the boy we're all wild about? Who's the wonder of the day?'. Years later the tune changed when Lindbergh's relations with the media soured.

The aviators gather

In early May 1927 Lindbergh was flight-testing his aircraft, the *Spirit of St Louis*, when news arrived that the veteran French pilots Charles Nungesser and François Coli had taken off from Paris for New York. Lindbergh began planning an alternative flight from California to Hawai'i. One day later Nungesser and Coli were overdue and to this day their fate remains unknown. Lindbergh flew east and arrived in New York on 12 May.

Two Paris-bound aircraft and crew were already in New York waiting for the weather to clear. One of the aircraft had recently completed a 51-hour test flight, more than enough time to reach Paris. On the evening of 19 May, Lindbergh called the Weather Bureau for an updated forecast. It was raining, with low clouds in New York, but the forecasters reported clearing conditions

The right side of the Spirit of St Louis*' instrument panel, with Lindbergh's tally for hours of fuel consumed in pencil near the top.*

along the coast. Lindbergh decided to take off in the morning. He could not sleep that night as he went over details in his mind, particularly concerning the fuel load.

Non-stop and solo – New York to Paris

The *Spirit of St Louis* had never taken off with a full load of fuel. In April, another trans-Atlantic contender had crashed and burned on take-off on a test-flight. On the morning of 20 May the ground was soft and wet, and Lindbergh was concerned about clearing telephone wires at the end of the runway. But with a push from the ground crew and several bounces, Lindbergh took off, cleared the wires and headed to Paris. Over land he looked for features to fix his position, but over the sea he navigated by dead reckoning alone; the instability of the aircraft made using a sextant impossible. To save weight he did not carry a radio.

Lindbergh flew in a great arc that took him over eastern New England, Nova Scotia and Newfoundland. Eleven hours into the flight he left North America behind, and flew into the night over the Atlantic. Over the ocean he had to divert around cloud masses when ice formed on his wings. His Wright J-5 engine operated flawlessly, but he had problems with his compass and he was unsure about where he would make landfall.

The aircraft's unique design made it unstable and Lindbergh had to remain in full control throughout the flight. He fought off sleep by thrusting his head out of the side windows, getting a blast of cold wet air. During the night Lindbergh was accompanied by apparitions in his cockpit, a phenomenon also noted by Shackleton during his 36-hour crossing of South Georgia and described in T. S. Eliot's *The Waste Land*.

After 27 hours in the air Lindbergh spotted fishing vessels and, soon after, a deeply indented coast. He matched the shoreline to his chart and found that he was over southwestern Ireland, not far off his intended track. He flew over Cornwall in late afternoon and noted that Blériot had crossed the English Channel a few miles to the north 18 years earlier. Lindbergh saw his second sunset since taking off as he approached Cherbourg, 32 hours into the flight.

Soon, the glow of Paris was visible and Lindbergh flew around the Eiffel Tower. His directions to Le Bourget airfield were a sketchy 'northeast of the city'. Here, his experience as an airmail pilot landing in cornfields at night paid off as he picked out the unlit runway from the dark landscape. He was confused by the headlights of cars clogging the roads approaching the airfield, unaware that thousands of Parisians were rushing to greet him as soon as he landed. At 10.22 on the evening of 21 May 1927, Lindbergh landed *Spirit*

Map showing Lindbergh's great circle route between New York and Paris.

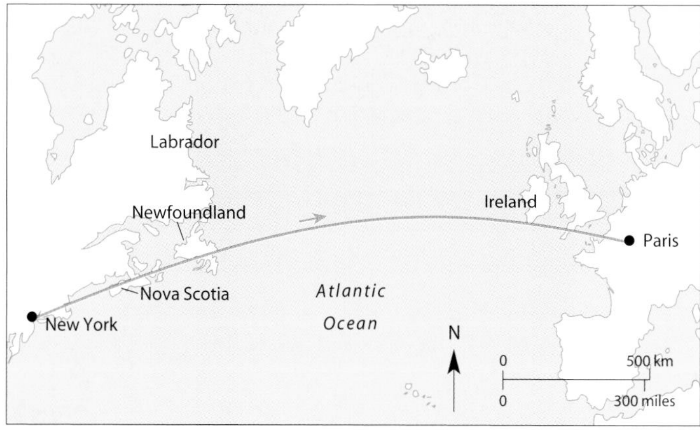

of St Louis at Le Bourget. He had flown his aircraft for $33^1/_2$ hours.

Overnight Charles Lindbergh was transformed from 'Flying Fool' to 'The Lone Eagle'. He went on to explore other air routes across the globe, which are now flown by thousands every day, including the great circle route between New York and Paris. His achievements brought acclaim and gave him the freedom to pursue his own interests to advance aviation.

Lindbergh's fame took a heavy toll, both personally and professionally, and he had nothing but disdain for the popular press. He argued against America's involvement in the Second World War and published writings that were racist in tone. He was the 20th century's first true celebrity, and, like others, he fell from grace. He later recovered his stature, travelling constantly, and advocating protection of the environment and the preservation of traditional cultures.

Eight days after he had reached Paris, Lindbergh's arrival at Croydon Aerodrome had the same effect on the crowd: a mass rush on to the airfield by thousands of well-wishers.

62

CAROLLE DOYLE

Women Pioneers of Flight

1930, 1937

Courage is the price that Life exacts for granting peace,
The soul that knows it not . . . knows not the livid loneliness of fear.
Nor mountain heights where bitter joy can hear the sound of wings.
AMELIA EARHART, 1927

When Charles Lindbergh completed the first solo flight across the Atlantic in 1927 (p. 254), he heralded the great age of aviation pioneers. A year later Amelia Earhart became the first woman to fly across the Atlantic; the fact that she was a passenger and, in her own words, 'as useful as a sack of potatoes', didn't stop the world's press clamouring for her story. Four years later she did fly solo across the Atlantic, landing her Lockheed Vega safely in an Irish field.

Amelia Earhart with her Lockheed Vega, in which she flew solo across the Atlantic.

The late 1920s and 1930s were heady times for the infant aviation industry. Men and women pushed back the boundaries of flight proving over and over again that air travel was possible. They shrank our world to a span of hours rather than years, but the price exacted was high.

Amelia Earhart

Earhart was not the first woman passenger to attempt the Atlantic crossing, but she was the first to survive. The 'sack of potatoes' was a qualified pilot who had already taken her Kinner Airster to 4,267 m (14,000 ft) in 1921, setting a new altitude record for women.

Her solo flight across the Atlantic in 1932 was not without incident. A few hours into it she encountered severe storms in which the aircraft was thrown around. Climbing up to try to fly above the clouds the wings began to ice up, making the aircraft ever more sluggish until it suddenly went into a spin. Earhart managed to pull out and level off just above the white-capped waves. Setting the aircraft down in a field of cows, 'Lady Lindy', as she was affectionately called, had proved that women could match men in both courage and ability.

Three years later she became the first person to fly solo across the Pacific from Honolulu to California. This 3,875-km (2,408-mile) flight was followed

Earhart became one of the icons of the new age of aviation and achieved great celebrity – her glamorous image was used in advertising.

later that year by another record-breaking solo flight, this time from Mexico City to Newark, New Jersey. On landing, crowds surged towards the aircraft and the woman who had become one of the icons of the new age of aviation.

Amelia Earhart was 39 when she set out on the flight which will forever be associated with her name. No woman had yet flown around the world – it was a tantalizing prospect. With her navigator Fred Noonan, Earhart would pilot the Lockheed Electra, labelled the 'flying laboratory' because it had been fitted with a Bendix RA-1 radio receiver, a radio direction-finder and other trial instruments. Ground-to-air communication was still in its infancy, however, and Fred would navigate by their position in relation to the stars and sun.

On 20 May 1937 the Electra took off from Oakland, California, crossing the United States in three days and on to Natal in Venezuela. Natal was the jumping off point for Africa, and as they crossed the Atlantic, Noonan navigated by using a bubble octant to measure the line of the sun to the earth. Earhart descended through cloud and haze towards the coast, but they were 190 km (120 miles) north of the intended destination, Dakar.

It took four days to fly across Africa to Khartoum in Sudan. Often there was nothing beneath the wings but uncharted forest and deserts. Earhart skirted the Arabian peninsula, overflew the Arabian sea and landed at Karachi after 13 hours 22 minutes. It was the first time that anyone had flown from Africa to India.

The Lockheed Electra piloted by Earhart soars over Bay Bridge, Oakland, in 1937.

One piece of equipment that Earhart usually took with her was her powder compact, so that she would always be ready to face the press which greeted her when she landed after her epic flights.

The flight across India was uneventful, but the airfield at Calcutta was waterlogged. Laden down with fuel for the flight to Burma, the Electra barely cleared the trees. There was a brief respite in Darwin, Australia, before the flight to Lae, New Guinea, on 29 June. Here they prepared for the long, 4,223-km (2,556-mile) flight across the Pacific to Howland Island.

In the Pacific the USS *Itasca* was waiting, while on Howland Island a high-frequency radio direction-finder had been set up. But this was 1937, radio signals were weak and static interference often made communication impossible. It was vital that Fred Noonan's chronometer should be accurate to the second, but he had to wait for two days before a clear enough time signal from Adelaide could be heard. His chronometer was three seconds out. Weather forecasts transmitted from Pearl Harbor were also difficult to receive. On 2 July Pearl Harbor got through and forecast a headwind of 12 m.p.h. This would lengthen flight duration to 18 hours. Just before take off Fred managed to get a time signal from Saigon, it showed his chronometer was still three seconds out. Heavy with fuel the Electra turned into wind and lifted off. Shortly after, Lae received an update on the weather from Pearl Harbor which now forecast the headwind at 26.5 m.p.h. Earhart and Noonan never received this information.

Communication with the USS *Itasca* was fitful. Until the Electra was an estimated 322 km (200 miles) from the ship Earhart's voice could hardly be heard. Every time Earhart transmitted the *Itasca* answered immediately in morse code, but neither Amelia nor Fred understood morse. As for the direction-finder on Howland Island, it was switched on hours before the flight and by the time the Electra was within range the batteries had run down. We will never know how far the Electra was from Howland Island, but for Earhart and Noonan the flight was over; the biggest search in history was about to begin.

Amy Johnson

Seven years before Amelia Earhart's fatal flight a young British woman was making headlines. On 24 May 1930 Amy Johnson became the first woman to fly solo from England to Australia, just one year after gaining her pilot's licence.

On 5 May, Johnson had taxied her two-year-old de Havilland Moth, *Jason*, into wind, and the open cockpit biplane had rumbled across Croydon's grass aerodrome. It was so heavily laden with fuel, spare parts and tools that Johnson just managed

In 1930 Amy Johnson flew solo from England to Australia – the first woman to do so. Seven years later, Amelia Earhart set out on an attempt to be the first woman to fly round the world, but the flight ended in tragedy when she disappeared in the Pacific.

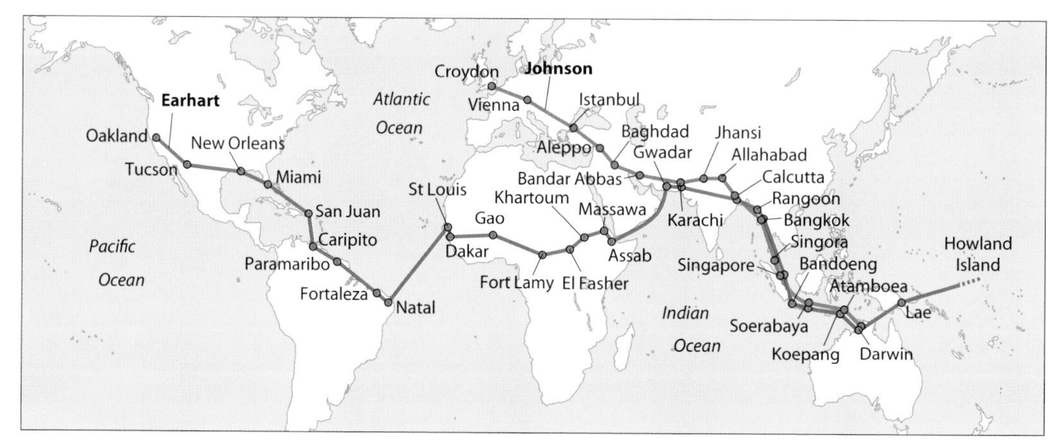

to lift off at the second attempt. The tools were her own as she was the first woman to be issued with a mechanic's licence.

When the great barrier of the Turkish Taurus Mountains loomed up, Johnson found that the biplane could not climb over them: the air was too thin and she risked literally falling out of the sky. She followed narrow, twisting gorges which suddenly blurred into cloud. Diving down she came out with one wing-tip virtually scraping the side of the canyon. Four days out she risked being enveloped by a sandstorm over Iraq – she could only land in the midst of the desert and wait it out.

Time was ticking by, for Johnson's intention was to beat the 15-day record of Bert Hinkler who had been the first person to fly solo from England to Australia in 1928. With monsoon rain beating down on the open cockpit she landed on a football pitch in Rangoon, Burma. The biplane slid towards a wire fence and the lower wing crumpled. Incredibly, two days later the repaired aircraft took off, but the record was now out of reach. Johnson landed at Darwin 19$^1/_2$ days after starting out. In her own eyes she had failed, but to the world, she had become the British Earhart, and to the British public if not to herself she was undisputed 'Queen of the Air'.

Over the next six years Johnson's record-breaking solo flights took her from Siberia to Japan and twice from England to South Africa. An attempt to fly to New York with her husband and co-pilot, Jim Mollison, in 1933 ended in a crash. The Mollisons stayed with Amelia Earhart to convalesce and the two women became firm friends.

Earhart's disappearance in 1937 caused Johnson to doubt her own ability. Separated from her husband and in deep depression, she reluctantly joined the Air Transport Auxiliary in 1940. A year later she crashed into the Thames Estuary in bad weather.

Neither Johnson's nor Earhart's bodies have ever been found, and to this day there is lively speculation on whether or not they did indeed crash. The sad fact is that the sky is uncompromising, it neither shows pity nor forgives the slightest human error. But in one way the speculators may be right, for surely icons can never die.

Above *Johnson ready for take off in her Gipsy Moth at Croydon Aerodrome, southern England, before her solo flight to Australia.*

Earhart (left) and Johnson (right) walking down the beach together in Atlantic City in 1933. Both showed immense courage in their aviation exploits; both died tragically.

RICHARD EVANS

The Long March

1934–35

Speaking of the Long March, one may ask 'What is its significance?' We answer that the Long March is the first of its kind... in history... Has history ever known a long march to equal ours? No, never!

MAO ZEDONG IN A REPORT TO A CONFERENCE OF COMMUNIST PARTY ACTIVISTS, DECEMBER 1935

The Long March was a heroic physical undertaking. But it also had great political significance. It allowed the Chinese communist movement both to survive and to escape from control by the Communist International in Moscow. And it enabled Mao Zedong to set foot on the ladder that led him to the leadership of China.

Mao used the term Long March to describe the march of the First Front Army of the Chinese Red Army of Workers and Peasants from its base in the southern provinces of Jiangxi and Fujian to a new base in China's remote northwest. Although it was one of several by contingents of the National Red Army from south to north, it was the one which mattered. If it had come to grief, many of the veterans and most of the leaders of Chinese communism would have foundered with it; and the whole movement might well have failed.

Mao Zedong, Zhou Enlai, Bo Gu and Zhu De (Commander-in-Chief of the Red Army) in Shaanxi in 1937.

Survival

During the summer of 1934, the situation faced by the First Front Army was grim. It had found no effective way of holding ground against the steady advance into its base of several hundred thousand Nationalist troops. Annihilation threatened. In this predicament, the three men in charge of military planning decided that the army could only hope to survive by abandoning its base. These were: Zhou Enlai (later China's prime minister for 26 years), Political Commissar of the whole Red Army; Bo Gu, a Moscow-trained civilian in charge of the day-to-day running of the Communist Party; and (exotically) Otto Braun, a German with military experience who had been sent to China by the Communist International.

The march – described to begin with as a 'shift' – began on 16 October. The marchers consisted of about 85,000 troops and several thousand civilians, many of whom were porters. There were about 30 women, including the wives of Mao Zedong and Zhou Enlai.

Five weeks later, the army fought its first big battle, at a river crossing, and suffered badly. It lost about half its strength and all its heavy stores and equipment. This threatening experience led

to a series of meetings of the Communist Party's politburo. At the fourth of these, held at Zunyi in Guizhou, the group of three was dismissed, and Mao Zedong became both a member of the party's Secretariat – its senior executive body – and military adviser to Zhou Enlai. Strategically, it was decided that the army should aim to establish a new base north of the Yangtze.

From start to finish the march was a test of physical and moral stamina. Commanders and civilian leaders sometimes rode, but the 'fighter' in the ranks always walked. Each wore plaited straw sandals, which needed frequent replacement, and a thin cotton uniform, and he normally carried a rifle or light machine gun, with ammunition, and a canvas bag for rations. More often than not, he slept in the open and the food he ate, bought or confiscated, was often uncooked.

Physical obstacles and political discord

The army, now about 30,000 strong, finally succeeded in crossing the Yangtze in May 1935. Thereafter, it encountered few enemy troops, but faced a series of formidable natural obstacles. These included a river, the Dadu, which flows through deep gorges, a mountain range with snowfields on either side of its only pass, and a waterlogged plateau, about 160 km (100 miles) wide, on the high watershed between the basins of the Yangtze and the Yellow rivers. The second and third of these claimed lives.

This stage of the march was also marked by a strategic dispute between Mao and his associates and Zhang Guotao, political chief of the Fourth Front Army. His army and the First Front Army met in central Sichuan in mid-June. Three months later, after a series of meetings and the division of the combined armies into two columns, Zhang turned south and Mao went north. Mao's column – only about 7,000 strong – marched northeast into Shaanxi. There, in mid-October, it found a haven: a base created and held for years by a local element of the Red Army.

An itinerary kept by one of the units in Mao's column shows that the march covered a total of 9,463 km (5,880 miles), the distance as the crow flies from Moscow to Beijing. To call it the Long March, as Mao did two months after it ended, is therefore entirely fair.

A later Chinese propaganda poster to spotlight Mao Zedong's leadership role during the Long March. This was the view of the Long March that the Chinese communists wanted everyone to accept.

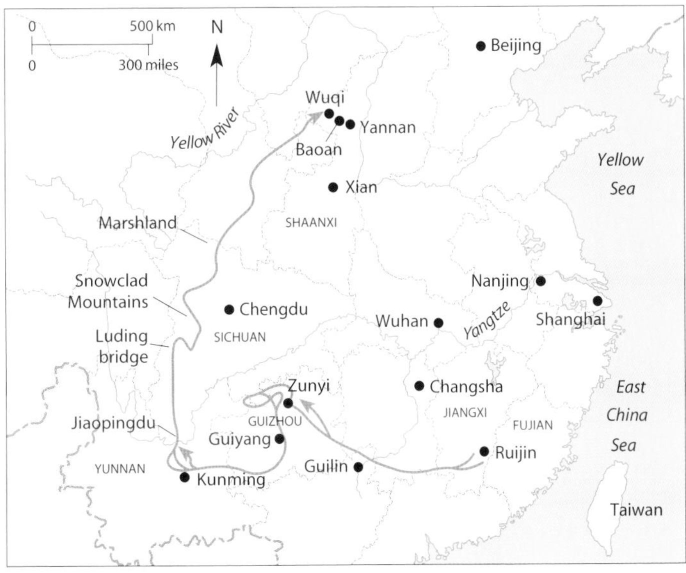

Map of the route of the Long March: the majority of the participants walked the entire length on foot.

Thor Heyerdahl & the Kon-Tiki

1947

To us on the raft the great problems of civilized man appeared false and illusory, mere perverted products of the human mind. Only the elements mattered. And the elements seemed to ignore the little raft.
THOR HEYERDAHL, 1950

Thor Heyerdahl sailed from South America to Polynesia on a raft made of balsa wood to demonstrate that it could be done. In 1936, while living for a year on Fatu-Hiva in the Marquesas, Heyerdahl had abandoned his zoology research and begun an intensive study into the origins of Polynesian race and culture. He started to think about the different theories of how the peoples of the South Pacific had initially reached the islands. By observing the ocean currents he became convinced that the islanders could have come from the east, from Peru – a theory that was revolutionary at the time.

After the interruption to his researches caused by the Second World War, and overcoming both financial difficulties and academic opposition, Heyerdahl flew to Ecuador where he hoped to find enough balsa logs to build a raft. He was determined to prove that balsa sailing-rafts could have crossed the Pacific from Peru to Polynesia.

Heyerdahl modelled his boat on Inca craft which had been seen and described by Pizarro (p. 105) in the 16th century. He used no modern materials, such as nails or wire, but knew he needed freshly felled trees. These he found in the forests of Ecuador – 12 huge balsa logs were

An early 17th-century drawing of a balsa-wood raft off the coast of Peru, the boat on which Heyerdahl based the Kon-Tiki *craft.*

floated down the Palenque River to the Pacific and the balsa raft was built in Callao Bay from nine logs bound together with rope. No one thought Heyerdahl had any chance of sailing safely across the Pacific, telling him the raft was too small, too fragile and too porous. Enough rations for six men for four months were stowed under the bamboo deck, along with 56 small cans of fresh water – a meagre amount for the journey.

Crossing the Pacific

The *Kon-Tiki* was named after a forerunner of the Incas – the legendary sun-king who had vanished from Peru and appeared in Polynesia some 1,500 years ago. Heyerdahl and his five Nordic companions finally left Callao in Peru on 28 April 1947 and were towed out to sea by a tug. In the beginning manoeuvring the raft was difficult, but they worked out a method of steering and were soon in the Humboldt Current which carried them swiftly in the right direction. The softness of the balsa wood turned out to be an advantage as the ropes wore their way slowly into the wood and were protected, rather than being worn away as some of the doom-mongers had predicted.

On the night of 30 July they saw and heard hundreds of seabirds, an indication that land must be close. Their next difficulty was how to stop the *Kon-Tiki*; three days after the first land sighting they found themselves drifting towards the notorious Takume and Raroia reefs. They managed to land on an uninhabited island, but the *Kon-Tiki* was smashed and, with the exception of the nine balsa logs which survived the battering, it became in Heyerdahl's words 'an honourable wreck'. They had crossed over 6,437 km (4,000 sea miles) in 101 days. The raft was restored and is now housed in the *Kon-Tiki* Museum in Oslo.

The Kon-Tiki *at sea: Heyerdahl compared it to an 'old Norwegian hay loft' when he first saw it completed.*

The crew of the Kon-Tiki*: Thor Heyerdahl is third from the left.*

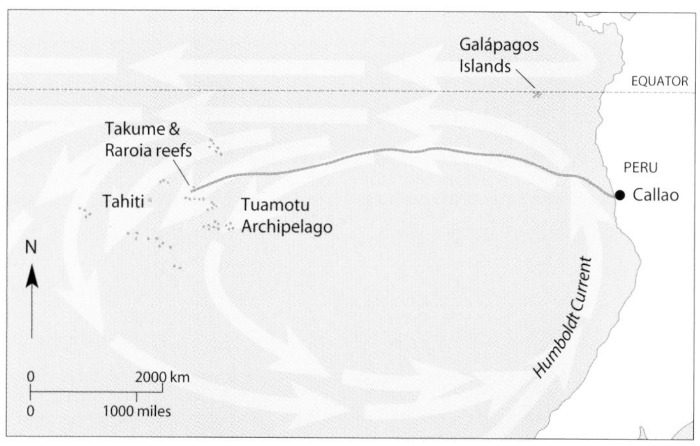

The route taken by the Kon-Tiki *across the Pacific on the 101-day crossing.*

Heyerdahl sailed Ra II *– a smaller and more compact version of* Ra I *– from Morocco to Barbados in 57 days.*

Aftermath

The journey caught the public imagination worldwide in the most extraordinary way; 20 million copies of Heyerdahl's account of it were sold and it was translated into 70 languages. Heyerdahl had set out to prove that the earliest settlers to reach Polynesia *could* have come from South America; it was never his intention to prove that they had definitively followed this route. Academic opinion was, however, dismissive: 'A nice adventure' was how Sir Peter Buck, then the leading authority on Polynesia described the crossing; Professor Karsten from Finland thought the whole thing faked; and Professor Birket-Smith from Denmark thought it best if the subject were 'killed by silence'.

Heyerdahl started his career when specialization was first taking a hold and he was regarded by academia as embracing too many disciplines. His methods were certainly unorthodox and he was a natural showman, but perhaps the academics were also jealous that he spent so much time away from his desk on expeditions. He suffered from rebuffs and a lack of academic recognition all his life, something he minded deeply.

The *Ra* expeditions

Another question that intrigued Heyerdahl was whether there was a link between the cultures of Central America and those of Egypt and the Indus Valley. He had first seen reed boats on Lake Titicaca in the Andes and began to wonder whether it would be possible to build and sail a papyrus reed craft across the Atlantic. In 1969 he saw reed boats on Lake Chad, decided to build one in Egypt, and on 25 May 1969 he set sail for America on *Ra I* with a crew of seven. After 56 days and 5,000 km (3,107 miles) they had to abandon ship, a week short of their destination. Undeterred, Heyerdahl built the smaller and more compact *Ra II*, which left Safi in Morocco on 17 May 1970; after an uncomfortable journey they reached Barbados in 57 days, abolishing the theory that no boat could have crossed the Atlantic before Columbus.

By steely determination and vision Heyerdahl demonstrated again and again that established theories about civilizations and movements of people were not necessarily correct. He believed that 'We have been blindfolded too long by the European attitude that everything began with us. In reality, many great civilizations throughout the world terminated with our arrival.' However, most scholars today, on the basis of archaeology, linguistics and genetics, still dismiss Heyerdahl's theories and believe that Polynesia was indeed settled from the west and that American civilizations were not influenced by Egypt.

STEPHEN VENABLES

65

Scaling Everest

1953

When we realized by their unmistakable gestures that they had been to the top, we temporarily went mad. I found myself embracing Ed and Tenzing, weeping not a little, and I think the others did the same.

JOHN HUNT'S DIARY, 30 MAY 1953

They spent the night perched on two stepped ledges cut from the snow at over 8,400 m (27,560 ft) above sea level – higher than any human being had ever camped before. The temperature was -27°C (-16.6°F) and the tent was buffeted by gusts which shook hoar frost from the fabric. Oxygen hissed through face masks, helping the two men sleep intermittently. At 4.00 a.m. they lit the paraffin stove to make a hot drink for breakfast. Then they wriggled out of their down sleeping bags and fumbled with icy fingers to pull on huge unwieldy high-altitude climbing boots and crampons.

At 6.30 a.m. they clambered out of the tent into brilliant white light. In the blue valley shadow 4,000 m (1,312 ft) below them they could just make out the monastery at Thyangboche, where the monks had blessed them two months earlier. Tenzing Norgay thought, 'God is good to us'. For him God was synonymous with Chomolungma, this holy mountain which his British and Commonwealth companions called Everest.

Porters carrying some of the 1953 expedition's 13 tons of supplies and equipment up the Khumbu Glacier to base camp. The peaks immediately behind mark the border with Tibet.

GEORGE MALLORY

When George Mallory set sail for India in 1924 he hoped desperately that this would be his last attempt on Everest – the mountain which had come to dominate his life over the last three years. He had only joined the 1921 reconnaissance reluctantly, but having found a way on to the Tibetan side of the world's highest mountain, and then, in 1922, climbed within striking distance of the top, he now believed that the summit was a real possibility – almost a certainty.

Mallory was just one of several remarkable pioneers – George Finch, Geoffrey Bruce, Edward Norton, Howard Somervell, Sandy Irvine and Noel Odell – pushing higher into thin air than anyone had been before, inventing high altitude mountaineering as they went along; but Mallory's eloquence, his literary aspirations, his good looks and his elegance as a climber seemed to single him out as the public hero of Everest. For a climber whose motivations were aesthetic, the harsh, brutish nature of climbing high on Everest's North Face seems to have had little appeal, apart from that vague abstract notion of 'challenge' and the lure of fame and glory. Mallory wanted desperately to reach that summit.

After many setbacks, caused mainly by appalling weather, two summit attempts were made in 1924. On the first, Edward Norton reached a point calculated at 8,573 m (28,126 ft) above sea level, climbing alone, without oxygen equipment. The second attempt was made by George Mallory. Despite his ethical and aesthetic misgivings about artificial aids, he decided to take oxygen equipment and chose as his partner the expedition's engineering genius, Sandy Irvine. Their last message to the outside world was a note sent down from Camp Six on 7 June 1924. The following day Noel Odell spotted them somewhere on or near the crest of the great Northeast Ridge, heading for the summit. Then the clouds closed in.

They were never seen alive again and it was only in 1999 that Mallory's body was found high on the North Face, lying where he had died after a battering fall, a length of broken rope still tied round his waist. Irvine's body is believed to lie slightly higher up the face. It is conceivable that the two men fell on the way back from the summit and many theories have been propounded to prove that this could have happened. But perhaps it is preferable that the exact nature of their deaths remains an unsolved mystery.

Above *Mallory and Irvine leave camp at the North Col for the last time, carrying heavy oxygen cylinders for their attempt at the summit.*

Below *Mallory's handkerchief, goggles, altimeter and wristwatch, found with his body in 1999.*

Edmund Hillary turned to him and checked, 'Okay?'. Every breath was an effort and words were a luxury. Tenzing smiled, 'Yes – ready', and the two men moved forward, kicking steps in the dazzling snow. It was 29 May 1953 – the defining day two separate life journeys had converged on top of the world.

Yak-herder and bee-keeper

Tenzing Norgay was born just a few miles from Everest, in Tibet. As a boy he helped tend yaks on the meadows beneath the mountain. Later, his family settled amongst the Sherpa people, just to the south of the mountain, in Nepal. Like many Sherpas, Tenzing travelled to Darjeeling to find work and in 1935 signed on to carry loads for an Everest expedition led by Eric Shipton – the fifth of seven unsuccessful British attempts on the north side of the mountain.

Thousands of miles away in New Zealand, the young Hillary avidly read the accounts of those attempts on Everest, while honing his own mountaineering skills in the Southern Alps, between working in the family bee-keeping business. His own chance to explore the Himalaya finally came in 1951, with an expedition to an unclimbed peak in India. At the end of that trip he was invited to Nepal to join Eric Shipton's reconnaissance of the hitherto untouched south side of Everest, just opened to foreign expeditions. It was an enchanting journey through the high valleys of the Sherpas, leading to the Khumbu Icefall.

By climbing this 900-m (2,950-ft) cataract of fractured, chaotic ice, Hillary and his British companions proved that Everest could potentially be climbed from Nepal. In the following year a Swiss expedition almost succeeded in doing that, pioneering the long route up the icefall into the hidden hanging valley which George Mallory, back in 1921, had named Western Cwm. From the head of this cwm the Swiss and their Sherpa team laboured up a 1,200-m (3,927-ft) high ice face to the wind-blasted saddle of the South Col, final staging post for the Southeast Ridge leading to the summit.

Fighting bitter winds, camping with inadequate equipment, labouring under the weight of malfunctioning oxygen sets, the Swiss Raymond Lambert struggled to about 8,600 m (28,215 ft) above sea level – probably higher than anyone had climbed before – before admitting defeat. His companion on this summit attempt was the leader of the Sherpa team which had helped establish the long chain of camps to the South Col – Tenzing Norgay.

Now a highly respected mountaineer, Tenzing had developed a passion, not just to work in the mountains, but to *climb* to the highest summit of all. Despite illness and exhaustion, he returned for the second Swiss attempt in autumn 1952, but early winter winds halted the expedition at the South Col, leaving the summit prize open for 1953.

Hillary, realizing that Tenzing was probably destined for a summit attempt, forged a strong partnership with the Sherpas' headman.

The final campaign

The 1953 Everest Expedition was planned initially by Eric Shipton, but at the last minute he was sacked by the organizing committee and replaced by a new leader, John Hunt, whose leadership skills were fully tested in gaining the loyalty of Shipton's affronted team. Ever the diplomat, Hunt listened carefully to the team and accepted their recommendation to include in the team two tough New Zealanders, George Lowe and Edmund Hillary. Hunt also agreed that

The southern route to the summit, pioneered by the Swiss in 1952 and perfected and completed by the British in 1953.

Right *Nowadays the Khumbu Icefall is equipped comprehensively with alloy ladders. In 1953 John Hunt's expedition had only a few ladders, which they supplemented with tree trunks, carried up from the lower valleys.*

Opposite *Tenzing Norgay on the summit of Everest at 11.30 a.m, 29 May 1953. On his raised ice axe are the flags of Britain, Nepal, the United Nations and India. The photo was taken by Edmund Hillary.*

Tenzing Norgay should be 'sirdar' – boss of the Sherpas, on whose load-carrying skills the expedition's success depended; on arrival in Kathmandu Hunt invited Tenzing also to be a full member of the climbing team.

And so the long journey which had preoccupied British climbers since 1921 finally reached its climax, galvanized by the charm, efficiency and determination of John Hunt and supported by the finest equipment available, above all reliable oxygen sets. Building on Swiss experience, the British expedition built a pyramid of eight camps to the South Col, from where Tom Bourdillon and Charles Evans almost reached the summit on 26 May, turning back reluctantly from the South Summit, when their oxygen began to run out. It was now the turn of Hillary and Tenzing.

'Tuji Chey, Chomolungma – I am grateful'

The first team's view of the final knife-edge ridge gave Hillary some idea of the final bridge which had to be crossed on 29 May. Starting much higher, from the precarious Camp Nine, he and Tenzing reached the South Summit early in the morning. Ever thorough, Hillary was doing mental arithmetic all the way, calculating oxygen rates, keeping enough gas in reserve for this final effort. An airy knife-edge ridge led to a 12-m (40-ft) high cliff, where Hillary chimneyed up between rock and snow, praying that the snow would not collapse and send him hurtling 3,000 m (10,000 ft) down the Kangshung Face. Tenzing followed. Beyond the difficult step, the ridge eased off over a series of gentle hummocks until, at about 11.00 in the morning, the two men found themselves looking down the far, northern side of the mountain into Tibet. There was no further to climb.

Hillary, with fitting Anglo-Saxon reserve, held out his hand; but Tenzing flung his arms around the huge man's shoulder, thumping him on the back. Then he posed for the historic photo, ice axe held aloft with the flags of India, Nepal, Great Britain and the United Nations. Late that afternoon, as the two climbers returned to the South Col, George Lowe was the first person in the world to hear the good news in the immortal words never intended for a wider audience: 'We knocked the bastard off'. Tenzing, according to his biographer, just uttered a humble Buddhist prayer: 'Tuji Chey, Chomolungma – I am grateful.'

ROBIN KNOX-JOHNSTON

Single-Handed Around the World

1968–69

No one thought a solo non-stop circumnavigation was possible at that time, in fact everyone took a delight in telling me it was impossible.

ROBIN KNOX-JOHNSTON

Robin Knox-Johnston seated in front of the pile of supplies he took with him on his round-the-world voyage.

It was a challenge whose time had come. In 1967 Francis Chichester had sailed alone around the world, with just one stop in Australia. To circumnavigate the world single-handed without a stop was the last great sailing challenge. But could it be done? Chichester's boat *Gypsy Moth IV* had needed a major refit at the halfway point and he had returned slightly disorientated for a few days. Could any boat survive 300 days at sea, including a passage through the whole length of the Roaring Forties. What food would keep for that length of time? Would the sailor go mad after so long at sea without any human contact?

The Sunday Times newspaper was quick to spot the promotional opportunity and offered a trophy, the Golden Globe, for the first person to succeed. Four of us announced our intentions, joined in time by five others – in all six British, two French and one Italian. The rules were simple. Sail alone, without outside assistance, non-stop around the world leaving the Capes of Good Hope, Leeuwin and Horn to the north. The paper adopted us, but their assessment of people's chances ruined any opportunity I had of gaining sponsorship. They had no concept of the thorough training Merchant Navy Officers received, nor what building my boat, *Suhaili*, in Bombay and sailing her home via the Cape of Good Hope had taught.

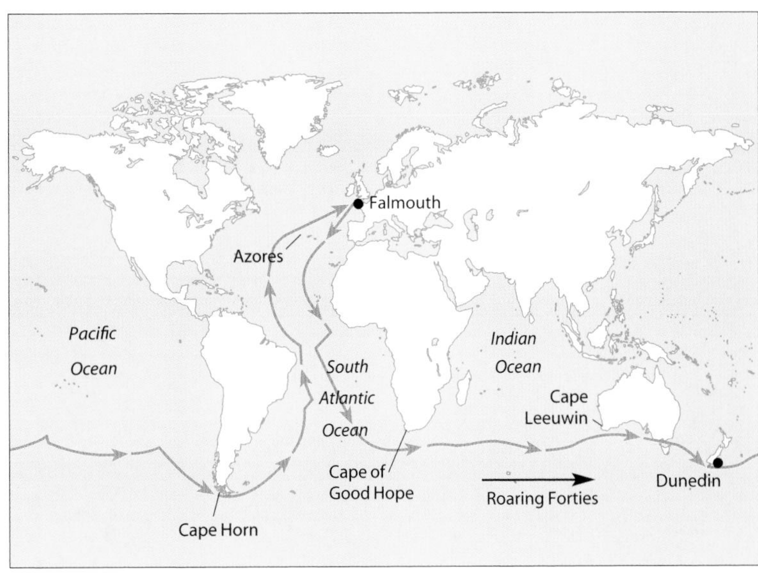

The route of Robin Knox-Johnston's successful single-handed non-stop voyage around the world.

Setting sail

It was decided arbitrarily by *The Sunday Times* that the race would start in October 1968 – too late for those of us with small boats, so three of us sailed in June: Chay Blyth, John Ridgway and myself. It was two months before the newspaper's favourite, Frenchman Bernard Moitessier sailed, but his boat was longer and so faster.

The first objective was to clear the crowded waters of the English Channel and reach open sea. Being unable to keep watch 24 hours a day, this was plain self-preservation. Then south and through the calms at the equator and round the high pressure system of the South Atlantic. I was already having some problems. My boat was leaking quite badly and it was necessary to spend two days at the equator working 1.5 m (5 ft) below the surface to tack a strip of copper over the leaking seam.

Further difficulties arose as soon as I got into the Roaring Forties. A storm struck, and in those waters that means giant waves, and *Suhaili* was knocked down so that her masts went under water. The damage was serious. The cabin shifted with the force of the blow, the water tank connections were knocked off and all the stored water was contaminated, the radio was soaked and its transmitter failed, and the self-steering was broken. Rain water could be collected in the sails and the self-steering was repairable, involving a very cold dip in those icy waters, but the loss of communication in those pre-satellite days meant that from then on I could neither tell people where I was, nor call for help if I got into trouble.

More storms accompanied me as I crept towards Australia, but I had adjusted to the constant wet clothing and primitive living conditions, my body had risen to provide the muscle required for the constant demands being made and I was

JOSHUA SLOCUM

Joshua Slocum was the first person to sail alone around the world, with stops en route. Born in Wilmot, Nova Scotia, in 1844, he subsequently became a naturalized American citizen. Having gone to sea as a cook at the age of 12, he led an adventurous life in the Merchant Marine and by the age of 25 was Master of a schooner. At one time he was part owner of the *Northern Light*, one of the finest American clipper ships, and later, as Master and owner of the *Aquidneck*, he was wrecked in Brazil. He built a 11-m (35-ft) canoe from pieces of the wreckage and sailed it back 8,046 km (5,000 miles) to New York with his family as crew. His book describing this voyage, *The Voyage of the Liberdade*, was published in 1894.

So it was a highly experienced mariner who, in 1892, was given the remains of a traditional 11-m (35-ft) sloop *Spray*, which he rebuilt himself. In 1895 he set off alone around the world, calling at Gibraltar, the Magellan Strait, Australia and South Africa, returning to Newport, Rhode Island, in 1898. He was able to support himself during this voyage by lecturing, and his book, *Sailing Alone Around the World*, published in 1900, is one of the great sailing classics. Slocum set off again in *Spray* in 1909 and was never heard of again, presumed run down at sea.

Returning to Falmouth on 22 April 1969, after 313 days alone at sea. For much of the time Knox-Johnston was without a radio to communicate with the outside world after a giant wave had soaked it.

learning all the time how to help a small boat to survive in those watery Himalayas. So when the self-steering finally broke beyond repair off Australia I felt confident of everything except the state of the boat. Maintenance and repairs were taking more and more time and the sails, which had started machine sewn, were now almost completely hand stitched.

Five hours aground off Dunedin gave me a chance to catch up with the competition from a journalist. I was well in the lead, Blyth and Ridgway had retired, and Moitessier was more than four weeks behind. I pressed on into the southern Pacific and towards Cape Horn. Preserving the boat by keeping north in less wild conditions cost more than 10 days as I ran into Easterlies, and I was concerned that Moitessier would catch me as I rounded Cape Horn on 17 January 1969. Much later I learned he had rounded the Cape 20 days behind me, a comfortable gap.

The Atlantic south to north is some 12,875 km (8,000 miles), but it seemed like the home straight. Off the Azores I managed to send a message to a British ship which reported me to Lloyds, the first news of me for over four months, and 17 days later I recrossed the start line off Falmouth. Moitessier withdrew in the South Atlantic, Nigel Tetley was approaching the Azores, spurred by the messages of fast progress from Donald Crowhurst. He pushed too hard and his boat broke up 1,610 km (1,000 miles) from the finish. Crowhurst's boat was found abandoned a month later, floating in the Atlantic, and his logs showed that, despite his claims, he had never left the Atlantic. He was never found. Of the nine boats that set out, just one returned to its start port.

ROBIN SCAGELL

67

To the Moon and Back

1969

The Moon I have known all my life, that two-dimensional small yellow disk in the sky, has gone away somewhere, to be replaced by the most awesome sphere I have ever seen.

MICHAEL COLLINS, APOLLO 11 ASTRONAUT, ON REACHING LUNAR ORBIT, 1969

The *Apollo 11* spacecraft carrying Neil Armstrong, Buzz Aldrin and Michael Collins left Cape Kennedy, Florida, bound for the Moon on 16 July 1969. But the mission really started eight years previously, with another historic flight – that of the Russian Yuri Gagarin (see box, p. 277), the first man in space, on 12 April 1961. It seems incredible that when the two American astronauts finally stepped on to the lunar surface it was less than 12 years since the first primitive Russian sputnik had orbited the Earth in 1957.

Within days of Gagarin's flight, President Kennedy was asking his Space Council what the US could do to upstage the Russians. 'Do we have a chance of beating the Soviets by putting a laboratory in space, or by a trip around the moon, or by a rocket to land on the moon, or by a rocket to go to the moon and back with a man. Is there any other space program which promises dramatic results in which we could win?' he wrote in a memo on 20 April 1961. 'Are we working 24 hours a day on existing programs? If not, why not?'

Journey to the Moon

On that July day, well within the end of the decade that Kennedy had promised, three astronauts lay on their backs at the top of a mighty *Saturn V* rocket, facing heavenwards. All three were space veterans, in 1960s terms. Mission commander Neil Armstrong, 38, had the classic NASA astronaut background – aviation mad as a boy, he got his pilot's licence at 16, even before his driving licence. He was a Navy air ace in the Korean war and had a degree in aeronautical engineering. Armstrong's first space flight was aboard the two-man *Gemini 8* spacecraft in March 1966, in which he carried out an essential part of the whole *Apollo* plan – the first space docking.

Sitting alongside Armstrong was Edwin 'Buzz' Aldrin, who was just a few months older. Also a veteran of the Korean war, Aldrin had studied astronautics at Massachusetts Institute of Technology, where his thesis was on the techniques for rendezvous of craft in space – techniques that were subsequently adopted by NASA. Aldrin set a record for spacewalking on the 1966 *Gemini 12* mission.

The Apollo 11 *astronauts: (left to right) Neil Armstrong, Michael Collins and Buzz Aldrin.*

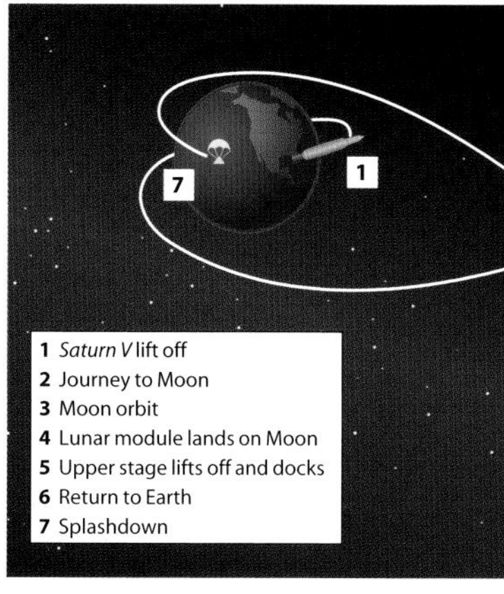

Right Apollo 11's *trajectory took it 384,000 km (240,000 miles) to the Moon. It had been preceded by two manned flights:* Apollo 8 *and* Apollo 10, *which both orbited the Moon but did not land.*

The Apollo *capsule was perched on top of the 111-m (363-ft) tall* Saturn V *rocket, one of the most powerful ever built.*

The third man of the crew was Michael Collins, like the other two men born in 1930, but a few weeks younger than Armstrong. From a military background, he too had been in space aboard a *Gemini* mission, as pilot of *Gemini 10* in 1966, which included a docking and a spacewalk.

Eleven minutes after blast-off the *Apollo* craft was in orbit and the three astronauts were weightless. Two and a half hours later, a rocket motor was ignited to send them on their way to the Moon. Unlike earthly voyages, a space mission is mostly unpowered coasting. Apart from mid-course corrections, the route is established by the timing of that initial rocket burn. But in the case of the *Apollo* missions it had been decided early on that there would be two actual craft – the command and service module (CSM), named *Columbia*, which would be the main vehicle, and the more delicate lunar landing module (LM), *Eagle*, which would undertake the landing itself. The LM was stored in a separate compartment, and during the trans-lunar coast it was necessary to rotate the CSM and dock with the LM. This done, the astronauts were able to settle down for a three-day coast to the Moon.

Landing in the Sea of Tranquility

On day four, the astronauts passed behind the Moon as seen from Earth, and while on its far side initiated rocket burns that would slow them down sufficiently to remain in lunar orbit, only 100 km (62 miles) above its surface. Armstrong and Aldrin transferred to the lunar module, and on 20 July 1969 the two craft separated. 'You cats take it easy on the lunar surface,' said Collins.

Following a coast period, the powered descent to the Moon took just 12 minutes, mostly under computer control. But after five minutes an alarm light flashed on the computer's control panel. 'Program Alarm, it's a 1202,' said Armstrong. Mission control in Houston realized that this was a computer overload alarm, and advised 'Roger, we're GO on that alarm' – meaning continue with the mission. But the computer was bringing *Eagle* down into a large crater and Armstrong decided to overshoot downrange. Finally, he brought the craft down on to the surface of the *Mare Tranquillitatis* (Sea of Tranquility) with only 30 seconds of fuel remaining. 'Houston, Tranquility Base here. The *Eagle* has landed!' reported Armstrong with more than a touch of joy in the voice of a normally matter-of-fact pilot.

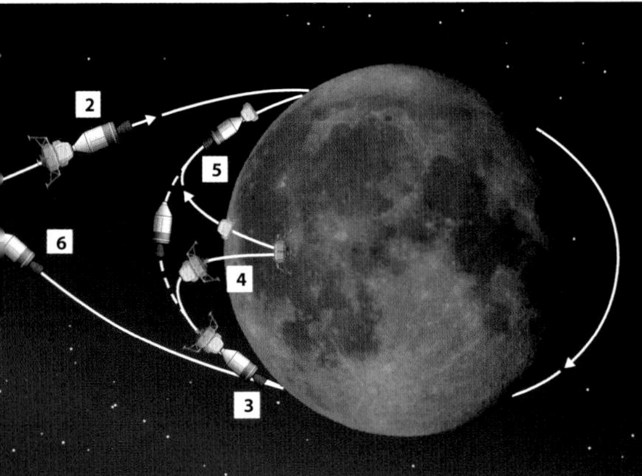

The actual moment of touchdown was something of a non-event for the participants. With lunar gravity only one-sixth of that on Earth, there was very little jarring. Fine dust from the rocket had blown across the landscape for a considerable distance, and the only evidence that they had actually landed was the appearance of a contact light triggered when a rod dangling from a footpad touched the surface.

It was over six hours after landing that Neil Armstrong finally made footfall on the lunar surface, uttering as he did so the famous line

THE FIRST MEN IN SPACE

The working background of **Yuri Gagarin** (1934–68) was probably as important to his selection as his aeronautical prowess. Trained as a metalworker, he learned to fly and joined the air force where he became a fighter pilot. He applied to become a cosmonaut in 1960 with just 230 flying hours to his name.

His single 90-minute orbit of the Earth included eating and drinking, which had never before been attempted in the minute or so of weightlessness possible using aircraft. Prior to this, it was uncertain whether the human body would continue to function properly when freed from gravity for the first time in its evolution.

Gagarin never went into space again after his flight. He died in 1968 in an air crash.

John Glenn (1921–) was not the first American to reach space – that honour belonged to Alan Shepard who made a sub-orbital flight in 1961 – but he was the first to reach orbit, on 20 February 1962. Glenn's background was quite different from Gagarin's. He had a distinguished war record, with 149 combat missions in the Second World War and the war in Korea, and after this became a test pilot. His orbital flight helped America to believe that its goal to reach the Moon was possible.

Back on the ground, Glenn was sidelined as an astronaut and eventually resigned to enter politics, becoming a Senator. But he was to reach space again aboard the Space Shuttle in 1998, becoming both the first and the oldest American to reach orbit.

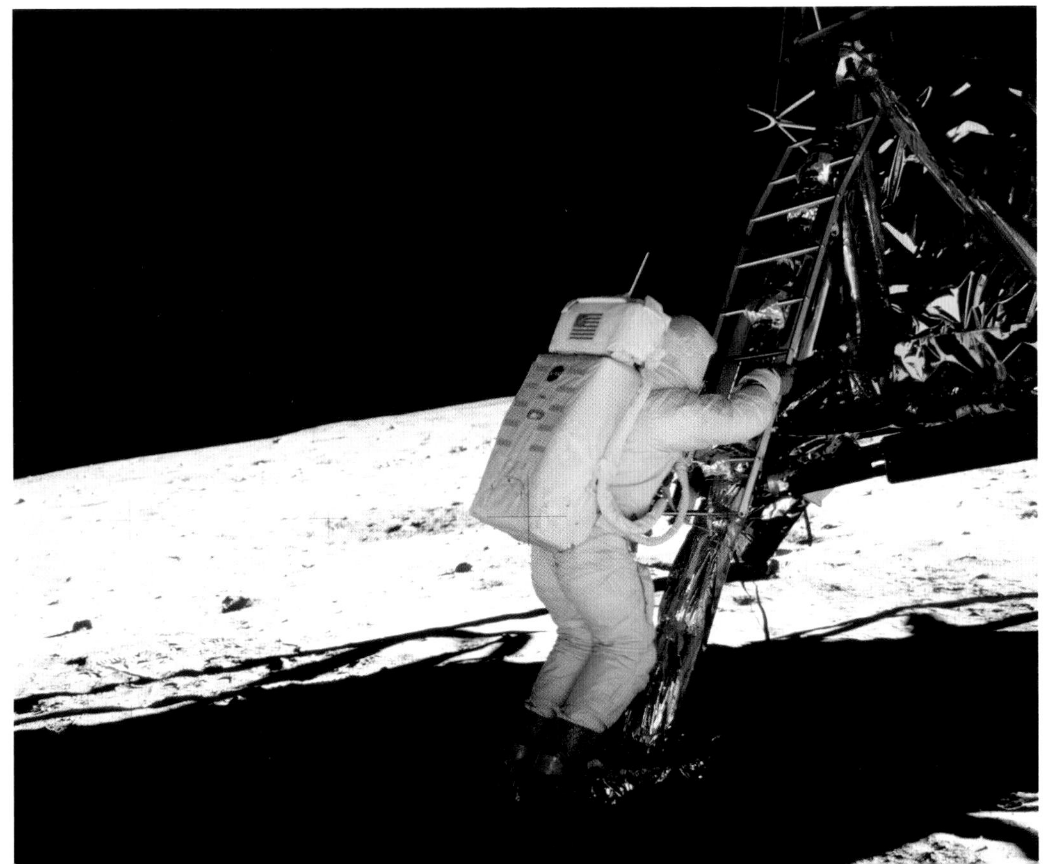

Buzz Aldrin steps on to the Moon. Neil Armstrong was the designated photographer, so almost all the photos are of Buzz.

Controversy continues to surround the 'waving flag'. In fact, the slow movements of the flag were the result of ripples in the fabric that continued in the absence of air.

'That's one small step for man, one giant leap for mankind'. Armstrong still maintains that he actually said '... for *a* man ...', which would make sense; but the transmission as received back on Earth gives no hint of this. The moment was viewed by cameras mounted on the side of the lunar module and was seen by an estimated 500 million people worldwide.

Aldrin followed Armstrong down the ladder and both men spent some time collecting rock samples, setting up experiments and testing out various means of moving on the lunar surface in their restrictive spacesuits. After only $2^1/_2$ hours of moonwalking they returned to *Eagle*, and less than 22 hours after landing on the new world they ascended back to orbit, where Collins had been waiting in *Columbia*.

Centre *The Lunar Module ascending from the surface of the Moon, just about to rejoin the Command Module, where Collins awaited.*

The legacy of *Apollo*

The three astronauts returned to fame and ticker-tape celebrations, but their legacy has been clouded by controversy in recent years. That the whole *Apollo* programme was devised for politics

rather than endeavour was never in question. The American public lost interest in the subsequent landings after the brief excitement of *Apollo 13*, in which an explosion in an oxygen tank during the outbound leg prevented a landing. The series was ended prematurely with *Apollo 17* in 1972 and humans have not left Earth orbit ever since.

A surprising number of people even question whether the landing ever took place at all and think instead that it was simulated in some NASA studio. How could the first step be filmed if there was no one there? And why did the American flag placed on the surface flutter if there is no air? Actually, the cameras were mounted on *Eagle* and the flag moved because of the lack of air and low gravity which meant that ripples in the fabric took a long time to die down.

Aldrin in particular has remained a great proponent of manned space flight, and in 2002 even swung a punch at a particularly dogged filmmaker. It will probably not be until the *Apollo 11* landing site is as well-visited by tourists as Botany Bay is today that the venture of these modern pioneers will finally be accepted by everybody.

NASA's finest hour: tickertape welcomes awaited the Moon heroes on their return, but public interest in Moon landings quickly waned.

ROBERT D. BALLARD

Voyages to the Bottom of the Ocean

1977

It is by logic that we prove, but it is by intuition that we discover.
HENRI POINCARÉ, 1904

On 12 February 1977, two ships left the Panama Canal. The Woods Hole Oceanographic Institution's R/V *Knorr* towed the R/V *Lulu* with its tiny three-man submersible *Alvin* lashed on deck. The Co-Chief Scientist of the expedition was Dr Robert Ballard who, eight years later, was to discover the *Titanic*. Their destination was the Galápagos Rift, a west to east spur of the Mid-Ocean Ridge, the largest mountain range on Earth, where the scientists on board planned to investigate the volcanic and tectonic processes going on deep beneath the Pacific Ocean. There, molten magma flowing upwards from within the Earth creates the ridge, like a blister swollen with heat, which is dissipated into the surrounding ocean water.

An undersea Yellowstone Park

Previous research had indicated that some process appeared to be 'mining' the resultant heat and, instead of spreading that flow equally out across the floor of the valley, might be concentrating it in hot springs similar to those observed above magma chambers on land. Yellowstone Park is a classic example, where melting snow trickles down through cracks in the ground towards the magma chamber that underlies this great volcano. As it travels downwards, the water is heated until it finally 'flashes' or boils, violently erupting above the ground in the form of Old Faithful or the numerous other geysers and boiling cauldrons that exist within the Park.

Clearly, geysers could not exist in the Galápagos Rift valley because the overlying pressure of the oceans at depths exceeding 2,000 to 3,000 m (6,560–9,840 ft) would not let it boil. But there should be hot springs, and that was what the 1977 expedition was hoping to find.

An unmanned submersible remotely operated vehicle called *Angus*, protected by a rugged steel cage that was designed to crash head on into ver-

Robert Ballard (in the foreground) and his team prepare to lower their unmanned camera vehicle Angus *into the ocean in hopes of locating their first undersea hot spring.*

tical rock cliffs and still go on working, was towed close to the ocean floor and collected a continuous series of 12,000 colour photographs.

Slowly, through the evening hours of 15 February, *Knorr* towed *Angus* along the east–west axis of the inner rift valley. All that was being recorded was the height of the vehicle from the bottom, the temperature of the water *Angus* was passing through and the tension on the cable. The greatest fear was that the vehicle would crash into rugged rocky terrain, in effect anchoring *Knorr* to the bottom. If that happened the cable tension would suddenly rise. If it exceeded 20,000 lb, the cable would break and *Angus* would be lost. The tension held at its normal 12,000 lb.

At 7.09 p.m. local time that night a small temperature anomaly lasting three minutes was transmitted to the surface recorder monitoring *Angus*' activities. The vehicle had passed over something warmer than normal, but they would not know exactly what the bottom looked like until the vehicle was recovered and the colour film processed in a lab aboard ship. After more hours on the bottom, during which no other anomalies were encountered, *Angus* was recovered. People gathered at the film-processing lab, anxious to learn what the vehicle had seen.

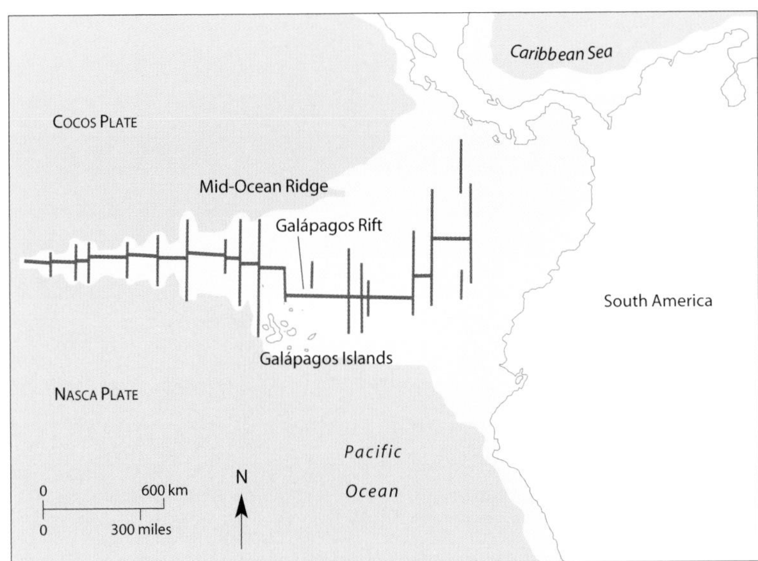

Map of South America and the eastern Pacific Ocean showing the location of the Galápagos Rift, where the first hot springs were located in 1977. The Galápagos Rift is a branch of the Mid-Ocean Ridge, caused by the separating Cocos and Nasca crustal plates.

In the lower left-hand corner of each frame a small red clock showed the time. As 7.09 p.m. approached *Angus* was passing over fresh lava flows covering the bottom, characterized by jet-black rocks with a glassy reflective surface – clearly very young flows. The water was crystal clear. But at 7.09 the scenery changed. The water became milky and clusters of large white clams, hundreds of them, could be seen wedged in between the lava rocks. This was something that had never been seen before. How could such large benthic (bottom-living) creatures survive on the surface of solid rocks in total darkness?

Oases of life

The manned submersible *Alvin* arrived on the afternoon of 16 February. At sunrise the following day it was lowered into the water. That day would cap off one of the great discoveries made in modern science. The hot spring or, more accurately, the hydrothermal vent *Alvin* entered and the observations made would reverberate within the scientific community for years to come.

The submersible Alvin *carries a pilot and two scientists to the floor of the ocean.*

Since *Alvin* was using the same transponders as *Angus* had used the night before, it was very simple to vector it to the same site. After a descent lasting an hour and a half, pilot Jack Donnelly brought Jack Corliss and Jerry van Andel to the bottom at a point less than 275 m (900 ft) from the clam beds. He then began driving along the lava floor towards the site. Along the way, the bottom looked as had been expected: it consisted of fresh but relatively barren lava flows.

When *Alvin* reached its goal, however, they observed a very different scene. At the same time, the temperature sensor began to beep. Warm water shimmered up from cracks in the lava flows. It was turning a cloudy blue as manganese and other minerals, carried from deep within the ocean bed, precipitated out of solution to form a solid coating on the cooler surrounding rocks. But that was not all. The sea floor was teeming with life. The scientists saw clams – giant specimens, 30 cm (1 ft) or more in length. Then shrimps, crabs, fish and small lobster-like creatures passed their viewports. *Alvin*'s robotic arm started to collect these – many were new to science.

Over the next several days they found more hot springs. The warmest water measured exiting

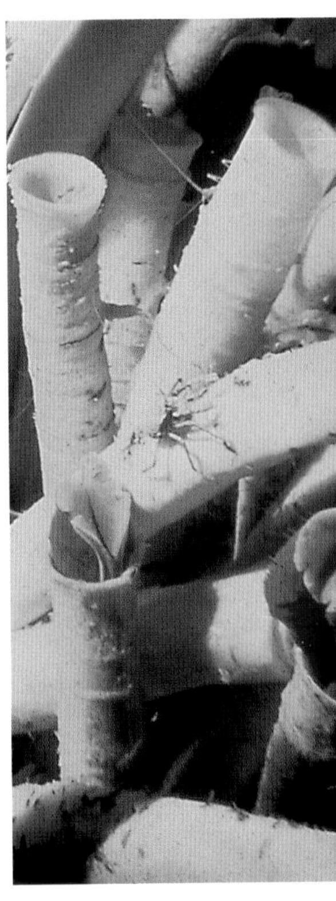

Above left *Giant tube worms, clams and mussels are among the unique benthic animal community that crowds around an active hydrothermal vent.*

Above *A close-up of giant tube worms living inside their protective tubes. Red feather-like gills protrude from the tubes and absorb the chemicals needed to replicate photosynthesis in total darkness through a process now known as chemosynthesis.*

from the vents was 73°C (163°F). With continuing guidance from *Angus*, their precisely targeted dives yielded rich rewards. One site was home to a population of hitherto unknown organisms resembling bright yellow dandelions, and each oasis produced more wonders: white crabs, limpets, small pink fish and clusters of vivid red-tipped worms that protruded from stalk-like white shells, or tubes. The largest tubes they observed were 3.65 m (12 ft) long. The animal itself filled over half this elongated stalk. With no eyes, mouth or any other obvious organs for ingesting food or secreting waste, and no means of locomotion, this was no worm, snake or eel, but no plant either.

A new process of life

The scientists began to speculate how the animals in these deep-sea oases got their energy and nutrients. Prior to this discovery, all life on Earth was thought to be due ultimately to photosynthesis, a process driven by the energy of the Sun. But here in the hot springs of the Galápagos Rift, in total darkness, life was thriving in far greater abundance than any previous theory could explain. What was responsible for this profusion of life?

When samples of the water coming out of the hot springs were collected by *Alvin* and brought to the surface, the awful smell of rotten eggs filled the lab. And when the clams were prised open, their flesh was blood red. Looking under the microscope, billions of tiny bacteria were visible that had taken over their bodies. Living in a symbiotic relationship with the clams and giant tube worms the bacteria were fixing carbon through chemosynthesis.

This process harnesses the energy of the Earth not the Sun to create a previously unknown carbon-based food chain. At these huge depths where the Sun's rays cannot reach, the tiny bacteria use toxic hydrogen sulphide dissolved within the hot spring water, along with oxygen and carbon dioxide in the ocean's water, to replicate photosynthesis.

This discovery has not only revolutionized our understanding of the origin of life on Earth, but is guiding the search for life elsewhere in the solar system and beyond.

JOHN CHRISTOPHER

Round the World by Balloon

1999

The way the public sees it is this. If we don't leave, we are idiots. If we do leave but don't succeed in our mission we are incompetent. But if we do succeed it's because anyone could have done it.
BERTRAND PICCARD, 1999

Just before dawn and the Breitling Orbiter 3 *undergoes final preparations before launch at Château d'Oex in Switzerland.*

Bertrand Piccard couldn't have summed it up better. Whether or not to launch was the major dilemma facing the round-the-world balloonists in the spring of 1999. This challenge had become a hotly contested race with up to eight teams battling it out to coax their fragile and wayward craft the thousands of miles needed to encircle the globe.

The key to a successful global flight is the jetstream. A band of wind moving west to east which forms in the northern hemisphere each winter as cool Arctic air squeezes against the warmer equatorial air-mass. However, by 1 March, when the silvery *Breitling Orbiter 3* ascended into the morning sunlight at Château d'Oex in Switzerland, the jetstream season was almost over and to most observers this latest attempt seemed hopeless.

The launch had been delayed after Richard Branson's balloon had strayed into forbidden Chinese airspace, causing the authorities to close the bamboo curtain to the other teams. It was only through persistent diplomatic approaches that Piccard obtained overflight permission for his Swiss-registered balloon. That and a promise to stay south of the 26th parallel, an almost impossible feat when you are flying at the mercy of the wind.

Joining him on this, his third global attempt, was British balloonist Brian Jones, but undoubtedly Piccard was the driving force behind the Breitling team. The grandson of celebrated stratospheric balloonist Auguste Piccard and son of Charles Piccard who had descended to the depths of the Pacific Ocean's Mariana Trench, here was a man striving to fulfil his destiny. Already an accomplished hang-glider pilot, he had become involved with ballooning after teaming up with Wim Verstreaten to take part in the Chrysler Transatlantic Balloon Race in 1992, which they won.

Significantly, that race proved that the Atlantic was no longer an insurmountable hurdle thanks to a new type of balloon known as a 'Roziere'. Resembling an ice-cream cone, this had a helium-filled sphere heated by a cone of hot-air to combine the advantages of both, resulting in a balloon which could take on the world.

The final attempt

Piccard and Jones knew that this was probably their last chance as the Swiss watch-makers Breitling had announced there would be no fourth *Orbiter*. To add to the tension further, ten days earlier the *Cable & Wireless* balloon had launched from Spain in a bid to fly with the slower southern winds around the bottom edge of China. There seemed little chance that the Breitling balloon would catch up, especially as it initially drifted southwest to Morocco, but this was a vital manoeuvre to line up for the Chinese target.

Gradually *Orbiter* curved eastwards across the deserts of northern Africa, and four days later they had weaved around no-fly zones over Egypt and Yemen to be greeted by news that their rivals had ditched off Japan.

By 9 March the Breitling balloon was well positioned to enter southern China, but, as the air traffic controllers reminded them, 'it is forbidden

SOLO CHALLENGER

Steve Fossett was undoubtedly the dark horse of the global balloon race. This quietly spoken businessman from Chicago had only flown in a balloon a few times when he and a partner tackled the Atlantic in 1994. Six months later he went solo, this time across the Pacific, and it was only a matter of time before he took on the challenge of a solo round-the-world attempt.

Fossett is a serial record collector. He started with sailing but quickly expanded his range of activities to include dog-sled racing across Alaska, driving in the Le Mans 24-hour race, climbing the tallest mountain in six of the seven continents, and of course flying. He has his own no-frills approach to such exploits, and for his global balloon attempts he opted to reuse the cramped capsule from his first Atlantic attempt. Unheated and unpressurized it was far from comfortable, but anything else would not have been the Fossett way.

He went on to make more attempts than anyone else – six solo and on one occasion hitching a ride with Richard Branson and Per Lindstrand. Repeatedly he pushed the record for solo balloon flights, although in 1998 severe weather almost cost him his life when he ditched off Australia. Undaunted by the success of the *Breitling Orbiter 3*, he persevered and in July 2002 he landed at Yamma Yamma in Queensland, Australia, after a successful global flight of almost 15 days.

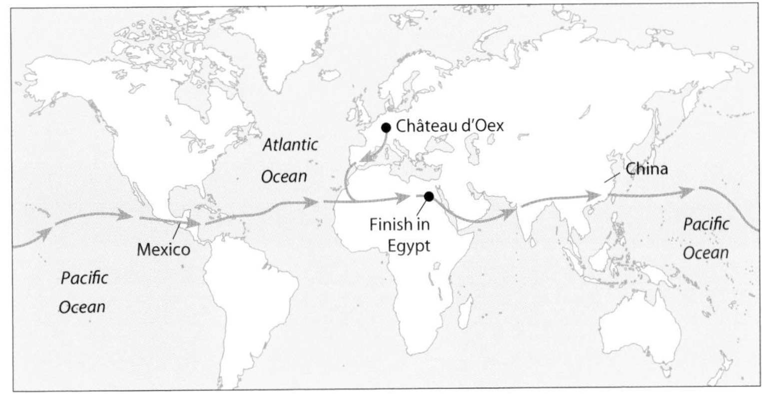

Map showing the route taken by Breitling Orbiter 3. *The route over China was crucial – the Chinese authorities had stipulated that the balloon had to stay south of the 26th parallel.*

to fly north of 26 degrees'. But, incredibly, for the first and only time during its long voyage, the *Orbiter* tracked due east in a straight line for 2,092 km (1,300 miles). At one point it drifted within 40 km (25 miles) of the restricted area before swinging back on course.

With China behind them they faced 16,000 km (10,000 miles) of the Pacific Ocean. Here the meteorologists advised a painfully slow low-altitude drift down to the Equator where faster jetstreams were expected to form. After six days of this the pilots were at their lowest ebb as their speed dropped to just 40 km (25 miles) an hour. Matters became worse as the aluminium-coated envelope blocked satellite communications with the control centre. For the first time Piccard and Jones contemplated the possibility of failure, and for the first time they admitted to each other that they were scared.

When the *Orbiter* eventually reunited with the jetstream it raced towards Mexico at 185 km (115 miles) an hour, but the euphoria was short-lived as both pilots suffered from the effects of prolonged breathing of the over-dry air of the capsule. Then the balloon exited the jetstream and started heading the wrong way. With the Atlantic still ahead and only four tanks of propane fuel left out of 32, their speed had to pick up or they would not make it. With his dream falling apart, Bertrand decided to risk everything by taking the *Orbiter* higher, and at 10,700 m (35,000 ft) he was vindicated as the instruments showed they were back on track and gaining speed.

On 20 March they passed the finish line at 9°27′ west, the point that their eastward journey had started over the red sands of Africa, and after 20 days in the air the *Breitling Orbiter 3* touched down in Egypt the following morning.

A celebratory picture of Piccard and Jones taken with a remotely controlled camera after landing, 21 March 1999.

ROBIN SCAGELL

Mars, Jupiter and Beyond

70

1977–

It may be that the old astrologers had the truth exactly reversed, when they believed that the stars controlled the destinies of men. The time may come when men control the destinies of stars.
ARTHUR C. CLARKE, 1970

The voyagers of the future will mostly be robots. No human has left the confines of the Earth's gravitational field since 1972, but instead machines with names such as *Voyager*, *Spirit* and *Cassini* have done the exploring for us by remote control. These robots have visited every planet in the solar system except Pluto, have dashed past comets (and been deliberately crashed into one), and have even touched down on a tiny asteroid and a giant moon.

They have undertaken some epic travels on our behalf. The twin *Voyager* spacecraft are now at the fringes of the solar system. The data they have sent back greatly advanced our knowledge of the outer planets, and they remain among the most productive of all space travellers. The timing of their launches made use of a fortuitous alignment of the planets which would not be repeated for 175 years. This is important because of the way planetary travel is carried out.

Every mission must carry all the fuel requirements for its journey at launch. The initial impetus to send the craft on its way from Earth orbit can be provided by a separate rocket that drops away, but after the initial burn that achieves a new orbit around the Sun most of the journey must be carried out by coasting. A craft needs enough initial velocity to escape being pulled into the Sun, though if it encounters a planet it can steal some of that planet's orbital momentum around the Sun. This is known as gravity assist, and it is the most economical way of visiting the planets.

The two *Voyagers*

In the 1970s and 1980s, the giant planets Jupiter, Saturn, Uranus and Neptune were ideally placed to make use of this technique. *Voyager 1* was launched two weeks after *Voyager 2*, on 5 September 1977, but it took a faster route and arrived at Jupiter first, 18 months later. During its dash past the planet it took 19,000 images of Jupiter and its major satellites. Jupiter is a gas world, with no solid surface. All we see are the tops of its swirling cloud layers, and time-lapse movies made during the encounter showed just how the planet's vast weather systems interact.

One of the biggest surprises came from the innermost of its four large moons, Io, which is

The planet Jupiter, photographed by Voyager 1, *with Io seen against the Great Red Spot and Europa to its right.*

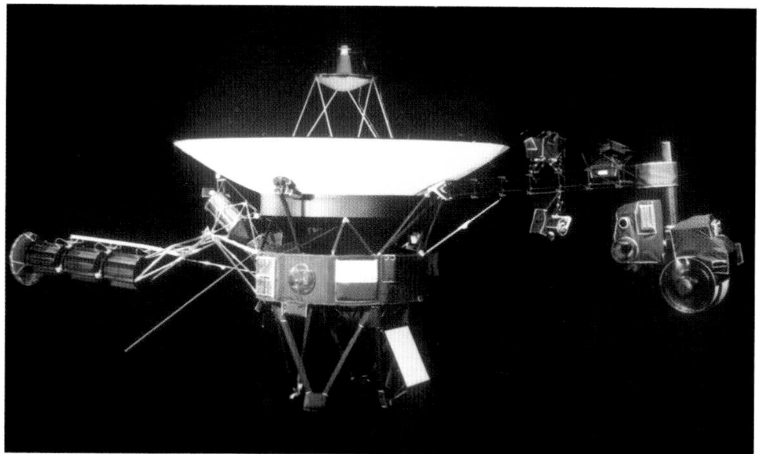

A Voyager spacecraft. The white dish is 3.7 m (12 ft) in diameter and the craft weighs 815 kg (1,796 lb) – about the same as a small car.

slightly larger than our Moon. Scientists expected it to be an inert world, but when navigation scientist Linda Morabito enhanced its image to search for a faint nearby star, she saw an anomaly which stunned her. It looked like a fountain on the moon's edge, and it turned out to be the first evidence for an active volcano beyond the Earth. In fact, Io's closeness to Jupiter churns its interior so much that it is the most active body we know.

Voyager 1 also showed that Jupiter has a ring surrounding it, much thinner and fainter than the well-known ones around Saturn – which *Voyager 1* reached 20 months later. Here, in addition to taking spectacular images, it measured the constituents of Saturn's upper atmosphere, finding a surprisingly low proportion of helium compared with the two larger gaseous bodies, Jupiter and the Sun. *Voyager 1*'s path close to Saturn's enigmatic cloud-covered moon Titan subsequently took it out of the plane of the planets' orbits.

Voyager 2 also encountered Jupiter and Saturn, which was the intended end of its mission. But it was still in fine shape, so a decision was taken to use Saturn's orbital motion to fling it towards the next planet, Uranus. This it reached over five years later, in 1986, and took thousands of images of that planet and its moons. Then it was on to Neptune, encountering that remote planet in 1989. Its images of the Neptunian system will probably not be repeated for decades.

The *Voyager* planetary mission has now been renamed the *Voyager Interstellar Mission*, though it will be many thousands of years before either craft leaves the Sun's gravitational influence. Their radioisotope generators are expected to run low sometime after 2020, after which they will cease transmission, but they will continue on their journeys. It is remarkable that the *Voyagers*, built with early 1970s technology, are still functioning billions of kilometres from home.

Exploring Mars

Flyby craft such as the *Voyagers* are like scouts who forge into unknown territory but cannot stop their headlong rush to investigate further. Real planetary exploration requires robots that can see, touch and feel, and act as much as possible as remote extensions of our own senses. The two Mars Exploration Rovers have been doing just that on the surface of the Red Planet.

Mars is the next natural target for human exploration after the Moon. Of all the planets it is the most like Earth. If you were to land there, a glance through the window might remind you of Chile's Atacama Desert – a sunny landscape of rocks, dunes, pale sky and even the occasional dust devil whipped up by the breeze. But venture outside unprotected and the sub-zero cold and thin carbon dioxide atmosphere would freeze and suffocate you, while the low atmospheric pressure, one hundredth that on Earth's surface, would cause your blood to boil within seconds. Humans will be there one day, but paving the way for us are robot pioneers.

Mars is a jinx on spacecraft. A third of all craft sent there have failed for one reason or another, leading to popular speculation about alien interference – though human error is mostly to blame.

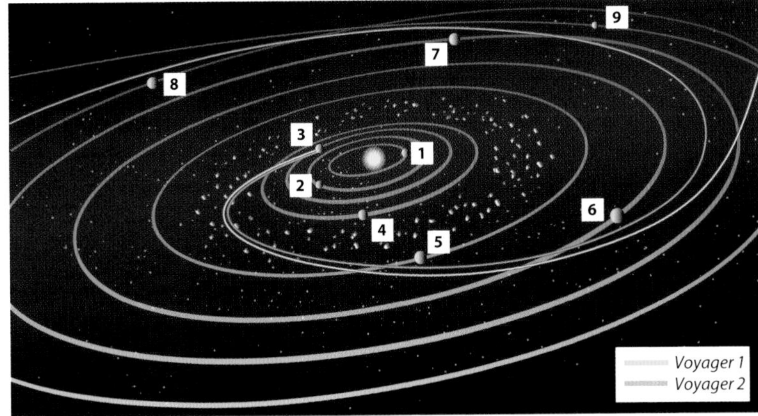

The Grand Tour of the Voyagers *around the solar system: 1 Mercury; 2 Venus; 3 Earth; 4 Mars; 5 Jupiter; 6 Saturn; 7 Uranus; 8 Neptune; 9 Pluto.*

At first it seemed that the Mars Exploration Rovers would suffer the same fate. First to arrive, named *Spirit*, reached the Martian surface on 3 January 2004, protected by airbags that automatically detached and deflated after landing.

Its first images overjoyed the mission controllers – a high-resolution panorama revealed a flat, rocky view of what is believed to be a long-dried-up lakebed. By 15 January *Spirit* had started to drive on to the terrain, but within days of starting to investigate its surroundings it was in trouble and was refusing to send any information back to Earth. All that was received was a simple acknowledgment that *Spirit* was still alive.

Solar panels gleam in this 360° view from 'Husband Hill' taken by the Mars Rover Spirit, *August 2005: a mosaic of 653 separate shots taken over three Martian days.*

The problem was traced to faulty onboard software that had not cleared its memory. Sending new software meant that *Spirit* was able to continue its work, joined at the end of January 2004 by its twin, *Opportunity*, on the other side of the planet. Both Rovers have travelled several kilometres, exploring craters, climbing hills and analyzing the rocks they have found.

The two Mars Rovers indicate the way forward for robot explorers in that they can be reprogrammed to think for themselves to some extent. In February 2005, for example, *Opportunity* was sent new navigation software that allowed it to steer its own way around obstacles, and it explored further in three Mars days than it had in 70 days after it had landed. Radio signals can take up to 20 minutes for the trip between Earth and Mars, so driving by remote control would be a slow business, involving a 40-minute delay between sending a command and seeing the result of the action.

Mission to Saturn

The *Cassini-Huygens* mission to Saturn has shown us strange new worlds, to quote *Star Trek*. *Cassini* arrived at Saturn in July 2004 and has been orbiting the planet with flybys of its curious icy moons. In January 2005 a European-built probe named *Huygens* was released at a predetermined time to plunge into the atmosphere of the hazy moon Titan, a moon larger than the planet Mercury. The pictures it took during its descent and from the surface itself showed a tantalizing world with clouds, shores and rivers – yet at temperatures of -180°C (-292°F). Here, methane takes the place of water and the probe came to rest on a slightly soft surface of ice and mud.

The outer solar system has many more ice worlds that deserve exploration, some of which may even harbour primitive forms of life. Jupiter's moon Europa is a prime target, as it is believed to have an ocean beneath its icy crust. The search for life drives much of our interest in the solar system; but even if other planets and moons are sterile, or without mineral wealth, the drive for exploration for its own sake will continue on worlds where human feet may never tread.

One day – the stars?

Robot missions to the planets take years, and scientists may spend much of their careers on a single voyage from inception to fruition. But will we ever be able to explore beyond the solar system? A *Voyager*-type mission to even the nearest star would take not just the lifetime of a human but of a civilization to yield results. However, miniaturized probes, maybe no bigger than a pen or even a needle, would be easier to send at high speed over vast distances. The power needed to accelerate such a microprobe to a good fraction of the speed of light is well within our capabilities, bringing the timescale back down to human proportions.

Astronomers have found planets around many other stars, though we believe that the natural limit of the speed of light will always mean journey times of tens of years even in our nearest stellar neighbourhood. We can simply speculate that one day it might be possible to bend the laws of nature sufficiently that faster-than-light travel may be feasible – but for the time being, travel to the stars is possible only in our imagination.

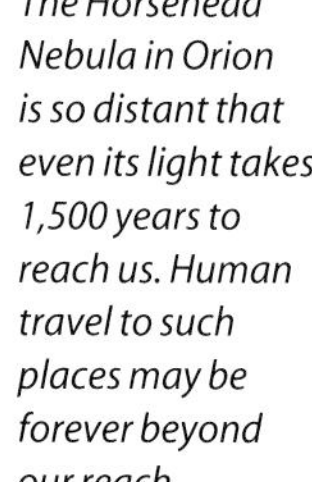

The Horsehead Nebula in Orion is so distant that even its light takes 1,500 years to reach us. Human travel to such places may be forever beyond our reach.

Further Reading

Ancient World

1 Out of Africa

Chen, C., Burton, M., Greenberger, E. & Dmitrieva, J., 'Population migration and the variation of Dopamine D4 receptor allele frequencies around the globe', *Evolution and Human Behavior*, 20 (1999), 309–24
Fagan, B. F., *The Journey from Eden: The Peopling of Our World* (London & New York,1990)
Fagan, B. F., *People of the Earth* (12th ed., Upper Saddle River, NJ, 2006)
Gamble, C., *The Palaeolithic Societies of Europe* (Cambridge, 1999)
Hoffecker, J., *A Prehistory of the North* (New Brunswick, 2005)
Lewin, R., *The Origin of Modern Humans* (New York, 1993)
Stringer, C. & McKie, R., *African Exodus* (New York, 1996)
Whybrow, P. C., *American Mania: When More is Not Enough* (New York, 2005), chapters 2 and 3

2 Into a New World

Adovasio, J., *The First Americans* (New York, 2002)
Dillehay, T., *First Settlement of America: A New Prehistory* (New York, 2000)
Dixon, E. J., *Quest for the Origin of the First Americans* (Albuquerque, 1993)
Dixon, E. J., *Bones, Boats, and Bison* (Albuquerque, 1999)
Fagan, B. F., *The Great Journey* (updated ed., Gainesville, 2004)
Fagan, B. F., *Ancient North America: The Archaeology of a Continent* (4th ed., London & New York, 2005)
Jablonski, N. G. (ed.), *The First Americans: The Pleistocene Colonization of the New World* (San Francisco, 2002)

3 Early Pacific Voyagers

Bellwood, P., *The Polynesians* (rev. ed., London, 1987)
Bellwood, P., *Prehistory of the Indo-Malaysian Archipelago* (rev. ed., Honolulu, 1997)
Irwin, G., *The Prehistoric Exploration and Colonisation of the Pacific* (Cambridge, 1992)
Kirch, P. V., *On the Road of the Winds* (Berkeley, 2000)
Lewis, D., *We, the Navigators* (2nd ed., Honolulu, 1994)
Thomas, N., Guest, H. & Dettelbach, M. (eds), *Observations Made During a Voyage Round the World* (by Johann Reinhold Forster) (Honolulu, 1996)

4 Egyptian Explorers

Lichtheim, M., *Ancient Egyptian Literature. Volume I: The Old and Middle Kingdoms* (Berkeley, Los Angeles & London, 1973), 23–27
Lloyd, A. B., 'Necho and the Red Sea: some considerations', *Journal of Egyptian Archaeology* 63 (1977), 142–55, especially 148–55
Markoe, G. E., *Phoenicians* (London, 2000)
Montserrat, D., 'Did Necho send a fleet around Africa?', in Manley, B. (ed.), *The Seventy Great Mysteries of Ancient Egypt* (London & New York, 2003), 254–55
O'Connor, D., 'Where was the kingdom of Yam?', in Manley, B. (ed.), *The Seventy Great Mysteries of Ancient Egypt* (London & New York, 2003), 155–57

5 Herodotus

de Sélincourt, A., *The World of Herodotus* (London, 1962)
Evans, J. A. S., *Herodotus* (Boston, 1982)
Gould, J., *Herodotus* (London, 1989)
Herodotus, *The Histories* (London, 2003)
Myres, J. L., *Herodotus: Father of History* (Oxford, 1953)
Romm, J. S., *Herodotus* (London & New Haven, 1998)

6 Xenophon

Briant, P., *From Cyrus to Alexander. A History of the Persian Empire* (Winona Lake, 2002)
Cartledge, P. A., *Agesilaus and the Crisis of Sparta* (London & Baltimore, 1987, repr. 2000)
Cawkwell, G. L. (ed.), *Xenophon. The Persian Expedition*, trans. Rex Warner (Harmondsworth, 1972)
Dillery, J. (ed.), *Xenophon Anabasis* (Loeb Classical Library, Cambridge, MA, 1998)
Lane Fox, R. (ed.), *The Long March. Xenophon and the Ten Thousand* (London & New Haven, 2004)
Rood, T., *The Sea! The Sea! The Shout of the Ten Thousand in the Modern Imagination* (London, Woodstock & New York City, 2004)

7 Alexander the Great

Cartledge, P., *Alexander the Great. The Hunt for a New Past* (new ed., London & NewYork, 2005)
Bosworth, A. B., *Conquest and Empire: The Reign of Alexander the Great* (Cambridge, 1988)
Briant, P., *Alexander the Great: The Heroic Ideal* (London, 1996)
Green, P., *Alexander of Macedon, 356–323 BC. A Historical Biography* (rev. ed., Berkeley & London, 1991)
Lane Fox, R., *Alexander the Great* (London, 1973)
Lane Fox, R., *The Search for Alexander* (London, 1980)

8 Pytheas the Greek

Cunliffe, B., *The Extraordinary Voyage of Pytheas the Greek* (London, 2001; New York, 2003)
Hawkes, C., *Pytheas: Europe and the Greek Explorers* (Oxford, 1977)
Roseman, C. H., *Pytheas of Massilia, On the Ocean: Text, Translation and Commentary* (Chicago, 1994)

9 Hannibal

de Beer, G., *Hannibal's March* (London, 1967)
Goldsworthy, A., *The Fall of Carthage: The Punic Wars 265–146 BC* (London, 2004)
Livy (Titus Livius), 'The War With Hannibal', Books XXI–XXX of *The History of Rome* (London, 1965)
Prevas, J., *Hannibal Crosses the Alps: The Invasion of Italy and the Second Punic War* (Cambridge, MA, 2001)

10 St Paul

Meinardus, O. F. A., *St Paul's Last Journey* (New York, 1978)
Morton, H. V., *In the Steps of St Paul* (Cambridge, MA, 2002)
Ramsay, W. M., *St Paul the Traveler and Roman Citizen* (repr., Grand Rapids, MI, 2001)
White, J., *Evidence and Paul's Journeys* (Hilliard, OH, 2001)

11 The Emperor Hadrian

Birley, A., *Hadrian, the Restless Emperor* (London, 1977)
Boatwright, M. T., *Hadrian and the Cities of the Roman Empire* (Princeton, 2000)
Life of Hadrian, in *Lives of the Later Caesars,* trans. A. Birley (London, 1976)
Speller, E., *Following Hadrian* (London, 2002; New York 2003)

Medieval World

12 Early Chinese Travellers on the Silk Road

Giles, H. A., *The Travels of Fa Hsien* (Cambridge, 1923)
Grousset, R., *In the Footsteps of Buddha* (London, 1971)
Hui-Li, *The Life of Heuen-Tsang* (London, 1911)

13 Early Voyagers to America

Fitzhugh, W. W. & Ward, E. I. (eds), *Vikings, The North Atlantic Saga* (Washington, DC, 2000)
Magnussen, M. & Pálsson, H., *The Vinland Sagas: The Norse Discovery of North America* (London, 1965)
Marcus, G. J., *The Conquest of the North Atlantic* (Woodbridge, 1980)
Wahlgren, E., *The Vikings and America* (London & New York, 1986)

14 Christian Pilgrimages

Harpur, J., *Sacred Tracks: 2000 Years of Christian Pilgrimage* (London & Berkeley, 2002)
Parks, G. R., *The English Traveller to Italy* (Rome, 1954)
Sumption, J., *Pilgrimage: An Image of Medieval Religion* (London, 1975)
Ure, J., *Pilgrimage: The Great Adventure of the Middle Ages* (London, 2006)

15 Muslim Pilgrimages

Amin, M., *Journey of a Lifetime: Pilgrimage to Makkah* (Northampton, MA, 2000)
Birks, J. S., *Across the Savannas to Mecca: The Overland Pilgrimage Route from West Africa* (London, 1978)
Long, D. E., *The Hajj Today: A Survey of the Contemporary Makka Pilgrimage* (Albany, NY, 1979)
Netton, I. R. (ed.), *Golden Roads: Migration, Pilgrimage and Travel in Medieval and Modern Islam* (Richmond, 1993)

16 Genghis Khan

Cleave, F. W. (trans.), *The Secret History of the Mongols* (Cambridge, MA, 1982)
Juvaini, Ata Malik, *The History of the World Conqueror*, trans. J. A. Boyle (Manchester, 1958)
Marozzi, J., *Tamerlane: Sword of Islam, Conqueror of the World* (London & New York, 2004)
Morgan, D., *The Mongols* (Oxford, 1986)
Rashid al-Din, *Jami al-Tawarikh* ('Compendium of Histories')

17 Marco Polo

Larner, J., *Marco Polo and the Discovery of the World* (New Haven & London, 1995)
Marco Polo, *The Travels of Marco Polo,* trans. R. Latham (Harmondsworth, 1958)
Wood, F., *Did Marco Polo Go To China?* (London, 1995)

18 Ibn Battuta

Dunn, R., *The Adventures of Ibn Battuta: A Muslim Traveler of the 14th Century* (Berkeley, 1989)
Gibb, H. A. R., *The Travels of Ibn Battuta*, Vols I, II, III, Hakluyt Society (London,1956); translation of *Rihla* of Ibn Battuta
Mackintosh-Smith, T. (ed.), *The Travels of Ibn Battutah* (London, 2003)

19 Zheng He, the Grand Eunuch

Levathes, L., *When China Ruled the Seas* (New York, 1994)
Mote, F. W. & Twitchett, D. (eds), *The Cambridge History of China, Vol. 7, The Ming Dynasty,1368–1644* (Cambridge, 1988)
Needham, J., *Science and Civilisation in China*, Vol. 1– (Cambridge, 1954–)

The Renaissance

20 Christopher Columbus

Columbus, Christopher, *The Four Voyages of Columbus,* trans. J. M. Cohen (Harmondsworth, 1969)
Cummins, J., *Christopher Columbus* (London, 1992)
Fernández-Armesto, F., *Columbus* (Oxford, 1991)
Flint, V., *The Imaginative Landscape of Christopher Columbus* (Princeton, 1992)
Thomas, H., *Rivers of Gold. The Rise of the Spanish Empire, from Columbus to Magellan* (London, 2003)

21 Vasco da Gama

Ames, G., *Vasco da Gama* (Harlow, 2005)
Bouchon, G., *Vasco de Gama* (Paris, 1997)
Diffey, B. W. & Winius, G., *Foundations of the Portuguese Empire 1415–1580* (Oxford, 1977)
Jayne, K. G., *Vasco da Gama and his Successors* (London, 1910; repr. New Delhi, 1997)
Ravenstein, E. G. S. (ed.), *A Journal of the First Voyage of Vasco da Gama* (London, 1898)
Subrahmanyan, S., *The Career and Legend of Vasco da Gama* (Cambridge,1997)

22 Ludovico di Varthema

Aubin, J., 'Deux Chrétiens au Yémen Tahiride', *Journal of the Royal Asiatic Society*, 3 (1993), 33–75
Giudici, P., *Itinerario di Ludovico de Varthema* (2nd ed., Milan, 1929)
Morrall, A., *Joerg Breu the Elder – Art, Culture and Belief in Reformation Augsburg* (London, 2001)
Schefer, C., *Les Voyages de Ludovico di Varthema traduits par Jean Balarin de Raconis* (Paris, 1888)

23 Ferdinand Magellan

Bergreen, L., *Over the Edge of the World* (New York, 2003)
Joyner, T., *Magellan* (Camden, ME, 1992)
Morison, S. E., *The European Discovery of America: The Southern Voyages* (New York, 1974)
Winchester, S., 'After dire straits, an agonizing haul across the Pacific', *Smithsonian* (April 1991), 84–95

24 Hernán Cortés

Clendinnen, I., *The Aztecs: An Interpretation* (Cambridge, 1991)
Cortés, H., *Five Letters to the King of Spain*, trans. J. Bayard Morris (New York, 1962)
Diaz del Castillo, B., *The Conquest of New Spain*, trans. J. M. Cohen (Baltimore, 1963)
Moctezuma, E. M., *The Great Temple of the Aztecs* (London & New York, 1988)
Smith, M., *The Aztecs* (Oxford & New York, 1996)
Thomas, H., *Conquest: Cortés, Montezuma and the Fall of Old Mexico* (New York, 1995)
Townsend, R. F., *The Aztecs* (London & New York, 1992)

25 Francisco Pizzarro

Hemming, J., *The Conquest of the Incas* (rev. ed., London, 2004)

Hemming, J., 'Pizarro, Conqueror of the Inca', *National Geographic*, 181:2 (Feb. 1992), 90–121

26 Francisco de Orellana

Carvajal, Friar Gaspar de, *Descubrimiento del Río de las Amazonas* (1543), trans. Bertram T. Lee, ed. H. C. Heaton (New York, 1934)

Cohen, J. M., *Journeys Down the Amazon* (London: Charles Knight, 1975)

Hemming, J., *The Search for El Dorado* (London, 1978)

Hemming, J., *Red Gold. The Conquest of the Brazilian Indians* (rev. ed., London, 2004)

Smith, A., *Explorers of the Amazon* (London, 1990)

27 Early Explorers of North America

Bolton, H. E., *Coronado: Knight of Pueblos and Plains* (New York, 1949)

Clayton, L. A. et al., *The De Soto Chronicles: The Expedition of Hernando de Soto to North America in 1539–1543* (Tuscaloosa, 1995)

Day, A. G., *Coronado's Quest: The Discovery of the Southwestern States* (Berkeley, 1940)

Favata, M. A. & Fernández, J. B. (trans.), *The Account: Alvar Nuñez Cabeza de Vaca's Rélacion* (Houston, 1993)

Winthrop, G. P. et al. (eds), *The Journey of Coronado, 1540–1542* (Golden, CO, 1990)

28 Francis Drake

Andrews, K. R., *Drake's Voyages: A Reassessment of their Place in England's Maritime Expansion* (London, 1967)

Drake, Sir Francis, *The World Encompassed by Sir Francis Drake* (London, 1628)

Kelsey, H., *Sir Francis Drake: The Queen's Pirate* (New Haven & London, 1998)

Loades, D., *England's Maritime Empire* (London, 2000)

Thompson, G. M., *Sir Francis Drake* (London, 1972)

29 Samuel de Champlain

Biggar, H. P. (ed.), *The Works of Samuel de Champlain*, 6 vols. (Toronto, 1922–36)

Bishop, M., *Champlain: The Life of Fortitude* (London, 1949)

Heidenreich, C. E., 'The Beginning of French Exploration out of the St Lawrence Valley: Motives, Methods, and Changing Attitudes toward Native People', in Warkentin, G. & Podruchny, C. (eds), *Decentring the Renaissance* (Toronto, 2001), 236–51

Heidenreich, C. E., 'Early French Exploration in the North American Interior', in Allen, J. L. (ed.), *North American Exploration: A Continent Defined*, Vol. 2 (Lincoln, Nebraska, 1997), 65–148

Litalien, R. & Vaugeois, D. (eds), *Champlain: the Birth of French America*, (Montreal-Kingston, 2004)

30 Early Searchers for the Northwest Passage

Davies, W. K. D., *Writing Geographical Exploration: James and the Northwest Passage 1631–32* (Calgary, 2003)

Delgado, J. P., *Across the Top of the World: The Quest for the Northwest Passage* (London & New York, 1999)

McDermott, J., *Martin Frobisher: Elizabethan Privateer* (London, 2001)

Quinn, D. B., 'The Northwest Passage in Theory and Practice', in Allen, J. L. (ed.), *North American Exploration: A New World Disclosed*, Vol. I (Lincoln, Nebraska, 1997)

Savours, A., *The Search for the North West Passage* (London & New York, 1999)

17th & 18th Centuries

31 Abel Tasman

Cannon, M. M., *The Exploration of Australia* (Sydney, 1987)

Clarke, C. M. H., *A History of Australia* (Melbourne, 1962)

Kernihan, G. H. (ed.), *The Journal of 1642* (Adelaide, 1964)

Sharp, A., *The Voyages of Abel Janszoon Tasman* (Melbourne, 1968)

Whitmore, R., *New Zealand in History*: history-nz.org/discovery1.html

32 Maria Sibylla Merian

Davis, N. Z., *Women on the Margins: Three Seventeenth-Century Lives* (Cambridge, MA, & London, 1995), 140–202

Rücker, E. & Stearns, W. T. (eds), *Metamorphosis Insectorum Surinamensis* (London, 1980). Facsimile edition of the watercolours in the Royal Library, Windsor Castle

Valiant, S., 'Maria Sibylla Merian: Recovering an Eighteenth-Century Legend', *Eighteenth-Century Studies* 3 (1993), 467–79

Wettengl, K. (ed.), *Maria Sibylla Merian, 1647–1717. Artist and Naturalist* (Ostfildern, 1998)

33 Ippolito Desideri

Allen, C., *A Mountain in Tibet: The Search for Mount Kailas and the Sources of the Great Rivers of India* (London, 1982)

Filippi, F. de (ed.), *An Account of Tibet: The Travels of Ippolito Desideri, 1712–1727* (based on Desideri MSS 'Historical Sketch of Tibet') (London, 1931)

Wessels, C., *Early Jesuit Travellers in Central Asia 1603–1721* (The Hague, 1924)

34 Vitus Bering

Divin, V. A., *The Great Russian Navigator, A.I. Chirikov*, trans. & ed. R. H. Fisher (Fairbanks, 1993)

Fisher, R. H., *Bering's voyages: Whither and Why?* (Seattle, 1977)

Frost, O. (ed.), *Bering and Chirikov: The American Voyages and their Impact* (Anchorage, 1992)

Frost, O., *Bering. The Russian Discovery of America* (New Haven & London, 2003)

Golder, F. A., *Bering's Voyages. An Account of the Efforts of the Russians to Determine the Relation of Asia and America*, 2 vols (New York, 1922/1925)

Steller, G. W., *Journal of a Voyage with Bering, 1741–1742*, ed. O. Frost (Palo Alto, CA, 1988)

Waxell, S., *The American Expedition*, trans. & ed. M. A. Michael (London, 1952)

35 James Bruce

Bredin, M., *The Pale Abyssinian* (London, 2000)

Bruce, J., *Travels to Discover the Source of the Nile*, ed. C. F. Beckingham (Edinburgh, 1964)

Moorehead, A., *The Blue Nile* (London & New York, 1962)

36 James Cook

Beaglehole, J. C. (ed.), *The Journals of Captain James Cook on his Voyages of Discovery*, 4 vols (Cambridge, 1955–69)

Beaglehole, J. C., *The Life of Captain Cook* (Cambridge, 1974)

Collingridge, V., *Captain Cook* (London, 2003)

David, A., *The Charts and Coastal Views of Captain Cook's Voyages, Vol. 1 – The Voyage of the Endeavour 1768–1771* (London, 1988)

Robson, J., *Captain Cook's World – Maps of the Life and Voyages of*

James Cook, R. N. (London, 2001)
Robson, J., *The Captain Cook Encyclopaedia* (London, 2004)
National Library of Australia/National Maritime Museum (Australia), CD ROM. *Endeavour – Captain Cook's Journal, 1768–1771*
http://www.captaincooksociety.com
http://pages.quicksilver.net.nz/jcr/~cooky.html

37 Jean-François de Lapérouse
Dunmore, J., *French Explorers in the Pacific, Vol. 1: The Eighteenth Century* (Oxford, 1965)
Dunmore, J., *Pacific Explorer: The Life of Jean-François de La Pérouse* (Palmerston North, 1985)
La Pérouse, J.-F. de Galaup de, *The Journal of Jean-François de la Pérouse 1785–1778*, trans. & ed. J. Dunmore (London, 1994)
http://pages.quicksilver.net.nz/jcr/~lap.html

38 Alexander Mackenzie
Gough, B., *First Across the Continent* (Norman, 1997)
Hamon, D., *Sixteen Years in Indian Country, 1800–1816* (Toronto, 1957)
Hayes, D., *First Crossing* (Vancouver, 2001)
Mackenzie, A., *Journal*, ed. W. Kaye Lamb (London, 1970)
Morse, E., *Fur Trade Canoe Routes of Canada* (Toronto, 1995)
Nute, G. L., *The Voyageur* (St Paul, 1931)
Twigger, R., *Voyageur. Across the Rocky Mountains in a Birchbark Canoe* (London, 2006)

39 Mungo Park
Gramont, S. de, *The Strong Brown God, The Story of the Niger River* (Boston, 1975)
Lupton, K., *Mungo Park, The African Traveler* (Oxford, 1979)
Park, M., *Travels into the Interior of Africa* (London, 2003)
Park, M., *Travels in the Interior Districts of Africa*, ed. K. Ferguson Marsters (Durham & London, 2000)

19th Century

40 Alexander von Humboldt
Botting, D., *Humboldt and the Cosmos* (London, 1973)
Bruhns, K., *Alexander von Humboldt eine wissenschaftliche Biographie* 3 vols (Leipzig, 1872); translated into English by J. & C. Lassiel, 2 vols (London, 1873)
Hall, F. & Pérez, J. F., *El mundo de Alexander von Humboldt: Antología de Texto* (Madrid, 2002)
Hein, W.-H. (ed.), *Alexander von Humboldt: Life and Work* (Ingelheim am Rein, 1987)
Humboldt, A. von, *Personal Narrative of a Journey to the Equinoctal Regions of the New Continent*, trans. J. Wilson, intro. by M. Nicholson (London & New York, 1995)
Kellner, L., *Alexander von Humboldt* (London, 1963)

41 Lewis & Clark
Allen, J. L., *Lewis and Clark and the Image of the American Northwest* (repr., New York, 1991). Originally published as *Passage through the Garden: Lewis and Clark and the Image of the American Northwest* (Urbana, 1975)
Jackson, D. (ed.), *Letters of the Lewis and Clark Expedition, with Related Documents, 1783–1854*, 2 vols (2nd ed., Urbana, 1978)
Jones, L. Y., *William Clark and the Shaping of the West* (New York, 2004)
Moulton, G. E. (ed.), *Journals of the Lewis and Clark Expedition*,13 vols (Lincoln, 1983–2001)
Ronda, J. P., *Lewis and Clark Among the Indians* (Lincoln, 1984)

42 Jean Louis Burckhardt
Belzoni, G., *Narrative of the Operations … in Egypt and Nubia* (London, 1820)
Burckhardt, J. L., *Travels in Nubia* (London, 1819)
Clayton, P., *The Rediscovery of Ancient Egypt* (London & New York, 1982)
Sattin, A., *The Pharaoh's Shadow: Travels in Ancient and Modern Egypt* (London, 2000)
Sattin, A., *The Gates of Africa: Death, Discovery and the Search for Timbuktu* (London 2003; New York, 2005)

43 Charles Darwin & the Beagle
Darwin, C., *Narrative of the Surveying Voyages of the HMS 'Adventure' and 'Beagle' between 1826 and 1836*, 3 vols (London, 1839)
Darwin, C., *Journal of research into the geology and natural history of the various countries visited by HMS Beagle under the command of Captain Fitzroy R. N. from 1832 to 1836* (London, 1840). Reprinted e.g. Darwin, C., *Voyage of the Beagle* (London, 1989)
Darwin, C. (ed.), *The Zoology of the Voyage of HMS. Beagle During the Years 1832–36*, 4 Vols (London, facsimile reprint 1980)
Darwin, C., *On the origin of species by means of natural selection …* (London, 1859, and later reprints)
FitzRoy, R., *Narrative of the surveying voyages of HMS Adventure and Beagle Between 1826 and 1839*, 2 Vols (London, 1839)
Keynes, R. D. (ed.), *Charles Darwin's Beagle Diary* (Cambridge, 1988)
Moorehead, A., *Darwin and the Beagle* (London & New York, 1969)

44 The Trail of Tears
Ehle, J., *Trail of Tears: The Rise and Fall of the Cherokee Nation* (New York, 1988)
Fleischmann, G., *Cherokee Removal, 1838: An Entire Indian Nation is Forced Out of its Homeland* (New York, 1971)
Foreman, G., *Indian Removal: The Emigration of the Five Civilized Tribes of Indians* (Norman & London, 1932)
King, D., *The Cherokee Trail of Tears* (Portland, OR, 2005)

45 Journeys into the Mexican Jungle
Brunhouse, R. L., *In Search of the Maya: The First Archaeologists* (Albuquerque, 1973)
von Hagen, V. W., *Maya Explorer. John Lloyd Stephens and the Lost Cities of Central America and Yucatán* (Norman, 1947)
von Hagen, V. W., *Frederick Catherwood, Architect* (Oxford, 1950)

46 Later Searchers for the Northwest Passage
Beardsley, M., *Deadly Winter: The Life of Sir John Franklin* (London, 2002)
Cyriax, R. J., *Sir John Franklin's Last Arctic Expedition …* (Plaistow & Sutton Coldfield, 1997; facsimile of 1939 edition)
Delgado, J. P., *Across the Top of the World: The Quest for the Northwest Passage* (London & New York, 1999)
Lehane, B. et al., *The Northwest Passage* (Alexandria, VI, 1981)
Ross, M. J., *Polar Pioneers: John Ross and James Clark Ross* (Montreal & Kingston, 1994)
Savours, A., *The Search for the North West Passage* (London, 1999)
Williams, G., *Voyages of Delusion: The Northwest Passage in the Age of Reason* (London, 2002)
Woodman, D. C., *Unravelling the Franklin Mystery: Inuit Testimony* (Montreal & Kingston, 1991)

47 Heinrich Barth & the Central African Mission
Barth, H., *Travels and Discoveries in North and Central Africa: being*

a Journal of an Expedition undertaken under the auspices of H.B.M.'s Government in the years 1849-1855, 5 vols (London, 1857–58; repr. 3 vols, London, 1965)
Boahen, A. A., *Britain, the Sahara and the Western Sudan 1778–1861* (London, 1964)
Caillié, R., *Travels through Central Africa to Timbuctoo and Across the Great Desert to Morocco performed in the Years 1824–28* (London, 1830; repr. 2 vols, London, 1992)

48 Search for the Source of the Nile
Brodie, F. M., *The Devil Drives: A Life of Sir Richard Burton* (London, 1967; repr. London, 1986)
Burton, R. F., *The Lake Regions of Central Africa: A Picture of Exploration*, 2 vols (London, 1860)
Maitland, A., *Speke and the Discovery of the Source of the Nile* (Newton Abbot, 1971)
Moorehead, A., *The White Nile* (London & New York, 1960)
Ondaatje, C., *Journey to the Source of the Nile* (Toronto, 1998)
Speke, J. H., *Journal of the Discovery of the Source of the Nile* (New York, 1864)

49 Crossing Australia
Cannon, M. M., *The Exploration of Australia* (Sydney, 1987)
Clarke, C. M. H., *A History of Australia* (Melbourne, 1962)
Moorehead, A., *Cooper's Creek* (London & New York, 1971)
Stokes, E., *To an Inland Sea* (Melbourne, 1986)
Webster, M. S., *John McDouall Stuart* (Melbourne, 1958)
http://www.slv.vic.gov.au/burkeandwills/

50 Into the Heart of Africa
Jeal, T., *Livingstone* (London, 1973)
Livingstone, D., *The Life and African Explorations of David Livingstone* (London, 1875)
McLynn, F., *Stanley: Dark Genius of African Exploration* (London, 2004)
Ross, A., *David Livingstone Mission and Empire* (Hambledon & London, 2002)
Stanley, H. M., *Through the Dark Continent, Vol 1 & 2* (London, 1878; repr. New York & London, 1988)

51 The Mekong River Expedition
Garnier, F., *Voyage d'exploration en Indo-Chine* (Paris, 1885); English translation in 2 vols: *Travels in Cambodia and Laos and Further Travels in Laos and Yunnan* (Bangkok, 1996)
Keay, J., *Mad about the Mekong: Exploration and Empire in South East Asia* (London, 2005)
Osborne, M., *The Mekong: Turbulent Past, Uncertain Future* (New York, 2000)

52 Travels in Arabia Deserta
Doughty, C., *Travels in Arabia Deserta* (London, 1888, and later eds)
Keay, J. (ed.), *The Royal Geographical History of World Exploration* (London, 1991)
Thesiger, W., *Arabian Sands* (London, 1959)
Ure, J., In Search of Nomads (London & New York, 2003)

53 The Northeast Passage
Kish, G., *North-east Passage. Adolf Erik Nordenskiöld, His Life and Times* (Amsterdam, 1973)
Leslie, A., *The Arctic Voyages of Adolf Erik Nordenskiöld* (London, 1879)
Liljequist, G. H., *High Latitudes. A History of Swedish Polar Travels and Research* (Stockholm, 1993)
Nordenskiöld, A. E., *The Voyage of the Vega round Asia and Europe*, 2 vols (London, 1881)
Nordqvist, O. A. 'Vega's voyage through the Northeast Passage', *Polar Geography and Geology* 7(1) (1983), 8–71
Vaughan, R., *The Arctic. A History* (Stroud, 1994), 59–64
De Veer, G., *A true description of three voyages by the North-east towards Cathay and China, undertaken by the Dutch in the years 1594, 1595 and 1596* (London, 1853)

54 The Pundits Explore Tibet
Hopkirk, P., *Trespassers on the Roof of the World* (London & Los Angeles, 1982)
Hopkirk, P., *The Great Game* (London, 1990; New York, 1992)
Hopkirk, P., *The Quest for Kim* (London, 1996; Ann Arbor, 1997)
Journal of the Royal Geographical Society: various contemporary accounts of the Pundits' journeys (1860s, 1870s & 1880s)
Survey of India Department, *Exploration in Tibet and Neighbouring Regions*, Part 1 and 2 (Dehra Dun, 1915)
Waller, D. J., *The Pundits. British Exploration of Tibet and Central Asia* (Lexington, 1990)

55 Exploring Central & East Asia
Allen, C., *Duel in the Snow* (London, 2004)
Hopkirk, P., *Bayonets to Lhasa* (London & New York, 1961)
Hopkirk, P., *The Great Game* (London, 1990; New York, 1992)
French, P., *Younghusband. The Last Great Imperial Adventurer* (London, 1994)
Pyasetsky, P., *Russian Travellers in Mongolia and China*, trans. J. Gordon-Cumming, 2 vols (London, 1884)
Rayfield, D., *The Dream of Lhasa: The Life of Nikolay Przhevalsky* (London, 1976)

Modern Times

56 Journeys Across Asia
Hedin, S., *My Life as an Explorer* (London, 1926)
Hedin, S., *Through Asia* (London, 1898)
Hopkirk, P., *Foreign Devils on the Silk Road* (London, 1980)
Tucker, J., *The Silk Road. Art and History* (London, 2003)
Walker, A., *Aurel Stein: Pioneer of the Silk Road* (London, 1995)
Whitfield, S., *Aurel Stein on the Silk Road* (London & Chicago, 2004)

57 To the North Pole
Cook, F., *National Geographic Magazine*, September 1909
Fleming, F., *Ninety Degrees North – The Quest for the North Pole* (London, 2001)
Herbert, W., *Across the Top of the World* (London, 1969)
Herbert, W., *The Noose of Laurels – The Discovery of the North Pole* (London, 1989)
Peary, R., *National Geographic Magazine*, September 1909

58 Race to the South Pole
Cherry-Garrard, A., *The Worst Journey in the World* (London, 1922, and later eds)
Evans, E., *South with Scott* (London, 1952)
Fiennes, R., *Captain Scott* (London, 2003)
Gran, T., *The Norwegian with Scott*, trans. E. J. McGhie (London,1984)
Solomon, S., *The Coldest March* (New Haven & London, 2001)
Wilson, E., *Diary of the 'Terra Nova' Expedition to the Antarctic, 1910–1912* (London, 1972)
Yelverton, D. E., *Antarctica Unveiled* (Boulder, 2000)

59 Shackleton & the Endurance
Alexander, C., *The Endurance* (London, 1998)
Huntford, R., *Shackleton* (London, 1985)
Lansing, A., *Endurance, Shackleton's Incredible Voyage* (London, 2000)
Morrell, M. & Capparel, S., *Shackleton's Way* (London, 2001)
Piggott, J. (ed.), *Shackleton, The Antarctic and Endurance* (London, 2000), 1–58
Shackleton, J. & MacKenna, J., *Shackleton, An Irishman in Antarctica* (Dublin, 2002)
Shackleton, E., *South* (London, 1919)
Thomson, J., *Shackleton's Captain. A Biography of Frank Worsley* (Ontario, 1999)
Worsley, Commander F. A., *Shackleton's Boat Journey* (London, 1974)

60 Women Travellers in Asia
Bell, G., *The Arabian Diaries*, ed. R. O'Brien (Syracuse, 2000)
Moorehead, C., *Freya Stark* (London & New York, 1985)
Stoddart, A. M., *The Life of Isabella Bird (Mrs Bishop)* (London, 1906)
Robinson, J., *Wayward Women* (Oxford, 2001)
Winstone, H. V. F., *Gertrude Bell* (London & New York, 1978)

61 First to Fly the Atlantic Solo
Berg, A. S., *Lindbergh* (New York, 1998)
Crouch, T. D., *The Blériot XI: The Story of a Classic Aircraft* (Washington, DC, 1982)
Lindbergh, C. A., *The Spirit of St. Louis* (New York, 1953)
Smith, R. K., *First Across! The U.S. Navy's Transatlantic Flight of 1919* (Annapolis, 1973)

62 Women Pioneers of Flight
Gillies, M., *Amy Johnson: Queen of the Air* (London, 2003)
Long, E. M. & M. K., *Amelia Earhart: The Mystery Solved* (New York, 1999)
Lovell, M. S., *The Sound of Wings* (London, 1989)
Luff, D., *Amy Johnson: Enigma in the Sky* (Shrewsbury, 2002)

63 The Long March
Salisbury, H. E., *The Long March: The Untold Story* (London, 1986)
Snow, E., *Red Star Over China* (London, 1937; rev. ed. New York, 1968)
Wilson, D., *The Long March 1935: The Epic of Chinese Communism's Survival* (London, 1971)

64 Thor Heyerdahl & the Kon-Tiki
Heyerdahl, T., *In the Footsteps of Adam* (London, 2000)
Heyerdahl, T., *The Kon-Tiki Expedition* (London & Chicago, 1950)
Heyerdahl, T., *The Ra Expeditions* (London & New York, 1971)
Ralling, C., *The Kon-Tiki Man* (London & San Francisco, 1990)

65 Scaling Everest
Douglas, E., *Tenzing – Hero of Everest* (Washington, DC, 2003)
Gillman, P. & L., *The Wildest Dream – Mallory, his Life and Conflicting Passions* (London, 2000)
Hillary, E., *View from the Summit* (London, 1999)
Hunt, J., *The Ascent of Everest* (London, 1953)
Venables, S., *Everest – Summit of Achievement* (London, 2003)

66 Single-Handed Around the World
Knox-Johnston, *A World of My Own* (London & New York, 1969)
Nicols, P., *A Voyage for Madmen* (London & New York, 2001)
Roth, H., *The Longest Race* (New York, 1983)

67 To the Moon and Back
Furniss, T., *One Giant Leap* (London, 1998)
Godwin, R. (ed.), *Apollo 11: The NASA Mission Reports*, 3 vols (Burlington, 1999–2002)
Light, M., *Full Moon* (New York & London, 2002)
Schefter, J., *The Race: The Definitive Story of America's Battle to Beat Russia to the Moon* (New York & London, 1999)

68 Voyages to the Bottom of the Ocean
Ballard, R. D. & Grassle, J. F., 'Return to the Oases of the Deep', *National Geographic Magazine*, 156 (1979), 689–703
Corliss, J. B. & Ballard, R. D., 'Oasis of Life in the Cold Abyss', *National Geographic Magazine*, 152 (1977), 441–53
Van Dover, C. L., *The Ecology of Deep-Sea Hydrothermal Vents* (Princeton, 2000)

69 Round the World by Balloon
Christopher, J., *Riding the Jetstream* (London, 2001)
Glines, C. V., *Round-the-World Flights* (Washington, DC, 2003)
Piccard, B. & Jones, B., *The Greatest Adventure* (London, 1999)

70 Mars, Jupiter & Beyond
Haines, T. & Riley, C., *Space Odyssey: A Voyage to the Planets* (London, 2004)
Kelly Beatty, J. et al. (eds), *The New Solar System* (Cambridge, 1999)
McNab, D. & Younger, J., *The Planets* (London, 1999)

Sources of Illustrations

a: above; b: below; c: centre; l: left; r: right

1 Museum für Kunst und Gewerbe, Hamburg; 2–3 © Joel W. Rogers/CORBIS; 4 The Art Archive/Biblioteca Nacional, Mexico/Dagli Orti; 5b Archaeological Museum, Beirut © Giovanni Dagli Orti; 5a Bibliothèque Nationale, Paris; 6b Biblioteca Nacional, Madrid; 6a Maria Sibylla Merian; 7b Private Collection; 7a NASA, Washington, D. C.; 11 Museo Navale di Pegli, Genoa; 12 British Museum, London, MS Or. 2780 f. 49 v; 13a Royal Geographical Society, London; 13b Photograph from the Peabody Museum of Archaeology and Ethnology, Harvard University, © President and Fellows of Harvard College, photograph by Hillel Burger, cat 99-12-10/53099.1(bowl) and cat 99-12-10/53100.2 (stem), neg T3866.1 Gift of the Heirs of David Kimball, 1899; 14a University of Newcastle upon Tyne; 14b Royal Geographical Society, London; 14–15 Georges Sourial/National Geographic Image Collection; 16–17 Photo Antonia Tozer/John Warburton-Lee Photography; 18 House of the Faun, Pompeii; 19 Natural History Museum, London; 20a ML Design; 20–21 Courtesy Richard Cosgrave, Photo R. Frank; 21 RMN, Paris – Photo R. G. Ojeda; 22 Ministère de la culture et de la communication, Direction régionale des affaires culturelles de Rhône-Alpes, Service regional de l'archéologie; 23 Kenneth Garrett/National Geographic Image Collection; 24–25 Courtesy of Meadowcroft Rockshelter and Museum of Rural Life, Pennsylvania; 25l Smithsonian Institution, Washington, D. C.; 25r ML Design; 26 ML Design, after Peter Bellwood; 27a Courtesy Peter Bellwood; 27b Robert Harding Picture Library Ltd/Photo Geoff Renner; 28 Courtesy Adrian Hodridge; 29 Photo Peter Hayman; 30 Werner Forman Archive, London; 31l Brooklyn Museum, New York; 31r ML Design; 32a British Museum, London, EA 25360; 32b Photo Heidi Grassley © Thames & Hudson Ltd, London; 33 Photo akg-images, London/Nimatallah; 34b ML Design; 34–35a © Jonathan Blair/CORBIS; 34b Antiquités du Bosphore Cimmérien; 35b British Museum, London, EA 25565; 36 © Sonia Halliday Photographs, photo by F. H. C. Birch; 37a British Museum, London, ANE 124017; 37b British Museum, London; 38a © Sonia Halliday Photographs; 38b ML Design, after Lane Fox, R. (ed.), *The Long March. Xenophon and the Ten Thousand* (London & New Haven, 2004), Map 1; 39 Photo akg-images, London/Nimatallah; 40 Photo akg-images, London/Gérard Degeorge; 41 © Sonia Halliday Photographs; 42al Photo Isao Kurita; 42ar British Museum, London; 42b ML Design, after Lane Fox, R.,*The Search for Alexander* (London, 1980); 43 Archaeological Museum of Pella, Greece; 45a British Museum, London; 45b Musée Cantonal d'Archéologie et d'Histoire, Lausanne; 45r ML Design, after Professor B. Cunliffe; 46l Naples Archaeological Museum; 46r British Museum, London; 47 Photo Araldo de Luca, Rome; 48 Photo Roger Wilson; 48a ML Design; 48b Photo Roger Wilson; 50 Aerial view of Caesarea; 51l Arian Baptistry, Ravenna; 51r ML Design; 52a Naples Archaeological Museum; 52b Robert Harding Picture Library Ltd/Photo Adam Woolfitt; 53 Werner Forman Archive/British Museum, London; 54 ML Design; 55a Photo Tony Mott; 55b Egyptian Museum, Vatican 1990, photo Scala, Florence; 56–57 Fujita Art Museum, Osaka; 58 Bibliothèque Nationale, Paris; 59 ML Design; 60a Bibliothèque Nationale, Paris; 60b Private Collection; 61 Viking Ship Museum, Roskilde. Photo Werner Karrasch; 62a ML Design; 62b Parks Canada/B. Pratt/ H.01.11.11.13 (72); 63 British Library, London; 64 Archivio di Stato, Bibliothèque, Lucques, MS 107 f. 29 r; 65 Bibliothèque Nationale, Paris, MS Fr 90-87; 66a MAS, Barcelona; 66bl ML Design; 66b V&A, London, M813-1926; 67 Canterbury Cathedral, Canterbury; 68 Bibliothèque Nationale, Paris; 69 Reza/National Geographic Image Collection; 70a ML Design, after *Saudi Aramco World*, vol. 55, 1, 2004; 70 Photo John G. Ross; 71 National Palace Museum, Taipei; 72 British Library, London; 72–73 Photo Antonia Tozer/John Warburton-Lee Photography; 73 Bust of Tamerlane; 74a ML Design; 74 Edinburgh University Library, Or. MS 20 f. 124v; 75 British Library, London, Royal MS 19 D I, f. 58; 76a Bibliothèque Nationale, Paris; 76bl Metropolitan Museum of Art, New York, Purchase, Bequest of Dorothy Graham Bennett, 1993 (1993.256); 76br from *The Book of Ser Marco Polo*, by Sir Henry Yule, 1875; 76–77 Private Collection; 77 ML Design; 78–79 James L. Stanfield/National Geographic Image Collection; 79 Bridgeman Art Library/Private Collection; 80l ML Design; 80r Bibliothèque Nationale, Paris, MS Arabe 5847, f.22; 81 from *The Western Sea Cruises of Eunuch San Pao* by Lo Mou-Teng, 1597; 82a Drazen Tomic, after Jan Adkins 1993; 82b National Palace Museum, Taipei; 83l National Palace Museum, Taipei; 83r ML Design, after Levathes, L., *When China Ruled the Seas* (New York, 1994); 84–85 The Art Archive/Museu do Caramulo, Portugal/Dagli Orti; 86 from *Theatrum Orbis Terrarum* by Abraham Ortelius, 1570; 87 Photo akg-images, London; 88 © Reuters/CORBIS; 89a Biblioteca Columbina, Seville; 89b Private Collection; 90a ML Design; 90b from *Historia General de las Indias* by Fernández de Oviedo y Valdés, 1547; 91l Photo akg-images, London; 91r Academy of Science, Lisbon; 92–93 from *Civitates Orbis Terrarum* by Braun and Hogenberg, 1572; 93a ML Design; 94 Courtesy Biblioteca Casanatense, Rome; 95 from *Die Ritterlich* by Ludovico Barthema, 1515; 96a Photo Nigel Pavitt/John Warburton-Lee Photography; 96b ML Design; 97l Naval Museum, Seville; 97r Mariner's Museum, Newport News, Virginia; 98 ML Design; 99b British Museum, London; 99a Bibliothèque Nationale, Paris; 100a Courtesy The Lilly Library, Indiana University, Bloomington, Indiana; 100b Naval Museum, Seville; 101 Germanisches Nationalmuseum, Nuremberg, MS 22414; 102 Biblioteca Nacional, Madrid; 103a Bodleian Library, Oxford, MS Arch Selden A.1.67r; 103b ML Design; 104 Bibliothèque Nationale, Paris; 105 Bridgeman Art Library/Museo de America, Madrid; 106 Photo John Hemming; 107l ML Design; 107ra Dumbarton Oaks Research Library and Collections, Washington, D.C.; 107rb Royal Library, Copenhagen; 108a Art Institute of Chicago, Robert Hashimoto/Buckingham Fund, 1955.2587; 108b Photo John Hemming; 109 Museo del Oro, Banco de la Republica, Bogota; 110a ML Design; 110b Museu Barbier-Mueller Art Precolombi, Barcelona; 111a Private Collection; 111b Photo John Hemming; 112–13 © CORBIS; 113 Frans Hals Museum, Haarlem; 114 © Buddy Mays/CORBIS; 115al Library of Congress, Washington, D.C.; 115ar ML Design; 115b Etowah Mounds State Historic Site – Georgia Department of Natural Resources, Atlanta; 116 National Portrait Gallery, London; 117a National Maritime Museum, London; 117b British Library, London, Sloane Collection MS 61; 118 John Carter Brown Library at Brown University, Arizona; 119 ML Design, after Raymond Aker, 1999, Drake Navigators Guild; 120 Courtesy of Septentrion Publishers, Quebec; 121a ML Design; 121b Private Collection; 122 Library and Archives of Canada, Ottawa, C-118494; 123 The Curators of the Bodleian Library, Oxford; 124 British Museum, Department of Prints and Drawings, London; 125a British Museum, Department of Prints and Drawings, London; 125bl British Library, London, C.54.bb.33; 125r Bridgeman Art Library/Private Collection; 126b ML Design; 126–27 British Library, London, Add. MS 12, 2-6, f.6; 127 from *Navigatio Septentrionalis* by Jens Munk, 1624; 128–29 Photo RMN, Paris – Photo Gérard Blot; 130 British Library, London; 131 Rex Nan Kivell Collection, National Library of Australia, Canberra, NK3; 132 ML Design; 133a British Library, London, Add. 8946 f. 52; 133b British Library, London; 134a Maria Sibylla Merian; 134b Museum of the Swiss Abroad - Château de Penthes-Pregny/Geneva, Switzerland; 135l ML Design; 135r from *Metamorphosis* by Maria Sibylla Merian, 1705; 136a from *China Documentis Illustrata*, by Athanasius Kircher, 1667; 136b ML Design; 137a Royal Geographical Society, London; 137b Photo RMN, Paris – Photo Jean Schormans; 138 Courtesy of the Horsens Museum, Denmark; 139a Private Collection; 139bl Smithsonian Institution, Washington, D.C. 85-5537; 139br ML Design; 140 Bridgeman Art Library/Scottish National Portrait Gallery, Edinburgh; 141a Courtesy of the Lewis Walpole Library, Yale University; 141b ML Design; 142a Yale Center for British Art, Paul Mellon Collection, USA. Courtesy The Bridgeman Art Library; 142b Private Collection; 143 Museum of New Zealand, Te Papa Tongarewa, Wellington; 144 Australian National Maritime Museum Collection, Sydney. Reproduced courtesy of the Museum; 145a Private Collection; 145b ML Design; 146a British Library, London, Add. MS 23920 f.50; 146b The Royal Collection, Her Majesty Queen Elizabeth II; 146–47 British Library, London; 147 West Sussex, UK: From the Collection at Parham Park; 148 Rex Nan Kivell Collection, National Library of Australia, Canberra, NK1671; 149 Rex Nan Kivell Collection, National Library of Australia, Canberra, NK11756; 150b Rex Nan Kivell Collection, National Library of Australia, Canberra, NK2173; 150–51 Rex Nan Kivell Collection, National Library of Australia, Canberra, NK5066; 151b ML Design; 152 National Gallery of Canada, Ottawa, Transfer from the Canadian War Memorials, 1921, 8000; 152–53 Photo Joseph Gillingham; 152a ML Design, after Daniells, R., *Alexander Mackenzie and the North West* (London, 1969); 154a Canadian Museum of Civilization, Quebec; 154b Photo Joseph Gillingham; 155 National Portrait Gallery, London; 156al Bridgeman Art Library; 156ar from *Travels in the Interior Districts of Africa: Performed in the Years 1795, 1796 and 1797 with an Account of a Subsequent Mission to that country in 1805* by Mungo Park; 156b ML Design, after Lupton, K., *Mungo Park, The African Traveler* (Oxford, 1979); 157 Photo courtesy Tom Fremantle; 158–59 Photo akg-images, London; 160 Royal Geographical Society, London; 161 State Museum, Berlin; 162, 163, 164a British Library, London; 164bl ML Design, after Humboldt, A. von, *Personal Narrative of a Journey to the Equinoctal Regions of the New Continent*, trans. J. Wilson, intro. by M. Nicholson (London & New York, 1995); 164br British Library, London; 165 Collection of the New York Historical Society, 1971.125. Gift of the Heirs of Hall Park McCullough; 166a Missouri Historical Society, St Louis, 1921 055 0001. Gift of Julia Clark Voorhis in memory of Eleanor Glasgow Voorhis, 1921; 166b Commissioned by the Missouri Bankers Association; 167l Courtesy of the American Philosophical Society, Philadelphia; 167r Athenaeum of Philadelphia, 76.16. Gift of Milton Hammer; 168a Library of Congress, Washington, D.C., LC-USF34-070356-D; 168b ML Design, after Gilman, C., *Lewis and Clark. Across the Great Divide* (Washington, D.C., 2003); 169 Galerie Beruhauter Schweizer, Zurich; 170 ML Design; 170–71 David Roberts; 171 Photo © K. D. Politis; 172 Egypt Exploration Society, London; 173a British Museum, London; 173b from *Six New Plates* by G. Belzoni, 1822; 174 Bridgeman Art Library/Down House, Downe, Kent; 174–75 Diagram of *The Beagle*; 175a By

permission of the Syndics of Cambridge University Library, MS Add.7983 f.31r; 175b Royal Geographical Society, London; 176 Bridgeman Art Library/Royal College of Surgeons, London; 177a Private Collection; 177c Natural History Museum, London, 26425; 177c ML Design; 178 © David G. Fitzgerald; 179 The Oklahoma Museum of History, Oklahoma Historical Society, Oklahoma City, OK; 180a Archives and Manuscripts, Oklahoma Historical Society, Oklahoma City, OK; 181b ML Design; 181 American Museum of Natural History, New York; 182 Private Collection; 183a Michael D. Coe; 183b Frederick Catherwood; 184 © P. Pet/zefa/Corbis; 185a ML Design; 185b Private Collection; 186 Royal Geographical Society, London; 187 from *Narrative of a Journey to the Shores of the Polar Sea* by John Franklin c. 1910; 188 from *The U.S. Grinnell Expedition in Search of Sir John Franklin: a Personal Narrative* by E. K. Kane, 1854; 189a from *Once a Week*, Oct 1859; 189l&r National Maritime Museum, London; 190, 191 from *Travels and Discoveries in North and Central Africa* by Heinrich Barth, 1857; 192a from *Travels through Central Africa to Timbuctoo and across the Great Desert to Morocco, performed in the years 1824-1828*, Vol II, by René Caillié, 1830; 192–93 Bibliothèque Nationale, Paris; 193 from *Travels and Discoveries in North and Central Africa* by Heinrich Barth, 1857; 194l ML Design; 194r Photo John Warburton-Lee; 195 Royal Geographical Society, London; 196 from *The Lake Regions of Central Africa* by R. F. Burton, 1860; 197l&r Royal Geographical Society, London; 198 ML Design, after Ondaatje, C., *Journey to the Source of the Nile* (Toronto, 1998); 199l Private Collection; 199r State Library of New South Wales, Sydney; 200a Dixson Library, State Library of New South Wales, Sydney; 200b La Trobe Australian Manuscripts Collection, State Library of Victoria, MS 13071; 201l ML Design; 201r Mortlock Library, State Library of South Australia, Adelaide; 202al Unknown photographer; 202ar&b La Trobe Picture Collection, State Library of Victoria, Melbourne; 203a Christie's Images, London; 203b Granger Collection, New York; 204 Royal Geographical Society, London; 205a ML Design; 205 Photo Nigel Pavitt/John Warburton-Lee Photography; 206bl Photo Mary Kingsley; 206a By permission of the Syndics of Cambridge University Library; 206br Pitt Rivers Museum, University of Oxford; 207l Royal Geographical Society, London; 207r Christie's Images, London; 208 Private Collection; 209a from *Voyage d'exploration en Indo-Chine* by Francis Garnier, 1873; 209b Photo Antonia Tozer/John Warburton-Lee Photography; 210a ML Design, after Keay, J., *Mad About the Mekong: Exploration and Empire in South East Asia* (London, 2005); 210b from *Voyage d'exploration en Indo-Chine* by Francis Garnier, 1873; 211 from *Travels in Arabia Deserta* by Charles M. Doughty, 1921; 212a ML Design; 212–13 Royal Geographical Society, London; 213 Photo Julia Margaret Cameron; 214l&r Pitt Rivers Museum, University of Oxford; 215 National Museum of Fine Arts, Stockholm; 216a from *The Voyage of the Vega round Asia and Europe* by A. E. Nordenskiold, 1881; 216b ML Design; 217 Rare Books and Manuscripts Division, New York Public Library, Astor, Lenox and Tilden Foundations; 218 Private Collection; 219 Private Collection; 220al from Annie Marston, *The Great Closed Land*, 1894; 220ar ML Design, after Hopkirk, P., *Trespassers on the Roof of the World* (London & Los Angleles, 1982); 220b from Sir Thomas Holdich, *Tibet the Mysterious*, 1906; 221a Photo Amar Grover/John Warburton-Lee Photography; 221b, 222 from *Tibet the Mysterious* by Sir Thomas Holdich, 1906; 223a Russian Imperial Geographical Society; 223b from *To Kyakhty na istoki Zholtoy reki*; 224a Royal Geographical Society, London; 224b Private Collection; 225a Horse Source/Photographers Direct; 225b ML Design; 226–27 Royal Geographical Society, London; 228 Galaxy Picture Library; 229 from *Through Asia*, Vol. 1, by Sven Hedin, 1898; 230a Royal Geographical Society, London; 230b from *Through Asia*, Vol. 1, by Sven Hedin, 1898; 231 from *Scientific Results of a Journey in Cental Asia 1899–1902, The Tarim River*, Vol. 1, by Sven Hedin; 232al British Library, London; 232ar British Museum, London, MAS 0.1129; 232–33 from *Ruins of Desert Cathay* by Aurel Stein, 1912; 233a ML Design; 233b from *Scientific Results of a Journey in Cental Asia 1899–1902, Lop Nor*, Vol. 2, by Sven Hedin; 234 ML Design; 235, 236 Royal Geographical Society, London; 237a&b, 238 Courtesy Sir Wally Herbert; 239 Scott Polar Research Institute, Cambridge; 240a National Library of Norway, Picture collection, Oslo; 240–41 Photo A. Wild, Archifact Ltd/Antarctic Heritage Trust; 241a ML Design, after Fiennes, R., *Captain Scott* (London, 2003); 242 Scott Polar Research Institute, Cambridge; 243l British Library, London; 243r Scott Polar Research Institute, Cambridge; 244 Royal Geographical Society, London; 245 State Library of New South Wales, Sydney; 246 Scott Polar Research Institute, Cambridge; 247al Photo Cary Wolinsky; 247ar Royal Geographical Society, London; 247b ML Design, after *National Geographic*, November 1998; 248 Scott Polar Research Institute, Cambridge; 249 University of Newcastle upon Tyne; 250l ML Design, after Bell, G., *The Arabian Diaries*, ed. O'Brien, R. (Syracuse, 2000); 250r Royal Geographical Society, London; 251a, bl & br from *The Life of Isabella Bird* by Anna M. Stoddart, 1906; 252a Royal Geographical Society, London; 252b Private Collection; 253a National Portrait Gallery, London; 253c John Murray Archive; 253b Royal Geographical Society, London; 254 Getty Images; 255 National Air and Space Museum, Smithsonian Institute, Washington D.C.; 256a National Air and Space Museum, Smithsonian Institute, Washington D.C., Photo Carolyn Russo; 256b ML Design; 257 Getty Images; 258 © Bettmann/CORBIS; 259a Library of Congress, Washington D.C.; 259b Photos by Pacific Aerial Surveys, Oakland, California, www.pacificaerial.com; 260 Public Library, Medford, Massachusetts; 260b ML Design; 261a Courtesy Hull Daily Mail Publications; 261b © Bettmann/CORBIS; 262 Helen Foster Snow Collection, Brigham Young University, Utah; 263a Bridgeman Art Library/Private Collection; 263b ML Design, after Richard Evans; 264, 265a&b Thor Heyerdahl/ Kon-Tiki Museum, Oslo; 266a ML Design; 266 © Bettmann/Corbis; 267, 268a&b, 268a Royal Geographical Society, London; 269b Drazen Tomic; 270, 271 Royal Geographical Society, London; 272 Knox-Johnston Archive/PPL; 273 ML Design; 274 Knox-Johnston Archive/PPL; 275, 276 Galaxy Picture Library; 276–77 Drazen Tomic, after *Into the Unknown. The Story of Exploration* (Washington, D.C., 1987), p. 320; 277b, 278, 278–79, 279 Galaxy Picture Library; 280–81 Courtesy Dr. Robert D. Ballard; 281a ML Design, after National Oceanic and Atmospheric Administration, http://oceanexplorer.noaa.gov; 282, 283l&r Courtesy Dr. Robert D. Ballard; 284 Photo Chas Breton; 285 ML Design; 286 Winds of Hope; 287, 288a, 288–89 Galaxy Picture Library; 289a Drazen Tomic, after *Into the Unknown. The Story of Exploration* (Washington, D.C., 1987), p. 304; 290 Galaxy Picture Library.

SOURCES OF QUOTATIONS

p. 23 Fray Bartolomé de las Casas, *An Account, Much Abbreviated, of the Destruction of the Indies*, Franklin W. Knight (ed.), trans. A. Hurley (Indianapolis, 2003); p. 26 G. R. Forster 1778, N. Thomas et al., *Observations Made During a Voyage Round the World* (Honolulu, 1996),185; p. 29 M. Lichtheim, *Ancient Egyptian Literature. Volume I: The Old and Middle Kingdoms* (Berkeley, Los Angeles & London, 1973), 23–27; p. 36 Xenophon, Anabasis, IV, iii; p. 39 Arrian, Anabasis, VII, i; p. 44 Geminus, *Introduction to Celestial Phenomena*; p. 46 Polybius, *History*, 3.61; p. 59 Chang Yueh, *Tang Records of the Western World*; p. 91 Álvaro Velho, *Roteiro da Primeira Viagem de Vasco da Gama* (*The Diary of the First Voyage of Vasco Da Gama*); p. 101 Bernal Diaz del Castillo, *The Conquest of New Spain*; p. 109 Gonzalo Fernández de Oviedo, *Historia general y natural de las Indias Occidentales* (Madrid, 1851); p. 112 *The Journey of Coronado. An account of the expedition to Cibola which took place in the year 1540, in which all those settlements, their ceremonies & customs, are described. Written by Pedro de Castañeda, of Najara*; p. 116 John Wynter, *The Observations of Sir Richard Hawkins, Knight, on his Voyage to the South Seas, Anno Domini 1593*, (London, 1622), f.95; p. 123 Thomas James, *The Strange and Dangerous Voyage of Captaine Thomas James* (London, 1633); p. 131 Abel Tasman, annotation on a map of his voyage; p. 136 F. de Filippi (ed.), *An Account of Tibet: The Travels of Ippolito Desideri, 1712–1727* (based on Desideri MSS 'Historical Sketch of Tibet') (London, 1931); p. 138 F. A. Golder, *Bering's Voyages. An Account of the Efforts of the Russians to Determine the Relation of Asia and America*, 2 vols (New York, 1922/1925); p. 140 Horace Walpole, *The Letters of Horace Walpole, 4th Earl of Oxford*, ed. Helen Toynbee, 16 vols (Oxford, 1903–5), letter dated 10 July 1774; p. 143 *The Journal of Captain James Cook*; p. 148 M. Delattre, Rapport sur la recherché à faire de M. de la Pérouse, fait à l'Assemblée nationale, quoted in J. Dunmore, *French Explorers in the Pacific*, Vol. 1 (Oxford, 1965); p. 152 Alexander Mackenzie, *Journal*, ed. W. Kaye Lamb (London, 1970); p. 155 Mungo Park, *Travels in the Interior Districts of Africa*, ed. K. Ferguson Marsters (Durham & London, 2000); p. 161, 162 Alexander von Humboldt, *Personal Narrative of a Journey to the Equinoctal Regions of the New Continent*, trans. J. Wilson, intro. by M. Nicholson (London & New York, 1995);p. 164 to Joseph Hooker 1881 and *Voyage of the Beagle* (1989), 6 August, 1836; p. 165 G. E. Moulton (ed.), *Journals of the Lewis and Clark Expedition*,13 vols (Lincoln, 1983–2001); p. 169 Letter to his family, in *Scheik Ibrahim: Johann Ludwig Burckhardt, Briefe an Eltern und Geschwister*, Carl Burckhardt-Sarasin & Hansrudolph Schwabe-Burckhardt (Basel, 1956); p. 174 from Darwin's, 'Autobiography' published in Francis Darwin (ed.), *The Life and Letters of Charles Darwin*, 3 vols (3rd ed. London 1887); p. 178 Revd Evan Jones, December 30, 1838, Camp of the 4th Detachment of Emigrating Cherokees, Little Prairie, Missouri; p. 181, 182 John Lloyd Stephens, *Incidents of Travel in Central America, Chiapas, and Yucatán* (Washington, DC, 1993); p. 186 Published in the *Polar Record*, Vol. 5 (Cambridge, 1949), 349–50 and Ann Savours, *The Search for the North West Passage* (London & New York, 1999), 184; p. 190 Heinrich Barth, *Travels and Discoveries in North and Central Africa: being a Journal of an Expedition undertaken under the auspices of H.B.M.'s Government in the years 1849–1855*, 5 vols (London, 1857–58; repr. London, 3 vols, 1965); p. 195 John Hanning Speke, *Journal of the Discovery of the Source of the Nile* (Edinburgh & London, 1863); p. 203 H. M. Stanley, *Through the Dark Continent, Vol 1 & 2* (London, 1878); p. 208 F. Garnier, *Voyage d'exploration en Indo-Chine* (Paris, 1885); English translation in 2 vols: *Travels in Cambodia and Laos and Further Travels in Laos and Yunnan* (Bangkok, 1996); p. 211 C. Doughty, *Travels in Arabia Deserta* (London, 1888); p. 215 A. E. Nordenskiöld, *The Voyage of the Vega round Asia and Europe*, 2 vols (London, 1881), vol. 1, 336; p. 234 R. Peary, *National Geographic Magazine*, September 1909; p. 239 R. F. Scott, *Scott's Last Expedition: The Journals of Captain R. F. Scott* (London, 2003); p. 243 H. Ludlam, *Captain Scott* (Foulsham, 1965), 227; p. 249 G. Bell, *The Arabian Diaries*, ed. O'Brien, R. (Syracuse, 2000); p. 254 C. A. Lindbergh, *The Spirit of St Louis* (New York, 1953); p. 264 Thor Heyerdahl, *The Kon-Tiki Expedition* (London & Chicago, 1950); p. 280 H. Poincaré, *Mathematical Definitions in Education* (1904); p. 287 Arthur C. Clarke, in *First on the Moon: A Voyage with Neil Armstrong, Michael Collins, Edwin E. Aldrin Jr*, G. Farmer & D. J. Hamblin (London, 1970).

Index